Bootlegged Aliens

POLITICS AND CULTURE IN MODERN AMERICA

Series Editors:
Keisha N. Blain, Margot Canaday, Matthew Lassiter,
Stephen Pitti, Thomas J. Sugrue

Volumes in the series narrate and analyze political and social change in the
broadest dimensions from 1865 to the present, including ideas about the ways
people have sought and wielded power in the public sphere and the language and
institutions of politics at all levels—local, national, and transnational. The series
is motivated by a desire to reverse the fragmentation of modern U.S. history
and to encourage synthetic perspectives on social movements and the state, on
gender, race, and labor, and on intellectual history and popular culture.

Bootlegged Aliens

Immigration Politics on America's Northern Border

Ashley Johnson Bavery

PENN

UNIVERSITY OF PENNSYLVANIA PRESS

PHILADELPHIA

Published by
University of Pennsylvania Press
Philadelphia, Pennsylvania 19104-4112
www.upenn.edu/pennpress

Printed in the United States of America
on acid-free paper

10 9 8 7 6 5 4 3 2 1

Library of Congress Cataloging-in-Publication Data

Names: Bavery, Ashley Johnson, author.
Title: Bootlegged aliens : immigration politics on America's northern border / Ashley Johnson Bavery.
Other titles: Politics and culture in modern America.
Description: 1st edition. | Philadelphia : University of Pennsylvania Press, [2020] | Series: Politics and culture in modern America | Includes bibliographical references and index.
Identifiers: LCCN 2019054907 | ISBN 9780812252439 (hardcover)
Subjects: LCSH: Immigrants—Government policy—United States—History—20th century. | Immigrants—Michigan—Detroit—History—20th century. | Illegal aliens—Michigan—Detroit—History—20th century. | Automobile industry workers—Legal status, laws, etc.—Michigan—Detroit—History—20th century. | United States—Emigration and immigration—Government policy—History—20th century. | Detroit (Mich.)—Emigration and immigration—Government policy—History—20th century. | United States—Ethnic relations—History—20th century. | Canada—Emigration and immigration—Government policy—History—20th century.
Classification: LCC JV6483 .B39 2020 | DDC 325.7309/042—dc23
LC record available at https://lccn.loc.gov/2019054907

Contents

Abbreviations

Archival Collections

ACHR	American Catholic History Research Center and University Archives, Washington, D.C.
ADA	Archdiocese of Detroit Archives, Detroit, Michigan
BDPL	Burton Historical Library, Detroit Public Library, Detroit, Michigan
BFRC	Benson Ford Research Center, The Henry Ford Museum, Dearborn, Michigan
BHL	Bentley Historical Library, University of Michigan, Ann Arbor, Michigan
DLA	Diocese of London Archives, London, Ontario
LAC	Library and Archives of Canada, Ottawa, Ontario
NARAI	United States National Archives I, Washington, D.C., Subject Correspondence, Records of the Immigration and Naturalization Service, Record Group 85, Records of the Immigration and Naturalization Service (INS)
NARAII	United States National Archives II, College Park, Maryland, U.S. State Department Records
NAUK	National Archives of the United Kingdom, Kew, London
RL	Walter P. Reuther Library, Archives of Labor and Urban Affairs, Wayne State University, Detroit, Michigan
UMSC	Labadie Collection, University of Michigan Special Collections, Ann Arbor, Michigan
WPLA	Windsor Public Library and Archives, Windsor, Ontario

Organizations

AFL	American Federation of Labor
ANOCL	Anti-National Origins Clause League

AWU	Automobile Workers Union
CIO	Congress of Industrial Organizations
CP	Communist Party
DAR	Daughters of the American Revolution
DFL	Detroit Federation of Labor
DOJ	Department of Justice
DOL	Department of Labor
INS	Immigration and Naturalization Service (1933–present)
IS	Immigration Service (1891–1933)
RCMP	Royal Canadian Mounted Police
SAR	Sons of the American Revolution
UAW	United Automobile Workers

Introduction

In May 2018, Attorney General Jeff Sessions told hundreds of Hondurans, Guatemalans, and Salvadorans seeking asylum in the United States to "enter America in the lawful way and wait your turn."[1] Sessions's assertion that migrants should apply for legal immigration status, a common refrain among nativist policymakers of the 2000s, relies on the idea that their own ancestors passed through inspection lines at Ellis Island before assimilating into the factories and farms of early twentieth-century America. *Bootlegged Aliens* challenges this narrative by demonstrating that instead of "waiting their turn," thousands of Europeans once crossed the border without legal papers, seeking refuge from anti-Semitism, violence, and poverty.

Bootlegged Aliens explores how immigration quotas of the 1920s launched an era of policing and profiling that categorized certain Europeans as "foreigners" and excluded them from the benefits of citizenship in the decade that followed. On the borderland between Detroit, Michigan, and Windsor, Canada, defining, policing, and marginalizing these "foreigners" became a profoundly local affair that denied those without citizenship access to jobs, labor unions, and, ultimately, the federal welfare state. Before World War II, grassroots nativist groups, unions, and politicians created policies that curtailed the rights of aliens, a process that occurred both locally and, because of Detroit's location on the international border, transnationally. The employment practices and precedents established in this northern industrial borderland shaped national immigration policies that cast suspicion on European foreigners across America's industrial core. By the outbreak of World War II, concerns about illegal Europeans had waned, but the policing and employment tactics that developed on America's northern border would influence wider policy toward immigrant employment and welfare for decades.[2] *Bootlegged Aliens* disrupts the narrative set forth by President Donald Trump and his contemporaries that positions

Europeans as the legal immigrants of America's past, who disembarked at Ellis Island and proved their worth with hard work in industrial factories. On the contrary, politicians had once cast Russians as anarchists and Italians as gangsters, and they worried that Poles might be bringing crime and disease to America as they crossed the border illegally.

Before immigration quotas, Europeans migrated to the United States with relative ease. For instance, in March 1914, Ukrainian Andrew Boyko stepped off the steamliner *Pomonia* at Ellis Island and headed for Detroit, a booming industrial center where workers could earn five dollars a day in the automotive industry. After ten years as a lathe hand in Henry Ford's factory, Boyko married a Ukrainian Canadian woman and settled in suburban Garden City, Michigan. Boyko and his wife frequently crossed the international border on a ferry to Windsor, where they visited family in the small border city's Ukrainian community. On his streetcar ride to work, Boyko sometimes witnessed Ku Klux Klan parades and graffiti attacking foreign-born Europeans like himself, but daily nativism did little to deter him from crossing the border, securing a job, or finding housing in America's Motor City. And if Boyko had sustained a workplace injury and lost his job, the city of Detroit's welfare department would have processed his application alongside those of native-born citizens.[3]

The lives of European immigrants changed in 1921 and 1924 when Congress passed immigration quotas limiting the number of Europeans allowed into the United States. Quotas meant new immigrants faced exclusion, policing, and the constant threat of deportation. In 1927, when Filip Kucharski began plans to leave Warsaw, Poland, to join his brother Artur in Detroit, he faced U.S. immigration quotas that barred him from entering the United States at Ellis Island. But hope was not completely lost for Kucharski. In the late 1920s, Canada still encouraged immigration, and Kucharski boarded an ocean liner bound for Montreal and made the journey to Windsor, a Canadian city just opposite the Detroit River to America's Motor City. After a few days in Windsor, Kucharski paid a smuggler to row him across the river, where he joined his brother in a boarding house in Hamtramck, Michigan.

As immigrants without citizenship, the Kucharski brothers experienced levels of exclusion that would have been inconceivable to immigrants like Andrew Boyko just ten years prior. Filip Kucharski, who had no entrance papers, lived in constant fear of deportation and could only find a temporary job shoveling debris and snow for a pittance outside Chrysler Motor

Company. Kucharski's brother Artur had legal papers but no citizenship, and when the Ku Klux Klan distributed literature threatening to expose illegal workers at his Chrysler plant, Artur's foreman fired him to avoid an investigation. Without jobs in the first year of the Great Depression, the Kucharski brothers crossed the Ambassador Bridge into Windsor, but in Canada, they encountered less work and a local government that had begun using deportation to clear city welfare rolls. Worried they might be picked up by local police or welfare investigators, the Kucharski brothers secured false American citizenship papers from a local counterfeiter and tried to cross the border again. But the U.S. Border Patrol stationed at the bridge noticed their crudely forged papers and sent the brothers to a holding cell where they recounted their saga to an Immigration Service inspector. Despite their pleas and Artur's insistence that he was still a legal immigrant, the inspector issued deportation orders for them both, on the grounds that they were "Likely to Become Public Charges" in the United States. Within a few months, immigration inspectors loaded both brothers onto a deportation train to New York, where they boarded an ocean liner bound for Europe.[4]

Bootlegged Aliens focuses on the Detroit-Windsor borderland to uncover a local and transnational history of how unions, politicians, and law enforcers shaped wider immigration policy and ideas about who deserved the benefits of an emerging welfare state. In the 1910s, new immigrants faced nativism from politicians, patriotic societies, and anticommunist organizations, but they found jobs and housing across America's industrial North. This all changed in 1921 and 1924 when Congress passed immigration quotas that wrote long-standing nativism into federal law. New quotas meant smuggled immigrants like Filip Kucharski faced policing and employment practices that criminalized and excluded them from American society. Over the next decade, policing and welfare practices expanded to affect Filip's legal brother Artur, excluding entire communities of ethnic Europeans regardless of their legal status. After quotas, one's citizenship began to dictate whether a migrant could find work, cross the border, join a union, or seek benefits from the state. In Detroit, activism and policy developed both locally and transnationally to create categories that would shape wider immigration regulations and practices about citizenship.

Local, federal, and international policies were mutually constitutive. Thus, *Bootlegged Aliens'* narrative moves between Windsor, Detroit, Ottawa, and Washington, D.C., often in a single chapter, to argue that local

Figure 1. An immigrant smuggler rowing three alien clients from Windsor to Detroit. In the wake of 1920s immigration quotas, smuggling became commonplace and associated entire European nationalities with urban crime. Courtesy of the U.S. National Archives, Washington, D.C.

practices in both the United States and Canada influenced federal policy, and once Congress passed laws, it was up to local welfare workers and immigration inspectors to enforce new immigration policy. What emerges is a story that chronicles the ways in which local violence, policy, and practice began to dictate federal immigration policy, demonstrating that, ultimately, it was city welfare workers and politicians who determined which applicants would receive jobs and federal aid. *Bootlegged Aliens* seeks to demonstrate that it is impossible to fully understand how immigration, welfare, and citizenship laws develop without telling a profoundly local story.

Detroit's role as a northern borderland made it distinctive, while its place as America's third largest city in industrial manufacture meant it shared common problems with other American urban centers. Detroit ranked just after New York and Chicago in manufacturing output, and like these metropolises, the Motor City had a large immigrant population that generated concerns about crime, labor, and welfare distribution.[5] Detroit's situation as a borderland, however, exacerbated many of these issues and added concerns over unauthorized immigration, day labor, and border crossing that tended to characterize cities like San Diego, Tucson, and El Paso during and after World War II. Thus, Detroit had immigration problems that mirrored other industrial centers, but its border with Canada threw issues over immigrants into sharp relief.

Exploiting migrants without citizenship papers has a long history in the United States. In 2019, agribusinesses in Texas, Arizona, and California employed undocumented migrants from Mexico for low wages, but restrictive laws passed one hundred years before allowed employers to exploit workers at the very moment key manufacturing centers like Detroit became so important to America's industrial economy. Soon after quotas took effect, companies like Ford, Chrysler, and Packard began hiring migrants like Filip Kucharski who, because they had no papers, would work under harsh conditions for little pay. When these workers challenged their employers, joined unions, or sought better conditions in Windsor, they faced layoffs and deportation raids that extended across the entire Detroit-Windsor borderland. Thus, *Bootlegged Aliens* uncovers the northern industrial origins of an exploitative system that emerged on America's border with Canada and remains central to debates about America's borders.

Bootlegged Aliens also argues that Canada became crucial to the development of American immigration and citizenship policy. In fact, when the New Deal promised a liberalization of American immigration policy, conservative Detroit politicians looked to Canadian immigration practices for nativist inspiration. The book's main focus remains on Detroit, but because the automobile industry extended transnationally into Windsor to form a larger metropolitan region, ignoring Canadian politics obscures part of this local story. When the United States enacted immigration quotas, effectively closing the border, Canadian businesses and politicians insisted on keeping the border open to Canadian border crossers who held positions in American industries. By the Depression, however, the Canadian government began to target immigrants, rounding them up for deportation or banishment to relief camps on Canada's frontier. Detroit's proximity to such policies meant local conservative politicians and nativist leaders invoked Canadian policies as a viable alternative to the leftist proposals of local politicians and soon the federal government.

In Detroit, New Deal policies incited a nativist backlash that linked "the foreigner" to communism, union activism, and welfare cheating. Subsequent nativist lobbies prompted the federal government to take a harder line on immigrants. This challenges scholarship by historians that argues European ethnics achieved broad acceptance during the Depression through inclusion in labor unions and New Deal social programs.[6] *Bootlegged Aliens* finds that while by 1936, New Deal labor policies had allowed for the rise of the United Automobile Workers (UAW) and federal work programs had employed tens of thousands of immigrants in very public Works Progress Administration (WPA) jobs across urban centers, they continued to face criminalization, policing, and exclusionary laws that stalled their acceptance into the workplace, unions, and federal welfare programs. Indeed, in response to the federal government's leftward turn, Detroit's conservative leaders and nativists began to cast union members and WPA workers as communists and foreigners, making it possible and politically popular to bar noncitizens from state programs in the years that followed. In 1939, the Roosevelt administration ceded to local nativist lobbies by barring all noncitizens from federal programs. Against the backdrop of the New Deal, local police, federal enforcers, and nativist politicians and activists used the success of organized labor and the growing welfare state to demand harsher checks on immigrants.

By focusing on Europeans along America's often-overlooked northern border, *Bootlegged Aliens* uncovers how grassroots actors, city policies, and international pressures shaped the development of American immigration laws between two world wars. Historians and legal scholars have produced important work on the ways in which immigration quotas and restrictions redefined the boundaries of American citizenship, but their work tends to focus on policy in Washington, D.C.[7] Mae Ngai, in particular, investigates how immigration restrictions between 1882 and 1924 turned Asians and Latinos into "illegal aliens," a development she argues allowed white European immigrants to become citizens by the 1930s.[8] Though her book includes a chapter chronicling European deportation, its focus on high-level policy decisions in Congress, the Department of Labor, and America's legal system obscures the complexities of local nativist struggles.[9] By using Detroit as an entry point to examine how the intertwined stories of deportation, anti-immigrant activism, and clashes over labor played out on the ground, this book finds that certain Europeans faced stigmatization as "illegal aliens" or "foreigners" well into the 1930s. Thus, even as liberal lawmakers began to negotiate reforms to naturalize law-abiding Europeans and reunite families, in Detroit, southern and eastern Europeans without citizenship faced nativist harassment, job loss, and barriers to welfare.[10] This sustained European exclusion formed a crucial part of America's long history of deporting, expelling, and barring people from its shores.

Bootlegged Aliens profiles the Border Patrol and Immigration Service's robust policing operations on America's northern border to argue that on the U.S.-Canada border, "foreigners" earned a disadvantaged position in the state. A wealth of borderland literature focusing on the U.S.-Mexico border explores the ways in which policing and the local politics of immigration rendered Mexican immigrants foreign, renegotiated boundary lines, and shaped the emergence of agribusiness and border regulation across the Sunbelt.[11] By focusing on the U.S. border with Canada, *Bootlegged Aliens* broadens this scholarship to underscore how immigration into major industrial centers like Detroit shaped immigrant hiring practices and influenced federal policies toward noncitizens.

Detroit's ethnic Europeans faced constant policing that associated their national groups with crime and made punishing them a popular option. A robust new literature on the American carceral state has shed light on the ways in which African Americans negotiated policing and incarceration throughout the twentieth century.[12] Kelly Lytle Hernández has joined this literature to the history of immigration by exploring how in Los Angeles, the U.S.-Mexico border intensified policing and turned the city into a center of mass incarceration.[13] Few scholars, however, have sought to understand where ethnic Europeans fit into this story of policing.[14] *Bootlegged Aliens* draws on the methodologies of incarceration scholars to argue that certain Europeans, particularly those of Jewish and Catholic origin, faced policing that paralleled punishment meted out to African Americans in America's Motor City.

But policing and deportations never stripped European immigrants of their claims to whiteness. Unlike African American, Mexican, and even some Arab migrants to the city, Europeans could live where they wanted and, if they naturalized, could gain access to the same jobs and benefits afforded to native-born Americans. This interpretation challenges literature on whiteness that argues employers, politicians, and cultural elites categorized Irish, Italian, and various Slavic immigrants as nonwhite and that these groups had to fight to achieve their white insider status.[15] *Bootlegged Aliens* finds that though ethnic workers faced exclusions through the

Depression era, they retained a higher racial status than non-European migrants to the city, a point that the book emphasizes by discussing the ways African American, Mexican, and Arab migrants negotiated Detroit's deportation and employment practices.[16]

Scholars of unsanctioned immigration struggle with questions about numbers because it is difficult to count people who worked every day to stay off the record. Even official reports prove problematic because Department of Labor officials often underplayed or exaggerated statistics. But more important than the physical numbers was the fact that local and federal officials became genuinely concerned about undocumented immigration on the U.S.-Canada border. In 1928, Commissioner General on Immigration Harry E. Hull reported, "Detroit earns its reputation as the 'worst in the country' for immigrant smuggling."[17] And by 1930, officials conjectured that around one thousand illegal immigrants crossed into the city each month.[18] Regardless of the actual numbers, a study of this region is critical to uncovering how southern and eastern Europeans negotiated rising fears about illegality and exclusion in ways that often paralleled the experiences of Asians and Latinos in the decades that followed. Studies examining border crossing in the urban North tend to focus on vice, liquor, and drug smuggling.[19] While vice and liquor were integral to the development of cross-border networks along the U.S.-Canada border, the illegal migration of people across this boundary, particularly between Detroit and Windsor, remains largely neglected.[20] *Bootlegged Aliens* brings the conversation over citizenship and illegality to the industrial North, focusing on the role of local immigrants, politicians, and employers in forging federal immigration law and practice.

A history of European immigrants from the 1921 Emergency Quota Act to the beginning of World War II reframes what it meant to be foreign in America's interwar era. Beginning with federal quotas, which Congress drafted in 1921 and finalized in 1924, allows the book to pick up where many histories of European immigration end. *Bootlegged Aliens* uncovers the ways in which new immigration laws opened an era of policing, employer exploitation, and the state-sponsored harassment of European foreigners.

The book's first three chapters focus on the implementation of federal immigration quotas from 1921 to 1929. Overlapping chronologically yet moving forward in time, they examine the enforcement of quota laws, immigrant pushback to new quotas, and their economic consequences for a border region that relied on open trade and immigration. Chapter 1 argues that 1921 and 1924 quotas essentially closed the Detroit-Windsor border with immigration inspectors and U.S. Border Patrol officers, a development that built Windsor into a city of automobile branch plants and robust immigrant smuggling. The rise in immigrant smuggling associated all Detroit foreigners with illegal immigration and crime, a development that alarmed established northern European groups. Thus, Chapter 2 follows Detroit's Irish, Scandinavian, and German immigrants in their lobbies to keep their quotas high under the National Origins Act, a move they hoped would keep their ethnic groups from the stigma of undesirability. And while their efforts failed to overturn quotas, they managed to disassociate their ethnic groups from stigmas of illegality, a development that becomes clear in 1928, when the Detroit police launched a deportation drive that targeted southern and eastern European neighborhoods of Detroit. Chapter 3 delves into the politics of employment, exploring how unions, employers, and two federal governments engaged in economic arguments that negotiated border crossing as an Anglo-Canadian privilege. At the heart of this controversy were twenty thousand Canadians who commuted from Windsor to Detroit each day for work. Union efforts to end the practice incited an international struggle that ended with the U.S. Department of State negotiating an agreement with Canada that allowed Anglo-Canadians and British nationals to keep commuter cards yet restricted commuters of foreign origin. New economic sanctions made the border between "desirable" Anglo-Saxon North Americans and "undesirable" ethnic Europeans more important than the international boundary.

The Great Depression decimated the automobile industry, creating widespread unemployment in both Detroit and Windsor that made local citizens favor nativist policies with renewed vigor. Chapter 4 chronicles how unemployed workers in Detroit and Windsor responded to the Depression by electing leftist reform mayors, but despite Mayor Frank Murphy or David Croll's views on immigration, both local leaders oversaw extensive deportation drives. In Detroit, the federal and local government cooperated to return thousands of Mexican immigrants and citizens to Mexico, while Europeans faced increased deportations in both the United States and Canada. Ultimately, the chapter argues that during the Great Depression, local deportation policies in Detroit and Windsor began to coexist comfortably with leftist political programs, tethering hard-line immigration policy to growing welfare initiatives.

The final three chapters analyze immigrant policy in Detroit during the New Deal era, when the politics of immigration became entangled with issues of labor and welfare. Chapter 5 uses the battle over immigrant registration in Michigan, which pitted the city's major union, the Detroit Federation of Labor (DFL) against employers and ethnic groups. Though the Michigan Registration Act of 1931 did not make it through judicial review, it did alienate foreign-born Europeans from the labor movement. When in 1933, the DFL joined with a local communist union to organize the automobile industry against Briggs Body Company, many foreign-born workers stayed home, ultimately undermining the union's efforts. As noted in Chapter 6, President Franklin Roosevelt's New Deal brought liberalized labor laws and inclusive immigration policies to the region, but these changes also incited a local nativist backlash. By 1935, the UAW managed to organize skeptical ethnic workers, but savvy nativists and employers used the strength of the UAW to cast all its members as communists and foreigners. Chapter 7 introduces Detroit's campaign against welfare fraud to argue that Mayor Richard Reading harnessed resentment toward New Deal policies to cripple the UAW and cast foreigners as welfare cheaters. Local pressure to purge foreigners from welfare reached the federal government, and by May 1939, the Roosevelt administration cut all aliens from the WPA, costing ten thousand Detroiters their only means of support. A year later, Congress passed the 1940 Registration Act, a move that would not have been possible without the prior two decades of anti-immigrant activism.

The book ends with an epilogue that sheds light on the long history of debates over migrant labor, trade, and crime. In the twenty-first century, unauthorized immigrants from Latin America, Africa, and Asia have become crucial to the service, agricultural, and construction industries in the United States. Just across the U.S.-Mexico border, maquiladoras, or border factories, employ local workers at low costs to manufacture goods for American industries. American employers' increasing reliance on these migrants has provoked backlash from politicians, unions, and right-wing groups who blame undocumented workers for cash-strapped welfare programs, for spikes in urban crime, and, of course, for taking American jobs. The election of Donald Trump has brought these issues into sharp relief, but *Bootlegged Aliens* demonstrates that struggles over immigrant labor, welfare, and noncitizenship have a long history and that they once focused on the U.S.-Canada border. Moreover, while many contemporary politicians cast the undocumented as a racial threat from Central and South

America and the Middle East, *Bootlegged Aliens* highlights the fact that certain Europeans once faced stigmas as "illegal immigrants" and "non-Americans." While today race looms large in such discussions, during the interwar era, politicians and newspapers used the concept of foreignness to convey the potential danger these newcomers posed to the nation, suggesting that they possessed political and social traits that meant they could not become true Americans. Both in the 1920s and today, employers have used these stigmas of "foreignness" and "racial otherness" to exploit immigrant populations for the inexpensive labor they provide.

Ultimately, *Bootlegged Aliens* demonstrates that Europeans have not always been legal. By the Depression era, immigrants like Andrew Boyko, the Ukrainian profiled in this book's opening, found themselves associated with illegal entry and had to constantly prove their allegiance to the state. Some did this by seeking naturalization. But as Boyko found, the process was far from simple. Under the terms of the 1906 Naturalization Act Boyko would have needed to take out his "first papers" or "declaration of intention" to naturalize at any federal court, a process that came with a five-dollar fee. In the next two to seven years, Boyko could have petitioned the court for naturalization, or final citizenship papers. Boyko may not have had five dollars to spare to take out his first papers, and the 1906 law's final requirement, that the petitioner be "familiar with English and the Constitution," would have certainly intimidated him.[21] Thus, thousands of immigrants like Boyko steered clear of the naturalization process, finding themselves in legal limbo as immigration laws created regulations around them.

By uncovering the stories of Europeans who chose not to Americanize or could not become citizens, *Bootlegged Aliens* argues that it was in the spaces between citizenship and illegality that state and local officials determined the boundaries of new laws. In 1927, Secretary of Labor James Davis reported to Henry Ford's *Dearborn Independent* that "hundreds of thousands, and possibly more than a million" immigrants lived within America's borders who were technically legal because they entered before 1921 quota laws yet could not apply for citizenship for lack of documentation, funds, or language skill. These "men without a country," as the article calls them, could not vote, practice law, settle on public lands, or reunite their families.[22] Harassed by nativists and relegated to the worst jobs in industries across the nation, these men and women offer an alternate history of European Americans and the local industrial origins of America's immigration state.

Chapter 1

"Illegal Immigrants" in an Industrial Borderland

One January afternoon in 1923, Immigration Inspector Earl Coe stood on Detroit's Woodward Avenue Ferry Dock with a pair of binoculars raised toward Windsor, Canada. As Inspector Coe watched his breath freeze in the winter air, he detected a slight movement across the river. The inspector squinted, and just as he lowered his binoculars, four figures "shrouded in white sheets" loomed toward him across the frozen Detroit River. When Coe approached the apparitions and asked them to disrobe, he discovered two Belgians and one Italian accompanied by a Canadian liquor smuggler. The group had planned to slip into the United States undetected, but Inspector Coe stopped their journey toward American jobs and homes. The inspector formed part of a growing state apparatus tasked with policing immigration on the Detroit-Windsor border, and to many Americans, the shivering Europeans and their guide represented a criminal threat to the United States and Canada that, during the 1920s, could be characterized by a single word: foreignness.

As a key borderland for unauthorized immigration in the industrial North, Detroit became central to an emerging struggle over nativist demands, federal immigration restrictions, and their regulation on the ground. Inspector Coe questioned the smuggler and learned the man was a Polish immigrant himself and a member of a larger smuggling ring that brought liquor and immigrants over the frozen Detroit River daily.[1] When snow blanketed the borderland and the Detroit River thickened with ice, the smugglers covered their clients in sheets or white plasterers' suits, gave them steel-cleated shoes to prevent them from slipping on the ice, and guided them across the river to Detroit's ethnic neighborhoods, where the newcomers sought work in automobile factories.[2] The practice became such a problem that immigration inspectors began referring to it as "ghost walking" and soon identified dozens of "ghost-walking gangs" operating on both sides of the international boundary.[3] Officials in Detroit complained that even the most powerful binoculars could not detect "white-sheeted figures creeping over the snow-blanketed ice."[4] The "ghost walkers" represented one sensational group in a growing industry that specialized in smuggling people into the nation. These smuggling operations developed in response to America's new immigration regime, which, in turn, created a regulatory apparatus on the U.S.-Canada border that would bring policing and federal regulation to local communities for the first time.

The new federal immigration laws of the 1920s prompted a rise in smuggling, but in Detroit, a key site of illegal immigration, employers, immigrants, smugglers, and federal enforcers determined the consequences of new laws. In 1921, responding to nativist lobbies set in place by local chapters of the Ku Klux Klan and patriotic societies, Congress passed the Emergency Quota Act, temporarily curbing immigration from southern and eastern Europe. In 1924, the Johnson-Reed Act established permanent quotas for immigrants from these European nations and barred all Asians from the United States.[5] But despite the federal legislation, automobile companies resented the restriction on their labor. To ensure that the Detroit-Windsor border would continue a long-standing tradition of open trade and border crossing, major employers established branch plants in Windsor and, in some cases, disregarded new laws altogether by employing smuggled immigrants in their factories. By the mid-1920s, immigrant smuggling became a major underground industry in the Detroit-Windsor region, and immigration inspectors like Earl Coe soon joined forces with local police and new Border Patrol officers to find and deport undocumented immigrants.

Newcomers who were caught smuggling became entangled in a local immigration apparatus geared toward facilitating fast and easy deportation. When, for example, Inspector Coe caught the two "ghost-walking immigrants," he sent them to Detroit's main police station for interrogation. Another immigration inspector, Earl Watson, questioned the men and determined they were both "likely to become a public charge" in the United States. Watson then sent them to Toledo's Lucas County Jail to await a deportation train running from Chicago to New York, where they left the United States on the ocean liner *America* as convicted criminals.[6]

The rise of smuggling, policing, and deportation gave nativists who had long practiced grassroots harassment a legal outlet for their xenophobic ideas. After the federal legislations established new immigration quotas, groups like the Ku Klux Klan and the Daughters of the American Revolution (DAR), which had traditionally favored mob violence and letter-writing campaigns, respectively, began to condemn immigrants with a new label: "illegal immigrant." Soon smugglers, their immigrant clients, and even the inhabitants of ethnic neighborhoods across the city came to be indiscriminately associated with criminality. Over the next decade, hooded vigilantes protested Catholics and Jews on the streets of the Midwest, and nativist politicians passed federal immigration laws aimed at the immigrants they most associated with crime, liquor consumption, and general undesirability. Thus, politicians and congressmen crafted new immigration laws, but it was the employers, Border Patrol officers, and immigrants of industrial borderlands like Detroit who determined precisely how new federal regulations would operate on the ground.[7] These local actors created America's immigration policy by inspecting, interrogating, and profiling European groups, associating southern and eastern European nationalities with foreignness and crime.

Detroit and Windsor Before Immigration Quotas

The rapid growth of the automobile industry brought thousands of newcomers to the city, prompting Detroit's established residents to demand immigration laws aimed at closing the border. In the 1910s and 1920s, southern and eastern European, Arab, Mexican, and African American migration changed the ethnic and racial makeup of the city. Once new migrants reached Detroit, they found jobs, established neighborhoods, and, in certain cases, organized politically and gained a reputation for liquor smuggling and anarchist radicalism. These changes incited a nativist backlash from groups like the Ku Klux Klan and the Daughters of the American Revolution, whose members sought to close the border and restrict immigration from groups they saw as undesirable.

By the early 1920s, the presence of an international border had come to characterize Detroit, but it also exacerbated concerns over immigration. Before the 1921 and 1924 Immigration Acts, the Detroit metropolitan region spanned two nations, defied international boundaries, and attracted thousands of workers from around the world. According to Detroit's

Chamber of Commerce, the Woodward Avenue ferry dock represented a "gateway to America" for any foreigner crossing between the United States and Canada. Through this gateway, the Detroit Chamber noted that over eleven million Canadians, Americans, and other national groups crossed freely to work in the "many mercantile and industrial establishments of the city." On their way to coveted jobs in the auto industry, Canadians, Poles, Italians, and African Americans passed "ramshackle buildings, the relics of the older city," before the art deco hotels and department stores of Woodward Avenue drew their eyes upward to stained glass windows and gilded adornments, markers of wealth and success in a city that was fast becoming one of the most important in the nation.[8]

As Detroit expanded, it became America's third largest manufacturing city and its fourth largest in population, attracting a diverse coalition of workers from across the nation and the globe. The men and women beginning to consider themselves Detroiters hailed from rural Michigan, Italy, Poland, and Alabama; punched time cards at Packard and Cadillac; built engines and car bodies on a moving assembly line; and boarded streetcars and ferries home to bungalows in Detroit's east side, Highland Park, Hamtramck, and Windsor, Ontario. The common denominator among new and established Detroiters was the automobile, an invention that was in the process of changing from an item of luxury item to one of necessity in modern American life. Rather than allegiance to a common nation, a shared race, or even a single city, new inhabitants of the Detroit industrial borderland shared economic goals, hoping a job sweeping the floors of Saxon or Briggs Motor Company might yield enough savings to ensure a prosperous return to Europe or a mortgage in Detroit.

Detroit possessed the fastest-growing immigrant population in the nation, and soon vibrant ethnic enclaves developed across the city. By 1920, thirty thousand new Italians, twenty-four thousand Hungarians, ten thousand Belgians, five thousand Greeks, and five thousand Croatians settled in separate yet overlapping regions of Detroit.[9] In these neighborhoods, each ethnic group opened shops and dance halls and maintained their own native customs amid new industrial surroundings. Many of these immigrants settled in Black Bottom, a region named for its dark, fertile soil, and soon the neighborhood housed thousands of Irish, Italian, German, Romanian, and Russian Jews living in yet overlapping colonies and streets. Soon larger groups began to establish their own neighborhoods.[10] For instance, Hungarians established a settlement of small red brick bungalows in a southwest part of the city named Delray, a region that soon developed the largest Hungarian population outside of Budapest. On Saturday nights, Hungarian churches and clubs held raucous *mulatsags*, which roughly translated to "good times" and always included beer and dancing.[11]

Poles represented Detroit's largest immigrant community. In all, 138,000 Polish newcomers populated entire blocks of the city's east side, settling close to the industrial plants where they worked.[12] Felix and Teklunia Koscielski remembered how important it had been for them to rent a home in a Polish neighborhood, where they could buy Polish goods at a local store and where Felix could walk to his job at Cadillac. To mask the smell of soot and industrial waste that drifted through their open windows, Teklunia planted a garden with vegetables for canning and many varieties of flowers, which bloomed throughout the spring and summer.[13] While the Koscielski family remained in the heart of the east side, other Polish settlements extended west along the Pere Marquette railroad. When the Dodge brothers built their factory within the city limits of Hamtramck in 1910, Poles flocked to the region, expanding the small city's population to just under fifty thousand, 70 percent of whom spoke Polish in their homes.[14]

Poles formed the most visible and insular immigrant group in the Detroit region. By 1920, over 80 percent of the Polish population lived in blocks that they dominated, and some never crossed boundaries marked by local meat sellers and Polish churches. Most Poles shared a common working-class background and culture. When they reached Detroit, they took jobs as unskilled factory and railroad workers, attended mass at one of Detroit's thirty new Polish Catholic churches, and built their own wood-frame houses with three rooms all in a row.[15] City social workers complained it was impossible to integrate Polish newcomers into American society because they spoke Polish at home, married other Poles, and attended meetings of political organizations like the Polish Republican League, which, in 1923, had a membership of five thousand across Detroit.[16] Poles' commitment to their language and Catholicism would make them a major concern for nativist groups committed to keeping Detroit Anglo-Saxon and Protestant in the years that followed.

Famine, revolution, and pogroms also brought fifty thousand Russians to Detroit, who separated themselves by religion and added to the city's growing non-Protestant population.[17] Christian Orthodox Russians and Ukrainians settled alongside each other in the growing east side and found

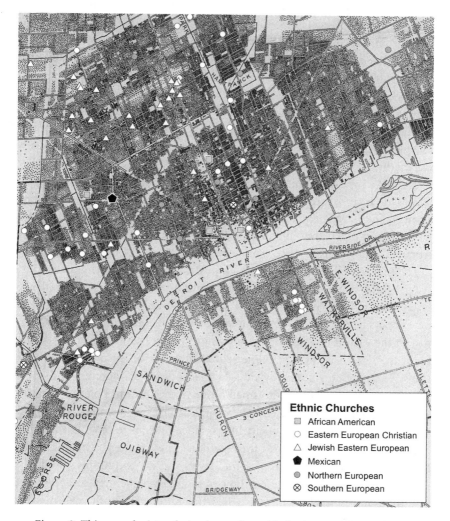

Figure 2. This map depicts ethnic places of worship in the Detroit-Windsor borderland. Note the separate cities of River Rouge and Hamtramck in Detroit and, across the river, the Border Cities of Ojibway, Sandwich, Windsor, Walkerville, and East Windsor. Map by A. Bavery, 2014, based on Floyd A. Stilgenbauer, "A New Population Map of Metropolitan Detroit," Wayne State University, 1936.

unskilled positions in all the major automobile plants. Another small colony of Russian and Ukrainian Christians ran the city's famed Eastern Market, vending vegetables, eggs, and cured meats to Detroit's east side immigrant communities.[18] But because 78 percent of Detroit's Russian immigrants were Jewish, locals began using the categories "Russian" and "Jewish" interchangeably. Jewish Russians settled alongside established Jews from Germany in Hastings Street and held a variety of jobs.[19] They were better represented than any other new immigrant group both in white-collar positions and in unskilled service and peddling work. Many labored as tailors, local vendors, and salesmen, giving them regular contact with other ethnic and national groups across the city.[20] Local nativists responded to Detroit's robust and highly visible Jewish community with virulent anti-Semitism from all levels of society. In 1920, industrialist Henry Ford penned *The International Jew: The World's Foremost Problem*, a widely circulated pamphlet that blamed Jewish Americans for communism in America, controlling the press, and even launching World War I.[21]

Jews even sold in Detroit's growing African American neighborhoods. After World War I, Detroit's black population increased by 611.3 percent, faster than any city in the nation. By 1920, an overwhelming 40,838 black newcomers had crowded into an area that became known as Black Bottom, just to the east of downtown.[22] Thousands of white southerners joined the black migrants, and at first, some settled side by side, priming racial tensions.[23] Black Bottom already housed the poorest immigrants, and soon African Americans moved into small frame homes next to Poles in a region known colloquially as the Kentucky district.[24] Black Bottom residents lived three hundred people to each city block. Open latrines festered in the summer humidity, pigs rummaged through trash piles on the street, and syphilis and pneumonia reached epidemic levels.[25] Poor conditions could not stem the tide of black migration, however, and over the next several years, one thousand new black migrants fled the American South each month, pushing the black community into the East Side Negro District and just north to Paradise Valley, an African American region that became central to black urban life.[26] While distinct ethnic white and African American neighborhoods began to emerge in this period, the boundaries of these neighborhoods remained fluid, and Poles, Italians, Russians, and African Americans often occupied the same city block.

African Americans came to Detroit because the automobile industry employed them in large numbers. A World War I labor shortage caused automobile companies to first seek out African Americans as an alternative labor group, and many companies soon recognized their willingness to work in difficult jobs. As early as 1917, officials at Packard Motor Company remarked that African American workers were "considerably better than the average European immigrant." Black workers earned a reputation for undertaking arduous tasks in the automobile industry with little complaint or demand for higher compensation. Consequently, by the mid-1920s, Ford and Dodge began to employ black migrants by the tens of thousands.[27] Automobile work marked an improvement from southern sharecropping, but companies still confined black migrants to the worst jobs of the industry. At Ford Motor Company, black workers labored almost exclusively in the foundry, while at Chrysler and Chevrolet they worked as paint sprayers and at Brigg's Body Company they wet-sanded car bodies.[28] Their presence in the city stirred racial anxiety among established Anglo-Detroiters, but they were not the only nonwhite migrants coming to the Motor City.

The promise of work also lured thousands of Arab immigrants to the Detroit region. Syrian Christians began coming to the city as peddlers in the early 1890s and, over the next several decades, attempted to identify themselves as white immigrants and Christians with ties to the Holy Land.[29] Their efforts were complicated, however, by the migration of several thousand Turkish, Kurdish, Afghan, Albanian, and Syrian Muslims. In the 1920s, somewhere between seven and sixteen thousand of these Muslim migrants settled in Highland Park and in other enclaves across the city. Most were young men who found work in Detroit factories and socialized not in mosques or mutual aid societies but in coffeehouses. Soon a handful of coffeehouses in Highland Park drew disparate Arab Americans together to share Turkish coffee, Middle Eastern food, and conversation about their new lives in a foreign city.[30]

News of Detroit's prosperity also drew around 1,500 Chinese to America's Motor City, where they settled throughout the downtown before finally establishing a Chinatown to the west of Woodward Avenue in the late 1920s. Detroit's first Chinese were savvy entrepreneurs who migrated from Chicago and opened restaurants and laundry establishments across the city.[31] Most notably, a wealthy Chinese restaurateur named Homer Gam traveled from Chicago to establish "King Yink Lo," Detroit's first Chinese restaurant, on the waterfront. The restaurant catered to sailors and introduced Detroiters to the popular dish, chop suey. Within a few years, Detroit had thirty-two Chinese restaurants, and Chinese laborers began to migrate to the city for work in these establishments and, they hoped, the automobile industry.[32] Because of the 1882 Chinese Exclusion Act, many Chinese were unauthorized immigrants and changed their English surnames to avoid detection. To signal family ties to their community, however, most Chinese kept their original names in Chinese characters. Thus, Chinese migrants developed ways to escape police detection while maintaining ties to their families in other cities and China.[33]

South Asian immigrants also migrated to Detroit's downtown, where they settled alongside other recent arrivals. Like the Chinese, these immigrants were barred under the 1917 Immigration Act, which established an "Asiatic Barred Zone," and in 1923, they lost the right to naturalize.[34] By 1920, the U.S. Census recorded 284 "Hindus" in Detroit, a group that would have comprised Hindu, Sikh, and Muslim immigrants from modern-day India, Pakistan, and Bangladesh. Many of these newcomers had wives and children, had taken steps to naturalize as citizens, and ran boardinghouses or worked in steady jobs at the docks, in iron foundries, and in automobile plants.[35] The numbers of South Asians were higher than those in the census, however, because hundreds or perhaps thousands of sailors on British ships from East Bengal and present-day Pakistan jumped ship in New Orleans and New York before migrating to Detroit. During and after World War I, a surge of these South Indian Muslims found work in automobile factories and crowded into boardinghouses in Detroit, eventually settling in a corner of Black Bottom alongside African Americans.[36]

In this era, five thousand Mexicans also came to Detroit from nearby sugar beet fields, giving the city the largest Mexican colony in the Midwest. Mexican migrants worked alongside Hungarians, Croatians, and Poles at Studebaker, Packard, Dodge, and Ford Motor Company.[37] As migrants sent news of their success home to Mexico, several thousand more Mexicans migrated north, many stopping first in Texas to pick cotton for a season before continuing onto Michigan.[38] Like Arab migrants, the majority of Mexicans were young men seeking higher wages in automobile work. Some found jobs at Ford, Chrysler, and Briggs, but particularly those with darker skin were confined to work in foundries alongside African Americans.[39] Unlike black migrants, however, Mexicans were not segregated into particular neighborhoods. Single men tended to crowd into boarding houses and apartments near the factories where they worked, and as housing became scarce in the city, they spread west into Corktown alongside Irish immigrants and, in some extreme cases, in boxcars on the southwest railroad yards or tent camps on the outskirts of the city.[40]

In the early 1920s, Henry Ford transferred the bulk of his manufacturing operations to the River Rouge Plant in Dearborn, and Mexicans followed other immigrant groups westward and established a region known as "Mexicantown." Mexican Detroiters raised funds for Our Lady of Guadalupe Church, which opened its doors in 1925. The church soon became the focal point of the southwest side Mexican community, drawing ten thousand Spanish-speaking migrants to the neighborhood. Soon Mexican women began to join husbands, fathers, and other family members, finding work as housekeepers, janitors, and laundry workers across the city. By the late 1920s, about twenty thousand Mexicans called Detroit home.[41]

The aforementioned migrants reached Detroit by ocean liners, train, and car, changing the ethnic and racial composition of America's Motor City so much that it became nearly unrecognizable to many of Detroit's older residents. Southern and eastern European, Arab, and Asian immigrants boarded ocean liners in the port cities of Hamburg, Naples, and Calcutta; disembarked at Ellis Island or docked in the port of New Orleans; and took trains to jobs in Chicago, Cleveland, and Detroit.[42] African Americans filled entire trains in Alabama, Georgia, and other southern states, hoping to leave sharecropping behind for fair wages and treatment in Detroit.[43] Most of Detroit's Mexican migrants did not leave their homeland for the Midwest but first crossed the border to work in the Texas cotton fields, where labor agents recruited them for work in the steel mills and packinghouses of Pittsburgh and Chicago. From these urban centers, many Mexicans headed to Detroit for work in automobile factories.[44] The newcomers, particularly those from Europe, concerned local leaders like Collector of Internal Revenue John Grogan, who warned readers of the *Detroit Free Press*, "Detroit is going to be flooded with the leftovers of Europe if something is not done."[45] Even more concerning was the fact that once in Detroit, migrants could cross into Canada at will, making it appear to established Detroiters like Grogan that undesirable immigrants entered Detroit from all directions.

Indeed, the practice of border crossing had long formed part of Detroit-Windsor residents' daily lives. Well before the automobile industry spanned the border, inhabitants of the region lived, worked, and traded across the two nations. Dating to the fur-trapping era of the 1700s, Detroiters had established the city as a trade outpost, an important port connecting Lake St. Clair to Lake Erie and a link to Montreal and the Atlantic.[46] In the 1850s,

Detroit-Windsor manufacturers tapped the region's rich iron mines to build a transnational stove-manufacturing industry that provided North America with heat and a place to cook. Most manufacturers were located in the city proper, but the industry depended on the iron mines dotting southern Ontario and Michigan's Upper Peninsula. Soon after the stove business took off, pharmaceutical companies moved in, spanning the border, with Park and Davis Company in Detroit and Bayer Aspirin in Windsor. As the once sleepy fur town gained a reputation for manufacture, it attracted European immigrants from Germany and Ireland who settled on both sides of the border.[47]

For workers in this era, the border represented little more than an imaginary line. Michiganders and Ontarians tended to disregard it, crossing at will for work or to visit family on either side. Robert Clark moved from London, Ontario, in the early 1900s because his parents found work in Detroit, but on long weekends and holidays, they returned to his mother's hometown of Oxenden, Ontario. Clark's informal migration was not uncommon. In his neighborhood, he recalled several children who returned to "the flinty mining towns of Quebec" or tiny farming communities in Sarnia, Ontario, never bothering to bring documentation of his travels between the two nations.[48]

Crossing from Windsor to Detroit in this era was fast, painless, and relatively unregulated. In 1919, a fleet of twenty ferries carried over ten thousand people to Detroit from the Windsor shore. In Windsor, a person hoping to cross the river needed to purchase a five-cent ticket and board the next boat for the Woodward Avenue Dock, a journey that took about twenty minutes. Once the ferry reached Detroit, two customs officers and an immigration inspector welcomed the boat, surveying the crowd for potential liquor smugglers, but they rarely demanded identification and had little chance to give each passenger more than a cursory glance. In 1922, after passage of the first federal immigration act, inspectors complained that it was impossible to "determine the status of each passenger included in this turbulent mass of humanity surging forward for quick passage through the gates." Once on the docks, immigrants boarded streetcars and lined up at taxi stands outside Detroit's main terminal, disappearing into the many ethnic neighborhoods of the city.[49] And while this constant stream of potential workers benefited employers, it prompted a segment of Detroit's native-born and established immigrant residents to demand restrictions on the cross-border labor flows.

Figure 3. Detroit Border Patrol officers frisking a group of European immigrants they have caught crossing the border from Windsor into Detroit. Smugglers had long ferried liquor and Chinese immigrants into the city, and with new federal immigration quotas, they began to help excluded Europeans across the border. Courtesy of the U.S. National Archives, Washington, D.C.

The Detroit-Windsor region's long tradition of international exchange, however, made closing the border difficult. Borderland residents had long used the international boundary between Detroit and Windsor to their advantage by crossing to avoid the local laws of each city. Canadians shopped in the cheaper department stores of Detroit, while many Americans purchased agricultural products in Windsor's markets.[50] In the early 1900s, young Catholics used Windsor churches to avoid Michigan's higher age requirements for marriage. On April 17, 1917, a young Italian couple boarded the Detroit-Windsor ferry to get married at Windsor's St. Alphonsus Church. Vittorio Ventmiglia was a twenty-four-year-old Italian-born laborer who had come to make his fortune in Detroit. He entered the church with Rosina Caradonna, a sixteen-year-old Italian American girl whose family had migrated from Brooklyn several years earlier. Rosina, or

Rose as she signed her name, could not marry Vittorio under Michigan's laws, which required a bride to be at least seventeen. In Canada, on the other hand, where the age of consent was fifteen, the couple received a quick Catholic ceremony at a respectable church before catching the evening ferry back to their new apartment on the corner of East Congress and Beaubien Street.[51] Indeed, hundreds of Detroit-Windsor residents like Rose and Vittorio used the border to their advantage, establishing cross-border networks that joined the two cities and would prove difficult to dismantle.

Beyond this relatively harmless small-scale border crossing, cross-border smuggling industries brought new concerns about crime and foreigners to the city. For decades, Chinese migrants had slipped across America's northern and southern borders to become America's first illegal immigrants.[52] Along the northern border in particular, many Chinese residents crossed legally from California to Vancouver to work on the Canadian Pacific Railroad in the 1870s. In 1882, when the United States passed the Chinese Exclusion Act barring all Chinese from immigration and citizenship, some of these migrants found themselves trapped in Canada, unable to return to family and friends in San Francisco and Seattle.[53] Within a few years, a smuggling network stretching from Niagara Falls to the Pacific Northwest developed to help Chinese cross into the United States.[54]

Detroit's proximity to industry and railroad lines made it an important spot for this early industry in unauthorized immigrants. By the 1910s, Chinese began to hide themselves in the crowds crossing between Windsor and Detroit each day, giving America's Motor City an early reputation as the "principal gateway" for smuggled Chinese.[55] Moreover, World War I passport regulations jumpstarted a small yet steady European smuggling industry along the U.S.-Canada border.[56] Opportunists in Windsor and Detroit's underworld seized the chance to organize smuggling rings that brought these Chinese and Europeans to the United States in boats, cars, and, in some instances, packed between furniture in freight boxcars.[57]

Early immigrant smuggling developed in tandem with a growing liquor smuggling industry. When Congress ratified the Eighteenth Amendment in 1919, trade in illegal liquor eclipsed the human smuggling industry. In response to new laws, organized gangs of liquor smugglers developed a prosperous illegal industry designed to transfer alcohol from Canada to Detroit. As the criminal trade developed, the strip of water between Port Huron and the St. Clair River gained a reputation as the "high road of rum."[58] In fact, 75 percent of all liquor smuggled into the United States during Prohibition crossed into the United States, using what became known as the "Windsor Detroit funnel."[59]

Foreign-born immigrants controlled the liquor smuggling industry, giving particular ethnic and national groups a reputation for crime. Detroit's notorious Purple Gang, a syndicate run by Jewish immigrants from Russia, rose to power by importing and distributing illegal liquor throughout the Midwest. Gang leaders Carl Jacoby and Abe Bernstein maintained control over the nation's liquor trade by relying on the St. Clair River to ship or bring hundreds of thousands of gallons of alcohol into Detroit. Beyond supplying local saloons, the Purples chartered vessels to take alcohol to other Great Lakes ports like Cleveland and soon newspapers dubbed them "the Jewish Navy."[60] Thus, even before smugglers began to transport aliens across the Detroit-Windsor waterways, Russian Jewish immigrants' involvement in the transport of illegal liquor laid the foundation for linking eastern Europeans to the city's growing criminal underworld. By 1920, when *The International Jew* reached mass distribution, Henry Ford most likely looked out on Detroit for evidence that "the liquor business of the world had been in the hands of the Jews."[61]

Despite growing anxiety over immigrants, certain business leaders, social reformers, and government officials thought they could turn new immigrants toward a singular American identity. These advocates of the movement known as Americanization spearheaded campaigns to offer instruction in English and American values.[62] The project was gendered. Settlement workers instructed women in American cooking and raising a proper American family, while business leaders focused on ways to turn immigrants into proper, efficient American men.[63] Henry Ford, in particular, believed deeply in Americanization and enrolled his immigrant workers in an English school that ended with a symbolic melting pot ceremony, featuring immigrants dressed in foreign costumes emerging from a cauldron as workers in American clothes.[64] Americanization advocates shared the paternalistic assumption that with their guidance, European immigrants of all backgrounds and religions could adopt Anglo-Saxon, Protestant beliefs and values.

A growing association between foreigners, crime, and political radicalism, however, shifted the conversation about immigrants from Americanization and incorporation to restriction and exclusion from the nation. In particular, a series of anarchist bombings and America's first "Red Scare" associated foreign-born Americans with political radicalism and violence. In April 1919, Italian anarchists sent bombs to important industrialists and businessmen, including John D. Rockefeller. In June, the anarchists intensified their efforts against America's establishment, this time planting bombs in the homes of congressmen and, most famously, Attorney General A. Mitchell Palmer, asleep in his Washington, D.C. townhouse.[65]

The bombings prompted a crackdown on political radicalism and a series of open raids across urban America that convinced many Americans that their institutions were under attack from radical foreigners. Strikes, many led by Italian, Finnish, and Ukrainian communists, ignited and spread like wildfire across industrial America. In Detroit, employers who had taken care to gain control of the city and local government became concerned when workers, especially the foreign born, protested their working conditions.[66] In 1919 alone, workers and unions staged forty strikes in the city, demanding higher wages, shorter workdays, and union recognition. Most notably, Wadsworth Manufacturing Company workers, Timken Axle Plant workers, the city's carpenters, and the streetcar operators all went on strike, sometimes for five months at a time.[67] As news of New York cart bombings and violent protests through Times Square reached Detroit's employers, they feared it was only a matter of time before Detroit became the next target of anarchist explosions.

In January 1920, local and federal police brought the Red Scare to Detroit, linking certain Europeans to terrorism and building the case for those who wanted ethnic Europeans' exclusion from the United States. On January 2, 1,500 Russian immigrants were enjoying a Russian play at the Turner Hall on Detroit's East Side when agents and police burst in with nightsticks. The police shouted, tipped over props, and smashed chairs, demanding that members of the United Revolutionary Workers present themselves immediately. Chaos ensued. Men and women, most of whom had no idea what was going on, screamed, grabbed children, and ran for the doors of the crowded theater. Several hours later, police took two hundred fifty "radicals" into custody. Similar raids rocked the city over the course of the next two days, targeting Finns, Poles, and native-born suspects in the workplace, the street, and their homes, arresting one thousand suspected radicals.[68] To avoid controversy, the police and Justice Department immediately released two hundred ex-servicemen, but they held the rest for days in the halls of the Federal Post Office Building in a set of rooms with one sink, one toilet, and no windows. Because they could not be deported under 1920 immigration laws, all the suspects were eventually released, but raids legitimized the growing connection many established Detroiters had begun to make between immigrants and crime.[69]

Ethnic European immigrants' association with anarchist violence exacerbated and legitimized the nativist anxiety many established Detroiters felt concerning the rapid demographic and political changes taking hold of their city. As southern and eastern Europeans crowded into factory jobs and African American neighborhoods grew, many longtime Detroiters yearned for the sleepy port city of the 1890s. Nativists tended to be white Anglo Americans or second-generation immigrants who remembered the years before southern and eastern Europeans, Mexicans, and African Americans had come to Detroit. On the whole, nativist Detroiters backed Prohibition; feared the threat they thought Orthodox, Catholic, and Jewish migrants posed to Protestant society; and associated newcomers with crime and political radicalism.

Detroit's most vocal and visible nativist organization was the Ku Klux Klan. The Klan took root in the industrialized North during the early 1920s with public rallies against not only African American migrants but also Mexican, Jewish, and Catholic immigrants working in urban factories. By the summer of 1923, the national Ku Klux Klan backed a platform of moral renewal, one hundred percent Americanism, antiunionism, anti-Catholicism, anti-Semitism, and racism. Hooded members attended night-time rallies, burned crosses on enemies' lawns, and circulated their national publication, the *Imperial Nighthawk*, on street corners.[70]

In Michigan, the Klan became part of mainstream life for many working-class whites. A segment of Detroit's Protestant community attended Klan picnics, lively parades, and mass celebrations, which, in many communities, became the center of family-friendly entertainment.[71] Taking advantage of a rising consumer culture, the 1920s Klan sold hats, flags, balloons, and even baby rattles branded with the KKK logos. Klan teacups and napkins became acceptable in many Anglo households.[72] These public displays of Anglo-Saxon supremacy helped turn the Klan into a formidable political organization in America's Motor City.

Detroit's 1920s Klan also terrorized the city's growing African American population, burning crosses on lawns and promoting violence against any black Detroiter who crossed the city's informal color lines.[73] African Americans who dared venture outside the boundaries of Black Bottom, Paradise Valley, or the crowded East Side Negro District faced Klan violence and

Figure 4. A Border Patrol agent and his partner escorting two captured immigrants at gunpoint. Scenes like this, which often ran in local newspapers, allowed the Ku Klux Klan to insist that new southern and eastern Europeans came to Detroit in illicit ways and represented a dangerous threat to the United States. Courtesy of the U.S. National Archives, Washington, D.C.

harassment. In 1925, when a middle-class black doctor named Ossian Sweet attempted to buy a bungalow in a white working-class neighborhood, the power of mob violence became painfully clear. No sooner had Sweet and his family moved in than hundreds of white neighbors surrounded the home, many of them masked in white Klan hoods. The mob's goal was to scare the Sweet family back to their home in Black Bottom, but violence broke out when someone hurled a stone through the Sweets' new window. From inside, one of the terrified African American men fired two shots, wounding one white man and killing another. The trial that followed heightened racial tensions throughout the city and eventually led to Sweet and his friends' acquittal, a surprising move from an all-white jury. But despite the outcome, the public trial made up-and-coming African Americans think twice before moving out of black neighborhoods.[74]

While the Klan used mob violence to enforce segregation, its members began to advocate for legal reform to America's immigration laws because it represented a concrete and respectable way to promote Anglo-Saxon America. In the early 1920s, the Klan's *Imperial Nighthawk* devoted more space to immigration restriction and reform than to any other topic, accusing immigrants from southern and eastern Europe of being "more alien" than northern Europeans and arguing that Jews and Italians were genetically prone to "commercialized vice, bootlegging, and dope selling."[75] Klan leaders used the language of citizenship to suggest only those eligible for membership in their hooded organization should become full Americans. They called initiation rituals "naturalization" ceremonies and individuals ready to take the oath "aliens."[76] These ceremonies drove home the idea that only by joining the ranks of organized Anglo supremacy could one become a true American.

Klan rhetoric soon crossed the border. Protesting the increase in immigration to Windsor, Anglo-Canadians founded the Cu Clux Clan of Canada. In late 1923, a Finnish language newspaper called *Vapaus* or "Freedom" charted the rise of Klan membership in Windsor. Canadian "Clan" members terrorized the Drouillard Road neighborhood, shattering the windows of Polish bakeries and painting crosses on the side of Windsor's synagogue.[77] When the *Border Cities Star* chose to run a series of articles lauding the achievements of Windsor's Polish and Hungarian communities, the "Clan" left a burning cross on the lawn of the newspaper's main Windsor printing house. The *Star* ran a photograph of the scene, claiming that many had seen the blackened cross "wrapped in oil-soaked cotton wood, blaze merrily, despite a heavy downpour."[78] Indeed, Detroit-Windsor's long history of exchange meant that even nativist ideologies and organizations crossed the border.

The Ku Klux Klan represented the most radical and vocal of the nativist groups in the Detroit-Windsor borderland, but as concern over illegal immigrants heightened, nativist ideas became common in the mainstream press. In 1920, Henry Ford famously used his newspaper, the *Dearborn Independent*, to chronicle the threat posed by what he called the "Jewish Menace." Other city newspapers printed subtler yet equally negative descriptions of Jewish life. The *Detroit Sunday News Tribune* called the Hastings Street Jewish neighborhood "Detroit's Ghetto," complaining that Jews crowded into unhealthy apartments, sometimes two to three families in one room.[79] By regularly associating Jewish immigrants with various urban ills, the press helped reinforce the idea that the immigrants, not their circumstances, were to blame for Detroit's crowded neighborhoods.

Local patriotic societies like the American Legion, the Sons of the American Revolution (SAR), and the corresponding Daughters of the American Revolution (DAR) also joined the movement to restrict immigration from nations in southern and eastern Europe. In 1921, Oswald Ryan, the American Legion's press commissioner, asked the nation's legislators to keep America from becoming "the biological dumping grounds of the world."[80] Detroit's Sons of the American Revolution jumped on the bandwagon, printing leaflets that claimed an invasion from "various anti-American and pro-foreign groups" threatened Protestant "God fearing Americans" across industrial America. But the DAR, an organization of wealthy white women, provided the most persistent and vocal opposition to new immigrants. From the parlors and drawing rooms of Detroit's elite Indian Village, Arden Park, and Palmer Woods, DAR women circulated petitions, blacklisted local businesses, and, most importantly, wrote hundreds of letters to their congressmen that demanded new federal immigration laws to stop the immigrants they thought presented "an egregious affront to the integrity of American values."[81] The rise of nativist activism Detroit and other industrial centers helped build the momentum federal policymakers needed to reform U.S. immigration laws.

Immigration Quotas and Smuggling

In 1921 and 1924, Congress heeded the demands of nativists across the nation with federal immigration quota laws they claimed would stymie the rise of immigration and crime in the industrial North and Midwest. But racialized immigration laws were hardly groundbreaking. Chinese laborers had first faced exclusion in 1882 with an act that was renewed in 1890, 1900, and 1907, when a so-called Gentlemen's Agreement extended restrictions to Japanese laborers while allowing well-to-do Japanese students and businessmen entry. Moreover, in 1917, a new Immigration Act required a literacy test at Ellis Island, a measure that nativists hoped would exclude thousands of Catholic and Jewish farmers. The 1917 act also created an "Asiatic Barred Zone," which labeled all individuals from Southeast Asia, with the exception of Japan, ineligible for immigration.[82] By 1920, immigration laws excluded contract laborers, Asians (except for Japanese and Filipinos), certain criminals, individuals who did not meet certain moral standards, persons with disabilities or diseases, paupers, radicals, and illiterates.[83] But despite this laundry list of excluded categories, more than 800,000 immigrants entered the country in 1920, and many Americans blamed them for the rise of crime and terrorism in urban regions.[84]

Congressional officials hoping to restrict immigration looked to the rise of grassroots nativism across the industrial North and Midwest and decided the moment was right to act. Albert Johnson, a Republican representative from Hoquiam, Washington, and chair of the House Committee on Immigration, proposed a two-year suspension of all immigration to give lawmakers a chance to remake immigration laws. Vermont Senator William Dillingham countered the ban with a quota system for Europeans. Dillingham had headed a joint commission created by Congress in 1907 to investigate America's immigration problem. The Dillingham Commission remains the largest immigration study ever conducted in the United States, and as Katherine Benton-Cohen argues, it launched an era of hard-line immigration policy with legacies that continued into the twenty-first century.[85] After the study released, Dillingham backed a bill that included a provisional quota system. New quotas would allow 5 percent of the number of foreign-born immigrants from each nation listed in the 1910 census. When the bill returned to the House, lawmakers approved it by lowering the annual quota to 3 percent and reducing total immigration to 350,000. The 1921 Emergency Quota Act marked the first time Congress had legislated a numerical cap on immigrants, and its passage spurred restrictionists in Congress to demand a permanent version.[86]

By 1922, national labor unions and business organizations set aside their quarrels over wages and workdays to lobby for permanent quotas. Samuel Gompers, head of the American Federation of Labor, argued that quotas presented a rare opportunity to stop a "rapidly revolving labor supply at low wages" from coming to the United States. Despite his own background as a Jewish immigrant, Gompers felt "a regular supply of American wage earners at fair wages" presented a key opportunity for the union movement.[87] For this very reason, the American business world traditionally resisted immigration quotas. But after the Italian anarchist bombings of the early 1920s, the New York Chamber of Commerce changed its immigration stance.[88] The Chamber's executive secretary, Charles T. Gwyne, warned the business world "to revise its policy concerning cheap labor." Inexpensive labor was not worth it, he argued, if the workers practiced radical politics and plotted violence against their bosses.[89]

Invigorated by business and labor support, restrictionists launched a campaign to permanently write nativism into American immigration law. In January 1922, Representative Johnson and Senator David Reed of Pennsylvania introduced an immigration bill to the House with the explicit hopes of maintaining "the Nordic integrity of America."[90] Johnson did not shy from nativist and racist language. To justify quotas for Polish immigrants, he claimed "eighty-five to ninety percent [of Poles] lack any conception of patriotic or national spirit and the majority of this percentage is morally incapable of acquiring it."[91] In a *New York Times* editorial, Johnson asserted that empirical evidence demonstrated that "the Poles, Austrians, and the nationals of the different Russian States who apply for visas are the most undesirable type of emigrant."[92] Thus, while the bill's creators portended fairness toward all immigrants, they sold the quota system explicitly as a way to keep America Anglo-Saxon and Protestant.

Representative Johnson also drew on new eugenicist studies to link new southern and eastern Europeans to crime. In 1922, the House Committee on Immigration commissioned a eugenics specialist at Carnegie Institute, Dr. Harry H. Laughlin, to analyze crime within immigrant groups. Laughlin's study, "Analysis of America's Melting Pot," came out the following year and concluded that immigrants from Great Britain, Scandinavia, Ireland, Germany, and the Netherlands had the lowest crime rates. In contrast, he argued, "New immigration from southern and eastern Europe runs relatively high in this type of social defect as we find it in custodial institutions of the U.S." Laughlin himself puzzled over whether the higher crime rates of new immigrants reflected "a difference in training or a biological difference," but the question mattered little to Congressman Johnson, who used the study to emphasize the dangers of southern and eastern European immigration.[93]

Once in Congress, debates over permanent quotas presumed that the United States should have a quota system, but legislators diverged over which nationalities deserved entrance over others. Representatives argued about whether quotas should be based on the new 1920 census, whether the Western Hemisphere should remain outside the quota system, or whether the Gentlemen's Agreement with Japan should stand.[94] The final Immigration Act signed by President Coolidge in May 1924 looked like this: the baseline of the quota system was pushed back to 1890 and the percentage lowered from 3 to 2 percent of foreign-born residents. Congressman Johnson argued that 1890 represented the ideal quota year because southern and eastern Europeans had yet to immigrate in large numbers to the United States and quotas would be highest for the "most desirable" German and British newcomers. But 1890 quotas were still temporary. After two years, the law provided for a special committee that would determine the "national origins" of the United States according to the new 1920 census and designate final quotas. Finally, to address legislators from the Southwest's demand for Mexican agricultural labor and those from the West's preoccupation with Asian immigrants, the new act placed no numerical limitation on Western Hemisphere immigrants and discarded the Gentlemen's Agreement with Japan.[95] This meant Mexican laborers could cross freely into farm labor from California to Texas, but wealthy Japanese students could no longer secure visas to study at Harvard or Yale. In effect, by 1925, new federal immigration laws sealed America's borders to all Asians and all but about six thousand Poles, three thousand Italians, and one hundred Greeks.

On the ground and in practice, quotas met resistance from business leaders who resented any check on their access to labor. Nowhere was this more apparent than in Detroit, where the city's Chamber of Commerce and the Michigan Manufacturers Association remained skeptical of quota laws, insisting that the immigrants coming to work in automobile factories were "of an unusually high caliber."[96] Closing the international boundary concerned the industrialists who relied on the migration and labor generated by an open border. To ensure the border would remain open, automobile companies expanded their factory operations in Canada, attracting new migrants to America's northern neighbor.

American manufacturers had begun using the border to circumvent such economic sanctions as far back as 1874, when the Canadian government passed protective tariffs that taxed American goods and favored those made in Canada. To circumvent Canada's "tariff wall," in the early 1900s, American firms like W. E. Seagrave Company (fire engines), J. T. Wing Company (metals), Saginaw Salt and Lumber, and Peters Cartridge built branch plants in Canada. By 1904, the automobile industry followed suit, and Ford Motor Company established Ford of Canada just to the east of Windsor. Two years later, Ford of Canada shipped automobiles across the Dominion and the British Empire with large export markets in India, New Zealand, and Australia.[97] As Ford's branch plant system became more and more lucrative, other automobile firms built their own plants in Windsor. By 1913, Hupp, Overland, Baker Electric, Tate Electric, Fisher Body,

National Auto Body, Dominion Stamping, and Kelsey Wheel all set up branch plants in Windsor.[98]

After the United States passed immigration laws, companies expanded their Canadian operations and thousands of excluded immigrants headed to Canada to work in the American branch plants. In 1925, Ford added two assembly plants to Ford of Canada, and the following year, Studebaker, Hudson, Chrysler, and General Motors all built branch plants in Windsor that employed a mixture of Anglo-Canadian and European-born workers. By 1927, over 40 percent of Windsor's residents worked at Ford of Canada, and 20 percent worked for another automotive plant. This mix of Canadian and immigrant workers churned out Model Ts and Ford Coupes for the Dominion of Canada and Great Britain. The branches and the automobiles they produced were exempt from the costly export taxes that applied to Detroit plants and could employ European immigrants who, before quotas, would have sought work in the United States.[99] Branch plants turned the Ontario border region into a major destination for both Canadians and immigrants excluded from the United States. As seen in Figure 2, the separate towns of Ojibway, Sandwich, Windsor, Walkerville, and East Windsor, also known as Ford City, expanded to border each other and became known as the "Border Cities," a sprawling region that filled with new immigrants and dominated the automobile industry.[100]

Canada responded to the influx of European immigration with its own set of racialized immigration policies. In 1910, Canada's Parliament allowed the state to exclude any immigrant "belonging to any race deemed unsuitable to the climate and requirements of Canada," and in 1923, Minister of Immigration and Colonization James Robb divided Europe into "preferred countries" and "non-preferred countries." Canada allowed free and open immigration from the "preferred countries" of Norway, Sweden, Denmark, Finland, Luxemburg, and Germany. Immigrants from the "nonpreferred countries" of Austria, Hungary, Poland, Romania, Lithuania, Estonia, Latvia, Bulgaria, Yugoslavia, and Czechoslovakia, on the other hand, could only enter as farm laborers, domestic workers, or if sponsored by family in Canada.[101]

The law reflected Canada's prejudice toward southern and eastern Europeans, but in practice, the system allowed tens of thousands entry. The provinces of Saskatchewan, Alberta, and Manitoba desperately needed farm labor, and southern and eastern Europeans learned they could travel to Canada on farm labor visas and work for a season in the west before heading elsewhere in Canada. For example, when Polish Anton Winowski disembarked at Montreal in 1926, he dutifully checked that he was a farm laborer and planned to head west to Manitoba. But instead of choosing arduous agricultural labor in the underpopulated western province, Winowski headed for Toronto, where he found work in a factory for several months. When he heard that automobile companies had opened dozens of branch plants in Windsor, Winowski boarded a train for the Border Cities, where he found work at Ford of Canada and settled on a Polish street.[102]

The growth of branch plants transformed the Border Cities from sleepy towns with a largely Anglo-Saxon population into a booming industrial region, where factories employed workers from dozens of nations. On Ottawa Street heading east toward Ford of Canada, where about a thousand Irish, Scotch, and English immigrants had previously settled in tiny row houses, between three and four thousand Poles crowded their families into the same homes. Sausage shops and Polish groceries wafted the smell of caraway and dill onto the crowded street, and Polish became the dominant language.[103] Soon three thousand Ukrainians settled on the parallel Shepherd Street and raised $2,750 to build the St. Vladimir and Olga Ukrainian Catholic Church, which opened in 1927 with an impressive brick façade and a Ukrainian school.[104] Fifteen thousand Hungarians also traveled to the city and, because they did not want to live or worship alongside other eastern Europeans, chose to rent homes on Drouillard Road, the street closest to Ford of Canada.[105] In this first year, European newcomers tended to associate with immigrants from their own national groups, attend their own churches and schools, and even work on assembly lines with workers who spoke Polish, Ukrainian, or Hungarian.

As in Detroit, established Windsorites feared the new immigrants who had rapidly changed the ethnic landscape of their city. In 1928, thousands of Poles, Italians, Ukrainians, Russian Jews, Greeks, Maltese, and Croatians began to call the Drouillard Road region home, prompting a Ford of Canada executive to disparage the "kaleidoscope of strange smells and foreign sounds that assault the senses when one exits the plant."[106] When housing on Drouillard Road became sparse, European immigrants began to settle to the east of the Ford plant in a company town once dominated by the French called Ford City. Ten thousand new immigrants settled in Ford City the following year, and as the town sprawled east and its inhabitants found work at Ford, Chrysler, Hudson, and General Motors, the city changed its name to East Windsor.[107] Among press and politicians, East Windsor soon became shorthand in general parlance for designating foreignness. For instance, when in a speech to the Canada Club, Windsor's mayor, Cecil Jackson, noted the "overcrowding and poverty rampant in East Windsor," his listeners understood he referred to the problem of new immigrants to the region.[108]

Living in the shadow of Detroit, thousands of East Windsorites thought they could escape local nativism and find higher pay in the ethnic neighborhoods and enormous factories of America's Motor City. Andor Bala, a Hungarian immigrant, worked part time at Studebaker's Canada assembly plant and lived in a boarding house where he shared a room with an Italian and two Poles. Despite his reliable job in Canada, Bala fantasized about working in Ford's main factory, where he could earn five dollars a day, a sum that would have quadrupled his Windsor earnings. Moreover, Bala wanted to leave the overcrowded Drouillard Road region for Detroit's Hungarian neighborhood of Delray, a region that, rumor had it, smelled of sausage and garlic even from the streetcar and had little contact with the rest of Detroit. But because Bala could not secure a quota visa, he married a fellow Hungarian in Windsor and stayed in the city the rest of his life.[109]

Unlike Bala, many Windsor immigrants who wanted work in Detroit found illicit ways to cross the border. In fact, the U.S. laws meant to curb immigration turned immigrant smuggling into a major industry in towns across the eastern Canadian border, all of which had growing foreign-born populations. Immigration Service reports noted with concern that excluded Europeans had begun to populate the Ontario border towns of Kingston, Niagara Falls, and Cornwall, hoping to cross into the industrial centers of upstate New York. Smugglers in these regions tended to be local farmers, boatmen, or landowners who brought one to two immigrants across the border at a time for extra cash.[110] For instance, after American laws took effect, John Thibault, a French Canadian mill worker and rowboat owner living in Cornwall, Ontario, began a side business in smuggling. Thibault worked in a paper mill by day, but as hundreds of Europeans crowded into the city from Belgium and Hungary, he spread the word that for ten dollars, he could row anyone hoping to get into the United States across the St. Lawrence River at night. Before Immigration Service caught Thibault, the millworker surmised that he had taken "between a dozen and twenty aliens across the water."[111]

Informal smuggling grew in popularity in part because there were few laws in place to punish smugglers. The Immigration Service complained that in Buffalo, when a smuggler like Thibault was "apprehended and convicted," he was given "but a nominal fine and the entirely inadequate punishment of one day in jail, neither of which could be expected to in any way deter him from engaging in violations of our law."[112] But smuggling in underpopulated Ontario mill towns rarely exceeded several boatmen acting on an irregular basis.

The border region's largest smuggling industry developed in Windsor, Canada, where organized gangs drew on their experience in the liquor industry to take tens of thousands of Europeans into the United States. After the 1921 Emergency Quota Act, Windsor provided an ideal place to wait the year required to apply to the United States as a Canadian resident. But the 1924 Immigration Act ended this loophole by applying quotas to European residents of Canada. Many of the waiting immigrants had relatives in Detroit, leaving illegal immigration as their only choice to reunite their families.[113] By 1928, so many immigrants crowded into the Windsor region that the *Detroit News* dubbed it the "Ellis Island of the border cities" for the entire United States.[114]

Immigrants smuggled from the Canadian Border Cities to Detroit because they had no trouble finding work in the city's major American factories. Ford Motor Company had a history of employing undocumented workers, usually for short periods. For example, after entering the city illegally on the Detroit-Windsor ferry in 1924, Italian Innocenzo Blanco worked as a metal finisher at Ford for two periods in 1925 before being laid off and finding short-term contract work elsewhere in the city.[115] Similarly, Napolis Usoris, a Lithuanian farmer, flashed FMC badge J-3139 to immigration officials, confirming that he had worked in the Steam Hammer shop at River Rouge for several months in 1928.[116] Thus, even after the 1924 Immigration Act, companies like Ford continued to employ those who could not provide papers in part-time, underpaid positions, a system that, in the short term, benefited immigrants and allowed employers to fill the most difficult or seasonal jobs of the industry.

Soon thousands of Europeans migrated to Canada with the intention of making it to American industrial centers, where they hoped they might find jobs at automobile companies like Ford, Chrysler, and Packard. In late 1924, Belgian Jacob Smoor turned to smugglers in the Detroit-Windsor borderland, a choice he claimed represented his only way to "get out of Canada and get to the U.S.A." After World War I, Smoor left the poverty of his village when a postcard arrived from his cousin in Detroit. The card featured the flowered gardens of Belle Isle Park on one side and, on the

Figure 5. Passengers disembarking the Windsor-Detroit ferry at the foot of Woodward Avenue and presenting their documentation to an Immigration Service officer. The bearded man shown here would have undoubtedly faced further scrutiny in the wake of 1921 and 1924 immigration laws. Courtesy of the Walter P. Reuther Library, Archives of Labor and Urban Affairs, Wayne State University.

other side, recounted the cousin's success in America, where he earned five dollars a day in Henry Ford's Highland Park factory. The salary represented nearly twenty-five times the average wage in Europe, enough to prompt Smoor to investigate joining his cousin.[117] But new American immigration restrictions made Smoor think twice about applying for a Belgian quota visa, and instead, the farmer booked a ticket on a steamer to Canada. When he reached the Canadian port in Montreal, Smoor headed straight to the U.S.-Canada border, where he labored alongside hundreds of other Dutch and Belgian immigrants in the Dominion sugar beet fields of Chatham, Ontario.[118]

Sugar work was difficult and Smoor yearned to leave the fields for Detroit. One particularly grueling afternoon, an envoy of Belgian smuggler Julius Bennett visited the fields, promising healthy workers safe passage into the United States for only five dollars. Smoor jumped at the opportunity to get out of the "sugar shanties" of southeast Ontario and reach his cousin in America's Motor City. Once Smoor agreed, the Bennett gang supervised every step of his journey, from the sugar fields to the docks of Windsor. A lookout ushered him into a tiny rowboat that carried him and three fellow Belgians to Detroit, where an American-based gang member met the immigrants and offered them a warm dinner and a bed in a boarding house on the city's French-Belgian east side. Once he reached Detroit, Smoor found work as a sweeper in Briggs Manufacturing Company, a factory notorious for inhumane labor conditions and low pay.[119] Smoor represented one of thousands of immigrants who turned to smugglers after American quota laws. By 1932, city immigration officials reported that 20,144 deportable Europeans resided within Detroit and its surrounding communities.[120]

In 1924, Congress had appropriated one million dollars to the creation of a "land border patrol" under the Department of Labor to keep immigrants and smugglers from violating new laws. The Border Patrol's role would be to actively search for and apprehend unauthorized immigrants at the border, complementing the work of the Immigration Service, a corps of immigration inspectors (and predecessors of the Immigration and Naturalization Service) that, since 1891, had overseen the administrative aspects of admitting and deporting immigrants in America's principal ports of entry.[121] Over the next several years, the U.S. Border Patrol acquired uniforms, police powers, and a mandate to enforce U.S. immigration laws on the Canadian and Mexican borders.[122] By 1926, Border Patrol officers began to take on more military operations, and in Detroit, they conducted a series of raids on Jacob Smoor's Belgian street. When they determined Smoor had no papers, they sent him to the Immigration Service, which arranged for his deportation to Belgium.[123] Thus, both organizations worked in tandem to locate and arrange for the deportation of unauthorized immigrants in border regions across the United States.

Smoor's story from postwar Europe, to grueling automobile factory, to Detroit's deportation office characterized the lives of thousands of America's immigrant residents.[124] After Congress established restrictive quotas meant to keep certain Europeans out of America, these nationalities faced criminalization that turned them into a suspect group in American society. In the wake of the 1924 Immigration Act, press reports regularly called Europeans in violation of the law "alien criminals," "bootlegged aliens," or "surreptitious entrants."[125] These immigrants' ties to gangs did not help their efforts to assimilate into respectable immigrant society.

Southern and eastern Europeans made up the largest proportion of smuggled immigrants, but Arab and Muslim immigrants also engaged in smuggling. American immigration laws outright excluded and denied South Asian and Afghan Muslims the right to naturalize, making illegal entry and residence their only way to get into the United States. Turks, Syrians, Kurds, and Albanians could naturalize, but the 1924 Immigration Act set quotas that fixed immigration from their home nations to one hundred entrants each year. Migrants hoping to join family and friends in Detroit's sizable Arab community had to seek out immigrant smugglers.[126] An official report from the Syrian embassy in Damascus reported that new immigration laws did not work because they only limited immigrants who, after being rejected, were "content to remain in their homeland." Those intent on migrating to the United States found ways in through illegal routes in Cuba, Mexico, and, most prominently, Canada.[127]

Smuggled immigrants often remained linked to urban underworlds and the networks they provided for years after their initial crossing. Once Smoor made it safely to the Belgian east side of Detroit, he continued to rely on Bennett's smuggling syndicate. The Belgian gang gave Smoor and his fellow aliens housing and steered them toward employment in the beet fields of Michigan Sugar Company. In return, Bennett received sizable bribes from employers. Indeed, Immigration Service inspectors complained that by mid-1924, Bennett had smuggled over five hundred Belgian and Dutch aliens between the beet fields of southeast Ontario and northern Michigan.[128] Bennett himself asserted that the number was higher. While drunk in a speakeasy, he bragged to anyone who would listen that he had no trouble smuggling fifty to one hundred Belgians from Canada every week.[129]

Large smuggling rings like Bennett's operated on both sides of the U.S.-Canada border, throwing immigrants like Jacob Smoor into the center of Detroit's criminal underworld. The proximity between Windsor and Detroit facilitated easy smuggling between the two cities. And while smuggling began informally, it quickly developed into a sophisticated network of crime that extended not only into Canada but also reached nations in Europe. Major smugglers established networks that built on and sometimes rivaled the bootleg liquor industry along the Detroit-Windsor waterway, involving aliens in a vast network of crime and illegality. By 1929, the Immigration Service had identified seventy-five major smuggling gangs operating from Lake St. Clair in the north and extending along the Detroit

River as far south as Dearborn. The tiny islands dotting the west of the Detroit River served as ideal immigrant transfer points, and no spot of American shore was too remote for the skilled smuggler.[130]

Smugglers often specialized in a particular ethnic group and maintained deep ties to local churches, organizations, and meeting houses in that community on both sides of the border. Mike Haluchinski ran one of Detroit's largest Russian, Polish, and Ukrainian smuggling syndicates from the shores of Canada. Haluchinski was born in Canada to Russian parents, and though inspectors suspected he was responsible for thousands of eastern Europeans' entrance into the United States, he never personally stepped onto U.S. soil or was ever charged with a single crime. Instead, Haluchinski established a hierarchical system of runners, lodgers, and boatmen on both sides of the river and ran a complex business of alien smuggling using the Wabash Railway Ferry.[131] By exploiting the railway system, Haluchinski and his gang avoided the patrolled port regions on both sides of the border and did not have to offload their human cargo until they were miles from border checkpoints.

From the Canadian side, Haluchinski sent men like Polish-born Sam Zeleski to find prospective clients in Windsor's immigrant Drouillard Road area. Once Zeleski located five to six Europeans seeking to enter the United States, he collected $100 from each ($20 he kept himself) and hid them in an appointed boxcar bound for Detroit. When the boxcar reached the United States, railroad inspector Herbert Girard received $30 per immigrant to let the boxcar pass without inspection. On the outskirts of the city, it was up to Zeleski to offload the immigrants and usher them into an awaiting taxi to a barbershop in the center of Detroit that fronted an "alien depot." From here, Zeleski returned to Canada via boxcar, leaving the immigrants in the hands of Russell Scott, an American known as Haluchinski's representative on the U.S. side of the border. Scott took responsibility for bringing the immigrants to the city but also for finding them a place to live, telling them which cafeterias to frequent, and where to find work, building the network between smugglers and new immigrants in ethnic communities.[132]

Alien smugglers also tended to work alongside liquor smugglers, associating foreigners with Windsor's bootlegging world. In 1928, the *Detroit News* called the city both the "rum capital of America *and* the nation's greatest port of entry for smuggled aliens."[133] Immigration Service officials confirmed that sometimes liquor smugglers brought immigrants in with their liquor shipments.[134] The association between smuggled immigrants and liquor prompted local newspapers to complain about the "bootlegging of humans" and "bootlegged immigrants" in Detroit.[135] The fact that many new immigrants not only came into the United States in direct violation of the law but also entered in collusion with ethnic gangsters and liquor smugglers cast a subtle shadow of undesirability and potential criminality over their ethnic groups in urban centers across the nation.[136] While today on the U.S.-Mexico border, local authorities and politicians emphasize the link between Latinos and a rising narcotics trade, a similar discourse was apparent as early as the 1920s, when police and policymakers on the northern border labeled foreign-born Europeans "bootlegged aliens," connecting them to the illegal liquor trade.[137]

During the 1920s, a mix of European, Canadian, and American smugglers controlled the entire northern border, building the workforces of America's largest cities. Each smuggling operation managed an established territory, invented its own methods, and specialized in certain combinations of ethnic groups. For a preset fee, smugglers took immigrants from Windsor to Detroit before offering them passage to popular industrial centers in Chicago, Cleveland, New York, Flint, or Pittsburgh, as well as Detroit.[138] The industry mushroomed after the 1924 Immigration Act, ensuring that America's ethnic neighborhoods would continue to receive a steady flow of immigrants. Once in urban centers, smugglers involved legal immigrants in helping, hiding, and housing unauthorized newcomers, involving entire ethnic neighborhoods in the process of subverting and reworking the meaning of new immigration laws on the ground.

Enforcement and Deportation

As mentioned in the previous section, the federal government responded to reports of organized smuggling by militarizing the U.S.-Canada border with the U.S. Border Patrol. When Congress passed the Immigration Act of 1924, it appropriated one million dollars for the creation of a federal Border Patrol, a force that focused much of its early attention on America's northern border.[139] The first Border Patrol comprised 450 men, almost half of whom were stationed on the U.S. border with Canada. By 1925, the Department of Labor had established outposts in Detroit, Montreal, Niagara Falls, and Grand Forks.[140] In Detroit's District 11, which stretched from Lexington, Michigan, to Port Clinton, Ohio, men patrolled in pairs,

Figure 6. Two U.S. Border Patrol officers patrolling the Detroit-Windsor border from the water. In 1929, the U.S. Department of Labor bought three small boats to help officers stay ahead of smugglers, who brought dozens of immigrant clients across the Detroit River every day. Courtesy of the Walter P. Reuther Library, Archives of Labor and Urban Affairs, Wayne State University.

equipped with a .45 handgun, handcuffs, and a flashlight that doubled as a club.[141] Using their nine boats, fourteen motorcycles, and three Chevrolet sedans, the U.S. Border Patrol kept "thousands of immigrants" from entering through Detroit, a region they had begun to call "America's back gate." In the Border Patrol's first two years, civil service examination requirements meant that U.S. Postal workers and a handful of Immigration Service officials formed the bulk of the force. However, men trained to sort letters made poor patrol officers, and high turnover rates encouraged the Department of Labor to reinvent the new enforcement agency.[142]

The militarization of the Border Patrol fit within a broader Progressive Era move toward reforming urban crime for the sake of preserving order and disciplining ethnic and racial minorities. In the 1920s, Progressive reformers foregrounded crime control as a crucial component of establishing an orderly, modern state.[143] Historians have demonstrated how, in Baltimore and Philadelphia, police were central to this vision, and their efforts disproportionately targeted minorities, particularly African Americans.[144] In Detroit, however, the presence of an international border meant that the Border Patrol would join forces with the police to monitor immigrant populations more than in other urban regions. Thus, maintaining order came to mean policing ethnic Europeans who, in turn, gained a reputation for criminal behavior.

Reforming the Border Patrol began in Washington, D.C., but officers tested their new policing techniques at the local level. Because the Border Patrol was administered by the Department of Labor, federal officials decided all changes to the force. In 1927, Secretary of Labor James Davis sanctioned a move to model the Border Patrol on the U.S. Army. Officers were recruited from the military, received training in military techniques, and obtained distinctive new forest green uniforms, badges, and puttees or high boots.[145] In 1927, the *Port Huron Times Herald* compared patrolmen to military officers, claiming, "Shots in the dark and hand to hand encounters with desperate criminals are every-day possibilities in the work of border patrol."[146] The militarization of the Border Patrol cast the U.S.-Canada border as a war zone, labeling the smugglers and immigrants crossing the Detroit River enemies of the state.

On the Canadian side of the border, the Royal Canadian Mounted Police (RCMP) patrolled for illegal liquor and immigrant smugglers. The Canadian Parliament established the Royal Canadian Mounted Police in 1873 to police the Canadian Northwest and promote Anglo settlement of the region. A decidedly military force from its founding, by 1904, RCMP officers had undergone rigorous training before signing a three-year contract and receiving a gun, a bright scarlet uniform, and, of course, a horse.[147] In 1920, the force merged with the Dominion police, Canada's secret service, and assumed responsibility for guarding the border and investigating suspicious political activities in the Dominion. Because 79 percent of officers were born in the United Kingdom, they harbored a natural suspicion toward new southern and eastern European migrants and focused the bulk of their investigation on these ethnic groups.[148] In the Canadian Border Cities, the RCMP founded a headquarters in East Windsor, a heavily immigrant region near Ford's Canadian plant, and dedicated a good segment of its resources to investigating communism, liquor, and immigration violations.[149] Because those under investigation crossed so frequently between Detroit and Windsor, the RCMP worked closely with the newly formed Border Patrol. In 1925, U.S. Assistant Secretary of Labor Robe Carl White remarked that the "work of the Border Patrol . . . compares favorably with that of the Royal Canadian Mounted Police," urging further cooperation between the two nations.[150]

While Border Patrol and RCMP officers watched the physical boundary between the United States and Canada, Detroit police and Michigan state police added "bootlegged immigrant" to their list of violations as they made the rounds through ethnic neighborhoods. In a sensational 1924 *Detroit Free Press* spread that referred to smugglers as "bootleggers in humanity," Border Patrol officers remarked that they operated in "close cooperation" with local and state police forces to apprehend smugglers and immigrants.[151] A year later, a similar story profiling Michigan's state police sensationalized the force's role in curbing liquor and alien smuggling on the Detroit River, claiming that their "adventures rival tales of Texas Rangers of frontier days."[152] Indeed, bringing local police into the process of border enforcement meant that immigration regulation became intertwined with local politics.[153]

Both the local police and federal Border Patrol brought captured immigrants to a third agency, the Immigration Service, for interrogation and potential deportation. In the mid-1920s, the Immigration Service had a holding cell and interrogation room in Detroit's main police department, tying local police to the wider federal process of immigration control. For instance, when Border Patrol officers at the Woodward Avenue ferry docks suspected a young German woman, Gertrude Muller, of trying to enter the United States illegally, they sent her to the Immigration Service, where an officer interrogated her with the help of an interpreter. Within a few minutes, her story that she planned to study the Bible in the United States and had permission to enter as a missionary broke down. In the small Detroit interrogation room, Muller admitted that she could not secure a quota visa in Germany and hoped to enter the United States though Canada. With a confession in hand, the immigration officer sent her to a holding cell, where she awaited deportation to Germany. Thus, from its earliest years, the Immigration Service and Border Patrol became intertwined with the Detroit Police Department.[154]

The new enforcement regime did little to curb undocumented immigration or preserve order in the city. Instead, smuggling increased and smugglers invented ingenious ways to stay one step ahead of Border Patrol officers. When officers began checking rowboats, speedboats, airplanes, and boxcars, smugglers began to hide immigrants in everything from secret truck compartments to linen closets in Pullman railway cars.[155] One group even succeeded in getting immigrants across the border in ventilated coffins.[156]

Between 1927 and 1929, Detroit smugglers brought roughly two thousand Europeans into the United States each month, making undocumented European immigration in Detroit a key concern for U.S. policymakers.[157] Colonel Ruel Davenport, head of the U.S. Border Patrol, reported that Detroit and its surrounding territory constituted "the most vulnerable point in the U.S. armor against smuggling."[158] He informed the *Detroit News* that Detroit and Windsor accommodated "a vast army of expert boatmen" who profited off the thousands hoping to work in the U.S. automobile industry or continue on to other cities. While the Department of Labor never compiled official data concerning illegal immigrants in Detroit, Davenport's obvious concern over smuggling in America's automobile capital suggests that smugglers had more success in this region than in other popular smuggling spots like Buffalo, El Paso, or Havana.[159]

Some smugglers chose to hide the foreignness of European immigrants, bringing them across the border in plain sight. These smugglers dressed immigrants in clothes and styles meant to make them look less foreign. Immigration Service reports on illegal immigration noted with alarm that instead of shawls and kerchiefs, Russian women were wearing silk stockings. Smugglers sewed American manufacturers' labels into their clothes and taught them rudimentary English in case officials probed them with questions.[160] More than a simple change of clothes, this interchange taught new immigrants that their foreignness would become a liability in America. As soon as immigrants reached Detroit's Russian region where families crowded into apartment blocks along Russell Street, they donned the clothes of their homelands and resumed conversations in Russian, Yiddish, or Ukrainian.[161]

Smuggling became an international concern when rings expanded abroad to solicit prospective immigrants in Europe. Between 1927 and 1929, U.S. State Department officials discovered major gangs in Hamburg, Brussels, Paris, Prague, and Naples. These international syndicates stationed men outside American consulates and embassies to take advantage of locals who had been rejected because of filled quotas.[162] Foreign Service officers from Prague, Rome, and Damascus all confirmed that new American immigration laws decreased total immigration but encouraged thousands to leave for Canada "primarily for the purpose of entering the United States at a later date."[163] Officials at the American consulate in Warsaw reported a spike in forged visas alongside a new industry in falsified American birth certificates. Evidently, a number of young people in Warsaw had taken to learning excellent English and making "the fraudulent claim to birth in the U.S. in the hopes of obtaining American passports."[164]

Sensational tales of international crime syndicates and heroic Border Patrol officers cast a shadow of suspicion over foreign-born people living in the Detroit-Windsor region. Windsor's *Border Cities Star* reported regularly on international smuggling rings, claiming that European syndicates provided immigrants with falsified visas and tickets on steamships to Montreal.[165] In Detroit and beyond, newspapers began calling for the government to check the "interloping and menacing aliens" who brought their "tradition of banditry and private vengeance" to the shores of America.[166] By 1928, the press regularly printed the term "alien" alongside the words "criminal," "gangster," and "undesirable," giving noncitizens a reputation for any number of crimes.[167]

Reports linking undocumented immigrants in Detroit to foreignness and espionage also reinforced the connection between certain Europeans and political radicalism. Back in 1924, Director of the Bureau of Investigation William Burns had warned Commissioner General of Immigration William Husband that his forces needed to keep an eye on Detroit, where reports had emerged that communists intended to smuggle Russian and Polish communists into the United States.[168] And while this report never reached the local or national press, fears over radical alien communists remained at the forefront of nativist discourse over the next several years.[169]

The rise of smuggling criminalized foreignness itself, making anyone with an accent or foreign dress appear suspicious in the eyes of many Detroiters. By the close of the 1920s, local reports queried, "How are we to know whether these newcomers are criminals, bootleggers, or suspect people? Their communities are no doubt harboring unsavory characters at this very moment."[170] In the eyes of many Americans, Detroit was turning into America's back door for Europe's undesirables.[171]

American policymakers stoked concerns over illegal immigrants by publicizing wildly different estimates as official numbers. In early 1926, Assistant Secretary of Labor Robe Carl White informed the House Committee on Immigration that the United States contained 250,000 immigrants subject to immediate deportation. Commissioner of Immigration Harry E.

Hull, on the other hand, conjectured there might be as many as 1.3 million undocumented aliens hidden in America's cities, a number he calculated using a complicated formula involving returned immigrants and excluded aliens.[172] These estimates, which were published in newspapers across the United States over the next several years, alarmed many Americans and intensified nativist campaigns in borderlands like Detroit, where the issue of undocumented workers seemed particularly pressing and, as mentioned earlier, local policymakers contended that over twenty thousand deportable aliens resided within the city.[173]

Federal immigration quotas and the policing policies they sanctioned gave nativist groups the force of the law. In June 1924, the Catholic Vigilance Committee, a group of Klan members who felt Catholics were "taking over America," circulated flyers across Ford Motor Company's Highland Park factory. The leaflets encouraged workers to remain wary of their Catholic coworkers, who, after new immigration laws, might be "surreptitious aliens" or "harboring a bootlegged relative." And while the Klan had little evidence that Catholics were more likely to enter the nation illegally, the charge worked to associate Catholic immigrants with undocumented crossing. John Costiglia, an Italian Catholic at Ford, reported that his coworkers "looked at me funny" after the Klan circulated leaflets about potential illegal Catholics in his plant.[174]

Suspicion toward ethnic Europeans incited by nativists informed legal proceedings when the Border Patrol began encouraging Detroiters to inform on potentially illegal neighbors or friends. This system fostered mistrust and tension within immigrant communities. Constantine Polos, a Greek immigrant living without papers, noted bitterly that his neighbor turned him in to free up his apartment, which faced the street and had a window.[175] At Ford Motor Company, George Smith, a Scottish assembly worker with a thick accent, reported losing his job because the worker next to him accused him of crossing into Detroit illegally. The tip brought the Border Patrol to his door and landed him in interrogation for two days before he could prove his legal status. When he returned to the line, the foreman had given the informant his position.[176] The Border Patrol called informants a "legion of friends," claiming they formed an integral part of the state enforcement system.[177] However, the growing network of espionage encouraged native-born and immigrant Detroiters to harbor suspicion toward foreigners and made anyone who appeared foreign vulnerable to the jealousies of coworkers and neighbors. Indeed, encouraging informant networks involved ordinary Detroiters in a collective practice of border enforcement.

Detroiters, of course, did not limit their xenophobic concerns to ethnic Europeans. Like European immigrants, Arab migrants also gained a reputation for violence and potential criminality. But instead of focusing on their illegality, Detroit newspaper reports on Arab immigrants emphasized their religious and cultural differences, portraying them as savage, anti-Western, and potentially polygamist. In the 1920s, polygamy was uncommon in the regions of Turkey and Syria, from which most of Detroit's Arab migrants originated, and it certainly could not have been practiced in Detroit's Arab population of bachelors, many of whom were Christian. Nevertheless, press reports emphasized that the religious and marriage practices of Arab immigrants made them poor candidates for American citizenship and a potential threat to established Christian Americans.[178]

Immigration restrictions did not directly affect Mexicans, but rising nativism and racism meant they, too, gained a reputation as backward, criminal, and undesirable migrants. Because southwestern and western legislators insisted that they needed Mexican agricultural labor, the 1924 Immigration Act did not apply quotas to immigrants in the Western Hemisphere.[179] Thus, Mexicans could migrate to Detroit in large numbers, but when they got to the urban Midwest, they faced employers who viewed them as expendable foreign labor and fired them at the first sign of economic downturn or workplace unrest. When Mexicans did find work, southern and eastern Europeans and African Americans were the first to resent them, and fights often broke out on the shop floors of automobile companies between ethnic and racial groups.[180] Unlike African Americans, Mexican immigrants were not restricted spatially, but as they settled alongside new immigrants from Europe, they faced discrimination and violence from white ethnics who wanted to emphasize their own tentative superiority.[181]

Mexican migrants even faced discrimination from within their own Catholic parish. In 1927, members of Our Lady of Guadalupe Catholic Church wrote to Detroit's Bishop Gallagher that the Anglo priest the archdiocese put in charge of their church had no respect for their community or traditions. Instead of encouraging their faith, they reported, Father Gore had taken down the painting of Our Lady of Guadalupe from the church's altar, a move, they assured the bishop, was "to all Mexicans an insult."[182] The parishioners' letter revealed that even in an institution that was supposed to form the core of Mexican Detroiters' community, they had to negotiate with a church establishment that treated them as inferior.

Because Detroit's Mexican and Arab communities remained relatively small, southern and eastern Europeans became the favorite targets of angry nativists, and calling for immigration raids and deportation became a way for nativists to articulate their ideas with the language of the law. The DAR agreed that undocumented immigrants presented a troubling urban social problem. Working in Detroit's alien detention and deportation center, DAR members complained that detainees were "illiterate and largely degenerate," unable to appreciate the magazines their organization donated.[183] Jessie Dunham Crosbie Ballard, the DAR's head of Americanization, noted that detainees were unlikely to become good Americans and that, when caught, needed to be sent back to their nations of origin.[184] For these Detroit women, immigrants from southern and eastern Europe represented groups marked by foreignness, a trait that was fast becoming a crime in and of itself.

Across the border, the Canadian Legion led the charge against "nonpreferred," southern and eastern European immigrants. In a 1927 address to the Canadian Legion, Hon. Wallace Nesbit warned veterans that "the need of this country is not solely cheap labor" from eastern Europe. Instead, Nesbit suggested that Canada should be doing all it could to restrict immigration to prevent the "adulteration and corruption of its citizenship." In conclusion, Nesbit declared that Canada should look to America and establish quotas against the "unskilled and peasant classes" of Europe.[185] The Legion championed keeping Canada "100 percent British" and encouraged deporting or excluding anyone who did not fit the Anglo-Saxon archetype. The Legion hammered home the idea by funding a series of prominent British ministers on speaking tours across Ontario. In the summer of 1928, Lord Lovat, undersecretary of state for Dominion affairs, urged Toronto's Empire Club and the Canadian Legion to sponsor legislation meant to keep Canadian immigration "not 100 percent Britishers, but 110 percent Britishers." Lovat argued that Canada needed to follow America's example and deport those who did not fit Ontario's distinctly British character.[186]

This cross-border climate of nativism allowed local and federal enforcers to regularize deportation proceedings in Detroit and create a demand for a similar process in Windsor. And while no concrete evidence

links the DAR or Canadian Legion lobbies to the region's deportation practice, they created a culture in which raids, interrogation, and presumed
guilt became permissible and desirable. In the mid-1920s, deportations
began to run through Boards of Special Inquiry, which laid the burden of
proof on the immigrant. In such cases, rather than lingering over suspected
aliens' cases, immigration inspectors devoted the majority of deportation
proceedings to determining the cheapest and fastest way of getting the
immigrants in question out of the country. The process ran with harsh
efficiency, suspending the basic rights of suspects and giving them little
chance to prove their innocence. In fact, only one-sixth of immigrants facing deportation received legal representation.[187]

Deportations developed on both U.S. borders, but Detroit's position as
an industrial center made it particularly concerning to policymakers, who
worried it might become the illegal gateway to cities like Chicago, Cleveland, and New York. And Europeans formed the prime target of legal
deportation raids. In the year after immigration quotas took effect, Commissioner General of Immigration James Davis reported that with the help
of the Border Patrol and local police departments, the United States had
deported the largest number of "undesirable aliens" in its history. Of the
9,495 deported, nearly six thousand were sent back to Europe, while 1,914
faced deportation to Canada and 1,828 to Mexico.[188] These numbers
obscure the informal deportations and policing practices developing on the
U.S.-Mexico border during this period, but they also demonstrate that
Europeans, particularly those in Detroit, faced the bulk of the state's new
administrative expulsion system.[189]

The case of Lucca Casabella demonstrates a typical Detroit proceeding.
On December 17, 1928, the Border Patrol caught Casabella in the trunk of
a smuggler's car with three immigrants from Hungary, Greece, and Yugoslavia. After arresting the group, officers brought Casabella and his cohort
to the Detroit police station, where the immigrants waited in a cell for three
days. On December 20, the police ushered Casabella into the offices of the
Immigration Service, a formidable building on Detroit's main thorough-
fare, Woodward Avenue. Here the Italian waited in a holding room before
an interpreter and chief inspector summoned him for questioning. After a
short interrogation, Inspector Robert Jones decided that Casabella had
entered the United States illegally and ordered him deported to Italy on the
steamship *Dori* at the expense of the steam liner.[190] With his fate sealed,
Casabella still had to wait two months in a Detroit detention center before

joining an eastbound deportation train that began in Chicago and picked up deportable Europeans at several cities before ending in New York.[191]

Casabella's case illuminates several trends that can be traced back to earlier deportation practices against alien Chinese and that, by the 1920s, came to characterize the evolving process of deportation in America.[192] First, it shows that officials entered proceedings with the assumption that an immigrant was guilty. Second, it demonstrates the administrative nature of hearings, which rarely involved more than the immigrant's testimony and almost always ended in deportation. Instead of debating his guilt, administrators in the bureau focused on whether to send Casabella to Europe or Canada, how the deportation was to be funded, and which deportation train could best accommodate Casabella's journey to New York.[193]

Even the most straightforward U.S. government-funded deportations meant immigrants might be held in detention centers for months. Detroit had a short-term detention room at the foot of Woodward Avenue and at the city police department next to the ferry dock, but the nearest long-term detention facility stood sixty miles south in Toledo's Lucas County Jail.[194] Canadian officials visiting the jail reported that conditions inside were deplorable and that deportees were treated not as citizens of a friendly nation but as common criminals.[195]

Deportations, which were popular among local nativists and policymakers, also cast immigrants as feminized dependents on the state with a single phrase: "likely to become a public charge" (LPC). Immigration inspectors had employed what became known as the LPC clause since 1882 to exclude the poor, but its criteria were vague enough to give immigration officers complete discretion over deciding who fell into the "public charge" category. In New York at Ellis Island, for example, inspectors used the LPC clause to reject immigrants suspected of homosexuality or immorality, arguing that, if let into the nation, these "degenerates" were likely to fill the state's jails and insane asylums.[196] Immigration inspectors also routinely denied single women entry or deported them for LPC violations during the first two decades of the twentieth century, arguing that their gender made them predisposed toward dependence on the state.[197]

Along the Detroit-Windsor border, inspectors began to apply the LPC clause to all immigrants, in the process emasculating southern and eastern European migrants by placing them in a category traditionally reserved for women and homosexuals. As smuggling increased along the border, overworked Immigration Service officials used the LPC clause to summarily deport immigrants for a range of reasons. The Immigration Service deported Austrian Leopold Drapal under the LPC clause for professing anarchist beliefs, while Peter Kojainan faced deportation as a "public charge" for managing a prosperous Detroit prostitution business.[198] Though inspectors could have deported Kojainan or Drapal under immigration laws prohibiting anarchism and brothel ownership, two charges connected with masculinity and violence, they chose to use the LPC clause, which did not require evidence or justification.

By the mid-1920s, the Immigration Service labeled immigrants "public charges" to ensure their swift and unquestioned deportation. When Detroit Immigration Service inspectors interrogated Robert Van de Voore, a Belgian who had entered the United States at Buffalo and could produce no papers, they puzzled over what to do with him. Van de Voore was employed as a pastry chef at Century Bakery in Detroit and had little money to his name. However, he swore he had crossed the border legally and had lost his papers. Instead of spending time writing to Buffalo's immigration office or investigating Van de Voore's residency, inspectors stamped his file "likely to become a public charge" because he had only a few dollars in savings. Despite the fact that the Belgian had a steady income, inspectors sent Van de Voore to the Lucas County Jail, where he awaited a deportation train to New York.[199] Van de Voore's story represented a larger pattern in American deportations. From 1925 to 1928, the Detroit Immigration Service reported dozens of cases in which complicated or confusing immigration cases received an LPC stamp sending the immigrants in question to ocean liners bound for Europe.[200]

Ultimately, the 1924 Immigration Act closed a borderland with a history of open exchange and transformed crossing into a crime undertaken by smugglers. By the winter of 1928, Detroiters and Windsorites opened their newspapers to regular coverage of "bootlegged aliens" and "ghost walkers" draped in white sheets looming across the frozen border to Detroit.[201] Such reports helped associate all immigrant Europeans with potential criminality. To keep the border open to trade, key automobile companies opened plants across the border, ensuring that even more southern and eastern Europeans would head to Windsor for work and find their way across the border. Thus, policymakers in Washington, D.C. and Ottawa drafted immigration laws, but it was local enforcers, immigrants, and nativists who negotiated the meaning of new laws, and nowhere was this process more visible or fraught than in the Detroit-Windsor borderland. In the years that followed, local immigrant groups and nativists further negotiated the meaning of federal immigration laws, ensuring that southern and eastern Europeans would become the group most associated with foreignness and the corresponding stigma of criminality.

Chapter 2

Defining Undesirables and Protesting Quotas

In 1927, Austrian Leopold Drapal pretended to be a German and snuck past Immigration Service inspectors on the Windsor-Detroit ferry. Once in Detroit, Drapal found a good job as a machinist at the Cairing Tool Company, where no one ever asked him for papers. Inspectors discovered his illegal entry several years later when Drapal became involved in radical politics. Detroit police only checked his immigration status when they arrested Drapal for throwing a brick through the window of Detroit's Anti-Saloon League headquarters in the name of communism. Had Drapal not vandalized a building or declared himself a communist in the police station, it is unlikely that police would have uncovered his citizenship status or deported him to Austria. Similar cases involving Scandinavian, Irish, Dutch, and British immigrants dot the official records, all featuring a northern European immigrant who, upon arrest, could not produce papers and faced deportation.[1] Most employers, police, and working Detroiters assumed these immigrants were legal until proven otherwise, and in such cases, their status came as a surprise.

The same year, Detroit police conducted a routine immigration raid on Gillespie Construction Company, sure they would discover evidence of undocumented Italian laborers. Most of the workers produced papers on demand, but Sicilian worker Clementi Palazzola could not, so the police sent him to the Immigration and Naturalization Service (INS) for questioning. In what quickly escalated into a deportation deposition, Palazzola claimed to have entered Detroit in 1913. He said he had spent the previous thirteen years working on city sewers and digging ditches. Though Immigration Service inspectors remained suspicious, when Palazzola provided testimony from foremen, grocers, and local vendors that confirmed his tenure in the city, inspectors let him return to work. Even after they released him, however, the inspectors kept investigating and soon found an arrest record for Palazzola dating to 1909, just after the Italian had arrived in Hamilton, Ontario. The Hamilton police report convicted Palazzola of stealing a cart wheel and sentenced him to two weeks in jail. Armed with new evidence, Detroit INS brought a shocked Palazzola back to the immigration station and questioned him about the incident. The Italian assured police it was a mistake: "There was an old wagon in the alley and I took the wheel. I served two weeks because I had no money to pay the fifty dollar fine." But the explanation did not sway the Immigration Service, and they used the case to prove he had committed a "misdemeanor involving moral turpitude," which provided enough of a rationale to exclude Palazzola as an "immoral person" under the 1917 Immigration Act. To seal the case, inspectors also labeled Palazzola "likely to become a public charge" and arranged his deportation to Sicily. Unlike Drapal's case, police and inspectors sought out Palazzola in his workplace and worked to build a deportation case against him.[2]

Northern Europeans like Drapal received less policing and profiling than southern Europeans like Palazzola because their nationalities worked tirelessly to disassociate themselves from the stigma of immigration quotas. Indeed, the 1924 National Origins Act introduced quotas for all Europeans, but local immigration politics and enforcement practices on the ground ensured that only certain immigrants, particularly southern and eastern Europeans, would feel their full effects. By 1929, deportation raids on Italians, Poles, and Russians on Detroit's east side became regular occurrences, while deportations of aliens like Austrian Leopold Drapal were portrayed as surprising anomalies. Perhaps the discrepancy can be explained in part by popular eugenicist theories, but in Detroit, organized British, Finnish, Irish, Austrian, and German activists played a key role in casting southern and eastern Europeans as the criminal immigrants. In an organized protest that ultimately failed to overturn the National Origins Act, northern Europeans did succeed in identifying their groups as respectable, law-abiding immigrants. This positive identity meant their neighborhoods faced few deportation raids, and in the years that followed, their nationalities rarely had to prove their citizenship or allegiance to the nation. For a brief moment, however, northern Europeans fought fiercely against quotas, demonstrating that such laws challenged their perceived acceptance in

American society. And in Detroit, their efforts to cast southern and eastern Europeans as the immigrants worthiest of discipline helped sustain targeted policing and deportation for decades.[3]

In Detroit and other immigrant-heavy cities like New York, Boston, and Chicago, immigrants who felt victimized by new quotas set out in protest. This sustained focus on portraying their groups as ethnically desirable complicates literature on whiteness and ethnicity that argues immigrants became white as a direct result of 1924 immigration quotas.[4] Investigating the pushback and protest to new quotas demonstrates that Europeans viewed quotas as a litmus test for their acceptance in mainstream Anglo-Saxon society. In fact, when compared to Mexicans or African American migrants, ethnic Europeans benefited from their status as white immigrants, but during the 1920s and 1930s, they had difficulty shaking stigmas of foreignness and criminality.[5] Thus, eager not to be cast as foreign, northern Europeans took great pains to protest quotas and emphasize their respectability.

The Midwest's large German and Scandinavian populations and Detroit's proximity to the border made America's Motor City a key site of protest. The National Origins Act changed the quota census year from 1890 to 1920, a move that meant the German and Irish quota would be cut by half and Scandinavians by several thousand. To combat this perceived slight, northern Europeans formed the Anti-National Origins Clause League (ANOCL), a group devoted not to overturning immigration laws but to raising the visa numbers of their own nationalities.

The ANOCL's immediate goal failed when President Herbert Hoover signed the National Origins Clause as a follow-up to the 1924 Immigration Act in 1929, but their larger objective of establishing their superiority as immigrants succeeded. This trend developed across the urban Midwest and eastern seaboard, but in Detroit, border crossing and concerns over illegal immigrants heightened the stakes for immigrants deemed criminal or undesirable. By the late 1920s, despite the fact that Germans bootlegged liquor, Irish smuggled across the border, and Austrians such as Leopold Drapal engaged in political radicalism, these groups managed to disassociate themselves with criminal enterprises. Northern European organizers in Detroit and across the border in Windsor instead argued that southern and eastern Europeans were the criminal immigrants. Consequently, when Detroit police and the Border Patrol launched a "deportation war," they limited raids and searches to southern and eastern European regions of the city, a move that further reinforced these ethnic groups' association with crime. By 1930, those against immigration began to advocate nativist policies through the language of crime control, a move that had broad appeal and long-term repercussions for the immigrants cast as potential criminals in the nation.

Quota Politics

Northern Europeans were not the first group to protest new immigration laws. In fact, American immigrants protested new quotas from the start. Though the 1924 Immigration Act passed with overwhelming support in Congress, pushback from nations in Europe, the powerful Michigan Manufacturers Association, and prominent Catholic and Jewish organizations made lawmakers fear that quotas might be dismantled at any moment. Senator David Reed and Congressman Albert Johnson personally assured the State Department that quotas would not jeopardize fragile global alliances and enlisted the New York Chamber of Commerce to persuade Detroit's industrialists to step in line. However, the congressmen faltered when religious organizations and foreign-language newspapers claimed new laws branded certain immigrants inferior and marginalized entire nationalities.[6] To obscure the nativist underpinnings of the act, Johnson and Reed included a "national origins clause" in the 1924 Immigration Act. The clause promised that by 1927, a Department of Commerce committee would use social science to devise new nondiscriminatory quotas.

Representative Johnson and Senator Reed anticipated pushback from world leaders in Europe and the American businesses that relied on European labor, but protest on the international business front was limited, and quota laws faced their fiercest opposition in America's immigrant communities. The United Kingdom, a nation with high quotas, expressed concern that American immigration policies created an administrative headache for British consular officials who were expected to send documentation or funds to reclaim their citizens.[7]

Similarly, officials in Canada complained that deportations meant their immigration office had become constantly tied up in American demands for documentation.[8] Romania also expressed distress. In early 1924, the Romanian premier wrote to the Canadian undersecretary of state, urging Canada to encourage American lawmakers to lift quotas, which would "dearly wound the pride of the Rumanian people." Romania, he claimed, was attempting to recover from a world war and needed to send its citizens abroad to generate the revenue for financial recovery.[9]

Many nations responded positively to quotas, hoping new laws might reverse world emigration and immigration patterns. While some Canadian officials objected to American immigration laws, Canadian Prime Minister William Lyon Mackenzie King anticipated that closing America's gates might allow "at least some hard working Canadians" to find work in high-paying American factories.[10] A number of eastern European nations that had already tried to slow emigration to bolster their own economies expressed relief that America had finally closed its borders.[11] The Lithuanian minister to Rome, Petras Klimas, told an American consular official that restrictions were "considered as a boon by the Lithuanian government." A postwar population exodus, Klimas worried, would decimate Lithuania's labor force and the 1924 Immigration Act actually saved the Lithuanian government from making unpopular restrictions on emigration.[12] Ministers in Poland and Czechoslovakia expressed similar sentiments, arguing that their states might rebuild only if their citizens stopped emigrating and began establishing businesses, farms, and factories on their soil.[13]

For their part, major American employers were skeptical of any regulation on their labor supply, and Detroit, America's third largest manufacturing center, came to the forefront of this opposition. Detroit's Chamber of Commerce, which represented a diverse body of elite Detroiters, including automobile dealers, lawyers, real estate agents, stock brokers, investment bankers, postal workers, druggists, and merchants, claimed its constituents simply could not afford to lose their access to inexpensive immigrant labor.[14] The Chamber's official publication, *The Detroiter*, insisted that policymakers ought to listen to their needs. After all, the magazine reasoned, Chamber members had the latest cars, the most up-to-date fashions, and the best homes in the city; were patrons of the finest restaurants and hotels; and, above all, paid 85 percent of the city's taxes, making them the city's most respectable and influential inhabitants.[15] Regarding immigration, Chamber members argued that the city was by no means a "dumping ground" for "undesirables" and that the Italians and Greeks operating the machinery and punch presses of their factories were legal, respectable workers who posed no threat to American values.[16]

While the Detroit Chamber took a moderate immigration stance by downplaying the supposed threat immigrants posed to urban life, the

Michigan Manufacturers Association directly opposed quotas. The Lansing-based organization, which represented 90 percent of the state's manufacturers, viewed new laws as a threat to unbridled labor policies. In the winter of 1922, the organization called a special midwestern conference in Chicago with the headline, "Help Prevent a Labor Shortage!" The meeting called for "strenuous efforts" to bring about an amendment to the immigration laws in the name of all industrialists who relied on immigrant workers.[17] Specifically, the organization advocated laxer immigration quotas toward farm laborers, a group in particular demand throughout the Midwest.[18]

To combat business opposition, Representative Johnson and Senator Reed enlisted the New York Chamber of Commerce to speak out in support of restrictions. The organization's vice president, Charles Gwyne, lobbied across the nation, calling "cheap labor un-American" and claiming that industries unable to survive on American labor "should be abandoned."[19] Native-born, naturalized European American and African American workers, the Chamber reasoned, would make better workers.

The prospect of immigration laws energized African American organizations in industrial cities. The Detroit Urban League (DUL), an organization dedicated to advancing the living and working conditions of black Detroiters, had long implored the Employers Association of Detroit to stop hiring foreigners. The DUL reasoned that African Americans provided a superior alternative to immigrant labor, an asset to the city of Detroit rather than a liability. The organization even compared black migrants to European and Mexican immigrants, reminding employers of the desirability and increasing scarcity of workers who were both "native born Americans" and spoke English.[20]

Many black Detroiters resented foreign-born Europeans because, despite their citizenship, African Americans continued to face the worst working and living conditions in Detroit. Ford Motor Company, the largest single employer of black workers in the region, confined African Americans to the foundry, where they poured iron and worked in extreme heat. The foundry soon earned a reputation as the most dangerous placement and its workers suffered burns, inhaled fumes, and weathered frequent bouts with pneumonia and tuberculosis. Despite the foundry's reputation as the "black department," nearly 50 percent of its workers were white, and most of these were recent immigrants. To compensate white workers, however, Ford offered a "foundry premium" that the company did not extend to African Americans. By the mid-1920s, white workers, even those without citizenship, earned an average of 11.3 percent more than their African American coworkers.[21] In housing, African Americans faced similar discrepancies. The majority of black Detroiters crowded into the Black Bottom district and could not find housing elsewhere because real estate agents and landlords had written racially restrictive covenants into deeds and rental agreements. Such covenants, which became a popular way to enforce de jure segregation across the urban North and the West, barred landlords or renters from accepting African American housing applications.[22] And while some African Americans continued to live alongside ethnic whites and a handful of new migrants, particularly Bengali and Indian Muslims, the majority of whom settled in and around Black Bottom, real estate covenants increased segregation in northern industrial centers.[23]

The fact that European immigrants who spoke little English could find better pay and housing stirred resentment among black communities across the nation. A look at discussions of foreigners in the *Chicago Defender*, a black newspaper with a circulation across urban America, demonstrates the bitterness felt by certain African Americans.[24] In a letter to the *Defender*, St. Louis citizen Henry C. Little argued that unlike Portuguese immigrants, black Americans were "full-blooded citizens" and deserved to be treated as such.[25] Similarly, an anonymous black Chicagoan wrote that "members of our Race" lived alongside Jewish, Polish, Italian, Greek, and Armenian immigrants and taught them "our language, our psychology, and our customs." But unlike African Americans, he argued, "only the newcomer seems to benefit."[26] The article demonstrates the frustration of the author, a black American, who, despite his language skills, citizenship, and understanding of American culture, faced more barriers to acceptance in his home nation than new immigrants.

Consequently, the Detroit Urban League favored immigration quotas. When the New York Chamber of Commerce began to pressure employers across the nation to back immigration quotas, the DUL assured Detroit's businesses that African Americans made excellent replacement workers.[27] Amid local and national pressure, Detroit's business community fell in line and began to view immigration restrictions as an inevitable set of new laws that corporations and employers would need to negotiate to their own benefit.

While the American business community relented on quotas, the immigrant and religious groups affected by the 1924 Immigration Act redoubled their protest. American Catholic leaders argued that new laws would legitimize the nativist rhetoric published by "self-styled patriotic societies" like the Daughters of the American Revolution, a group that claimed Catholics made "unacceptable immigrants" and often carried diseases.[28] The National Catholic Welfare Conference (NCWC) did not engage the DAR pamphlets but instead protested quotas in Congress. New immigration laws, the NCWC reasoned, would not curb poverty, reduce disease, or stop foreign languages from being spoken in urban streets. Instead, the Catholic organization warned that restrictions would "anger immigrants against America by the patent discrimination, which this proposed." Catholic bishops from across the United States urged Congress to make quotas fair so as not to "justify the egregious demands of patriotic groups" like the DAR and the American Legion.[29]

Arab Americans, particularly Syrians, used religion to argue that they deserved higher quotas and, at the very least, the chance to become citizens.[30] Between 80 and 90 percent of Syrian immigrants in the United States before 1924 were Christian, and they relied on this fact to emphasize their desirability as opposed to Muslim Arabs or Muslim Indians. For instance, Syrian immigrants portrayed themselves as victims of Ottoman oppression in search of justice and acceptance in the United States. But ironically, because quotas accounted for nationality, not religion, Syrian Christian lobbies helped ensure that Syrian Muslims, Turks, and Albanians would receive quotas regardless of faith. Indian Muslims, on the other hand, were subject to Asian exclusion laws and could not become naturalized citizens.[31] Ultimately, a segment of Detroit's large Muslim community objected to their very small quota numbers yet refrained from voicing sustained protest in a fight they may have felt powerless to win.

Jewish Americans, on the other hand, voiced their objections to quotas early and loudly. Jewish organizations agreed that quotas would mark foreigners, particularly Jews, as inferior. The American Jewish Congress and B'nai B'rith International called upon Congress to dismantle restrictive quotas. *Novoye Russkoye Slovo*, a Russian Jewish publication with a national circulation of seven hundred thousand, claimed quotas would divide Americans into "class A citizens" who were native born and "class B citizens" who were "born on the wrong side of the Atlantic."[32]

Like the Jewish press, foreign-language newspapers lambasted the new immigration laws. New York Italian newspaper *La Follia* called quotas "un-American, inhuman and despicable." *Il Progresso*, a national left-leaning Italian paper, objected to quotas because they linked Italians to illiteracy, criminality, and general undesirability. Quotas would only be admissible, the newspaper argued, "only when they are equal for all nations." New York's *Russky Golos* took the lobby a step further, claiming that Congress was "throwing a bone to the KKK and the American Legion." By February 1924, the State Department organized a report for Congress with vehement complaints from a range of Lithuanian, Russian, Polish, Hungarian, and Italian papers, all citing the distinctly "un-American" nature of new laws.[33]

Other foreign newspapers attacked quotas for misrepresenting their national groups. Basing quotas on the 1890 census, many immigrants argued, could not account for the breakup of the Austro-Hungarian Empire, which changed borders and produced immigrants whose identities did not align with the states from which they originally immigrated. American census takers, they complained, often listed Czechs as Austrians and confused Hungarians, Lithuanians, Russians, and Poles.[34] This inaccuracy, they reasoned, made the entire quota system flawed. Rather than offer an equitable solution to America's immigration system, the Polish newspaper *Amerikai Magyar Hepszaba* charged quotas with "enacting racial and religious discrimination into law," under the guise of equity.[35] Thus, Catholic and Jewish organizations and immigrant newspapers introduced the idea that low quotas corresponded with the value the American state had placed on their nationalities, turning the battle for quotas into a symbolic struggle over acceptance in American society.

Protest worried Representative Johnson and Senator Reed, who wanted a permanent set of American laws that could not be called biased or unfair toward any ethnic groups. Their solution, the national origins clause, drew on statistics and census data to offer new quotas that would not explicitly discriminate against certain groups for ethnic reasons. The national origins clause, which was scheduled to take effect in 1927, involved three important changes to American immigration law. First, it discarded the provision designating quotas at 2 percent of each nationality's foreign-born population under the 1890 census and capped total immigration at 150,000. Second, it allocated new quotas according to the "national origins" (a deliberately confusing concept) of America's total population rather than its foreign-born population. And finally, to make the law appear unbiased, lawmakers chose 1920 as the year to base America's new national origins quotas. Those in favor of restrictions hoped new quotas would appear nondiscriminatory while still favoring Anglo-Saxon nations.[36]

In the spirit of the Progressive Era, the national origins clause promised to use statistical analysis in order to maintain the racial and ethnic makeup of the United States. A "scientific" study of the origins of the American people in 1920 would serve as the basis of the new quotas.[37] Senator Reed argued that unlike the 2 percent formula, which used numbers of foreign entrants to determine quotas, national origins quotas should "roughly correspond with the national origin of our whole population," including those of American citizens. National origins quotas, he claimed, would promote a "united and homogeneous" nation, unsullied by "foreign points of view, foreign loves, foreign hates, foreign newspapers, foreign colonies and foreign propaganda."[38] Nativist policymakers hoped that by couching new quotas in the language of social science, the American public, including the Catholic and Jewish establishment, would view the quotas as a way to maintain America's identity.[39] In a hearing before the House Committee on Immigration, Senator Reed assured Congress, "I think most of us are reconciled to the idea of discrimination. I think the American people want us to discriminate." The key issue for Senator Reed became finding a discriminatory system that Americans would support and tolerate.[40]

Not surprisingly, national origins quotas proved difficult to quantify. Dr. Joseph A. Hill, a statistician at the U.S. Bureau of Census, chaired the Quota Board and immediately set out to determine the national origins of America's 1920 population.[41] Hill and the committee analyzed surnames and scrutinized incomplete census data from 1850 to 1890, which only began recording immigrants in 1820 and designating immigrants by "race or people" in 1899. And as immigration protesters had noted, post–World War I boundary changes left many Europeans in a category that was nearly impossible to classify by national origin.[42] For example, Heinrich Petersen, an immigrant of German descent whose family emigrated from Szczecin at a time when the town was part of the German Empire, suddenly became Polish when the Quota Board used the world's post–Versailles Treaty boundaries to classify national origins.[43] Ultimately, new quotas proposed by the board mixed prewar and postwar boundaries and incomplete U.S. census data to impose a system of classification legitimized by social science.[44]

The architects of the 1924 Immigration Act were thrilled with the new quotas and hoped ethnic Americans would view them as a compromise. John Bond Trevor, a lawyer who helped Senator Reed and Representative Johnson devise the quota system, claimed that the national origins plan presented the only "method which represents native born American stock in the quotas and at the same time will keep the foreign elements of our country from lodging complaints."[45] The national origins plan doubled the quota for British immigrants, while Poles and Italians enjoyed a slight increase in their admitted numbers (one thousand and two thousand, respectively), and other southern and eastern European groups received similar numbers. The slight increases, policymakers reasoned, would make it seem as though Congress had addressed the concerns set forth by Jewish and Catholic organizations. The largest changes were to the German and Irish quotas, which new formulas cut in half, and to Scandinavian nations, where immigrants lost nearly two-thirds of their entry slots.[46] The law's architects lamented the loss of Scandinavian numbers, but they saw it as necessary if they wanted to lower German quotas in favor of British migrants.[47]

In Detroit, business organizations immediately objected to new quotas. The Michigan Manufacturers Association (MMA) voiced the concern of automobile companies, which relied on the skilled Germans who formed the backbone of machinist labor. Lowering German quotas, the MMA argued, threatened to stymie innovation and production in the industry.[48] The Chamber of Commerce made its concern public in its magazine, *The Detroiter*, which soon added "ending national origins" to its list of organizational objectives.[49] But Detroit's businesses had little power to change federal policy, and within a few months, they dropped the issue.

Higher quotas mollified Detroit's Italian Americans, who felt slighted by the 1890 plan. The *Tribuna Italiana* noted that national anti-Italian sentiment might be on the decline because new laws promised to raise Italian visas from 3,845 to 5,802.[50] The *Voce del Popolo*, a local Italian antifascist paper, expressed similar views toward new quotas, which editor Father Joseph Ciarrochi claimed were quite "favorable to Italy." Ciarrochi, a priest at Detroit's Santa Maria parish who had achieved local celebrity status with his stand against the Italian mafia and Mussolini, encouraged Italians to send for skilled friends and family to fill new quotas, asserting that within a few more years, all Americans would begin to say, "The Italian immigrant stock of today is fine!"[51]

While some Italians viewed higher quotas as a sign that Anglo America was ready to view them as more than impoverished workers and bootleggers, others remained skeptical of federal reform. The Sons of Italy, a national Italian organization of 300,000, protested national origins quotas on the grounds that any and all restrictions stigmatized the hardworking immigrants already in the United States. In early 1927, Vincent Esperti and

Paul Bommarito, supervisors of Detroit's Lodge 215, claimed any legislation including quotas "evinces a spirit of animosity against Italy and avow-
edly discriminates against all Italians." In Detroit, where a border threw
issues of smuggling and immigration into sharp relief, Esperti and Bommarito argued new laws were highly "un-American and destructive of faith
and confidence" in the American nation.[52] The Sons of Italy maintained
that any laws ranking certain nationalities above others would cause unfair
treatment and promised not to back down on discrimination laws. And
indeed, ethnic protest to national origins would keep immigration law at
the forefront of American politics for the next five years.

Immigrant Protest in Detroit

The northern European nationalities facing lower entry quotas became the
most outraged with the new National Origins Act because they thought
their groups were so desirable that they should face no quotas at all. In
1927, Detroit's Scandinavians, Germans, Belgians, Dutch, and Irish immigrants formed the Anti-National Origins Clause League, a group that
reached a membership of 500,000 across Michigan and argued that quotas
and their enforcement unfairly targeted members of their "respectable"
nationalities. While the ANOCL failed to convince the government to raise
their quotas, northern European activists succeeded in distancing their
nationalities from the stigma of illegal entry after the act passed. By the late
1920s, ANOCL efforts ensured that southern and eastern Europeans, not
immigrants from Ireland or Germany, earned a reputation for crime and
illegal crossing.

Inhabitants of northern industrial regions with large immigrant populations like Boston and New York also protested the national origins plan.
The Board of Alderman of Chelsea, Massachusetts, a working-class industrial region just across the Mystic River from Boston, launched a protest on
behalf of their immigrant constituents. The national origins plan, they
argued, was "based on a hazy and unsound foundation of facts" and would
"be interpreted to the detriment of the Celtic, Teutonic, Slavic, and Scandinavian races." Drawing on a gendered notion of the hardworking immigrant, the aldermen insisted that restrictive laws made Europeans "resent
the imputation and undesirableness cast upon those nations of Europe,
from whose virile manhood and womanhood the very structure of this
country was built on." Indeed, dozens of letters from Boston, Connecticut,

and New York poured in imploring President Hoover to think twice before signing immigration laws that would humiliate immigrants.[53]

Large populations of Germans and Scandinavians in the Midwest, however, meant the majority of protest stemmed from this region, particularly from Detroit. Indeed, ANOCL rallies drew leaders from Detroit's more established immigrant communities into common conversation. On January 2, 1928, thousands of northern European immigrants packed into the Arena Gardens Skating Rink to voice their concern over new quotas. Local Danish minister and spokesman for the group, Reverend Sven Jorgensen, took the stage first, reminding the audience that the "desirability of the Scandinavian race" made new quotas an insult. Next, Recorder's Court Judge Frank Murphy spoke on behalf of the city's Irish Catholics, decrying the "Anglo-Saxon supremacy" that had shaped Detroit politics. Archbishop Michael Gallagher echoed Murphy's concerns about Anglo-Saxon elitism and added that new laws "unfairly targeted Catholics" and made upstanding churchgoers appear suspect to Protestant Detroiters.[54] Figures like Jorgensen, Murphy, and Gallagher united certain immigrant groups, but their cries of outrage did not extend to all immigrants or even to all Catholics. By positioning their national groups as respectable, hardworking immigrants, the ANOCL implied and often stated that it was southern and eastern Europeans who should be barred from the boundaries of America.

New quota laws turned the politics of immigration into a personal struggle for many Europeans. In 1926, just as quotas took full effect against Scandinavians, Bergljot Nilssen warned her mother-in-law in Norway that "the new law is unnecessarily strict" and that getting her nephew Eigil into the United States would be tricky. Despite the fact that Eigil was a sober and respectable farmer, she lamented, it would be impossible for him to secure a visa under new quota laws.[55] Cases like Bergljot's, which expressed concern that quotas targeted nationalities considered respectable, soon became common in Detroit and inspired immigrants to join the ANOCL.

The ANOCL gave immigrants like Bergljot an outlet for their frustration. By the spring of 1927, Detroit's ANOCL held monthly rallies in the city and began to circulate literature and petitions throughout the United States.[56] In particular, ANOCL publications questioned the "appalling exhibition of mathematical jugglery" on display in the new quotas, which the Senate called "accurate and scientific."[57] ANOCL President Joseph Carey, a second-generation Irish American lawyer from Detroit, assured policymakers in Washington that his organization did not object to the "spirit of immigration restrictions." Instead, Carey insisted that Irish, Scandinavian, German, and Dutch immigrants deserved a greater sign of respect for having "contributed much to American industry and life."[58]

As the organization gained popularity and influence across the city, ANOCL members began to vocalize precisely what its members thought about other immigrant groups. In letters to the House Immigration Committee, the ANOCL called southern and eastern Europeans and their American-born children "alien blocs, alien groups, and foreign groups." The letter expressed the indignation of Germans, Irish, Danes, and Finns that their nationalities had been categorized alongside the Poles and Italians who might soon "ruin America."[59] Indeed, their lobbies suggested that no matter how many generations these immigrants lived on American soil, they would never become full Americans.

Some German Americans even began to feel the ANOCL's attitudes toward southern and eastern Europeans were too liberal and joined the more radical Ku Klux Klan. In 1927, Otto Schultz, a naturalized German, received a letter from L. J. Black, kilgrapp, or secretary, of Detroit's Klan Number Sixty-Eight, accepting him into the Klan. On the evening of February 8, Schultz, a thirty-eight-year-old automobile worker, quietly slipped out of the apartment he shared with his brother-in-law and sister Lottie and headed toward the Danceland Arena, where he took his oath, or "naturalization," into the nativist organization. Schultz represented a growing segment of northern European immigrants who turned to the nativist rhetoric of exclusion and racism to legitimize their own claims to citizenship.[60]

Northern European activism gained national traction when Secretary of Commerce Herbert Hoover realized he needed the German and Scandinavian vote to win a presidential election campaign against Catholic Democrat Al Smith. One look at ANOCL letters and newspaper coverage of midwestern rallies against national origins made it clear that siding with new quotas would alienate a significant block of northern European voters. Though he had supported President Coolidge's efforts on immigration reform, when Hoover took Coolidge's place on the Republican ticket, he shifted his stance on immigration. In July, just four months before the election, Hoover released a statement claiming he remained in favor of overall immigration restrictions, but he had begun to rethink national origins quotas, which he suddenly viewed as "indeterminable, uncertain, and unsound."[61] In case this did not convince German American voters, he also emphasized his own German ancestry and his role in ending the German blockade as head of the U.S. Food Administration during World War I. To further assure voters of his commitment to repealing the National Origins Act, Hoover backed a Senate proposal to postpone quotas, arguing that they needed further analysis to truly reflect the American population.[62]

Hoover's political maneuvers shocked powerful nativists who feared immigration restrictions might be in jeopardy. The North American Civic League, a national patriotic society with a distinctly nativist platform, denounced the candidate for pandering to "temperamental and highly excitable" groups of immigrants. Likewise, the Sons of the American Revolution accused Hoover of ceding to the demands of "anti-American, pro-foreign groups."[63] However, nativist complaints could not persuade the candidate to change his stance. Hoover knew that even if he infuriated nativist groups, their members were unlikely to cast a vote for his opponent, New York Governor Al Smith, a Catholic who advocated shifting quotas to favor southern and eastern Europeans.

Ultimately, backing a move to postpone and reexamine national origins quotas secured Hoover the votes he needed to win the election. By November 6, 1928, 26 percent of the nation's German-language newspapers had endorsed Hoover and the German and Scandinavian votes split. According to the *New York Times*, Smith predictably won the majority of Poles, Italians, Greek, Czechs, Slovaks, Slovenians, and Croatians but only half of German voters. Scandinavians turned out in even larger numbers for Hoover, with nearly 60 percent of their population casting votes for the Republican's moderated platform.[64] After Hoover's win, ANOCL organizers redoubled their efforts on behalf of their national groups. The organization expanded its membership across the United States and recruited over nineteen hundred ethnic organizations into an umbrella society that claimed to represent the interests of northern Europeans nationwide.[65]

The campaign fostered a culture of exclusion that clearly ranked certain Europeans higher than others and fed into the vision of the nation advanced by patriotic societies and the Klan.

Much as before, the ANOCL highlighted the confusion brought on by a new quota system and the difficulty in determining the "national origin of all Europeans." But the organization also made sure to place special emphasis on the fact that northern Europeans were "rarely bootlegged" and "almost always upstanding citizens."[66] President Carey urged Congress to base quotas on the 1890 census, which excluded Europeans who were "prone to corruption and less adaptable to the climatic, economic, and social conditions of the country."[67] By positioning their nationalities as less "aliens" and more "citizens of this country demanding their rights," the ANOCL set forth northern Europeans as the American immigrants most deserving of citizenship and equal rights.[68]

Continued congressional debate over quotas and immigration laws also brought Mexican immigrants under scrutiny. Soon many Americans began to conflate high quotas for southern and eastern Europeans with a call for Western Hemisphere quotas against Mexicans. For instance, in a letter to President Hoover, Mrs. Gladys A. Roll of Des Moines, Iowa, condemned the president for keeping out desirable Scandinavians when she thought he should be stopping "the undesirable element that has crept into America from southern and eastern Europe" and placing some sort of cap on immigrants from Mexico.[69] When discussing Mexicans, Gladys Roll was most likely referencing a movement under way in Congress that proposed quotas for Mexican immigrants.

Unlike the national origins clause, the effort to end Mexican immigration crumbled under pressure from large agribusiness and grassroots Mexican activism. In 1926, John Box, a congressman from a tiny town in east Texas, introduced the Box bill, which would cap Mexican immigration to 2 percent of the 1890 census, but the bill failed to gain traction.[70] Despite a general inclination toward nativism, congressional leaders feared confrontation with powerful farmers who relied on Mexican labor across the southwest. Box did not give up easily, and over the next several years, he used the stock market crash of 1929 and the corresponding economic depression to justify numerous proposals to end Mexican and even Canadian immigration, all of which failed.[71] Despite the failure of congressional action, discussions over restricting Mexicans emboldened nativists to continue lobbies against immigrants from across the southern border. In a letter to the *Detroit Free Press*, C. M. Goethe, president of the Immigration Study Commission, called for the United States to close the "Mexican back door" and end the immigration of "Mexican undesirables" to the United States. And while the United States never extended quotas officially to Mexico, anti-Mexican nativism led to the Mexican repatriation movement of the Depression era, a topic that will be covered further in Chapter 4.

Immigrants did not protest in Windsor because the Canadian government maintained relatively lax immigration laws. Despite the Canadian Legion's calls to close Canada's borders to all but British citizens, Minister of Immigration Robert Forke insisted that Canada would continue to welcome immigrants from Scandinavia, Germany, and Luxemburg. When questioned about southern and eastern Europeans, he assured concerned Canadians that steamship companies would admit "only those men as they could guarantee to find work for."[72] But in reality, thousands of southern and eastern European farmers and domestic workers could still secure visas to Canada and, after a season in western Canada, head to Windsor or the United States.

Consequently, Windsor's population of southern and eastern Europeans continued to grow. Most European newcomers lived on Windsor's west side or in the autonomous region adjacent to Ford Motor Company known as Ford City. By 1929, the region had a large population of Poles, Ukrainians, and Italians, many of whom had crossed over from the United States to work in Canadian branch plants. Soon, however, several hundred Serbs and Croatians made their way to Ford City for unskilled work. Radoje Knejevitch, editor of the *Voice of Canadian Serbs*, remembered of the Serb community, "They were not specialists, carpenters and so, but poor people who had strong muscles and many only 20 or so years."[73] Indeed, new Serbian and Croatian immigrants tended to be young men with little job training, a group perfect for low-wage automobile work but who would also face first layoffs in times of economic hardship.

Many of these new immigrants ended up in Windsor after brief stints at farm labor. For instance, Serbian Pavle Popov left Yugoslavia in 1927 at the age of twenty-four for work on a farm in Harrow, Ontario, a tiny town just south of Windsor. Instead of the economic windfall he had imagined might help him support a wife and children, Popov found himself in a tiny town surrounded by a strange language and only earned one dollar each day. Popov ran into some luck, however, later that year when he found work constructing the Ambassador Bridge, the international suspension bridge that would connect Detroit to Windsor. By 1928, he found a job at Ford of Canada, and two years later, he had saved enough to bring his wife and children to Canada.[74]

As Windsor became more international and nativism increased, businesses sometimes refused to employ immigrants to set themselves apart. In May 1929, the Windsor Spark Plug Plant advertised that its business was "100 percent Canadian." Not only did the company use all Canadian raw materials, but it also employed a staff "made up entirely of residents of the border cities." The fact that the company did not employ immigrants or groups usually referred to as "newcomers to the Border Cities" became a point of pride.[75] Thus, as in the United States, new Slavic and eastern European migration patterns ensured that nativism and pro-Canadian activism would continue to inform the city's local politics.

In the United States, President Hoover found he could no longer ignore nativist groups' insistence that national origins quotas presented a legitimate and scientific immigration system. In March 1929, the American Legion, DAR, and the Immigrant Restriction League merged to form the Allied Patriotic Societies.[76] The organization claimed that the National Origins Act was the only plan that would "preserve the blood of the United States in its present proportions." Countering the arguments of the ANOCL, the group emphasized the exclusive desirability of Anglo-Saxons, reporting that people from England and Scotland were far more likely to marry Americans and assimilate than Norwegian, German, or Danish immigrants. The society admitted that these northern Europeans might one day become Americans but claimed that they were alien enough to be good candidates for exclusion.[77] The Ku Klux Klan also joined the campaign, sending thousands of telegrams and letters to senators and representatives in Washington urging policymakers to support national origins.[78] In July 1929, the Senate passed the final National Origins Act and, having secured the German and Scandinavian votes, President Hoover signed it without hesitation.

With the passage of the National Origins Act, the Anti-National Origins Clause League dissolved. ANOCL President Joseph Carey chastised Hoover for reversing his immigration policy and deceiving "good Americans" for votes. In a letter to Assistant Secretary of Labor Robe Carl White, Carey wrote, "We feel that pledges of our President should be carried out" and that the northern Europeans of America "look forward to a future date for the cancellation of the 'national origins' plan."[79] But Hoover never revisited the national origins question, and the new quotas formed part of America's permanent immigration system.

Despite the ANOCL's failure to meet its immediate goals, the organization did succeed in distancing northern Europeans from the stigma of illegal immigration and crime. At a moment when deportations were on the rise and nativism thrived, Irish, German, and Scandinavian immigrants avoided association with crime and illegality. Finns and Swedes still faced deportations, but these proceedings tended to be the result of accidental arrest.[80] Poles, Russians, Italians, and Romanians, on the other hand, began to negotiate a world in which deportation raids in their ethnic halls, workplaces, and neighborhoods had become commonplace.[81]

Nativism, Criminalization, and Deportation

Associating southern and eastern Europeans with crime allowed local politicians to code nativist agendas with the language of crime control. In Detroit's 1929 mayoral election, this meant that traditional nativist voters joined northern European members of the ANOCL to back Charles Bowles, a candidate who had once been associated with the Ku Klux Klan. Instead of discussing ethnic undesirability, however, Bowles, focused on a message of crime control. Promising to end urban crime was not overtly nativist, but in a city where southern and eastern Europeans had gained a reputation for bootlegging and border smuggling, calls for reform meant addressing immigration issues. And as mayor, Bowles set to work with local law enforcement to launch a "deportation war" that targeted southern and eastern Europeans. By the onset of the Great Depression, deportations targeting ethnic workplaces and neighborhoods became a popular way to address anxieties about the problems immigrants supposedly brought to America.

The 1929 election offered Detroiters a clear choice. On one side was Catholic Democrat John W. Smith, who had already bested Bowles in the 1924 mayoral election and entered the race confident that his voting base would again come through. Yet Smith failed to grasp the extent to which nativist rhetoric would galvanize Anglo-Americans and the northern Europeans who so desperately wanted to be accepted as Detroiters. By promising a "tough line" on crime and an even "tougher line" toward aliens, Republican candidate Charles Bowles appealed to thousands of voters who may not usually have supported a candidate with a Klan background. In a campaign that newspapers dubbed the "most bitter ever staged in Detroit," Bowles proposed a platform that exploited nativist fear and exacerbated standing divisions between ethnics and African Americans.[82]

The Klan seized on this moment of economic uncertainty to put its preferred candidate in office.[83] Bowles paid lip service to moderation and disassociated himself from his Klan backers enough to gain broader support, but the Klan campaigned hard for Bowles in public rallies. Just a month before the election, in September 1929, thousands of Klan members and concerned Detroiters crowded into Danceland Arena, a giant hall in the heart of the city, to hear Klan leader and Alabama Senator Richard Heflin endorse Bowles. Heflin addressed Detroit's white middle and working classes in a southern drawl, citing the evils of "evolution, Poles, and the Catholic Church." Amid applause, Heflin passed out nomination sheets featuring Bowles's photo and a promise to rid the city of crime and Russian aliens in the same sentence, suggesting the two were related.[84]

Bowles's platform called for criminal reform and Anglo-Protestant respectability, a move that emphasized to Detroiters that it was newer Catholic and Jewish immigrants who posed the threat to American laws and values. Supported by the *Detroit News* and the *Detroit Free Press*, Bowles portrayed himself not as a hooded vigilante armed with a burning cross but as an upstanding Michigander with the people's interest at heart. On the campaign trail, he emphasized the fact that he had never "traveled below the Mason-Dixon line," making him a true local. Indeed, Bowles was born in Yale, Michigan, where he attended public schools before attending the University of Michigan. Appealing to Detroit's working-class Protestants, Bowles brought up his membership in Detroit's Congregational Church along with fraternal orders such as the Masons, the Elks, the Odd Fellows, and the Eagles. He also promised to appoint a new chief of police and end urban crime, pitting himself against his opponent, Mayor John Smith, who he claimed had spent three and a half years presiding over "one of the most lawless periods in Detroit history."[85]

In perhaps a surprising turn, Bowles reached out to African American voters, claiming that they should unite against a common Catholic, immigrant enemy. Tactical alliances between Klan affiliates and African American activists were not unprecedented. In 1922, black Nationalist leader Marcus Garvey met with the Ku Klux Klan to organize a détente of sorts, proposing that African Americans and whites keep to themselves.[86] Perhaps drawing on this precedent of communications between white supremacists and black Nationalists, Charles Bowles assured Detroit's African American community that if they voted for him, he would leave them in peace. He reminded black Detroiters that as a judge in the Recorder's Court, he had worked to save the all-black St. Paul Zion A.M.E. Church, while his opponent, John Smith, "was so prejudiced that he refused to sit even in school by a colored boy." Immigrants and Catholics, he noted, formed the real threat to Protestant society.[87]

Bowles's sudden appeals to Detroit's black community did little to garner African American support, but the move did make him appear more moderate in the eyes of many white voters. This turn to moderation helped build the "Bowles stronghold," the press's new name for his coalition of working-class and elite Protestant supporters.[88] By voting for the new Bowles, who the Klan surrounded with a "Protestant halo" of respectability, many whites could support maintaining the Anglo status quo without participating directly in Klan politics.[89]

Despite his insistence on Protestant superiority, many northern European Catholics voted for Bowles. Joseph Carey, Irish Catholic immigrant, fierce advocate for northern European rights, and former president of the Anti-National Origins Clause League, suggested Bowles "might be good for the Irish." Reasoning that no one would be "the worse for a purge of some Italians and Poles," Carey urged northern Europeans to claim their "respectability and thrift" and stop "voting for immigrant interests."[90]

Catholic John Smith, on the other hand, appealed to immigrants with promises of liberal unemployment benefits and relaxed alcohol laws.[91] Calling dry laws "the rankest sort of joke," Smith likened himself to the average working-class voter, with a life straight from "a tale by Horatio S. Alger."[92] The child of a single mother and war veteran, Smith joined a union and became the superintendent of a construction company before Governor Chase Osborn appointed him deputy labor commissioner and eventually sheriff of Wayne County. As sheriff, Smith mediated a peaceful labor dispute involving "foreign workers in Wyandotte who did not know how to express their grievances."[93] Such stories made Smith a hero in the eyes of thousands of southern and eastern European workers. The *Tribuna Italiana D'America* reminded "all of immigrant Detroit" that Smith had no affiliations with the Klan and had lobbied against immigration restrictions in 1924. To them, Smith represented immigrants and their interests, while Bowles wanted to deport them.[94]

But on November 6, 1929, Bowles's platform of Protestant cultural politics and crime control won him the election with a margin of eight thousand votes. In an inaugural speech broadcast across Detroit, the new mayor promised to end corruption and open a new era. His administration, he predicted, would quash the "vicious criminal element of foreign origin" threatening the industrial North.[95]

As mayor, Bowles launched a system of profiling and deportation that solidified growing links between southern and eastern Europeans and crime. Because northern Europeans had managed to establish their respectability with ANOCL protests, or perhaps also because they mobilized for Bowles during the campaign, the mayor left their neighborhoods out of deportation efforts. By emphasizing the "desirability" of German, Irish, British, and Scandinavian immigrants, Mayor Bowles and city police suggested that there was something inherently criminal and un-American about other national groups. Soon local newspapers drove home the idea that the only way to purge the streets of "Italian gangsters," "Russian smugglers," and "Hungarian conmen" was to deport them.[96]

Using local police to carry out deportation raids in the name of crime control was not a new tactic. Beginning in the 1880s, police in Boston and New York, two port cities with large numbers of Irish immigrants, rounded up poor and criminal newcomers for return to Ireland. Their efforts laid the groundwork for an 1891 federal measure allowing the deportation of anyone deemed "excludable" under standing immigration laws. By the turn of the century, Massachusetts and New York rounded up and deported large numbers of poor Irish immigrants, reasoning that without money, they would certainly turn to a life of crime.[97]

During the Prohibition era and in the early years of the Great Depression, police in major cities used what they termed "deportation drives" to control local immigrant communities. In Chicago, for instance, police rounded up residents of immigrant neighborhoods indiscriminately, bringing them to district stations for interrogation and eventual release. Sometimes prosecutors charged them with minor violations, but only a small proportion of those arrested ever made it to immigration officials for further questioning. Thus, deportation drives were less about actual deportations and immigration laws and more about local social control and demonstrating police might. In particular, police eager to stem criticism over Prohibition-era police corruption increasingly used deportation drives to demonstrate their competence as a law enforcement agency.[98]

Though Detroit's police records of the period no longer exist, it stands to reason that local police carried out deportation raids for similar reasons. To demonstrate police competence and the law enforcement prowess of the new Bowles administration, in the fall of 1929, Detroit's Immigration Bureau director, John Zurbrick, instituted a "deportation war" that resulted in thousands of arbitrary arrests and as many as a thousand deportations.[99] To wage his "quiet war," Zurbrick organized a partnership with the Detroit Police Department, urging Police Chief Thomas C. Wilcox to interrogate anyone arrested or even suspected of "suspicious activity."[100] The local society newspaper *Detroit Saturday Night* applauded Zurbrick's efforts, declaring him a local hero for targeting the 2,815 noncitizens in Detroit area penitentiaries. Every day, it reported, Zurbrick and his inspectors visited the police headquarters, selecting "Slavic and Italian looking" suspects and plying them with "astute questions" meant to uncover whether they had entered the country illegally.[101] Supported by the local press, Zurbrick assured the public that because of his policies, "the word is being passed that Detroit is not a safe place for the foreign-born crook."[102] But of course, policing extended beyond local prisons and into immigrant neighborhoods, conflating law-abiding immigrants with those behind bars and vice versa. And while it is impossible to know just how many first- and second-generation immigrants local police rounded up, comparing Detroit drives to those in Chicago suggests that the number of immigrants coming into contact with aggressive policing was in the tens of thousands.

As in Chicago, Detroit deportation drives reassured local residents worried about immigrant crime. It is unlikely that raids actually sent more than about a thousand European immigrants for deportation between 1929 and 1930, but roundups targeted far larger numbers of first- and second-generation Europeans.[103] Moreover, press reports on the correlation between crime rates and foreigners behind bars turned Detroit into a national symbol of how targeted deportations supposedly diminished crime in urban centers.[104] Ultimately, the campaign cast suspicion on Detroit's Hungarian, Russian, Polish, and Italian neighborhoods, making it appear as though scores of undocumented criminals lurked behind the Italian groceries, Greek restaurants, and Hungarian sausage shops of ethnic Detroit.

With the triumph of his "deportation war," Zurbrick doubled down on raids in southern and eastern European neighborhoods. Speakeasies in Polish Hamtramck became a favorite spot for police in search of potential "bootlegged aliens." For instance, as Peter Wiconciwski enjoyed a bit of moonshine in a blind pig on the edge of Hamtramck, police stormed the building, knocked over tables, and cuffed Wiconciwski against the wall. After being transported to the local police station, Wiconciwski parried questions concerning his drinking habits and citizenship status. He admitted to partaking of the occasional drink but insisted that he was not an illegal resident because, though he did not have final papers, he came to the United States from Poland in 1916 before Congress passed immigration restrictions. And while police could not deport Wiconciwski, they sent him back to Hamtramck with a $500 fine, signaling to other immigrants that the police meant business.[105] In fact, by 1930, this practice became so clearly linked to new immigrants, a group lawmakers assumed were not citizens, that the federal government increased the penalty for Prohibition violations to a felony specifically so local authorities might better "deport alien violators of the prohibition law."[106] Ultimately, Immigration Service officials and

police looking for crime in particular ethnic neighborhoods found it, reinforcing the popular nativist idea that it was the Poles, Italians, Hungarians,
and Russians who smuggled from Europe to Canada and directly into
Detroit's underworld.

The immigrants who were slated for expulsion faced long jail terms
while they negotiated the administrative hurdles set in place by a state relatively new to large-scale deportations. A 1929 *Detroit Free Press* article entitled "Many Hang on Rim of U.S. Melting Pot" reported that between 100
and 115 aliens were detained at the Wayne County Jail at any given time,
where they endured the "prolonged and nerve-wracking" process of appealing and submitting to deportations. To offset costs, the federal government
sent the county about five thousand dollars each month, while the aliens
waited for monthly deportation "classes" to be compiled between Detroit,
Jackson, and Ann Arbor county jails. Once assembled, the U.S. Department
of Labor paid another several hundred dollars for each immigrant's train
trip to Montreal, where they would wait another several weeks before being
loaded on an ocean liner back to Europe.[107]

In an uncharacteristically sympathetic look at the plight of migrants
caught up in a "deportation mill," the article profiled a Scot, portraying him
as an unlucky yet morally upright immigrant. Despite the fact that most
deportees were of southern and eastern European origin, the *Detroit Free
Press* introduced Ebenezer P. Hay, a man who wanted to become an American yet was "about to be shoved off the rim [of the melting pot] with his wife
and small child." While most European deportees were southern and eastern
Europeans whose expulsions garnered little sympathy from readers due to
their supposed criminal proclivities, the image of Anglo-Saxon Ebenezer Hay
alerted readers to the often unfair and arbitrary nature of new laws. Coverage
of Hay's deportation demonstrates that when northern Europeans got caught
up in immigration proceedings, they tended to be portrayed as unfortunate
victims of laws not meant for them in the first place. Thus, even when British,
Scot, German, and Scandinavian immigrants found themselves subject to
immigration quotas and deportations, they skirted the labels of criminality
imposed upon those from other regions.[108]

Like northern European men, the press portrayed women held for
deportation as victims rather than threats. The *Detroit Free Press* mentioned
a dozen young women held in the Detroit County Jail in separate quarters
from the male inmates. The paper profiled Pauline Zaluskowski in particular, a Canadian resident of Polish origin who "was caught in the tolls in

immigration legislation" and might face deportation to Canada or Poland. Instead of hardened lawbreakers, women tended to earn a reputation as hapless victims.[109]

Concerns over gender sometimes overlapped with immigration and miscegenation laws, bringing African American Detroiters under the purview of immigration officials. In a case the *Detroit Free Press* called a "grotesque affair," Canadian Lena Montgomery married a local "Detroit Negro" named Odie Montgomery. Under unclear circumstances, Lena faced deportation to Canada in 1925 but returned immediately and asserted that because Odie was her husband, she was entitled to citizenship and residency in the United States. At this time, the state legislature was embroiled in a battle with the National Association for the Advancement of Colored People (NAACP) over a miscegenation bill that would prevent an African American from marrying "any white person."[110] In the face of Ku Klux Klan fury and protest, the state judiciary committee yielded to the NAACP and tabled the bill. In practice, however, local administrators continued to scrutinize interracial marriage, a fact that became clear in the case of Lena and Odie Montgomery. Because of his marriage to a Canadian white woman, Odie, to whom the *Free Press* refers to simply as "the Negro," faced a ludicrous set of questions over his own citizenship, which, as a migrant from the sharecropping South, he could not prove. Despite the fact that he had resided in Detroit for thirty-eight years, Odie joined his wife in prison, where both faced an uncertain future and possible deportation to Canada.[111]

Deportation drives also targeted non-European immigrant groups more directly, a development that would only worsen as joblessness mounted during the Great Depression. Members of Detroit's Arab American community noted a constant concern that members of their groups might be sent back to the Middle East. In some cases, this kept them from political activism. For instance, pan-Muslim leader Duse Muhammad Ali, an Egyptian immigrant of Sudanese heritage, refrained from discussing the plight of Arab Americans in Detroit for fear of being deported.[112] Considering the precarious position of their local leader, it is most likely that the hundreds of Arabs in Highland Park and Dearborn, Michigan, also lived under constant fear of government raids and questions. Abraham Younan, a thirty-eight-year-old Syrian who faced deportation after returning from a brief trip to his home country, felt the full impact of America's new immigration policies. To argue his case, Younan hired immigration attorney O. Guy

Frick, who claimed Younan should not be deported because it would leave his two American citizen children as dependents on the state. Upon consideration, a federal judge ruled against Younan's deportation.[113] Younan's case demonstrates the obstacles Arab immigrants faced, most of whom did not have access to lawyers. And though the *Detroit Free Press* article reporting Younan's case makes no mention of his religion, with the first name Abraham, it is likely he faced better treatment than Muslim Syrians or Turks in the region.[114]

As the Great Depression continued, local police and immigration officials applied the deportation practices they had developed to expel Europeans to return thousands of Mexican migrants across the southern border. Mexican repatriation is examined further in Chapter 4, but it is important to note that just a few years prior to this, deportation drives targeted southern and eastern Europeans, associating their groups with crime. In response to European deportation, grassroots immigrant groups and local police ensured immigrants from southern and eastern Europe would face the bulk of anti-immigrant activism and enforcement.

Between 1927 and 1930, immigrant battles over new quotas helped rank immigrants by desirability, a move that mattered when city governments began deciding where to send police and INS officials. Therefore, in Detroit, despite the fact that ANOCL protests failed to overturn new immigration quotas, they fed into and solidified a national perception that northern Europeans tended toward thrift, sobriety, and respectability, making them ideal candidates for citizenship. Because Detroit was a major international borderland, the tendency to rank immigrants by desirability informed a growing economic debate over which immigrants, if any, should be allowed the privilege of border crossing for work. While similar local systems developed in New York, Boston, and Chicago, the presence of an international border made the issue of immigration particularly pressing in Detroit. Ultimately, the ANOCL's cross-border rhetoric helped establish northern Europeans as desirable, respectable immigrants and played a key role in convincing politicians, employers, and two federal governments to allow Canadian and British immigrants to commute daily between Windsor and Detroit. By the Great Depression, quotas still barred certain northern Europeans from the United States, meaning thousands smuggled across the border into American industrial jobs. But once these British, Irish, German, and Scandinavian immigrants made it to the United States or even to Canada, they benefited from local practices that coded them as legal insiders regardless of their immigration status. Southern and eastern Europeans, on the other hand, faced regular raids, accusations, and questions that labeled them as outsiders, a distinction that would have profound consequences as immigration officials, employers, and unions negotiated requirements around who was eligible for industrial work on either side of the border.

Chapter 3

The Problem of Canadian Day Laborers

While northern European immigrants battled over quota numbers in Detroit's city hall and the U.S. Congress, employers and unions along the border negotiated the ethnic politics of crossing the international boundary for work. After Congress passed the 1924 Immigration Act, between fifteen and twenty thousand Canadian, British, and European day laborers boarded the Windsor ferry each morning for jobs in industrial Detroit. Seventy-year-old Robert Yates began making the round-trip journey across the Detroit River in 1891. Yates was born in Ontario, lived his whole life in Windsor, and spent his entire working life as a watchman on the Detroit ferry dock. When the United States established new immigration quotas, Yates had to pay an eight-dollar head tax to the Immigration Service and secure a commuting card that allowed him to resume the daily route from Windsor to Detroit.[1] As a Canadian citizen and a skilled laborer with long-term employment, Yates represented a subset of high-status immigrants who managed to hold on to their border crossing privileges with only an administrative inconvenience.

Five thousand non-Canadian day laborers would not be so lucky. In 1926, Detroit's labor movement seized on a national push for immigration restriction to pressure the Immigration Service to pass General Order 86, extending immigrant status to all commuters from Canada. This meant Jack Smith, a young British-born mechanic who lived in Windsor and worked at Ford Motor Company of Detroit, had to secure a quota visa from the American consulate to keep his job. When Smith learned all British quota visas were filled for 1926 and 1927, he lost his ability to cross the border along with his position at Ford and moved in with Canadian relatives.[2] John Bitner, a Czechoslovak immigrant living in Ford City, Canada, faced the same problem. When Order 86 took effect, Bitner lost his position at Packard Motor Company, meaning his wife Anna had to provide for their four children with mending and washing.[3] The *Border Cities Star* and the Border Cities Chamber of Commerce profiled dozens of barred immigrants, condemning the regulation for curtailing the "rights of Canadian residents who happen to be born elsewhere" and closing a border where residents depended on "the open exchange of people."[4]

At its core, barring commuters like Smith and Bitner represented an economic issue. But the battle over immigration was also, in Detroit, always intertwined with the struggle over foreignness. As quota laws incited arguments about immigrant crime and respectability, employers, diplomats, and labor leaders used the growing culture of xenophobia to advance their own arguments. Employers' organizations and diplomats wanted to keep the border open and maintain free trade agreements that encouraged international commerce. But as southern and eastern Europeans gained a reputation for border crime and smuggling, industrialists dropped their lobbies and instead began to advocate restoring quotas for Anglo commuters, a group already associated with desirability.

In opposition, the Detroit Federation of Labor (DFL) used nativism and anti-Semitism to close the border to the day workers. It is unlikely that the DFL viewed commuters as more than an economic threat, but by casting border crossers like John Bitner as dangerous (even racialized) foreigners poised to infiltrate American society with foreign ideas and criminal tendencies, the union attracted supporters who otherwise would never have sided with organized labor. By warning working Detroiters that some of the commuters crossing the border might have the same ethnic backgrounds as the immigrant groups linked to crime and deportation, the DFL gained popular support. The union's nativist turn left employers and diplomats, who hoped to keep the border open to commuters, with no choice but to counter with their own ethnic argument and insist that most border crossers were British and Canadian. Ultimately, the commuter controversy demonstrates how nativist ideas about immigrant desirability crept into and soon dominated an issue that represented an economic struggle over open borders and labor.

Organized Labor Protests

The commuter controversy began as a local labor dispute and gave labor unions a reputation for nativism that would prove difficult to shake. It pitted the DFL, which had long hoped to close the border to day laborers, against key employers who wanted to minimize regulations on their workforce. When Congress passed the 1924 Immigration Act, the DFL took advantage of the national political mood to launch an attack against workers who lived in Canada and labored in American industries. DFL President Frank X. Martel claimed day laborers, or commuters, worked as "inveterate scabs" and complained that the proximity of the border meant new immigration laws were "largely nullified" in Detroit.[5] According to Martel, commuters crossed the border and picket lines in the same stride, harming the union movement, undermining labor conditions, and challenging America's newest immigration laws.

DFL leaders saw the 1924 Immigration Act as the perfect opportunity to push for change. The Detroit union was a subsidiary of the larger American Federation of Labor (AFL) that historically catered to craft workers, musicians, and skilled laborers of the auto industry, meaning that the union had little interest in unskilled workers or new immigrants from Europe. DFL members' ancestors had immigrated to the Motor City several generations earlier from northern European nations, and they tended to identify not as German or Swedish Americans but as Americans. In the automobile industry, they held skilled or semiskilled positions, and many felt threatened by the influx of ready workers from southern and eastern Europe.[6]

Labor unions have had a long history of anti-immigrant activism. As noted in Chapter 1, the AFL's first president, Samuel Gompers, a Jewish immigrant himself, thought immigrants undermined unions' chances to demand higher wages and organize.[7] But union efforts against immigrants can be traced to the post–Civil War years. In the 1870s, Denis Kearney, the charismatic leader of San Francisco's Workingmen's Party, spearheaded a move for Asian exclusion.[8] And in Boston, the Knights of St. Crispin, America's largest trade union at the time, rose up in protest when a major shoe company brought in Chinese workers to break a strike. Over the next ten years, labor unions, particularly the Knights of Labor, lent their support to the Chinese Exclusion Act, which would bar Chinese from citizenship and immigration for decades.[9] Thus, the DFL's stand against commuting immigrants fit within a long tradition of union activism against immigration.

President Martel himself reflected the values of the DFL as an organization. He gained national notoriety in the 1910s as a leader of Detroit's Typographical Union and waged several successful campaigns on behalf of the union. In his personal life, Martel identified as a Catholic and a Republican and favored restraint and tact within the labor movement.[10] He blamed undocumented immigrants and commuters from Canada for the DFL's inability to organize effective strikes, particularly within the automobile industry, and he even went so far as to label Detroit a "trade union desert" because immigrants and "hyphenated Americans" continued to saturate its workforce.[11]

Detroit's placement at an international borderland and America's third largest industrial center made commuting from Canada an ideal option for residents of the entire Windsor border region. In 1926, the Border Cities Chamber of Commerce, an organization dominated by contractors, bankers, and medium-sized business owners on the Canadian side of the border, reported that day laboring across the Detroit-Windsor borderland represented the "largest international crossing in the world." The tradition, which began in the mid-nineteenth century and grew steadily with the city's industrial might, was legal under the laws of both nations and proved mutually beneficial to immigrants and employers on either side of the border. In order to facilitate easy crossing, the Immigration Bureau even printed commuter cards, meaning Canadians could cross easily, flashing their cards to immigration inspectors before proceeding to jobs across the city.[12]

For some savvy European immigrants, day laboring provided a loophole around new immigration laws. Native-born Canadians formed the majority of commuters, but soon after restrictions, thousands of Europeans moved to Windsor and established residency, intending to cross daily into the United States. Soon the practice became a way for five thousand Brits, Scots, Russians, Poles, and Romanians to legally circumvent U.S. quota laws by applying for commuter cards as Canadian residents.[13] Thus, commuting kept the border open even after laws drafted in Washington had ordered it closed.

Canadian day laborers continued to come to the United States because American employers recruited them. For instance, Fedor Bachila emigrated from Russia to Canada in 1912 and became a naturalized citizen. While working at GM of Canada in Windsor, he gained unparalleled skills as a machinist and toolmaker, prompting American Twist and Drill Tool Company to offer him a job. The position came with a considerable pay raise, making Bachila's daily ferry ride a worthy investment.[14] The Border Cities Chamber of Commerce supported Bachila and his fellow day laborers because they spent their money on Canadian property and goods. The Chamber asserted that the "freedom of intercourse" between the United States and Canada was a "highly important asset in the development of Detroit" and helped an economic system beneficial to all of North America.[15]

Employers in Detroit jumped at the opportunity to hire Canadian commuters. Ford, Dodge, GM, and Packard all encouraged day laborers because they worked for less and built competition within the labor market, an important component in weakening organized labor. Employers even used day laborers as strikebreakers. In 1925 and 1926, when Detroit's metal polishers and carpenters unions organized a walkout, employers looked to Windsor for temporary employees. Within a few days of each strike, Windsor residents boarded the ferry to closed factories, causing two strikes to fail and business to resume as usual within the month.[16] Windsor's *Border Cities Star* reported that "the businessmen of Detroit consider the border as merely an imaginary line" and saw no trouble importing labor from the Canadian side, especially when unionized Americans threatened to shut down production.[17]

Such practices challenged the DFL's efforts to organize in a city dominated by powerful businessmen and divided across ethnic and racial fault lines. But the union could do little to curb the legal practice until federal immigration quotas closed the border by the mid-1920s. Despite the fact that quotas did not apply to Canadian immigrants, DFL President Martel lobbied tirelessly to extend quotas to day laborers. For Martel, ending commuting became a personal crusade that meant gaining control of the labor force and dealing a blow to the tremendous strength of American industrialists.[18]

Martel himself most likely viewed Canadian commuters as nothing more than an economic threat to organized labor. His own background was French Canadian, meaning his family would have negotiated its fair share of anti-Catholicism and nativism. Martel's father, Charles Henry Martel, was born in Montreal, but like many young French Canadians, when he had trouble finding work in the French-speaking city, he moved to London, Ontario, where he worked as a blacksmith. As a French Canadian in Ontario, Charles Martel faced anti-Catholic, anti-French discrimination, harassment, and violence, and in 1878, he followed thousands of his countrymen across the border in search of peace and acceptance in the growing French Canadian colony of Saginaw, Michigan.[19] Charles Martel lived in Saginaw for the next thirty-five years, and it was here that he married Michigan-born Lena Martel and had four children: Mary Louise, Elmer, William, and Francis Xavier, all of whom learned to speak fluent French.[20]

Perhaps given his own immigrant background, Frank Martel cast commuting as first and foremost an economic threat to American workers. Citing a citywide unemployment rate of one hundred thousand, he argued that closing the border to Canadians would allow twenty thousand American workers to find jobs again and "spend their money in Detroit," a prospect meant to appeal to naturalized and native-born Americans across the Motor City.[21] Ending commuting, he argued, promised to bring thirty million dollars in wages back to Detroit, where they could serve "the needy people in our community and add much in the way of prosperity to the city."[22] Embedded in this economic argument was Martel's hope that homogenizing the workforce might finally allow the DFL to organize the skilled mechanics, painters, and glass makers of Detroit and, with time, the entire auto industry.[23]

Martel sought the support of the national labor movement, but the AFL shied from the Detroit controversy for fear of alienating Canadian union affiliations. In letters to AFL Secretary Frank Morrison, Martel implored the larger union to use its influence to push the commuter controversy to the forefront of national labor politics. He assured Morrison that the DFL did not oppose the fifteen thousand Canadian workers who crossed the border but wanted to make sure five thousand European residents of Canada had to secure quota visas to the United States to keep their jobs. European day laborers, he reasoned, "have never joined unions in Canada." Instead, he argued they had immigrated to Canada "with the sole objective of getting into the U.S. in defiance of the quota law."[24] Despite the AFL's historic support of restrictionist immigration laws, Morrison parried Martel's requests by asking for more numbers and details. Ultimately, Morrison feared taking a stand in what he must have viewed as a relatively minor border dispute that could hurt AFL efforts to establish a transnational labor alliance with Canadian unions. When pressed, Morrison replied to Martel with sympathy, yet he refused to become involved for fear of "overstepping the legal responsibilities" of the international labor movement.[25]

In an effort to gain citywide and national traction, Martel began to frame the struggle in the language of nativism. Despite the fact that commuters were not immigrants, the *Detroit Labor News* announced that the

question of "immigrant labor" had "slumbered long enough," demanding
that the city uphold and enforce America's new immigration laws.[26] The
DFL campaign gained support from native-born workers and soon from
elites who championed deportation drives and increased policing along the
border but who otherwise would not have sided with organized labor.[27]
Commuting from Canada represented a perfectly legal practice, but by
identifying Canadian border crossers with the specter of undocumented
immigration, Martel endeavored to link the two groups. In 1926, he began
to write furious letters to congressmen, judges, local officials, and law
enforcement agents that claimed alien day workers frustrated the opportunities of "real American-born workers."[28] Martel's savvy rhetoric, which he
used to advance the DFL's economic goals, built on the fears about aliens
taking American jobs that had become the mantra of groups like the KKK
and the American Legion.

The DFL soon pointed the finger at city employers for violating immigration laws. Tapping into the growing public anxiety over immigration
violations and labor, DFL reports claimed certain companies had become
notorious for hiring both day laborers and "bootlegged immigrants" to
keep their costs down. High on the list were Crowley Milner Department
Store, the Book-Cadillac Hotel, Park-Davis Laboratories, and "all the major
automobile moguls," companies the DFL claimed "routinely ignored
American immigration laws" by hiring day laborers and unnaturalized
workers. DFL reports never provided sources beyond "city authorities," but
by naming specific department stores and automobile companies, the
reports linked Canadian day workers to the larger issue of smuggled aliens,
illegality, and potential crime in the city.[29]

Union lobbies encouraged the Department of Labor to act, but new
regulations still proved too soft for the union. On April 22, 1927, the
Detroit Labor News predicted that the Department of Labor was on the
verge of issuing a total ban on "all foreign-born Canadians," and an
"elated President Martel" reported, "The efforts of Labor are at last bearing
fruit."[30] A week later, the Department of Labor passed General Order 86,
which barred Canadians from seeking new work in Detroit and required
existing day workers to obtain certificates from their employers in order
to keep their jobs. Order 86 also applied 1924 immigration quotas to all
commuters, effectively closing the border loophole to Windsor's European
born.[31] The new regulation meant Europeans would stop crossing daily for
work, but it also legitimized commuting for fifteen thousand naturalized

and native-born Canadian day workers. Thus, when the order passed, Frank Martel declared Order 86 a first victory in what he would turn into a war against ending all Canadian day labor.[32]

Diplomatic and Business Pushback

Order 86 met immediate opposition from businesses and foreign policy experts on the grounds that it disrupted free trade and challenged friendly relations between the United States and Canada. On the Canadian side, the Ontario government claimed regulations signified "an unfriendly act" from their neighbor to the south, an act that might threaten labor relations between the two nations.[33] Both the Detroit and Border Cities Chambers of Commerce agreed, noting that open labor and an open border had bolstered the industrial might of the Detroit metropolitan region.

Detroit business interests and manufacturers viewed new immigration orders as a check on their industrial autonomy. L. J. Flint, president of King Motor Car Company, asserted closing the border was just another Department of Labor ploy to keep employers out from "under the thumb" of Washington.[34] The Detroit Chamber of Commerce agreed, adding that barring five thousand commuters represented a symbolic check on their power and would do little to alleviate unemployment. On the contrary, he argued, the publicity could "create an influx of ten thousand workers from other parts of the U.S." who would scramble to take displaced commuters' jobs.[35] Indeed, Detroit businesses viewed Order 86 as an unwelcome regulation on their access to labor and promised to fight regulations at every turn.

Canadian protective tariffs ensured that Windsor's economy would remain tied to American industry. In 1920, Windsor's industrial commissioner Maclure Sclanders identified 206 separate industries in the Border Cities, over half of which were American. Protective tariffs, he argued, had helped the region shift from the "small town category into the truly metropolitan." Automobile plants like Ford of Canada, Fisher Body, Studebaker, and Kelsey Wheel Company dominated the region's economy. An automobile industry slump in 1921, however, drove thousands of Canadian and newly emigrated Europeans across the border in search of comparable work in Detroit's factories. A segment of these workers chose to move across the border, but others kept their homes in Windsor and made the daily commute across the border to work.[36]

Commuters soon became crucial to the economy of the entire Canadian border region. The Canadian Chamber of Commerce noted that 97,396 people lived in Windsor and the tiny border towns of Tecumseh, Riverside, Ford City (later East Windsor), Walkerville, Sandwich, Ojubway, La Salle, Amherstburg, Sandwich West, and Sandwich East. Of these residents, the Chamber estimated at least 31,146 depended on a head of the household or provider who crossed daily for work in the United States. Canadian businesses that relied on the revenue generated from returning day workers feared American labor hoped to end all commuting and close the border, a move that promised to plunge one-third of "Border Cities" residents into poverty.[37] Canadian newspapers agreed, noting that Order 86 alone meant at least 14,000 workers and their dependents would be "deprived of a means of livelihood."[38] Ending day labor for workers like Scottish James Campbell meant the tool maker no longer had wages to bring back to Walkerville and spend in restaurants and bars. Multiplying this loss by five thousand workers and another nine thousand dependents meant less business for local Windsor establishments. Perhaps worse for the city, when workers like Campbell lost their American jobs, they turned to municipal welfare funds. After Order 86 barred Campbell from crossing for work, he registered himself, his wife, and his two children for help with coal, bread, and milk from the Walkerville welfare office.[39]

The Border Cities Chamber of Commerce insisted that day laborers formed crucial cogs in America's industrial machine and that the "freedom of intercourse between both nations" formed a major "asset in the development of Detroit." To drive home this point, the Border Cities Chamber profiled the histories of upstanding day laborers like George Sterling and Harry Belfoy, both British subjects who held skilled jobs as metal polishers at Fisher Body Company. The loss of Sterling and Belfoy's unparalleled skills, the Chamber argued, would cost Fisher "upwards of two hundred dollars in recruitment and training."[40] The *Border Cities Star* echoed Canadian business, reminding the Department of Labor that the "flow of commerce and labor" had always been integral to both sides.[41]

When the U.S. Department of Labor refused to reverse Order 86, the Canadian business community turned toward diplomacy to reinstate the rights of certain commuters. In the winter of 1927, the Border Cities Chamber of Commerce recruited a group of lawyers from Toronto and New York who claimed the Jay Treaty of 1784 allowed British peoples to cross the border for work. The Jay Treaty was signed in the wake of the Revolutionary

War and for over a century had been "buried away in dusty tomes and unknown to thousands." However, Article III of the treaty clearly stated that "British subjects can pass freely across the international border" separating the United States from Britain.[42] The Jay Treaty, Canadian businesses argued, meant any immigrants of English, Irish, Scottish, or Canadian descent could legally cross into Detroit for work.

Frank Martel balked at the treaty, arguing that modern labor concerns had rendered the agreement obsolete. The DFL president reminded Detroiters that the United States had signed the Jay Treaty over a century before "to meet conditions that existed when Michigan was a wilderness and Detroit was a frontier trading post." The treaty, he concluded, was meant to protect "Indians dwelling on either side of the boundary line" and promote "inland navigation" of unchartered Michigan and Ottawa territories. Now that Detroit had developed into a key industrial center and Canada was no longer beholden to the United Kingdom, Martel reasoned, the Jay Treaty mattered little.[43]

Martel's assessment of the treaty was essentially correct. Indeed, the framers of the U.S.-British treaty could hardly have predicted the fact that the Detroit-Windsor industrial region would become America's center for automobile trade. Even the Detroit Chamber of Commerce agreed that invoking a treaty "wrought in the wake of Revolutionary zeal and uncertainty" hardly upheld the case for foreign day laborers. The Detroit Chamber conceded that though it objected to regulations against labor in general, Order 86 made sense in the context of new American immigration quotas.[44]

But Canadian lawmakers seized the chance to fight on behalf of British subjects. In May 1927, E. G. Odette, Liberal member of Parliament for the Windsor region; Mayor Jackson of Windsor; and Mayor Daniels of Walkerville formed a delegation to protest Order 86. The Windsor Delegation, as it became formally known, wrote complaints to Ottawa, London, and Washington, D.C., urging the U.S. Department of Labor to recognize the "rights of His Majesty's subjects under the Jay Treaty or other treaties." If Order 86 could not be amended to allow British commuters, the delegation threatened to close the border to U.S. immigrants or tax U.S. exports to Canada.[45]

Such threats prompted Detroit businesses to call for an end to disputes over border labor. In a memo to the State Department, the Detroit Board of Commerce noted that Canada exported $474,690,028 in goods to the United States. In particular, Detroit automakers relied on raw materials like wood, sand, and iron ore from Ontario. The Chamber noted that a "loop-hole in immigration policy" would be worth avoiding any import conflicts with Canada.[46]

Ending day labor from the United States to Canada also had the potential to cause a management crisis for major automobile companies. While twenty thousand largely blue-collar workers journeyed from the Border Cities to Detroit each day, 250 white-collar workers boarded the Detroit-Windsor ferry in the opposite direction. These American day laborers worked for companies like Packard and Ford, which relied on American managers and skilled tradesmen to help run the Canadian assembly lines and report back.[47] Most were trusted American employees who had been selected to take on managerial or training responsibilities across the river. For instance, Christopher York had worked as an auto body builder, a difficult and skilled trade, for Packard for ten years before the company promoted him to the Canadian plant as an overseer of the Canadian branch. York had recently purchased a house in a desirable northwest region of Detroit and had little interest in moving his wife and two small children across the border. To reach his new job in Windsor, York boarded the ferry each day, handing his work papers to a Canadian immigration inspector, who rarely raised an eyebrow. Each month, York submitted a report to Packard in Detroit, notifying the parent company of any administrative problems or hints of labor unrest on the Canadian side of the border.[48] Retaining skilled supervisors like York allowed major companies like Packard to keep control over transnational business operations.

In response to complaints from both sides of the border, the U.S. Department of State arranged a meeting with the Windsor Delegation. On a sunny May afternoon, a state department official met with the Canadians to assess the transnational labor conflict. Mayors Daniels and Jackson revealed that they understood Order 86 not as an extension of American immigration laws but as a response to the "agitation created by the DFL." The mayors acquiesced on the issue of southern and eastern European commuters, admitting that Poles, Hungarians, and Czechs had few grounds to maintain their commuting status. However, the mayors maintained the position that barring British subjects constituted a violation of U.S.-British treaty law. Moreover, the Windsor Delegation admitted they feared the DFL ultimately aspired to end all commuting and close the border. Such a move, the delegation argued, would be "unfair and unwise" because the DFL "does not involve even five percent of the population of Detroit."[49]

Ultimately, the Windsor Delegation's demands perpetuated the growing demand that day labor rights be reserved for Anglo-Saxon commuters.

Soon the local labor dispute turned into an international border controversy over the rights of British subjects. In Ottawa, Canada's External Affairs Office issued a statement that asked the United States to "abide by treaty laws" and treat British subjects with the respect they deserved.[50] London's Foreign Office also weighed in on the day laborers, noting that "though their direct importance to the U.K. is small," the office "wishes that the U.S. would uphold the Jay Treaty."[51] Wary of souring friendly dealings with Canada and even the United Kingdom, the U.S. State Department urged policymakers in Washington and Detroit to back off the commuter issue.[52]

Though the controversy was essentially a diplomatic one, the politics of ethnicity soon crept into the debate. Secretary of State Frank Kellogg warned, "Ontario, Ottawa, and London view the regulations as an unfriendly act against their subjects and what problem should we have with British and Canadian workers in American plants?" Kellogg's insistence that northern Europeans presented no threat to America was likely influenced by wider northern European efforts to prove their own respectability. Implicit in the declaration, of course, was the fact that policymakers should focus on southern and eastern Europeans, groups that more and more Americans thought posed an actual threat to American cities.

America's patriotic societies soon took up the British and Canadian commuters' plight, which they linked to the national origins clause, an amendment to immigration law that promised higher quotas for the British. Elizabeth Smith of Detroit's Daughters of the American Revolution asked presidential candidate Herbert Hoover to support the National Origins Act and intervene on behalf of British subjects protected under the Jay Treaty in the same letter, arguing, "The right kind of immigrant is needed to grow our cities."[53] Detroit's American Legion agreed, adding that the American government "need not cave to a handful of union men."[54] Though nativism and anti-immigrant sentiment formed central components of both the DAR and the American Legion's identity, their nativist rhetoric only extended to non-Anglo immigrants. In their eyes, opening the border to Anglo-Saxon migrants and stymying the efforts of organized labor both represented positive developments for Detroit society.

Amid growing international controversy, AFL President William Green made a futile attempt to curb the DFL's zeal. When unions in Great Britain and Canada began sending him angry letters, Green urged DFL President Martel to examine the problem in a "broad nationalistic point of view" and move "beyond local situations."[55] But Martel ignored the international and instead penned a passionate letter to Secretary of State Frank Kellogg. Martel insisted, "Too long have the officials of the U.S. government and Washington interpreted the immigration law in the interest of business and people outside the U.S. rather than those it sought to protect within the U.S."[56] For Martel, closing the border to five thousand commuters had transformed into a larger battle pitting labor against powerful industrialists and their access to foreign-born labor.

American employers across the nation sided with Detroit businesses and Anglo day laborers, casting Martel as a petty union leader unable to see the larger dynamics of U.S.-Canada trade relations he threatened. The *New York Journal of Commerce* asserted that ending commuter privileges would constitute a "most unnecessary affront to a friendly neighbor," a move that might provoke retaliation from Canada.[57] Businessmen in the *Boston Transcript* claimed that the Department of Labor had acted "rather stupidly," first in ceding to "unimportant local labor interests" and next in threatening the "time honored daily pilgrimages of British residents of both countries across the border."[58] To these large business organizations, letting several thousand British foreigners cross the border each day for jobs they already held represented an absurd controversy that reached international proportions.

Lobbies on behalf of British subjects worked. In June 1927, six months after the Jay Treaty turned the day labor issue into an international affair, the U.S. Department of Labor decided to allow 1,200 additional British subjects to cross the border daily for jobs in Detroit. The Department of Labor made no mention of the Jay Treaty or international business pressure, but the increase coincided with the number of British subjects barred by Order 86.[59] It meant that Jay Cox, an English laborer living with his family in Windsor, could apply for a commuter card and resume his position as a metal polisher at Fisher Body Company.[60] The change, which did not represent an official shift in policy, mollified U.S. and Canadian business interests. By the summer of 1927, day labor became a privilege reserved largely for Anglo-Saxons on the Detroit-Windsor border.

The Demise of Day Labor

Local employers and diplomats disguised their preference for Anglo commuters with arguments about treaty laws. But when southern and eastern

Europeans began to demand the same rights, it became clear that ethnicity played a key role in dictating who would be allowed to cross the border for work. A New York attorney stepped in to help these southern and eastern Europeans sue for commuting cards, and in turn, the DFL intensified its campaign. President Martel exploited the nativism and anti-Semitism already prevalent in Detroit to cast commuters as dangerous foreigners who had discovered a new loophole in U.S. immigration laws. At the ferry docks, union members also resorted to strong-arm tactics, harassing day workers as they disembarked and, in a few extreme cases, physically forcing them back onto boats. By emphasizing the foreignness of commuters, President Martel had finally discovered a way to animate widespread support against them in Detroit, and by the onset of the Great Depression, DFL intimidation and harassment limited commuter numbers to a few thousand.

Reeling from the British "adjustments" under General Order 86, President Martel began using nativist rhetoric to portray naturalized Canadians as violators of new immigration laws and threats to America's Anglo-Saxon values.[61] This move was likely more opportunistic than genuine in that even Martel himself did not fit the Anglo-Saxon ideal he invoked and Martel's middle name, Xavier, revealed his Catholic origins. Regardless of his own family's background, Martel condemned Order 86 for "helping the foreign-language speaking aliens" of the city. In the *Detroit Labor News*, he condemned Order 86 for "nullifying the Johnson immigration law" and giving naturalized Canadians "an extra legal status which under the law they would not enjoy." Despite the fact that by the summer of 1927, only about five hundred European-born Canadians held commuting cards, Martel emphasized the "Russian worker," who he claimed had a "higher status and more privileges under Order 86 than he could ever otherwise have enjoyed under the immigration law."[62] By choosing a "Russian worker" to represent commuters, Martel tapped into the anti–eastern European rhetoric championed by the Ku Klux Klan and even business leaders like Henry Ford.

The DFL's nativism turned explicit in July, when the *Detroit Labor News* published a series of political cartoons featuring ethnic commuters. In a cartoon entitled "Prepare for the Invasion" (Figure 7), Order 86 stands merrily at the Detroit-Windsor border, ready to let in a dark-skinned man labeled with the words "Foreign Labor." The foreign-born day laborer in question has a hat pulled over his face and a smoking pipe coming out of his mouth as he leaps over the Detroit River, presumably toward jobs in Detroit industries.[63] The depiction of the Canadian day worker as a dark-skinned gangster type (rather than a British or Canadian automobile

Figure 7. "Prepare for the Invasion," *Detroit Labor News*, July 1, 1927. The
Detroit Federation of Labor's newspaper depicts a commuter from Windsor
to Detroit leaping over America's immigration laws with General Order 86,
which allowed anyone from the British Empire to cross the border for work.
Despite the fact that most commuters were British or Anglo-Canadian, the
man is drawn with a dark face, an appeal to nativists who feared the influx of
southern and eastern European immigrants to Detroit. Reprinted courtesy of
the Metropolitan Detroit AFL-CIO.

worker) was meant to concern nativist Detroiters who already feared the
demographic change and potential crime they thought certain Europeans,
Mexicans, Arabs, or African Americans brought to Detroit. By drawing on
the racialized fears held by many established and second-generation
Detroiters, the Detroit Federation of Labor linked commuting to the changing racial population of Detroit. Despite the fact that this was not actually
the case, and most commuters were northern European or Canadian, the
depiction demonstrates the way a labor organization sought to exploit
standing racial and ethnic concerns about immigrants.

While the DFL disseminated xenophobia, former commuters stuck in
Canada yearned to resume their Detroit jobs. The Department of Labor's

unexpected decision to restore commuter cards to 1,200 British laborers gave thousands of debarred Canadians and ethnic Europeans renewed hope that they might also find or resume work in Detroit. In 1927, former commuters wrote letters to prominent immigration attorneys in Ottawa, Toronto, and New York, explaining their cases and asking that their commuter rights be restored. In response, Eli Goldsmith, a prominent New York immigration attorney, boarded a train to Detroit to assess the situation. After discussing the matter with officials on both sides of the border and reading the terms of the Jay Treaty, Goldsmith declared with confidence, "Order 86 is illegal in every particular." He assured "native-born Canadians, naturalized Canadians, and British-born residents of Canada" that he could easily reopen the border and overturn the regulation.[64]

To challenge General Order 86, Goldsmith filed injunctions on behalf of seven Windsor men who he deemed particularly qualified for day labor in Detroit. But Goldsmith failed to grasp the intense anger toward foreigners developing across Detroit. For the case, Goldsmith represented one native-born Canadian, two Englishmen, and four naturalized Canadians from Poland, Yugoslavia, and Greece. On the morning of November 8, the seven men, three of whom had dark complexions and spoke English with eastern European accents, filed onto the Detroit-Windsor ferry dock to appear before a board of special inquiry. The men making the final decision were senior immigration inspectors who spent their days approving deportation orders that returned large numbers of eastern Europeans back across the Atlantic. The inspectors examined the plaintiffs at length, asking Greek-born Nicolai Dimitroff why his tailoring business might suffer without cross-border clients and what Polish-born Alexander Perlmutter thought he could contribute to America's labor market. After a quick deliberation, the board refused entry to all seven Canadians, calling the situation a potential "foreign invasion."[65] For the inspectors, the foreign-born Canadians most likely resembled too closely the hundreds of undocumented Poles, Greeks, and Yugoslavs they interrogated and deported each month from Detroit's ethnic neighborhoods.

The DFL retaliated by casting Goldsmith as a foreigner himself who cared more about fellow Jews than "real Americans." Goldsmith was indeed a Jewish lawyer from New York with a history of fiercely representing eastern European immigrants slated for deportation. In a letter to Secretary of State Frank Kellogg, President Martel used thinly veiled anti-Semitic language, claiming Goldsmith represented the "corrupting influences of foreign outsiders" and a "threat to American democracy."[66] The *Detroit Labor*

Figure 8. "The American Mussolini," *Detroit Labor News*, December 2, 1927. In this cartoon, the Detroit Federation of Labor's newspaper portrays Eli Goldsmith, the New York lawyer who filed an injunction on behalf of immigrant commuters, as a fascist "American Mussolini" with a sheriff star and a large club, poised to bludgeon Uncle Sam. By depicting Goldsmith with a hooked nose and three-piece suit, the illustrator reminds readers that the lawyer is a Jewish outsider. Reprinted courtesy of the Metropolitan Detroit AFL-CIO.

News invoked dual concerns over fascism and Jews in a political cartoon entitled "The American Mussolini" (Figure 8). The cartoon depicts a racialized Jewish man, presumably Goldsmith, clad in a three-piece suit and a sheriff star, looming over Uncle Sam with an enormous club labeled "INJUNCTION." In a speech bubble, the Jewish thug reminds Uncle Sam, "I'm the ruler."[67] With the cartoon, the DFL drew on concerns that Jewish lawyers, stockbrokers, and elites, particularly from Washington and New York, sought to undermine and control American institutions and laws, posing a threat to America as real as Mussolini's fascism in Europe.

The Detroit Federation of Labor's appeal to nativism and anti-Semitism shifted the border controversy from economics to a growing local fear of foreigners. And the tactic worked instantly. The Daughters of the American Revolution, a group that, just seven months earlier, had filed petitions on behalf of British commuters protected by the Jay Treaty, wrote letters asking Secretary of State Kellogg to "stay strong against the Jewish influences threatening to open the gates of Detroit."[68] The Allied Patriotic Societies of Detroit followed suit, demanding that Kellogg "close the border to the criminal foreigners" poised to violate America's immigration laws.[69] For patriotic societies, commuters now represented a potential criminal invasion or threat to American values, demonstrating the powerful effect the DFL's nativist lobbies had on Detroit society.

But rising nativist and anti-Semitic rhetoric appeared only to reinforce Goldsmith's resolve on behalf of the Canadian commuters. Realizing he would have little success appealing to the Immigration Service, an organization committed to limiting immigration, the New York lawyer took the day laborers' case up with the Detroit District Court. To test the validity of Order 86, Goldsmith held a mass meeting of former commuters at the Armories of Walkerville. In the building that had once held World War I munitions, Goldsmith assured 255 Canadians, Brits, Yugoslavs, Romanians, and Hungarians that he would get them back to their Detroit jobs.[70]

After a year of litigation, Goldsmith and his clients celebrated their first victory. Goldsmith's argument against Order 86 relied on the claim that the local Immigration Service could not "contravene American immigration law." To prove that Order 86 impeded federal law, Goldsmith directed 250 immigrants to crowd into the U.S. consulate in Toronto and formally apply for nonimmigrant visas. William Thomas Gristy, an English-born machinist living in Ford City, Canada stood first in line. When his request was denied, Gristy and 250 other Canadian residents boarded the 11 p.m. Windsor ferry and offered an affidavit recounting their experience to a notary public standing on the docks. Goldsmith then brought the affidavits to Detroit Federal Court Judge Charles Simons, who ruled that in sixty-one of the cases, General Order 86 marked "the only bar to their entry" and granted them injunctions.[71] While several injunctions went to Canadians with foreign-sounding surnames like Dimitroff, Semeniuk, and Kuzniar, the other 85 percent went to men and women with surnames like Gristy, Cox, Smith, and Thomas.[72] Though it is impossible to know definitively, this evidence suggests that Goldsmith understood that cases on behalf of immigrants with Polish and Greek surnames garnered far less sympathy than those with Anglo-Saxon plaintiffs. In other words, he probably realized anti-immigrant prejudice was keeping his clients from winning and adjusted his tactics.

Perhaps Goldsmith hoped a success on behalf of Anglo-Saxon day laborers might open the door for a round of new cases, but legal troubles at the border sent the lawyer back to New York. While Goldsmith shuttled back and forth between Washington and the Detroit borderland, demanding affidavits and consulting experts on immigration law, the Windsor police court charged him on two counts of "operating an employment agency without authority." Goldsmith heard nothing of the Windsor charges until two weeks later, when the court issued a bench warrant for his arrest. Exhausted from weeks of litigation and no doubt tired of the legal hurdles erected along the border, Goldsmith boarded a train to Windsor and paid fifty dollars bail to ensure his appearance in court. With the help of a local lawyer, Goldsmith managed to get the charges dropped, but he returned to New York for good, remarking only that "the whole affair smacks with organized labor."[73]

The Detroit Federation of Labor never took credit for Goldsmith's court date, but the union had begun to deploy extralegal tactics to end day labor. By 1928, the DFL positioned men at the ferry pier to harass day workers. Each morning, DFL members stood at the docks, pointing out commuters, shouting insults at them, and sometimes forcing them back onto the ferry. Michael Dropnik, a Polish-born Canadian with a card allowing him to commute to his job at Chrysler, claimed he lost his job and his commuting privileges because a union member would not let him through. Afraid a DFL man on the dock might hit him with a rock, Dropnik returned to Windsor and crossed the river the next day, hoping to explain the situation to his foreman. But by the next morning, Dropnik's job had been filled, and without American work, the U.S. Immigration Service revoked his commuter card.[74]

As jobs became scarce during the Great Depression, employers ceded more and more to union pressure and stopped employing Canadians. Citing the scarcity of work for even citizens, Frank Martel began to seek out and notify employers that their hiring practices violated immigration laws. Although the Canadian commuters were legal workers, the DFL's tactics often worked. The Border Cities Chamber of Commerce noted that employers had become reluctant to hire Canadians who caused "such great upset from the men in organized labor."[75] By 1929, only about five thousand day laborers made the journey to Detroit each day.

Many employers and officials ignored Martel's letters, particularly if the Canadians in question were Anglo-Canadian workers. In November 1929, Martel contacted Detroit's school inspector, E. D. Williams, to warn him that a firm working at Roosevelt High School employed three Canadians to fix its boilers. Williams did not fire Canadians William Davis, Miles Davis, or Walter Hayward, and after a week, Martel wrote a second letter to the inspector demanding that the men be fired. When Williams refused to discharge the Canadians, Martel sent the school inspector a newspaper clipping featuring a New Orleans contractor who faced a $100 fine or sixty days in jail for employing aliens.[76] Martel kept writing to Williams about the Canadians over the next several months, suggesting that the inspector never looked into the matter and that he perhaps had more important things to do than fire repairmen who spoke English and looked like Americans.[77]

By the late 1920s, it was Canadians born in southern or eastern Europe who faced the most scrutiny. Michael Gardas, a Polish-born Canadian, worked for Hudson Motor Company for six years before his foreman discovered he was Canadian and asked him to leave, citing "external pressure to get rid of foreigners." Gardas responded by assuring his foreman, "I have never caused any trouble for any union. I want nothing to do with strikebreaking. I am not a scab." But the foreman replied, "You certainly don't sound American" and fired Gardas.[78] Thus, new border laws made foremen and other Americans link foreigners or those speaking with an accent to potential trouble with the law.

The battle over commuting on the Detroit-Windsor border began as an economic controversy between labor and employers. But when northern Europeans protested quotas by asserting their own desirability, the politics of ethnicity crept into the debate. Soon the Detroit Federation of Labor called commuters "bootlegged aliens" and "criminals" to advance its economic demands, and employers and diplomats did the same, insisting that British and Canadian workers be allowed to commute on the grounds that they represented the most desirable immigrant groups. Growing opposition to commuting taught businesses and the DFL that inciting local fear of foreignness trumped arguments over free labor and trade. Thus, in the years that followed, the DFL doubled down on its insistence that certain immigrants were inherently unfit to become American workers and used

the anti-immigrant momentum generated by the campaign against commuters to introduce a state law that would register all aliens in Michigan.
The union's turn from economic discussions to nativism worked, and by
the late 1920s, day laboring became a privilege reserved for a handful of
lucky Anglo-Saxon, skilled workers. In the longer term, however, efforts to
cast southern and eastern European border crossers as potential criminals
alienated members of slighted ethnic groups from the labor movement and
ensured that the divide between ethnic Europeans came to matter more
than the physical border separating the United States from Canada.

Chapter 4

Reform, Repatriation, and Deportation During the Depression

As state benefits expanded in the United States and Canada, so too did the demand for hard-line immigration policy. In the early years of the Great Depression, city politicians on both sides of the Detroit-Windsor border backed harsh new immigration policies even as state and federal officials attempted to keep the border open to trade and commerce. In fact, by the end of 1929, local politicians and businesses promised to make the U.S.-Canada border crossing easier than ever. Though business organizations had essentially lost the battle over commuting from Canada, on November 11, 1929, they cheered at the opening of the Ambassador Bridge, the first extension bridge to connect two North American nations. The bridge between Windsor and Detroit had been in the works for nine years, and as Michigan Governor Fred Green and Ontario Minister of Mines Charles McRae cut a symbolic ribbon, they spoke of friendship and open borders, messages that were punctuated with a backdrop of fireworks and an American band playing "O Canada" while a Canadian one played "America."[1] And Detroit and Windsor's leaders had much to celebrate. The fiscal year of 1929 had seen record automobile production, and though the stock market crash meant a few layoffs began in the fall, the downturn produced little worry among optimistic employers and workers.[2] With a bridge that would reduce border crossing to ten minutes, businesses, politicians, and labor interests predicted the 1930s would bring fewer border regulations, increased immigrant traffic, and more opportunity to the borderland.[3] Within a few months, however, the Great Depression had begun to devastate the automobile industry, and local politicians on both sides of the border sanctioned harsh immigration policies in the name of preserving jobs and benefits for citizens.

The Depression put pressure on policymakers in Washington, D.C. and Ottawa to deport noncitizens, but it was local politicians and law enforcement agents who carried out the particulars of expelling Europeans and Mexicans. While in the 1920s, nativist leaders with ties to the Klan spearheaded strict border policing and deportation drives, by the early days of the Depression, leftist, pro-immigrant leaders faced mounting pressure to advance deportation and repatriation drives. In 1930, Detroit and Windsor voters elected Frank Murphy and David Croll as mayors of their cities, respectively. Both new mayors ran on platforms advocating robust welfare benefits and social programs, but they faced criticism when residents worried that immigrants might benefit from costly new initiatives. Consequently, to garner support for their welfare plans, both mayors presided over large-scale deportation and repatriation drives meant to keep European and Mexican immigrants off the city and national payroll.

By 1930, local deportation policies in both Detroit and Windsor began to coexist comfortably with leftist political programs, a development that tethered hard-line immigration policy to growing welfare initiatives. Scholars of Canadian deportation and Mexican repatriation during this period have understood European and Mexican removals both in isolation and as unfortunate federal responses to the Great Depression.[4] But in practice, it was local mayors who negotiated the groups that would benefit from new programs and those who would not. In Michigan and the Midwest, where deportation drives began in the early 1920s, politicians and police transitioned seamlessly to rounding up and deporting noncitizens of European and Mexican origin, a move that crossed the border into Canada. Thus, transnational deportations turned the Depression era into a moment when Europeans and Mexicans faced intense stigmatization and profiling, a finding that challenges work on the Depression and New Deal that tends to focus on how the cultural politics of the 1930s helped ethnic Europeans assimilate into American society.[5] Examining the politics of deportation and municipal aid on the Detroit-Windsor border reveals that after weathering the policing and stigmatization of the 1920s, noncitizens and new immigrants became excluded from local welfare programs in both the United States and Canada, ensuring they would be excluded from social programs throughout the Depression era.

The Depression and Welfare in Detroit and Windsor

The Depression decimated the automobile industry, prompting voters in both Detroit and Windsor to seek dramatic political change. For Detroiters, this meant ousting Mayor Charles Bowles and taking a chance on Frank Murphy, a local judge who promised work programs, expanded city welfare, and an end to political corruption and crime. Windsorites followed Detroit's lead and elected Mayor David Croll, a Jewish, Russian immigrant, who promised the municipal government would take an active role in administering welfare to unemployed workers. But voters seeking expanded welfare wanted new programs to be reserved for citizens, and as city governments increased spending and as unemployment showed no signs of abating, Mayors Murphy and Croll faced local pressure to address unemployment and city debt by expelling recent arrivals to their cities.

The Great Depression hit Detroit particularly hard. By the late 1920s, Americans had only begun to view cars as daily necessities, and as they lost their jobs, most people put their precious savings into mortgages, rent, and grocery accounts. This plunged Detroit, a region that depended on the automobile industry, into economic turmoil. In 1929, the automobile industry had employed 450,000 workers, and by 1932, this number fell to 243,000, leaving hundreds of thousands of Detroiters out of jobs.[6] With less work to go around, automobile workers who had never thought twice about immigrant laborers began to worry that noncitizens, particularly unauthorized immigrants, were taking precious factory positions. Barry Smith, an American-born Packard worker, noted that as the factory cut back positions and he watched his fellow workers negotiate bread lines, "foreigners in my friends' jobs" became more and more conspicuous.[7] Growing resentment meant more and more native-born workers began blaming "bootlegged immigrants" for stealing jobs they thought should be reserved for Americans.

But in a city where over 25 percent of the population was born abroad, outright nativism went only so far.[8] When it came to choosing a mayor in 1930, Detroit voters sought a leader who would promise to support all workers regardless of ethnic origin while also promoting jobs and relief for Detroit citizens. Frank Murphy, a leftist Catholic Recorders Court judge, represented the perfect candidate to fit this role. The son of Irish immigrants and an established member of the community, Judge Murphy managed to speak to immigrants' needs while still occupying the space of a respectable, second-generation northern European.

In September 1930, Frank Murphy entered a four-way recall election with promises of new jobs and crime control in Detroit. The election was an unexpected event, brought on by the recall of Mayor Charles Bowles, who Detroit's business community accused of corruption. Consequently, the race was bitter, pitting business-backed John Engel against Catholic Democrat John Smith and Charles Bowles, the Klan-endorsed mayor who refused to drop out of the race.[9] Judge Frank Murphy entered the race with calculated reluctance, only declaring his candidacy when voters petitioned him to run, and crafted a careful image of himself as the respectable son of hardworking immigrants. Beyond proposing increased welfare benefits and pensions to the unemployed, Murphy advocated a reorganization of the police department and a more concerted focus on cleaning up urban crime.[10]

Judge Murphy made criminal reform part of his platform to set himself apart from the corruption of career politicians, particularly Mayor Bowles. But in the wake of a eugenics movement that had associated African Americans, Mexicans, and southern and eastern Europeans with inherent criminal tendencies, pledges to end urban crime naturally invoked racist and nativist associations in the minds of voters.[11] When Murphy became mayor of Detroit, a city where the border heightened concerns over illicit immigration, his promises to address urban crime translated to crackdowns on immigration. Thus, the Murphy administration opened an era of robust deportations and repatriations for Mexicans and noncitizen Europeans across the city.

As a candidate, however, Judge Murphy earned tremendous support from black and Mexican Detroiters. Walter White, head of the National Association for the Advancement of Colored People (NAACP), urged Detroit's black community to unite behind Murphy for his fairness as a judge in the widely publicized Ossian Sweet trial outlined in Chapter 1.[12] Young Judge Murphy presided over the trial with a level of "even handed justice" that, Walter White claimed, "unfortunately, the Negro defendant could duplicate in few courts of law, north or south."[13] Judge Murphy's subsequent popularity among both working-class and professional African Americans earned him 80 percent of votes in predominantly African American Wards 3, 5, and 7.[14] Detroit's Mexican population also organized in favor of the judge, printing banners that read in Spanish: "Vote Judge Frank Murphy for Mayor. A man who understands and will represent the people. He has always demonstrated special interest in minorities."[15]

Murphy also united the city's ethnic European communities.[16] The judge convinced Detroit's German Protestant Bund organizations, which tended to shy away from Catholic candidates, to rally behind Murphy's campaign in large numbers and vote for his promise of a "new life and regenerated Detroit."[17] Religious and secular southern and eastern European organizations also campaigned vigorously for Murphy, and after decades of being harassed by the Klan and Protestant anti-Semites like Henry Ford, Detroit's 68,000 Jews turned out in favor of the judge.[18] Thus, Murphy brought together a broad coalition of ethnically, racially, and economically marginalized Detroiters, groups that felt the consequences of the Great Depression with more intensity than many of Detroit's wealthier Protestant residents.

On September 9, 1930, Frank Murphy won 31 percent of the votes, enough to give him the majority, and became the mayor of a city plagued by unemployment and teetering on bankruptcy. Before the Depression, the city of Detroit administered a small amount of aid to unemployed citizens and noncitizens through its Department of Public Welfare. Detroit's relief funds plummeted during the economic crisis because 95 percent of its relief money came from public sources, as opposed to cities like New York, Chicago, and Philadelphia, where around 65 percent of their relief relied on public funds. Thus, as demands for relief rose, the city nearly went bankrupt trying to keep up with an ever-increasing caseload.[19]

Even if a Detroit resident qualified for welfare, the funds were not enough to support a family. In 1930, a family of five on relief rarely received more than $6.50 a week for food and coal.[20] Moreover, the Welfare Department was highly decentralized, and individual welfare workers made decisions about aid and the neediness of families on a discretionary basis, leading to uneven distributions of aid. For example, in 1930, Morrici Chrokeich, a Russian national with a wife and small child, received $5.40 and a milk ration every two weeks, while Italian Vito Calvariso, an Italian with three children and a wife, received $7.70 weekly along with coal and milk rations.[21] All in all, during the Depression, the median earning for a family plummeted from $33.05 to $10.82. Neighborhood fire houses distributed stew, bread, and coffee each evening, creating lines that stretched for miles, sometimes attracting 1,700 individuals at a time.[22] As single men lost their jobs and the ability to pay for boarding houses, major factories set up cots in open warehouses that, at the very least, provided shelter from icy winter winds and spring rain. Fisher Body factory opened "Fisher Lodge," housing

1,500 men, and Studebaker packed another 1,300 homeless men into its drafty buildings.[23] But local factories only offered partial and temporary relief, and as the economy showed no signs of improving, jobless workers turned to their family, friends, and the city government for aid.

The Depression hit immigrant newcomers to the region particularly hard. In largely Polish Hamtramck, local welfare workers refused to offer relief to families with fewer than three children, meaning multiple families often crowded into one home to claim they represented a single household.[24] Many immigrants turned to kinship networks for support. For instance, single Polish immigrant Wladyslav Sciecki relied on the charity of a family friend from the "Old Country." After he lost his factory job and his part-time work as a farmhand in Smith Creek, Michigan, Sciecki moved into Anna Krazucewsky's Hamtramck boarding house. Sciecki searched for employment for two years, all while living off the charity of his friend, compiling a debt of over $600 for his room and board. When Krazucewsky's husband lost his own factory job in 1932, she told him she did not want him to starve but that he would have to leave, reasoning, "We have our family to support."[25] Indeed, as the economy showed no signs of improvement, kinship networks broke down, putting more and more pressure on municipalities to help starving residents.

Like new Europeans, Mexican migrants faced disproportionate layoffs in the Depression's early days. Mexican workers were accustomed to being the last hired and first fired, but most expected the Depression's effects to be temporary and thought they would be back to work by the winter of 1930. When the Depression continued and unemployed Mexicans struggled to pay rent, faced overdue grocery accounts, and had furniture repossessed, they applied for city relief. When they could not get more than a few dollars from overburdened welfare workers, some Mexicans turned to petty crime in order to survive, a development that vindicated white Detroiters' growing assertion that Mexicans should be purged from the city.[26]

Black Detroiters also lost their jobs in large numbers. In fact, during the Depression, African Americans faced twice the unemployment rate of their white counterparts.[27] Despite the fact that they remained only 7 percent of the population, African Americans made up 30 percent of relief recipients, and by the early 1930s, nearly 80 percent of the city's African American community was unemployed. The most visible jobless African Americans were, of course, unemployed automobile workers, particularly those who had worked at Ford in the foundry. But African American women who had been employed in large numbers as domestic servants also faced layoffs. Thus, almost overnight, entire families of black migrants lost their only means of paying rent, heating their homes, or feeding their families.[28]

As unemployment spread, Mayor Frank Murphy pressured major automobile companies to offer relief to the thousands of former automobile employees vying for scarce city welfare resources. In 1930, Mayor Murphy formed the Mayor's Unemployment Committee (UC), an organization that joined policymakers with industrialists to provide food and support to laid-off workers.[29] For a company-run welfare model, the mayor looked to Flint, where General Motors had begun to supply laid-off workers with coupons for groceries in local stores. But in Detroit, Packard and Chrysler Motor Companies claimed they were teetering on the edge of bankruptcy themselves, and their city taxes would have to be enough to help unemployed workers. Mayor Murphy agreed, and the UC applied its heaviest pressure on Ford Motor Company, which paid no taxes to the city of Detroit because its factories were located in Dearborn and Highland Park. Henry Ford claimed that this exempted him from any welfare debt to Detroit, but the mayor reminded Ford that a full 15 percent of Detroiters on welfare were unemployed Ford workers.[30]

Pressure from city hall hurt Ford's image as benefactor to his employees. At Detroit's 1931 Labor Day Parade, thousands of marchers from across the automobile industry flooded the streets, waving placards stating, "We want jobs!" At the end of the parade, hundreds of former Ford workers followed a banner that read "WORKERS OF FORD MOTOR COMPANY." They wore masks to hide their identities from Ford investigators, but their message hit their mark.[31] Henry Ford, who wanted his future labor force to remain grateful and compliant, made a series of light concessions to the unemployed, the first being community garden plots to supplement unemployed workers' incomes. When the workers complained that community gardens did little to alleviate their real need, Ford offered food to unemployed workers in Dearborn. The Ford relief program provided former workers with sixty cents a day at the Ford commissary, a sum that would be deducted from the individual's paycheck when he or she resumed work at the company.[32]

When Mayor Murphy and city administrators continued pressing Ford to take responsibility for his unemployed workers, the industrialist launched his most public welfare program, the rehabilitation of Inkster, a mixed-race community adjacent to Ford Motor Company. Because black

Detroiters faced racial covenants that precluded them from buying land in Detroit, John Dancy, head of the Detroit Urban League, had negotiated with a white realtor to acquire 140 acres outside the boundaries of Detroit to sell to African Americans. Inkster had no paved streets, streetlights, city sanitation, or water, but the prospect of home ownership brought 1,195 African Americans to the newly incorporated city, making them 27 percent of the Inkster's population.[33] As soon as Inkster secured some basic municipal amenities, however, the Depression hit, once again turning off its streetlights, halting its garbage service, and, of course, leaving the majority of its residents unemployed. It is unclear why precisely Ford decided to intervene in Inkster, perhaps because it was so close to his factories and not within the political jurisdiction of Detroit proper.[34] Whatever his reasons, Ford's intervention in Inkster gave him a citywide reputation for coming to the aid of black Detroiters, and as a result, Mayor Murphy stopped pressing Ford to help unemployed workers.[35]

Instead of helping black Inkster residents, Henry Ford instituted a system of debt peonage for the city's African Americans that would inform his dealings with all of African American Detroit. To alleviate unemployment and hunger, Ford Motor Company rehired 500 black Inkster residents at the rate of $1 a day, using what would have made up the rest of their wages to set aside a general fund to feed, house, and restore city services for the people of Inkster.[36] This practice of withholding wages in return for welfare ended when the New Deal instituted a minimum wage, but Ford administrators devised ways to collect workers' debts voluntarily. Collectors even began to bribe relatives of indebted Ford workers with jobs under the condition that they would pay a portion of the debt. Under this system, it soon became almost impossible for African American workers to find work at Ford without first finding a debtor to sponsor.[37] The Inkster project looked uncomfortably close to sharecropping for many African Americans, but at the national level, black newspapers lauded Ford for remembering the plight of black migrants.[38]

Working-class city residents began to view Mayor Murphy as a benefactor, but another segment of Detroiters insisted that pressuring companies to support workers stymied business and encouraged laziness. In a letter to the *Detroit Free Press*, a man who identified himself as a member of the "uncommon herd" to distinguish himself from Murphy's working-class constituency, called a "Murphy Detroit" a "Detroit in which to live without working."[39] On its front page, the newspaper also ran a piece criticizing

Mayor Murphy for spending $17,000,000 on welfare relief in a year, claiming that other American cities like Chicago and Baltimore thought the "welfare experiment" had turned Detroit into a "honey pot for the unemployed."[40] These comfortable Detroiters argued that by providing cash, milk, and coal for the unemployed and pressuring companies like Ford to support their laid-off workers, Mayor Murphy encouraged the unemployed to demand something they did not deserve from their local government. But to a majority of working-class, ethnic, Mexican, and African American Detroiters, Mayor Murphy's welfare policies had turned him into a local hero.

Across the border in Windsor, unemployed workers also sought a way to combat the effects of economic crisis. Because Windsor's economy was tied so closely to Detroit's, when American manufacturers closed automobile plants, they also shut down their Windsor operations. By 1930, Ford and Chrysler of Canada had reduced automobile production by three-fourths and Packard, Fisher, and Studebaker closed their small assembly plants entirely, causing nearly one-third of Border Cities residents to lose their jobs, giving the region the highest unemployment rate in all of Canada.[41] When layoffs began, fourteen thousand Windsorites left to seek positions in Toronto and other major cities, but twenty thousand new unemployed migrants from farmlands flooded to the city in their place, growing the city's population to ninety thousand.[42] Windsor's 1931 census noted that ten thousand of the city's inhabitants were born in continental Europe or Britain.[43] As more and more plants closed and layoffs continued, Windsor immigrants and native-born Canadians turned to soup kitchens and charity organizations by the thousands.

Windsor also suffered when U.S. tariff laws caused an export crisis across Canada. In an effort to protect American industry and agriculture from foreign competition, President Hoover signed the 1930 Tariff Act, or Smoot-Hawley Tariff. The act effectively raised tariffs on over twenty thousand imported goods, but because Canada relied heavily on exporting agricultural goods to the United States, the tariff hurt Canada's economy. Windsor had long exported iron ore and sand to Detroit for automobile production, but high tariffs crippled mining companies, causing them to lay off more workers.[44]

In the face of an economic crisis of unprecedented proportions, Windsor voters elected a young Jewish immigrant named David Croll to the office of mayor. To working Canadians, Croll represented success against all odds. In 1906, he had immigrated from Moscow to Windsor and settled on Goyeau Street alongside other Jewish immigrants. Penniless and unable to speak a word of English, Croll and his five siblings sold newspapers on the streets. In time, however, he and his siblings learned the language and attended school, and they all earned higher degrees in medicine and the law. Despite his success, Croll had not forgotten his humble roots and credited city welfare and Jewish community centers with giving his family the opportunities they so desperately needed in those early years. Consequently, Croll ran for mayor on a platform modeled loosely after Frank Murphy's in Detroit, promising pensions, public works, and welfare to the unemployed.[45]

Croll's platform set forth a series of concrete plans that appealed to many Windsor residents. He vowed to reorganize the social service department, establish a community fund drive and a municipal coal yard, lower gas company rates, and create protections for small borrowers against rising interest rates. Above all, Croll promised to represent the "common man," and he used his own humble background to argue that he understood unemployed and destitute workers' plight.[46] Thus, less than three months after Frank Murphy won Detroit's mayoral race with promises of leftist reform, just across the border, Windsorites elected David Croll, making him not only the youngest but also the first Jewish mayor of a Canadian city.

True to his word, Mayor David Croll set out to reorganize Windsor's welfare system. The city's small welfare department had traditionally focused on distributing winter coal and milk rations to a handful of families with children and found itself unable to handle the sudden surge of requests from unemployed factory workers. In his first several months, Mayor Croll canvassed factories for jobs and petitioned the provincial government in Toronto to send money for unemployment relief.[47] When a group of widows petitioned him for help with food and coal for their families, the new mayor created a community fund that set aside municipal money for widows, the disabled, and immigrants who could not find work because of special circumstances. In an early large-scale public work program, Croll also sought to create jobs for unemployed men by launching beautification programs in Windsor's parks and school buildings.[48]

For a brief moment, it appeared that residents of the Detroit-Windsor region had set aside nativist convictions that might have otherwise rendered Jewish Mayor Croll and Catholic Mayor Murphy unelectable in favor of welfare reform and unemployment relief. Concerns over who deserved new benefits, however, reinvigorated rhetoric casting southern and eastern Europeans and Mexicans as undeserving criminals. Windsor officials critical of Mayor Croll began to blame "alien labor" from Europe and even the United States for taking the jobs of Canadian citizens.[49] As the Depression continued and municipal debts rose, officials in Windsor and Detroit began to advocate returning noncitizens to their nations of origin. Consequently, by the early 1930s, a transnational push for deportations targeted Detroit's Mexican and ethnic European communities on both sides of the border.

Deportation as Unemployment Relief

Mounting concerns over welfare and debt prompted President Herbert Hoover and Canadian Prime Minister Richard Bennett to support federal deportation and repatriation drives. And while debates over deporting recently arrived immigrants began in Washington and Ottawa, it was local mayors, police, and immigration inspectors who carried out deportations on the borders of both Canada and the United States. In the Detroit-Windsor borderland, a decade of associating noncitizens and recent immigrants with crime and unlawful employment in the automobile industry easily translated to blaming the same newcomers for taking a disproportionate share of local welfare.

In Detroit, despite the fact that native-born, white citizens received a large percentage of city welfare, black migrants and immigrants born in Europe and Mexico gained a reputation for dependence. In 1932, the Sub-Committee on Welfare Statistics informed Mayor Murphy that the foreign born comprised 41 percent of welfare recipients, while native whites represented 39 percent and African Americans the final 20 percent of individuals receiving relief. In case these numbers appeared insignificant, the report reminded city officials and businessmen that this meant proportionally to their population that 10.2 percent of foreigners and 17 percent of African Americans received welfare. Meanwhile, 3.8 percent of native-born whites depended on the city for extra aid.[50] The growing perception that ethnic Europeans and African Americans from the South used a disproportionate amount of city aid made exclusionary policies popular.

The first of these came from Washington, where President Hoover's new Secretary of Labor William Doak advocated deportations to mitigate the economic effects of the Depression. Doak was a former union organizer who associated southern and eastern European immigrants with lowering the price of labor and breaking strikes. When he joined the Department of Labor in 1930, Secretary Doak launched an ambitious drive to find and deport every unauthorized immigrant living within the boundaries of the United States. Though he admitted the move was drastic, he promised it would serve the dual purpose of reducing crime and unemployment.[51] Linking dependence and poverty to vice suggested that the two issues were intertwined and that new immigrants were predisposed to both.

The assumption that deporting new immigrants controlled crime and lowered welfare burdens prompted local leaders to adopt harsh deportation policies, often against their wishes. In Detroit, Mayor Murphy opposed increased deportations, but when his relief programs stalled, he endorsed police commissioner Thomas C. Wilcox's nightly "tip-over" raids in ethnic neighborhoods. Such raids gave police an excuse to enter any building, where they could demand papers from those inside. If an immigrant could not produce proof of legal status, the individual was sent to the Immigration Service. Mayor Murphy called the raids a crime control measure, but he also understood that they would deport hundreds on public assistance.[52] Thus, despite Mayor Murphy's personal discomfort with deportation, his administration began expelling immigrants to fulfill dual promises of crime control and public welfare for local citizens.

Deportations affected more European immigrants than their raw numbers suggest. In 1932, an official report from Detroit's District 11 recorded 2,356 deportations, which had been paid for by the U.S. government or steamship companies and sent immigrants back to Europe, Asia, the Middle East, and Africa. This represented a small proportion of the 22,001 noncitizens the report claimed remained eligible for deportation in the district or the over three hundred thousand foreign-born residents of Detroit.[53] As discussed in Chapter 2, research on deportation drives in Chicago during the early years of the Great Depression suggests that only a small number of those rounded up were ever deported. Indiscriminately detaining thousands of ethnic Europeans without warrants did, however, link those arrested and their ethnicities to urban crime. Moreover, deportation drives made it appear that local administrators and police remained committed to crime control.[54] Detroit's police records have been destroyed, making it impossible to calculate just how many immigrants local enforcers rounded up in the city's large-scale deportation raids. But comparing the Detroit case to Chicago suggests that to produce around two thousand actual deportations, police likely rounded up, interrogated, and incarcerated tens of thousands of first- and second-generation Europeans. This meant that in the early 1930s, entire neighborhoods of Italians, Poles, Russians, and Hungarians likely cowered in fear when they saw police walking down the streets and that, inversely, native-born Detroiters associated foreign districts with vice, crime, and questionable citizenship.

Investigations also encouraged noncitizens to drop welfare petitions or leave the city. In the early years of the Depression, noncitizens were eligible for city welfare, but constant welfare investigations made many foreign recipients hide from investigators and lose their access to funds. In June 1931, Detroit's district director of immigration, John Zurbrick, orchestrated "welfare checks" that sent thousands of noncitizens into hiding. Zurbrick and his inspectors paused the "deportation war" they had carried on for over two years to plan an investigation into the citizenship status of the thirty thousand Detroiters receiving benefits from the city.[55] Zurbrick claimed the check was for informational purposes, but he also hoped to intimidate alien welfare recipients and encourage them to drop claims. In fact, Zurbrick promised that the investigation would mean about three thousand welfare recipients would disappear from the city. To reach this estimate, the immigration inspector used numbers from the year before, when his team investigated five hundred welfare recipients in Dearborn and more than sixty were never heard from again. When the investigators checked their homes, they found some had moved to other parts of the city or to other states. Inspector Zurbrick reported that if his team kept up their work, the welfare department would have funds for three thousand more American citizens.[56] It is possible that a large number of those investigated were unauthorized immigrants, but it is more likely that they were legal noncitizens who feared an overly zealous deportation regime might find a way to send them or perhaps loved ones out of the country. When police conducted regular deportation raids in immigrant neighborhoods, any questions about citizenship from a city official would have created panic among Detroit's immigrant communities.

For Detroit's Mexicans, this is precisely what happened. In 1930, news circulated that 90 percent of Mexican workers at Ford Motor Company had lost their jobs, prompting Detroit police, federal immigration agents, and local Mexican officials to join forces to "repatriate" around fifteen thousand Mexican migrants, many of them American citizens, back to Mexico.[57] Mexican painter Diego Rivera became involved in the repatriation drive while living in Detroit painting murals for Henry Ford's son Edsel at the Detroit Institute of Art. Rivera felt Mexican workers would fare better in their homeland and helped establish the Liga de Obreros y Campesinos (Workers and Peasants League), an organization that educated local Mexicans about their repatriation rights and lobbied U.S. and Mexican policymakers for funding.[58] Detroit's first deportation train, which cost the U.S. and Mexican governments a combined $7,280, pulled out of Detroit's Central Station on a cold winter day in 1932 with 442 Mexican passengers. Newspapers stressed that the train held only "voluntary" repatriates but also noted the tears shed by mothers holding sobbing "black haired babies" as they "see dreams crash."[59]

Some Mexicans refused to board deportation trains south, prompting local police and immigration service to begin rounding up groups for deportation, using the "likely to become a public charge" (LPC) clause to justify coercive raids. As outlined in Chapter 1, the LPC clause dated to the 1882 Immigration Act and for over fifty years had given immigration inspectors the discretion to deport paupers, homosexuals, the disabled, or anyone they deemed likely to need public assistance.[60] In 1931, when Immigration Chief Zurbrick felt repatriation numbers had begun to lag, he directed roundups in the city's Mexican westside neighborhood to locate those who were deportable for any reason.[61] By the following year, he reported to the Commissioner General of Immigration and the Department of Labor that his bureau had "sent about 1,500 who had become public charges to Mexico."[62] Ultimately, the repatriation drive decimated Detroit's Mexican community, leaving only about 1,200 Mexicans in the city by 1938.[63]

The Communist Party's International Labor Defense (ILD) became the most vocal opponent of repatriation drives in Detroit. While police worked with Rivera to identify Mexicans for return to their homeland, the ILD distributed circulars written in Spanish attacking repatriation and calling Rivera a "renegade of the Communist Party." The pamphlets also condemned the Mexican government for failing to uphold its promise to provide land, agricultural tools, and food to repatriates.[64] But protest did little to stem the tide of antiforeign sentiment sweeping through Depression-era Detroit, and Detroit's Mexican community became one of its largest casualties.

Detroit's Chinese also faced government crackdowns during the early years of the Depression. Between 1929 and 1930, the city lost one-third of its Chinese population, reducing the already small community from about 1,500 to 500 residents. The *Detroit News* claimed that most of these Chinese left of their own accord, traveling to Chicago, East Coast cities, or even China to better weather the Depression.[65] And while this certainly may have been true, the press also noted that the police had begun to crack down further on Chinese smuggling rings and scrutinize the local Chinese community for documents.[66] While no evidence remains to prove Chinese were herded onto deportation trains alongside Mexicans, they certainly faced immigration checks and police roundups meant to reduce their numbers.

As repatriations emptied Detroit's Mexican and Chinese neighborhoods, policymakers used these models to encourage the "removal" of Europeans who found themselves "without employment and destitute." In February 1931, the Bureau of Immigration inaugurated a program that used a subsection of the 1917 Immigration Act to authorize and pay for the removal of aliens who "within three years of their landing in the United States have fallen into distress or need public aid." During the following year, inspectors interviewed and repatriated 2,637 aliens, mostly from "industrial states" such as Michigan.[67] Like Mexican repatriation candidates, potential returnees found themselves in the strange position of proving their financial desperation to a government that they had only recently tried to convince of their desirability.

Loneliness and memories of family in Europe prompted hundreds of Europeans to present themselves for voluntary removal. Panto Corovich, a Yugoslavian man who had lost a factory job, owed the grocer $30, and lived off the charity of a Yugoslavian friend, applied for removal to his hometown of Mena, where he could at least live in poverty with his wife and two children.[68] Like Corovich, Giuseppe Morano applied for removal to Italy after a full year of unemployment. When his debts mounted to $150, Morano told inspectors, "I have no job here, and my family is in Italy," making the Italian an ideal candidate for removal.[69] Voluntary removal offered Corovich and Morano a short-term solution to their unemployment, but in the midst of a worldwide economic crisis, it is unlikely that the men would find work in Yugoslavia or Italy. In truth, Depression-era removals allowed U.S. officials to deny responsibility for the very immigrants they had brought to American industrial centers en masse just a decade prior. By emphasizing immigrants' foreignness, Department of Labor leaders argued that these men and women should be cared for by governments abroad, not the United States.[70]

In some cases, the injuries sustained in American industries even quali-fied immigrants for removal. After five years in the coal mines of West Virginia and several years as a machine grinder in a Detroit factory, Hun-garian Istvan Mezano fell ill and checked in full-time at a Department of Public Welfare hospital. While receiving treatment, he took a day trip to Canada, a move that qualified him for repatriation as a "recently arrived immigrant." The next week, an Immigration Service inspector made a trip to the hospital and informed Mezano that as a legal alien, he would proba-bly soon lose his access to treatment, but because he had recently reentered the United States, he could return to Kerecsend, Hungary, free of charge.[71] To local officials, Mezano's decision to leave Detroit meant one more non-citizen cut from overburdened welfare rolls. But in a larger sense, Mezano's case demonstrates how the American state had begun to cast those born abroad as legal outsiders. This federal shift allowed local officials to send thousands of Mexicans onto repatriation trains and return other immi-grants to Europe to seek treatment for the injuries they sustained in Ameri-can industries.

Voluntary removals and repatriations became so popular that the Immi-gration Service began granting them to immigrants who were not impover-ished but just wanted to return home. In 1930, Ivan Petrumanjanez convinced the Immigration Service to recommend a funded removal for himself, his wife, and children on the grounds that if he remained in Detroit, he would need to apply for city welfare. With his small savings account, Petrumanjanez did not fit the law's requirement that he be "unemployed and destitute," but he argued that after losing his job, other factories would avoid him, reasoning, "I have grey hair and am an old man and they won't hire me." He supported his family with little trouble after selling his car, but he warned inspectors, "I will have to go to the welfare unless I go back to Jugo-Slavia." When questioned, his wife Lena con-curred, assuring inspectors, "My husband has no work and we don't want to go to the Welfare." Despite the family's ability to stay afloat, inspectors agreed that even the slightest chance they might apply for city welfare legiti-mized funding their tickets back to Yanahkit, Yugoslavia, where they planned to make a living by farming a plot of family land.[72] The Petruman-janez case shows that Immigration Service officers had become so eager to expel as many immigrants as they could from the nation that they over-looked the basic requirements of federal laws. While repatriation repre-sented a promising step for Petrumanjanez, local inspectors' zeal for increasing repatriation helped cast self-supporting immigrants as dependents on the state.

These repatriations did little to reverse the effects of the Depression, but they did reinforce the growing perception that welfare benefits should be reserved for American citizens alone. In Detroit, a city of 1.5 million, the nearly seventeen thousand individuals who returned to Europe or Mexico had little impact on the rising city debt. Nevertheless, Immigration Inspector Zurbrick assured the Department of Labor and the public that the removal system had "relieved the public welfare funds from the maintenance of indigent aliens." Framing the program as a public service, he noted that he often received gratitude from "aliens when they find that authority has been received for their removal."[73]

Detroit's Arab Americans, many of whom identified as European or white themselves, also returned voluntarily to their nations of origin to escape the Depression. These migrants, however, tended to pay for their tickets home, making it easier for them to return to the United States. By the early 1930s, Detroit's Syrian, Lebanese, and Turkish immigrants had established a key Muslim community in Highland Park and began to settle the southeast region of Dearborn to be closer to jobs at Ford's River Rouge factory. When unemployment spread though their community, many chose to return to French-controlled Syria or Lebanon. For instance, in 1930, instead of going on welfare, a prospect she found shameful, Fatima El Haje arranged for her family's return to Lebanon. When she reached her homeland, however, El Haje immediately regretted her decision. The French administrators had not invested in infrastructure and the region also suffered from depression and hunger. Consequently, El Haje spent the next years trying to arrange for her family's return, a feat she finally managed in 1937. Stories like El Haje's emphasized the fact that return to the Middle East or Europe rarely benefited immigrants and instead produced an uptick in applications for return visas in Washington, D.C.[74]

At the local level, repatriations not only associated foreign-born immigrants with welfare but also ensured that noncitizens would not have a stake in America's emerging welfare state. During the early days of the Depression, as mutual benefit societies and church organizations went bankrupt, American workers facing unemployment turned toward city and eventually federal welfare benefits.[75] This shift meant many working-class Americans began to depend on and demand state benefits, but the growing popularity of deportation and repatriation reminded southern and eastern

Europeans with no citizenship papers and nearly all Mexicans that they would not be welcome in this new America.

In a region where border crossing still formed part of the local culture, many Europeans who had become uneasy with American policies headed to Windsor. But in Canada, municipalities had begun enforcing an existing clause within federal immigration laws that allowed for the deportation of recent immigrants. For instance, after witnessing several raids on his Detroit street, Carlo Stazzi, an Italian with no papers, decided to cross the border to Windsor to live with his brother. Stazzi traversed the Ambassador Bridge on foot, but when he found no work in Windsor and by the winter of 1932, Stazzi registered for city welfare. By seeking public relief, however, Stazzi qualified for deportation as a "public charge," and the Windsor welfare commissioner sent his name to Ottawa. Soon Stazzi received a deportation order for his return to Italy.[76] Though in Canada, Stazzi was technically not illegal, he became subject to deportation under a subsection of Canadian law that reserved the right to deport any immigrants who had lived in Canada less than five years and sought public assistance.[77] In the early 1930s, federal laws and the local enforcement they required on both sides of the border turned the Detroit-Windsor region into a hostile place for foreigners.

The same year Windsor residents elected David Croll to be their mayor, Canada's wider population responded to the Great Depression by electing conservative Richard Bennett prime minister. Bennett ran a campaign replete with nationalist rhetoric that proposed austerity measures to reinvigorate Canada's economy. When he reached office, Prime Minister Bennett advanced an agenda promising to preserve Canadian jobs and resources for its citizens. Soon the Bennett administration looked to U.S. repatriation and deportation efforts to justify a similar move against any immigrant who had recently arrived in Canada and lost his job. This meant that by the end of Bennett's first year in office, his administration had deported 7,025 immigrants on welfare. The justification for deportations relied on British poor law tradition, which held local cities responsible for feeding and employing their residents. This localized welfare system worked when people stayed in one place, but the Depression forced thousands of men and women to leave cities in search of work, creating an army of "transient workers" moving from place to place.[78] Bennett argued that the "transient workers," many of whom were foreign born, threatened the welfare of Canadian cities and that the most humane and responsible action would be to help them leave Canada in much the same way the U.S. government returned Mexicans across the southern border. By 1931, Bennett encouraged cities across Canada to send the names of noncitizens to Ottawa, where his welfare officers would investigate their backgrounds and quietly issue deportation orders, beginning a process that arranged for the expulsion of thousands and raised relatively little outcry from the Canadian public.[79] Thus, federal policy from Ottawa spearheaded deportation efforts, but their implementation at the city level turned drives into local affairs, subject to the particular politics of a city's politics, inhabitants, and, in the case of Windsor, its placement on an international border.

Like its American neighbor, automobile plant closures hit Windsor particularly hard. Windsor's Mayor David Croll opposed tying deportation to welfare dependence, but rising unemployment incited familiar concerns that immigrants might be taking jobs from Canadian citizens. Between 1930 and 1931, Windsor Welfare Commissioner Clyde Curry worked with Windsor police to stop and question any "foreign-looking person" waiting for coal or asking for a grocery stipend. In the neighboring Border Cities of East Windsor and Sandwich, Curry encouraged local welfare departments to do the same.[80] The system became particularly effective in East Windsor, where long bread lines stretched down the city's immigrant region of Drouillard Avenue after Ford of Canada shut down 80 percent of its production. These lines soon became key sites for investigating immigrants, and welfare workers quietly questioned over a thousand Italians, Poles, and Russians, sending the names of those without jobs to the Department of Immigration in Ottawa.[81] And while Mayor Croll opposed deportations, he had no jurisdiction in East Windsor and could not stop Commissioner Curry from influencing local welfare workers.

When neighboring towns implemented deportation drives, Windsor leaders faced pressure to follow suit. In June 1932, administrators in the nearby towns of Kitchener and Oshawa, Ontario, launched programs to purge unemployed foreigners from their municipalities.[82] Oshawa was home to Chrysler of Canada, meaning that, like Windsor, its residents relied on a struggling automobile factory and thousands of new immigrants crowded the streets of the town. Welfare Commissioner Curry warned his Windsor constituents that once Oshawa expelled its immigrants, thousands would soon be "drifting in here to escape." It stood to reason, Curry concluded, that Windsor should follow the lead of Canada's other automobile center and expel its foreigners so as not to fall behind economically.[83]

Deportations in Oshawa motivated Commissioner Curry to launch a deportation drive without Mayor Croll's support. First, the Welfare Commission sent the files of ten Windsor immigrants to Ottawa's Minister of Immigration, promising that these men would be deported for seeking aid. Next, Curry established a deportation committee with welfare administrators who took to Windsor's streets, interrogating one hundred men and women in local welfare lines and rounding up any foreigners who had arrived within the previous five years.[84] Commissioner Curry asserted that his initiative would help get "rid of the undesirables from foreign lands clogging up the money meant for good Canadian citizens."[85] In practice, this meant that inspectors began to question anyone who looked ethnic, meaning that they had to rely on nativist profiling to single out immigrants, reinforcing the idea that foreign-born people did not deserve the same benefits as Canadians.

Mayor Croll refused to sign any deportation orders, forcing a standoff within the city government. For the mayor, a Russian immigrant himself, deportation struck a personal chord. In an article to the *Border Cities Star*, he reminded Windsor residents, "These people have to be treated as human beings." Over the radio, he assured residents that he was not out to protect criminal aliens or those hoping to "overthrow the government by force." However, he promised, "No man legally admitted into this country who has become poverty-stricken through no fault of this man is going to be deported so long as I can help it!"[86] The mayor's impassioned speeches earned him the admiration of immigrant communities on both sides of the border who felt their ethnic groups had been unjustly linked to the economic crisis.[87] But local Canadians and national leaders supported deportations as a way to cut down on crime and save money. In July 1932, Commissioner Curry announced that he would begin to take orders directly from Ottawa and began to deport non-Canadians without the mayor's approval. Curry asserted that while Mayor Croll "stood on his soapbox, immigration inspectors came to the city to carry out their jobs." The Welfare Department, he reported, had already sent twenty immigrants home to Europe, and administrators planned to investigate hundreds more with or without the consent of the mayor. When Prime Minister Bennett commended Curry's actions, the commissioner redoubled deportation efforts, writing off Mayor Croll's views as "simply out of fashion."[88] Thus, despite the mayor's efforts, local administrators continued to deport anyone they could, forcing even established immigrants to fear for friends, neighbors, and family members who might have immigrated in the past five years.[89]

The popularity of deportation drives in Windsor made it clear that despite the election of a mayor with a Jewish immigrant background, nativism continued to inform local policy, causing immigrants to worry about their security within Canadian society. Mayor Croll himself lamented, "Windsor no longer shows immigrants the same tolerance" that he as a young Jewish lawyer with a slight Russian accent had found in the city.[90]

Ultimately, the new Ambassador Bridge had made border crossing easier than ever, but Depression-era deportation practices restricted the movements of even legal immigrants. When the extension bridge opened and reduced crossing the border to a ten-minute drive, the region's pharmaceutical and automobile companies predicted that the border would all but disappear from the region.[91] Real estate developers in Windsor began advertising "Detroit adjacent properties" in the *Detroit Free Press* that came complete with a drawing depicting the proximity of the Border Cities to Henry Ford's River Rouge factory.[92] However, the Great Depression generated movements in Ottawa and Washington, D.C. to close North American borders and guard U.S. and Canadian national interests with tariffs and deportations. When car sales dropped and automobile factories began closing plants, federal pressure to deport immigrants reached the Detroit-Windsor borderland, meaning anyone who looked Slavic, Italian, or Mexican might face interrogation or police harassment.

Analyzing Depression-era deportation and border crossing in Detroit and Windsor reveals how local and transnational politics shaped American immigration laws. And while state and federal policymakers determined the opening of bridges and the passage immigration laws, local governments decided who could live, work, and receive benefits in particular cities. By the early 1930s, cross-border deportation efforts tied new immigrants to dependence on the state. And because deportations increased under progressive mayors, examining Detroit and Windsor's city politics reveals how hard-line immigration policies began to coexist comfortably within liberal administrations. As local leaders agreed to enact nativist immigration policies, the Detroit Federation of Labor (DFL) seized the opportunity to regulate the border with a campaign to register all aliens in the state of Michigan.

Chapter 5

Registering Immigrants in the Depression Era

In May 1931, at the height of the Great Depression, Michigan's state legislature passed an act that required all alien Michiganders to carry registration cards. Governor Wilber Brucker assured Detroiters that "only those who are here illegally need be concerned," but in reality, the act provided employers and unions a legal way to intimidate workers without citizenship regardless of their legal status.[1] The registration act required unnaturalized Detroiters to present themselves at the local Office of Public Safety, where a commissioner subjected them to fingerprinting, photographing, and lengthy interviews before issuing them a card marked "desirable and cleared for work." If local police caught an alien working without a registration card, the worker faced a fine and ninety days in prison followed by a trip to Detroit's immigration office for further investigation.[2] The Michigan Registration Act angered local immigrant groups who thought their members might be stigmatized by fingerprinting, and it also concerned employers who resented any checks on their access to free labor. These groups lobbied to ensure a federal judge would strike down the Registration Act before it could take full effect, but the battle over registration created lasting tensions between unions, employers, and immigrant communities in Detroit. For Joseph Kowalski, a Polish alien in the process of taking out his citizenship papers, the idea of registering with the state and especially leaving his fingerprints meant "we are seen as criminals by the government and the unions just because we are not born in America."[3] The growing resentment Kowalski and other immigrants felt toward labor and local government would weaken strikes and cause immigrants to distrust even leftist politicians throughout the 1930s.

The Detroit Federation of Labor (DFL) championed alien registration as part its wider struggle against border crossing from Canada, but angering Detroit's immigrant communities undermined the DFL's efforts to organize the automobile industry. The DFL had spent the previous four years struggling against employers and diplomats in a battle to close the border to commuters, and by 1930, the union doubled down on its commitment to casting undocumented workers as communist radicals and criminals. The DFL began by warning that the new Ambassador Bridge would mean an "influx of cheap foreign labor," reporting that in the bridge's first month, 35,817 immigrants had poured into the United States.[4] The numbers reported by the DFL reflected all border crossings and were actually no higher than traffic the month prior, but in an era when local politicians waged deportation and repatriation drives to keep foreigners off welfare in both Detroit and Windsor, the DFL easily won support for registering aliens. The union's registration drive, however, alienated immigrant communities from organized labor and crippled efforts to unionize the automobile industry.

In 1933, when the DFL lent its support to striking Briggs Body workers, a segment of ethnic Americans still resented the union for its role in alien registration and stayed out of the strike. Labor historians have argued that despite its failure, the Briggs strike represented an opening act in a larger story of automobile organizing, a conflict that taught automobile workers their collective strength and raised their consciousness. While this may be true, this chapter reexamines the Briggs strike as evidence of the deep ethnic divisions forming within organized labor, cracks that would be impossible to repair when the Congress of Industrial Organizations (CIO) and United Automobile Workers launched their unionization campaigns just two years later.[5] Ultimately, local efforts to deport, repatriate, and register immigrants kept entire segments of North America's population on the sidelines of the labor movement and, soon, America's emerging welfare state.

Registering Immigrants

The deportations and repatriations upending ethnic communities in the Detroit-Windsor borderland gave the DFL the momentum to campaign for alien registration, a move that brought even legal immigrants under police and political scrutiny. The DFL led the registration campaign in 1931, arguing that deportations alone would not combat unemployment. Drawing on a long tradition of anti-immigrant activism and a more recent battle against commuters in Detroit, the DFL objected to alien workers because they supposedly saturated the labor market and undercut wages in the midst of an economic depression.[6] President Frank Martel claimed alien registration presented no hardship to aliens in that "every native born American is registered at his birth; he is registered when he commences his attendance at school; he is registered when he avails himself of his right to vote, and he is registered when he joins a Trade Union." Registering aliens, he reasoned, would present no hardship to those who had legal papers and would only target unauthorized workers, facilitating "their deportation or proper assimilation."[7] But registration shifted local immigration debates to legal immigrants, reminding these newcomers that they were not welcome in local workplaces and unions.

Growing local support for deportation may have emboldened the DFL, but the larger American Federation of Labor avoided the issue. American Federation of Labor (AFL) President William Green wrote to President Martel reminding him the local union also needed to tread lightly when dealing with legal immigrants. As outlined in Chapter 3, President Green had urged the Detroit union to stop campaigning against Canadian commuters a few years before, and once again, he argued that mandatory registration would only "sow terror and dissent" among ethnic groups. In a broader sense, President Green also understood that organized labor needed to recruit ethnic workers and that there was no need to humiliate or alienate potential union members by demanding their fingerprints.[8]

But President Martel ignored Green's plea for moderation and insisted that the national union could not possibly understand the situation in Detroit, where an international border and now a bridge provided employers with access to an inexhaustible workforce. Registering immigrants, Martel argued, promised to open jobs for "American workers" and deal a blow to the automobile magnates who had managed to keep the city open shop longer than any other in the nation.[9] Like the problem of Canadian commuters, President Martel viewed registering immigrants as a labor issue and hoped a new law would allow the DFL to gain some measure of control over a workforce in which even skilled and semiskilled workers could be recruited from the ranks of Canadian or European-born workers and undermine union efforts to organize.

To gain statewide traction on alien registration, however, President Martel needed the support of Michigan employers, and he began peddling registration as a check on the only thing employers feared more than organized labor—communism. The same month the Ambassador Bridge advertised an easy route between the United States and Canada, Martel began writing to state officials and business leaders across the state, citing the "terror wrought by foreign-born communists" in the city. In a letter to Governor Wilber Brucker, he warned, "If left unchecked, communist agitators will destroy the institutions we hold dearest."[10] Instead of mentioning labor or organizing the workforce, President Martel positioned alien registration as a campaign that transcended industrial quarrels in a larger fight against communist foreigners.

The connection between foreign-born Europeans and radical politics was, of course, nothing new. In 1919, a wave of anarchist bombings had prompted terrified federal officials to deport hundreds of foreigners over the course of the following year in a Red Scare that linked Italian and Russian communities to political violence. Even after terrorist attacks slowed, the trial of Niccolo Sacco and Bartolomeo Vanzetti, which ended in the Italian men's execution in 1927, kept discussions linking foreigners to anarchism in national headlines.[11] Detroit's Communist Party had been actively involved in protesting the execution of the two Italian men, and by 1930, antileft activists and politicians joined anarchism, socialism, and communism under the term "isms," arguing that each represented an equal threat to American democracy.[12]

The DFL's insistence that foreigners were growing the ranks of Detroit's Communist Party was based in some measure of truth. By the Great Depression, Detroit's Communist Party had begun to recruit more workers than ever, and thousands of new members were born in Europe. The party's policy of nondiscrimination appealed to foreign-born workers tired of nativism and deportation drives, and its promise to fix a broken capitalist system spoke to the desperation and fear felt by many foreigners who found themselves in America, unemployed, with no extended family or safety net. Hundreds of Romanian, Polish, Hungarian, and Greek immigrants attended communist meetings and joined the party. In February 1930 alone, 1,059 Detroiters joined the Communist Party, giving America's Motor City one of the nation's fastest-growing communist movements.[13] Soon angry communists staged mass demonstrations in the heart of the city and circulated newsletters in Ford, Chrysler, and Packard plants demanding unemployment benefits and higher wages.[14]

In response, the Union League of Michigan, an organization dominated by the state's business elite, took the advice of DFL lobbyists and drafted an alien registration bill for the state legislature in Lansing. The Union League was a conservative social men's society with more than a thousand members, including Governor Brucker, directors of insurance agencies and banks, and Charles Mott and Lawrence Fisher, both vice presidents of General Motors.[15] While these economic leaders certainly disliked working with a labor union, they began to view DFL calls for alien registration as the only way to curb the threat of communism in Detroit. In early 1931, the league organized a fifteen-member Subversive Activities Committee that warned members of the ten to fifty thousand communists organizing within the city limits of Detroit.[16] Because foreign-born Russians, Italians, Finns, and Ukrainians had a particular reputation for political radicalism, the league reasoned that a registration bill might at the very least intimidate foreign-born workers and return to employers a measure of the control they traditionally wielded over Detroit's workforce. In fact, registering immigrants represented one of the less radical of the Union League's ideas. The league also advocated deporting naturalized workers and disenfranchising native-born members of the Communist Party.[17] Thus, as the registration campaign gained political traction in Lansing, legal and naturalized immigrants began to worry that their place in American society might be under threat.

The registration campaign shifted the focus of nativist groups and "patriotic societies" from undocumented aliens to legal immigrants. The American Legion lauded the bill and took the opportunity to demand even steeper legislation against migrants to Detroit. The veterans' organization coined the slogan, "Detroit for Detroiters First," demanding that employers only offer jobs to native-born Americans who had resided in Detroit for more than five years. The campaign targeted not just foreign-born but also black Detroiters, many of whom had migrated north in the wake of restrictive immigration laws and also gravitated toward the inclusive platform of the Communist Party.[18] Keeping "Detroit for Detroiters First," the legion claimed, would cut down on communism, crime, and political radicalism, three trends that, by 1931, were linked to foreign-born Europeans and the thousands of African American migrants crowding into the city's Black Belt and Paradise Valley neighborhoods.[19] Thus, registering aliens marked the first step in a movement that sought to document and ultimately expel all non-Anglos from the region.

In response, American Civil Liberties Union (ACLU) President Richard Baldwin launched a national protest on the grounds that the bill discriminated against foreigners living legally in America. The ACLU was founded to promote free speech during World War I, and in the 1920s, the organization channeled its efforts into litigating against anti-Catholicism, anti-Semitism, and racism across the nation. President Baldwin had a history of successfully obstructing efforts to pass federal alien registration laws and thought a win in Michigan might embolden nativist lawmakers intent on restricting the rights of America's foreign born. While the registration bill had been drafted by Detroit's business leaders and found support with patriotic societies, President Baldwin chose to fight the bill by writing to DFL President Martel. Baldwin may have hoped for sympathy from President Martel, who, by this time, supported his French Canadian father and lived on the city's Belgian east side. President Baldwin reminded the DFL leader that alien registration would be used "to intimidate alien workers in trade unions." Alien registration, Baldwin argued, would only serve to distance foreign-born workers from organized labor.[20]

But ACLU lobbies did little to weaken President Martel's resolve. And when communist protesters took to the streets, the union president redoubled his support for the Union League and alien registration. Between the fall of 1930 and the spring of 1931, the communist-led Trade Union Unity League staged regular protests, wielding signs that read, "Fight against the A.F. of L. which is the agent of the bosses!" Public protests infuriated President Martel, who wrote to the Union League, arguing that "registration would cripple the communists." The Union League agreed, expressing the hope that registration could end the Communist Party in all of Detroit. "If not, why would the communists protest so?" asked a Union League publication.[21] By 1931, the alliance between the city's largest labor union and its business elite promised to end communism and urban crime, but the new focus on legal immigrants incited local backlash.

Communist leaders pulled together a group of prominent Detroit reformers to condemn the bill. Under the auspices of the Detroit Council for the Protection of Foreign-Born Workers, an organization established in 1928 to combat nativism in urban centers across the United States, communist organizers encouraged prominent Detroiters to speak out against registration. Democratic Senator Charles M. Novak, Detroit Social Secretary Mrs. George T. Hendrie, and Methodist Reverend E. J. Warren all stepped forward with their objections. In a joint petition, they agreed that alien registration would "greatly intimidate foreign born workers" and was "hardly in keeping with American traditions."[22] By emphasizing the potential for harassment and unfair treatment in foreign-born communities across the city and encouraging prominent Detroiters to publish their concerns, communist organizers hoped to portray the bill as a civil liberties violation.

Ethnic communities in Detroit launched their own protest to the bill. In May 1931, in the gilded parlors of the Georgian-style Hotel Statler, Jewish, Hungarian, German, Polish, Italian, Greek, and Belgian representatives gathered to discuss ways to stop the bill from becoming a law.[23] Before forming lobbies, they raised awareness in Detroit's foreign-language press. The *Polish Daily News, Polish Worker, Hungarian News, Abend Post*, and the *Greek Progress* all emphasized how registration would build a "system of espionage" that would "stigmatize the foreign born" and "increase racial and national prejudice" throughout the city. The ethnic papers agreed that the DFL's drive to register foreigners would prevent "labor unity and cooperation."[24]

Ethnic societies that rarely engaged with each other united to voice their protest. The Lithuanian Workers of Detroit assembled a mass meeting of 5,390 in the Lithuanian Hall to condemn registration while the Allied Singing and Dramatic Society, Croatian Union of America, and Slovak Workers Society circulated petitions that protested placing their ethnic groups "legally in the same category as criminals."[25] Indeed, the threat of registration, fingerprinting, and possible deportation mobilized ethnic organizations, pitting them against the DFL and the employers who associated their nationalities with communism.

Ignoring the protest, on May 29, 1931, Governor Brucker signed the bill, requiring all aliens in Michigan to register with the state. The governor assured Detroiters that "only those who are here illegally need be concerned," but in truth, the act represented more than an administrative hassle for those not born in America.[26] Officially, the law required nonnaturalized residents to present themselves at the local Office of Public Safety, a new division within the Detroit Police Department, where a commissioner would document them with fingerprints, a photograph, and a lengthy interview before issuing a card marked "desirable and cleared for work." If local police caught an "alien" worker without a registration card, the worker faced a fine and ninety days in prison followed by prompt delivery to federal immigration officials.[27] Furthermore, Sections 12 and 14 of the law made the employment of an unregistered alien a misdemeanor. Employers in violation were liable to a fine of $100 or ninety days of imprisonment, marking it the first time employers were to be held responsible for their own part in violating immigration laws.[28]

Immigrants and Employers Fight Back

The Union League declared a victory with the passage of the Michigan Registration Act, but foreign-born Detroiters took to the street in protest. Groups of Lithuanians, Poles, and Italians claimed registration replicated "conditions existing in Czarist Russia."[29] Governor Brucker reminded foreign-born Detroiters that "all available jobs should go to those who are here lawfully" and that new sanctions would actually protect law-abiding immigrants from the "undesirable aliens" who were "prominent among those urging the overthrow of [the] government."[30] The Union League of Michigan heartily agreed and printed crisp copies of the new law for distribution in factories and neighborhoods across Detroit.[31]

The prospect of registration, particularly employer accountability, split Detroit's business community. Small to midsized business owners tended to favor registration. The Detroit Chamber of Commerce, for instance, which had a handful of key industrialists on its board but was run by employers and entrepreneurs with small staffs, applauded the new law. The Chamber still clung to Americanization programs meant to assimilate new immigrants, and by the Great Depression, they feared foreign-born communists might scare away potential investors.[32] To them, registration represented a way to expose and expel undesirable immigrants from the city, and it posed little threat to the small staffs in their automobile dealerships, drug stores, and law and real estate offices.

The Detroit Employment Managers' Club (DEMC), an organization representing larger companies, divided over registration. Some of its members bought into the argument that alien registration might end communism. In fact, a National Metal Trades Association representative, Jacob Spolansky, an immigrant from Ukraine, championed registration in the DEMC as the only way to separate the "undesirables" from the respectable immigrants. He argued that all eastern Europeans like himself should want an alien registration system because it offered a way to distance their nationalities from criminality. Spolansky became a fervent advocate for registering immigrants, so much so that by 1931, many Michiganders referred to the Registration Act as the "Spolansky Act."[33]

But when employers realized the Alien Registration Act meant regulating access to immigrant labor, the DEMC's larger manufacturers lodged their opposition to the act. The DEMC represented a number of major industrial operations, including Detroit's construction, steel, and tool companies, along with small automobile factories like Saxon, Hupp, and King, all of which relied on inexpensive immigrant workers and had little interest in wasting time on citizenship requirements. Giants like Ford and Chrysler also sent representatives to DEMC meetings, where members discussed how to retain good employees, discharge workers, and train foremen.[34] DEMC industrialists felt they should have free reign over "open shop" Detroit and resented any state intrusion into their hiring practices, particularly when these restrictions came with employer fines. While many industrial employers had begun to discourage the employment of noncitizens, they felt the choice should be decided by their management, not lawmakers in Lansing.[35]

The Michigan Manufacturers Association (MMA), an organization representing the largest industries in Michigan, opposed registration because it punished employers. The MMA advisory board included presidents of Chrysler, Buick, Cadillac, and Dodge and executives at Ford Motor Company, and its officers ran key industries throughout the state. MMA President A. B. Williams headed Postum Cereal Company, council member C. E. Bennett was the president of Novo Engineering Company, and Secretary A. R. Demory presided over Timken-Detroit Axle Company.[36] After Governor Brucker signed the registration law, John Lovett, MMA general manager, voiced the organization's outrage. He claimed the state had infringed upon the traditional jurisdiction of industry and insisted that "an employer has no way of knowing that certain aliens, particularly Canadians, are not American citizens."[37] The law also shifted a large burden of paperwork and detection to individual employers, a change that MMA executives claimed would be impossible to enact in large industries with multiple factories across Detroit and its suburbs.[38]

Like sanctions on commuting, these employers thought alien registration signaled an unwelcome state regulation that threatened their access to skilled immigrants. By the end of May, a group of manufacturers lodged a suit against the bill because some of their skilled employees had begun to resign rather than be subjected to "the humiliations of fingerprinting."[39] During the Depression, employers had no trouble finding unskilled workers. Indeed, an unemployed army of semiskilled and unskilled workers crowded outside the gates of major automobile companies each morning. Skilled workers, however, proved more difficult to find or train, and companies worried their noncitizen engineers and foremen might leave positions.[40]

As employers withdrew their support for the law, communist protesters focused on the Detroit Federation of Labor for betraying the interest of ordinary workers. Throughout the summer of 1931, communists staged mass protests in Detroit's most public places. On June 19, the secretary of the national Communist Party, William Z. Foster, even traveled to Detroit. On a sweltering summer afternoon, thousands of protesters crowded into Grand Circus Park, a public square adjacent to the financial district, to hear Foster speak out against the "blacklist alien registration law," which he warned would pit native-born Americans against the foreign born and "divide and defeat" the labor movement.[41] Indeed, many foreign-born and immigrant Americans had begun to see the DFL's campaign as evidence that organized labor did not represent their interests.

Jewish leaders also spoke out against the law, turning the repeal of the registration law into a battle over civil rights and Jewish discrimination.[42] Popular rabbi Leon Fram of Reform Temple Beth-El insisted that the law would only bring "czarism, terror, blackmail, and extortion" to Detroit's foreign-born communities. He worried that Detroit's 75,000 Jewish residents, a group already linked to criminality and political radicalism in the popular press, would face increased policing if the law took effect.[43]

Ultimately, however, Jewish and communist protest provided fodder for nativists. The Ku Klux Klan and the DAR both insisted that registering immigrants could stop the spread of "isms," a term used by nativists to refer to the evils of "communism," "Semitism," and "Catholicism."[44] By using the label "isms" to refer to all three issues, the nativist organizations reinforced the idea that the interest and members of all three groups overlapped and that all posed a threat to Protestant America.

The DFL worked to cast protest against the law as a fringe movement led by a handful of ethnic and religious minorities. Throughout the spring and summer of 1931, the *Detroit Labor News* published articles disparaging protesters as "hyphenated Americans," suggesting that they did not deserve the same rights or recognition as native-born American citizens. When Rabbi Leon Fram wrote to the paper asking that the DFL try to understand the pressures registration placed on foreign-born workers, the *Detroit Labor News* ran a piece entitled "The Rabbi Rants," which portrayed the Jewish leader as an unhinged peddler of un-American values.[45]

But it was small-scale ethnic employers that suffered most under registration, and their protest ultimately overturned the law. Immigrant businessmen challenged the legislation with several successful suits in the Sixth

Circuit Court of the U.S. Court of Appeals.[46] First, building contractor George Arrowsmith claimed the law represented an unrealistic administrative demand. Arrowsmith was born in Lancashire, England, and found himself subject to the registration law as an employee and a potential employer of immigrants. In June 1931, Arrowsmith brought in a group of Jewish lawyers led by Detroit's Theodore Levin to file a suit against Governor Brucker, the attorney general, and the Office of Public Safety on behalf of Arrowsmith, arguing that his livelihood as a contractor depended on employing workers of foreign birth. They claimed registration impinged on his "fundamental human rights."[47]

Levin and his fellow litigators also filed a suit on behalf of Francesco Dimeglio on the grounds that registration laws had the potential to bankrupt his barbershop and send him back to Italy. Dimeglio claimed that he crossed the Detroit River legally in 1923, in an era before immigration officials bothered to track entries or offer consistent entry documentation. Due to registration requirements, Dimeglio faced potential deportation and the loss of his Italian workers, many of whom had similar stories of lost papers or overlooked records.[48] Here, lawyers focused on the inherent unfairness and impracticality of the state's new registration law, which caused "unnecessary humiliation" for foreign-born Michiganders and demanded a sophisticated system of documentation that simply did not yet exist in the United States.[49]

Beyond impracticality and prejudice, Levin attacked economic burden the registration law placed on small companies. Chrysler, Packard, and Ford could pay the $100 fine for employing undocumented workers. However, if caught employing a worker without proper registration papers, owners of companies like Detroit Polonia Publishing Company faced a choice between bankruptcy or ninety days in jail. Detroit Polonia printed the city's largest foreign-language newspaper, the *Polish Daily News*, and had an exclusively Polish-born staff.[50] Editors of the Detroit paper were particularly concerned because Adolf Pasterz, a Polish-born feature writer, refused to register with the state on principle.[51] Instead of firing Pasterz, the editors joined the suit against registration.

In July, the Sixth Circuit Court of the U.S. Court of Appeals declared the law unconstitutional, marking a major triumph for civil rights groups, ethnic lobbyists, and employers across Detroit. In Cincinnati's District Court, Judges Arthur C. Denison, Ernest O'Brien, and Charles C. Simons listened to Theodore Levin argue that Michigan would turn into "an armed

camp" unless the federal government stepped in. After a lengthy deliberation, the court ruled that the power to regulate immigrants lay exclusively
with the federal government, not with individual states. Judge Denison
delivered the opinion, which focused not on ethnic discrimination but on
the economic burden registration placed on employers.[52] Thus, the decision
to repeal registration represented a victory more for advocates of laissez-
faire economic policy and open labor than for foreign-born Americans.

This detail was not lost on Jewish Detroiters. The *Detroit Jewish Chronicle* agreed that the verdict marked a victory for "human beings who happen
to be foreign born" but that it also exposed the nativism that continued to
dominate city politics. The paper's editors warned immigrant Detroiters
and their families that "there exists a general feeling of hatred against the
immigrants" and that the registration case only proved that "the country
at large is now imbued with an anti-alien spirit."[53] Indeed, many ethnic
Americans viewed the registration fight as proof that their groups might
never be accepted as full Americans by Anglo-Protestant citizens.

Instead of blaming employers or nativists, however, ethnic Detroiters
held the DFL responsible for the registration law. The *Detroit Jewish Chronicle* claimed that the DFL should have looked out for the needs of all workers and that it was "no friend to immigrant Detroit."[54] Frank Januszweiski,
editor of Detroit's *Polish Daily News*, the Polish daily with the largest circulation of any foreign-language newspaper in the city, urged his readers to
avoid unions and insisted that the labor movement was the enemy of hardworking Poles.[55] In a city with a Polish population of one hundred seventy
thousand, the insistence that the DFL and, by association, the AFL espoused
nativist views, encouraged thousands of ethnic readers to view labor with
suspicion. And as labor leaders attempted to organize automobile workers,
reluctant ethnic Europeans presented a problem for organized labor. It is
perhaps unsurprising that undocumented workers who lived in constant
fear of discovery and deportation chose to weather exploitation without
complaint. But after the DFL attempted to register all of Michigan's aliens,
many naturalized and legal immigrant workers began to view labor as the
enemy and chose not to participate in strikes the union endorsed.

Immigrants and Labor Unrest

As employers, unions, and nativists struggled over the question of foreign-
born labor, foreign-born workers without citizenship still needed to support themselves and their families. Because the Depression had placed

financial constraints on ethnic and religious charities and the city's largest union had a history of lobbying against their immigrant interests, a large segment of Detroit's noncitizen population turned to city employers, a group that tended to glance the other way when the question of documentation came up. This forged a tentative and troubled alliance between major employers, especially manufacturers, and workers without citizenship. The labor system that emerged was less formal than the welfare capitalism of the early industrial years but relied on a similar combination of coercion and benefits to maintain a stable workforce.[56] By 1933, when the automobile industry attempted to wage its first major strike against Briggs Body Company, many foreign-born workers still harbored enough suspicion toward organized labor to undermine the strike. In short, the Briggs disaster taught labor organizers that in a city where over 25 percent of the population was born abroad, any union hoping to stage a successful strike would need to convince immigrant workers that not all unions stood with the DFL's positions on immigration.[57]

Immigrants without citizenship, particularly those who could not prove their legal status, faced constant and consistent exploitation from major companies. Instead of benefits, employers like Ford, Chrysler, and Packard offered part-time, underpaid jobs to those men and women not legally qualified to work. In return, employers demanded that these laborers avoid radical politics or collective bargaining. At the slightest sign of rebellion, industrialists used deportation to instill fear in other restless employees. Ultimately, alien workers without solid proof of their legal status fell into an informal system in which manufacturers both denounced and relied on their work.

Many large employers ignored formal citizenship policies. For instance, Ford Motor Company (FMC), which, in 1933, employed over one hundred thousand industrial workers of thirty-six nationalities, officially required citizenship and naturalization. Yet in practice, Ford employed a number of undocumented workers. In an interview, a Ford representative claimed to prefer American citizens because they were "more loyal and more stable," but upon further questioning, the Ford official admitted that even in the midst of city registration drives, FMC did not "discriminate against noncitizens."[58] Indeed, while Henry Ford may have espoused nativist ideas and anti-Semitism, as well as encouraged Americanization, in practice, noncitizens, workers who were easily laid off or deported, made an appealing option for companies facing the specter of industrial unionization on the horizon.

Noncitizen Detroiters lucky enough to find employment during the Great Depression became the most vulnerable to layoffs in major industries. At a meeting of the Human Resources Association of Detroit, employers admitted that they did not check employees' papers until the necessity arose. Representatives from Timken-Detroit Axle Company, Chrysler, and Packard claimed that during times of depression, especially after the 1929 stock market crash, foremen checked to see who had taken out their final papers, a measure they had not bothered to undertake when they hired the workers. The companies claimed that "when layoffs are necessary, aliens are being dropped" before native-born Detroiters or even African American migrants.[59] The Detroit Chamber of Commerce even proposed a state "immigration service" to patrol both Michigan and international state lines and turn back migrants in search of jobs.[60] While employers never organized the service, they did begin to conduct random searches for papers and legality, giving them a way to justify layoffs with the added benefit of appeasing native-born workers and labor activists.

Hiring noncitizens also allowed Ford Motor Company to avoid paying even the smallest amount of welfare benefits. In 1932, Paul Maslone, an unnaturalized Austrian, had spent seven years working for Ford before his foreman reduced his workload to three to four hours each week. This was hardly enough to support his wife and two children, but Ford welfare workers insisted to the Dearborn Welfare Department that Maslone was not a candidate for relief because he had not applied for citizenship.[61] Maslone could not be deported because he came into the United States before 1924. But because he had no papers, he was ineligible for even the small garden plots and food rations Ford offered to unemployed workers. Thus, as city policymakers attempted to hold powerful industrialists accountable for the workers they had lured to the city, these employers countered by hiring alien workers at low wages and no chance of benefits.

Facing underemployment, unemployment, or deportation, undocumented workers naturally went to great lengths to keep their statuses a secret. George Duffy, an Irish immigrant who had let his first papers lapse and feared for his job at Ford, admitted that he bribed his foreman not to expose him. He claimed that workers in plants across the city paid foremen "cash and in kind for the privilege of holding their jobs." During the harsh winter of 1934, he even rode with an Italian worker who gave his boss eggs and chickens to keep from being fired or, worse, deported.[62] Back-door deals contributed to the development of an underground labor system that left undocumented workers constantly afraid a single wrong step might land them in the immigration office at the Detroit Police Department.

While alien workers kept their heads down, Detroit's 700,000 unemployed organized the Ford Hunger March.[63] In March 1932, communists led by William Z. Foster and the Trade Union Unity League planned a march from Henry Ford's unemployment office to his River Rouge plant, where they planned to present a set of demands to Ford, including improved working conditions and relief for thousands of laid-off Ford employees.[64] When three thousand former workers reached Ford's factory, the scene quickly devolved into chaos as protesters threw rocks at Ford strongmen and the Dearborn police fired shots into the crowd. Mayor Murphy sent Detroit police to quell the violence, but by the end of the day, five protesters were dead and sixty more had major injuries.[65]

Despite the fact that most alien Detroiters avoided any public action that might get them deported, the persistent association between foreigners and communism made newspapers and even some employers view the Ford Hunger March as an un-American, communist, and, above all, alien protest. Most marchers were native-born Detroiters, but reports suggested that foreigners were responsible for the violence. At the national level, a scathing article in the *Los Angeles Times* warned the nation that foreign radicals must be to blame for the protest, urging Washington to strengthen its "deportation laws as to permit the sending out of the country of alien radicals."[66] Closer to home, Traverse City's *Record Eagle* reminded readers that "if the immigration laws provided for registration," many of the "alien marchers would now be back in Europe."[67] The *Detroit Free Press* portrayed the march as a "riot" spearheaded by communists and foreigners, noting that the police had sent the names of those arrested to the Immigration Service, suggesting that many might not be in the United States legally.[68] Thus, even though it is unlikely that noncitizens or unauthorized immigrants played a major role in the march, the discourse emerging after the event cast foreigners with questionable legal status as major actors in the violent struggle.

The assumption that most marchers were aliens eligible for deportation prompted Ford Motor Company to begin using public deportation as a way to discourage communist organizing or strikes. Ford Motor Company was particularly concerned with communist organizers on its assembly lines. Beginning in 1930, Charles E. Sorenson, personal secretary to Henry Ford, began monitoring the circulation of the *Ford Worker*, a communist pamphlet distributed exclusively within the Ford Motor Company, which soon had a circulation of twenty thousand.[69] After the Hunger March, the Ford Service Department negotiated a series of deportation raids with the Immigration Service that targeted Ford workers in nearby Dearborn, Michigan. In July 1932, the Department of Labor arranged for the deportation of 105 Dearborn residents and planned another four hundred arrests throughout the month.[70] These raids took place everywhere from workers' homes to the assembly line, fostering an atmosphere of fear and mistrust that would have permeated every aspect of workers' lives. In the fall of 1932, Ford officials allowed immigration inspectors to handcuff and drag Thomas Kostopoulos off the shop floor as an "alien suspect," a clear message to workers on the assembly line who considered joining the Communist Party, staging protests, or simply asking for higher wages or more hours.[71]

Deportation drives cultivated an atmosphere of intimidation and fear that affected even immigrant workers with papers. Mike Kovacevich, a forty-year-old Croat from Yugoslavia, had been employed at Ford Motor Company's blast furnace for twelve years and had begun the naturalization process when local police picked him up and charged him with "illegal entry to this country." After holding him in the local jail for four days, the Immigration and Naturalization Service (INS) released him with a full exoneration, but the four days away lost Kovacevich his coveted position at Ford. To support his wife and three small children, Kovacevich applied for welfare from the city of Dearborn and fell hundreds of dollars in debt with the Wolverine Milk Company, Kozma Eagle grocer, and the local doctor for food, milk, and medical bills. Despite having committed no violations, being arrested and interrogated for immigration violations cost the Yugoslav and his family their only means of support.[72]

Indeed, the majority of Ford Motor Company's immigrant workers had citizenship or first papers, but some feared deportation raids might uncover undocumented family members. For instance, Ukrainian Nick Belenko immigrated legally to the United States in early 1924, took out citizenship papers, and found work at Ford Motor Company, where he earned fifty-seven dollars every two weeks. However, Belenko's wife Maria and their eight-year-old son Pytor could not secure quota visas and instead traveled to Canada and crossed the Detroit River illegally. Belenko was perfectly eligible to work at Ford and rose through the ranks of the River Rouge assembly line, but his undocumented wife and son made him vulnerable.

In 1932, his foreman caught him discussing the declining conditions and pay at Ford with another worker with known communist ties. Within a month, Immigration Service inspectors mysteriously received news of the Belenko family's undocumented members and brought Maria into their Detroit office for interrogation. After a series of brisk questions, Inspector Moriaty stamped Maria and Pytor's deportation order, authorizing their immediate return to Poland.[73]

It is impossible to determine whether Belenko's brief association with political radicalism precipitated his wife and son's deportation. But Belenko himself saw a clear connection, lamenting in his deposition to the Immigration Service, "I should not have spoken with those communists." Despite the fact that he was a citizen, Belenko felt he should have kept a lower profile to keep his family safe.[74] The Belenko case demonstrates that even if an immigrant could legally work, members of his or her family network might be subject to deportation, a reality employers used to manipulate and intimidate workers. In a city with over four hundred thousand legal foreign-born residents, thousands of immigrants likely feared for the livelihood of a brother, grandmother, wife, neighbor, or friend.[75]

Instead of helping undocumented workers trapped in a labor system operating through fear and deportation, the DFL continued to blame immigrants for taking jobs from native-born Americans. This choice further pitted immigrant workers against organized labor. After registration laws failed, DFL President Frank Martel encouraged the Department of Labor to hire two "Contract Labor Investigators" who would work in various industries across Detroit tasked with "ferreting out illegal alien entrances."[76] Both "Contract Labor Investigators" had solid ties to the American Federation of Labor. As its first investigator, the department appointed Frank H. Steele, a member of Detroit's Typographical Union and an active Odd Fellow. The Immigration Service felt Steele's membership in a fraternal organization known for nativist policies, not to mention his union activism, would help him "clean up bootlegged immigrants." Joe Frayne, who had served on the Immigration Service for twelve years, was the son of Hugh Frayne, an AFL representative in New York City and another supporter of strict immigration policy. Throughout the early 1930s, Frayne and Steele infiltrated communist meetings, took temporary jobs in factories, and frequented Polish, Italian, and Belgian streets on Detroit's east side, reporting any news of undocumented workers to immigration officials, who then launched full investigations.

Such efforts further connected foreign-born neighborhoods to communism and illegality while also reminding these immigrants that the DFL and, by extension, all unions were still the enemy.[77]

Concerned the Department of Labor would not devote sufficient energy to rooting the undocumented out of Detroit's workforce, Martel, who seemed to possess boundless energy, committed himself and the DFL's resources to the task. This proved particularly effective in cases involving the federal government. In early 1930s, Martel informed the U.S. War Department that contractors hired to erect new buildings on Selfridge Field were notorious employers of unauthorized immigrants. He claimed that Anthony Benton, a Belgian contractor, placed ads in a Belgian paper and gave "preference to alien low standard labor." Indeed, in employing alien and even undocumented bricklayers and masons, Martel claimed that Benton and "labor-skinning contractors" like him threatened the standards of the DFL's Bricklayers Union. In response, the Department of Labor sent immigration inspectors to check the naturalization statuses of each construction worker laying bricks on the field, creating panic and confusion among the francophone workers as they dusted the mortar off their ragged clothes and reached for crumpled documents. Many of the Belgians averted their eyes, offered false addresses to inspectors, and headed to bungalows and boarding houses on the city's far east side, most likely resenting the DFL and federal inspectors who had robbed them of a day's work and pay.[78]

By the early 1930s, alien workers in the Detroit-Windsor borderland negotiated exploitative employers, a hostile labor movement, and city governments preoccupied with wider unemployment. Economic conditions meant immigrants without papers had to endure low pay and harsh conditions to keep from being deported. But when even leftist, pro-immigrant mayors could not curb popular "repatriation" drives on either side of the border, legal immigrants began to fear they too might face removal. Mounting concerns over deportation and soon, registration, caused foreign-born residents of the region to view the employers, politicians, and union leaders who lobbied for such reforms with suspicion. When Detroit's labor movement finally organized an automobile strike at Briggs Body Company, both undocumented and legal foreign-born Europeans avoided the conflict. Immigrants' refusal to set down their tools meant that the Briggs strike was bound to fail.

Two months after Franklin Roosevelt won the presidency with promises of a New Deal for America, 450 tool and die workers walked out of a small plant of Briggs Manufacturing Company. The strikers, most of whom were British and Irish born, protested the 20 percent wage cut Walter Briggs had introduced in January 1933.[79] Briggs did not want to slow production and knew the skilled labor undertaken by strikers would be difficult to replace, so the company rescinded the wage cuts and the strikers cheered. Their success inspired similar strikes at two subsidiaries of the company, both of which worked. A couple of weeks later, metal finishers at the Briggs Highland Park plant set down their tools, and soon, Briggs workers across the city walked off their jobs, causing a three-month protest and the first major automobile strike to include skilled, semiskilled, and unskilled workers. At its height, 12,000 workers actively struck and about 100,000 workers could not work because Ford Motor Company had to close a number of its plants when it could not get automobile bodies.[80] The initial plants' success, however, remained the strikers' only win and the strike soon divided along political and ethnic lines. Internal divisions allowed Briggs to recruit strikebreakers and reopen the plants.[81] By February 1933, it became clear that the DFL's decade-long effort to bar, deport, and register foreign-born workers made many of these unskilled laborers wary of unions and striking in general. Ultimately, such divisions contributed to the strike's failure.

The fact that Detroit's first major mobilization of automobile workers began at Briggs Body came as no surprise. The company had a reputation for dangerous working conditions and low wages. Back in 1927, on a sweltering June afternoon, while thousands of workers in the Mack Avenue plant sprayed automobile bodies with proxylin, a highly flammable chemical meant to speed up the paint-drying process, a broken lamp tipped over, causing an explosion that engulfed an entire warehouse in flames. The fire, which could have been avoided with more ventilation, killed twenty-one workers and blinded fifteen others.[82] Making matters worse, Walter Briggs kept the incident quiet, paying off mainstream newspapers, policemen, and the fire department to downplay the issue. To grieving widows or the survivors who left the blast with permanent injuries, Briggs denied the incident entirely, claiming that missing workers had never come in to the plant that day and that the injured were dramatizing a routine workplace fire.[83]

Despite Briggs's efforts to deny the fire, news of the disaster got out and outraged workers, progressives seeking workplace reform, and newspaper columnists. But Briggs continued to deny the incident and insisted on offering the lowest wages in the city. Each morning the industrialist left Stone Hedge, his 9,000-square-foot English-manor-style mansion, passing

Figure 9. Men building car bodies at Briggs Manufacturing Company, a company with a reputation for having the the most dangerous working conditions and underpaid employees in the automotive industry and, therefore, a major employer of black and undocumented European workers. When, in 1933, thousands of Briggs workers went on strike, Detroiters did not need to ask why. Courtesy of the Walter P. Reuther Library, Archives of Labor and Urban Affairs, Wayne State University.

through lush gardens and a formidable wrought iron gate on the way to his office in Highland Park. In contrast, he paid his workers too little to afford anything more than the tiniest room in the city's overcrowded East Side neighborhoods. In 1927, he offered women twenty-one cents and men thirty-five cents an hour and refused to pay workers for idle time between shifts or jobs. When the Depression began, Briggs lowered wages by five to ten cents. This made Briggs "a last resort," attracting many black workers and immigrants who had recently arrived in Detroit, many of whom probably had no entry papers and certainly did not have citizenship.[84] DFL and communist labor activists called Briggs a "slaughterhouse," and ordinary workers joked, "If poison doesn't work, try Briggs," meaning that workers sought jobs at the factory only in times of "hunger and want."[85] So when a handful of workers put down their tools in protest, no one had to ask why.

The first tool and die workers to set down their tools had probably been planning the strike for quite some time. A few days after they left their jobs, other Briggs workers followed their lead, protesting low wages, speedup of production, unhealthful conditions, irregular employment, and long hours. As thousands of workers took to the frigid streets, Walter Briggs sent word of his refusal to acquiesce from sunny Florida, where he was taking a break from the icy city. Briggs declared that because of the Depression, times were hard and the strikers were "lucky to have a job."[86] This, of course, did not sit well with exhausted strikers, and by the end of January, over six thousand Briggs workers braved cold picket lines across Highland Park and Detroit, and Briggs decided to cut his vacation short.[87]

Labor organizers did not begin the strike, but key city unions jumped at the chance to organize the automobile industry. Soon after the strike began, the communist-led Automobile Workers Union (AWU) joined the strike effort, appointing Phillip Raymond, a charismatic local communist leader, to organize the strike.[88] Within a few days, four thousand workers from Murray Body joined the strike, a development that sent President John W. Murray into negotiations with Walter Briggs and other worried industrialists over how to stand their ground and avoid a total shutdown of the city. But the employers found themselves at a stalemate, and as the production of auto bodies stopped, the strike forced Hudson Motor and Ford's River Rouge plant to shut down.[89] By February, assembly lines throughout the city quieted and over one hundred thousand workers idled.[90] For a brief few months, Briggs workers and their compatriots held the attention of the entire nation.[91]

Eager not to be eclipsed by communist organizers, the Detroit Federation of Labor also lent its support to strikers. President Frank Martel disliked the communists' involvement at Briggs, but he also recognized the energy generated by a citywide strike and hoped the Briggs walkout could represent the perfect moment to challenge Detroit's open shop tradition. The union's paper, the *Detroit Labor News*, ran full-page spreads supporting strike efforts, lauding the "protest against intolerable conditions of employment."[92] In February, the DFL formed a special committee that asked for contributions from member unions to help the strikers in "prosecuting their war against starvation wages" and published the names and dollar amounts individual locales had offered to the Briggs strikers.[93] When police began to round up strikers for questioning and potential imprisonment, President Martel even used his political connections to bail strikers out of jail.[94]

The threat of deportation, however, divided foreign-born strikers from their native-born coworkers at Briggs. Simply put, foreign-born workers without papers or those with undocumented family members had more to lose than even the most desperate American citizen. For instance, as metal finisher John Buckley waved a sign in the faces of policemen outside the Briggs Mack Avenue plant, the most he feared was a lost job or perhaps a few days in jail.[95] But a large proportion of Briggs workers were not full citizens. Across all departments, half of Briggs' workforce was born in Europe, and of these, 20 percent were unnaturalized or undocumented workers. If police arrested foreign-born workers, they sent them to the Immigration Service for questioning, a move that might result in deportation for the striker or someone in the worker's family. Soon police began to search for signs of "foreignness" as an excuse to arrest and potentially deport workers, making foreign-born workers even more wary of joining picket lines.[96]

Black workers, who also found themselves exploited by industry and unwelcome in unions, shied from the Briggs strike. In 1930, three-fourths of the dangerous Mack Avenue paint-spray and wet-sanding department was African American.[97] Despite their high levels of exploitation, black workers in Detroit traditionally avoided organized labor. Detroit Urban League (DUL) President John Dancy urged workers to steer clear of unions, which he thought offered little to African Americans. In the 1920s, the DUL sent black strikebreakers to end the Timken Axle strike, and by 1934, Dancy asserted, "Of one thing I am convinced, and that is that the local (AFL) president is not warm toward negroes and I am against him and have told him so to his face."[98] Many black workers did join the communist AWU, but a larger number stayed away from picket lines or returned to work at the first sign of resumed production.[99]

Walter Briggs exploited the cracks forming within the ranks of strikers by offering former Briggs workers their jobs again with no penalty. At the end of January 1933, Briggs enticed enough former employees to cross the picket lines to resume production at Highland Park and to get his Mack Avenue plant up to about half capacity.[100] Eager to keep his new workforce safe from rioting strikers and perhaps, to protect their identities, Briggs housed seven hundred strikebreakers in temporary barracks, which he had installed in the Mack Avenue plant.[101] Meanwhile, just outside the gates, workers and unemployed friends stood outside the factories, singing, "Stay away you scabs! Stay away from here! We're here to fight for the workers right, so don't you interfere," to the tune of the "Farmer in the Dell." Furious picketers tried to figure out the nationality, race, or religion of strikebreakers, and rumors that alien and black workers were to blame swept the picket lines.[102]

Regardless of Walter Briggs's efforts, hundreds of foreign-born workers dotted the picket lines, and cries for solidarity crossed the international border. The *Canadian Hungarian Worker*, or *Canadai Magyar Munkas*, and the Finnish communist paper *Vapaus* both urged their readers to stay away from the Briggs factories and support Hungarians across the border.[103] Frank Majewski, a Polish-born framer at the Briggs Highland Park plant, told city investigators that he went on strike because he could no longer support his wife and five-year-old on Briggs wages. Majewski insisted that he had no interest in joining any unions but that he did attend two communist meetings because the organizers were the only group that seemed to understand the tremendous pressure placed on workers throughout the factories. Consequently, when workers walked out of the Briggs plant, Majewski followed.[104]

But many immigrant and African American workers avoided public picketing, and some even joined the strikebreakers. Strike organizers circulated leaflets that urged alien and African American workers to stand strong with their fellow workers, suggesting that some members of these groups had returned to work.[105] Walter Briggs placed particular pressure on foreign-born strikers. To disperse picketers, the industrialist enlisted fifty police officers and deputized one hundred thirty more men, encouraging them to arrest protesters for "agitation," "criminal syndicalism," and immigration violations.[106] Seeing their fellow workers hauled off to Immigration Service interrogation rooms most likely terrified many foreign-born workers, encouraging them to either return to work or stay home to avoid trouble. The targeting of immigrant workers infuriated the Automobile Workers Union, which condemned Briggs for attempting to "sow dissention and hatred between native and foreign-born workers" by rehiring workers without legal papers.[107] The same went for African Americans. Communist publications distributed on picket lines warned "American and foreign-born, white and Negro men" that the only way to "force employers to pay a living wage and give adequate relief to workers laid off from the plants" was to work together regardless of race or nationality.[108] Though no records exist listing the nationality or race of strikebreakers, the communists' plea asking workers to stand together regardless of race or legal status suggests that Detroit's most vulnerable inhabitants were not jeopardizing their jobs for higher wages.

Other ethnic groups refused to strike because they remembered the DFL's role in ending commuting from Canada and passing alien registration. The *Polish Daily News*, Detroit's most widely circulated foreign-language newspaper, condemned the strikers, a pivotal development in a city that remained 20 percent Polish.[109] The newspaper's editor, Frank Januszweiski, held a grudge against organized labor that dated to the Michigan Registration Act. Januszweiski had helped file one of the key suits used in overturning the registration law, and he still blamed the DFL for sowing hatred against foreigners. Thus, when the DFL lent its support for the strike, the paper urged upstanding Poles to distance themselves from what he called communist or criminal foreigners by avoiding strikes and labor unrest. Throughout the Briggs strike, the *Polish Daily News* discouraged its readers from taking to the picket lines, claiming, "Polish people should have no debt to the communists."[110]

Instead, the newspaper reported on the violence of strikers. In February, the *Polish Daily News* ran a story on how striking Briggs workers Arthur Besser and Nelson Farrer urged an angry crowd to throw rocks at a bus full of strikebreakers, causing the bus to veer off the road into a ditch. As the replacement workers, some of whom were Polish immigrants, cowered behind seats, strikebreakers launched stones and bricks through the windows of the bus. When the police arrived half an hour later, they found a group of workers bloodied and barricaded in a bus while strikers cheered. The piece ended by asking, "Is this how respectable Polish people ought to act?"[111] By discouraging labor organizing, the Polish-language newspaper tapped into the suspicion many immigrant workers already felt toward organized labor and its history of anti-immigrant campaigns.

By March 1933, the strikers negotiated a "compromise" with Walter Briggs that reopened factories and sent workers back to unventilated warehouses and underpaid assembly line work. Despite clear defeat, the DFL and Communist Party cited a set of lackluster concessions and promises from Briggs and officially declared the strike a victory. Automobile Workers Union leader Philip Raymond highlighted the role of the Unemployment Council in encouraging the unemployed to join picketing workers, claiming this move demonstrated "the possibility to win a strike despite great unemployment."[112] But behind closed doors, no one cheered. In a pointed note to DFL President Frank Martel, prominent social activist and leftist lawyer Maurice Sugar wrote, "I would like to let you know exactly what I think but profanity is prohibited in telegrams. It must have been an autoworker who said 'another such victory and we are lost.' "[113]

When the loss finally set in, communist strikers attempted to derive lessons from the three-month ordeal. Phillip Raymond conceded that the strike's main failure was that organizers had not done enough to reduce discrimination against foreign-born workers. He claimed the Briggs strike had painfully taught organizers that future strikes depended on the participation and support of all workers regardless of their citizenship or ethnicity.[114]

But the Detroit Federation of Labor did not share the communists' view and continued its campaign against the foreign born. Just a year after the Briggs disaster, President Martel revisited an old refrain, insisting the state could solve unemployment by registering aliens and policing motor companies that preferred "importing labor" to using native Detroiters.[115] As Depression conditions worsened and industrial workers demanded their own union, DFL organizers held fast to tactics that favored skilled Anglo workers and blamed outsiders for making the task of unity appear impossible.

Locked out of the organized labor movement, alien workers not inclined toward communism placed their faith in industrial manufacturers. Lithuanian Mike Ozols worked at Ford Motor Company through the 1930s and remained loyal to the company even amid widespread layoffs. By the end of 1933, when Ford laid off 15 percent of its staff, Ozols lost his position. Because he had never taken out citizenship papers, Ozols could also not apply for Dearborn welfare benefits. Regardless, Ozols assured Ford that he would never turn to organized labor. In a letter transcribed by his literate son, Ozols told his former employer, "Even though I am unemployed, I will always be grateful to Henry Ford for allowing me to work as long as he did. I will never bite the hand that once has given me everything." He went on to condemn organized labor for its "unfeeling treatment of those not fortunate enough to have full citizenship."[116] Ozols represented one of thousands of foreign-born workers who remained suspicious of organized labor, a fact that undermined union efforts to mobilize workers in Detroit.

Struggles over immigration policy in the early years of the Depression taught alien workers in Detroit not to trust labor unions or even leftist politicians promising change. In both Detroit and Windsor, even legal immigrants feared police might arrest family members, neighbors, or friends and deport them across the Atlantic. As the Depression showed no signs of abating and President Franklin Roosevelt opened a New Deal era with promises of relief, recovery, and reform to all regardless of legal status, many foreign-born Europeans breathed a sigh of relief. But immigration reform in Washington, D.C. caused local nativists, politicians, and newspapers to double down on efforts to link foreigners to communism and crime. Four months after the Briggs strike's end, the *Detroit Free Press* ran an article reporting that unknown numbers of Romanian, Serbian, Italian, Greek, Albanian, and Turkish "criminal aliens" and "alien racketeers" continued to smuggle into Detroit, where they supposedly found jobs at Ford's River Rouge plant and joined the ranks of local communist and labor agitators.[117] Thus, when the United Automobile Workers finally tried to unite all workers, the union faced hostility from local leaders and newspapers and from foreign-born workers who remained suspicious of organized labor.

Chapter 6

The Immigrant Politics of Anticommunism

On December 8, 1935, Officer Pete Miller swapped his police uniform and badge for a set of simple trousers and a white shirt and headed to Detroit's Finnish Hall to spy on a Communist Party meeting. Officer Miller was a member of Detroit's Special Investigation Squad, or Red Squad, a group in the Detroit Police Department tasked with monitoring and obstructing local communist activity. On this particular afternoon, Officer Miller filed into the great hall and scanned the several hundred people in the crowd, trying to remember faces, names, and accents, anything that might be useful in his report to the Detroit Police Department. Before long, William Weinstone, district organizer of the Communist Party and a Lithuanian-born Jew, stepped up to the podium and gave a speech urging the audience to fight employer corruption and recruit new supporters. Unaware that an undercover policeman stood in the crowd, Winestone named the Polish Language Association, Holy Cross Hungarian Church, and several union locals as key sites for recruitment.

Miller listened attentively, and when the meeting ended, he composed a report to the Detroit Police Department, detailing the organizations named at the meeting, also remarking on the "Jewish faces and foreign accents" he observed in the crowd. Armed with this evidence, Detroit police raided UAW Local 343, the Polish Language Association, and Holy Cross Hungarian Church, rounding up hundreds of "suspicious attendees" for questioning and sending forty "potential aliens" to the newly formed Immigration and Naturalization Service (INS) for further interrogation.[1] The Red Squad's persistent raids demonstrate that even as federal New Deal policies curbed deportations and legalized collective bargaining, local police ensured that intimidation, nativism, and profiling would continue to form part of the daily lives of ethnic European Americans. In fact, local nativist activism helped associate unions and communism with a single word: foreignness.

In Detroit, police and the violent nativist groups used fear of communism to legitimize local policing and vigilante justice that challenged the Roosevelt administration's turn toward immigrant inclusion. In Washington, D.C., New Deal officials slowed deportation raids and worked to extend welfare benefits to noncitizens. Moreover, new labor laws allowed for the rise of industrial unionization under the Congress of Industrial Organizations (CIO), a union that began to recruit immigrant workers. These policies have led scholars to suggest that the New Deal marked the beginning of the end of ethnic fragmentation and nativism, a development Lizabeth Cohen credits with facilitating the rise of a "CIO culture of unity."[2] Indeed, workers in Chicago, New York, and Detroit unified behind new industrial unions, but the rise of organizing also led to a nativist backlash from local police and workers who insisted certain Europeans could never become full Americans. Consequently, ethnic Americans, particularly the hundreds of thousands without citizenship, continued to be excluded from mainstream Anglo-Protestant society much longer than historians have suggested.

In the Detroit-Windsor borderland, police, union leaders, and citizens who did not agree with what they perceived as relaxed immigration rhetoric coming from Washington established harsh local practices that drew on and reinforced a transnational milieu of anticommunism. In 1931, the Canadian government banned the Communist Party, a move that allowed Prime Minister Richard Bennett's conservative administration to deport prominent communists, force thousands of immigrants into relief camps, and intimidate the labor movement. In the United States, the Roosevelt administration's immigration policy was much more complicated. The new Democrat continued Mexican repatriation campaigns and refused asylum to persecuted European Jewish refugees by the boatload, but his administration also slowed coercive tactics toward those Europeans lucky enough to already reside in the United States. In particular, Secretary of Labor Frances Perkins put a stop to deportation raids and insisted that noncitizens should be allowed access to federal work programs, filling relief lines and jobs with thousands of alien workers. Moreover, in Detroit, immigrant workers began to strike with the United Automobile Workers (UAW), giving them a stake in one of the key unions to emerge out of the New Deal state.

New Deal policies, however, infuriated citizens who thought the foreign born should be grateful for any opportunities afforded them in the United States. In 1935, the Black Legion, an offshoot of the Ku Klux Klan, praised Canadian policies on communism and began to terrorize Detroit's immigrant and African American neighborhoods. The Red Squad followed suit, justifying raids on immigrant workplaces and halls in the name of anticommunism, insisting that if the federal government would let immigrant communists run loose across the city, they would have to take matters into their own hands. By 1938, popular Detroit radio commenter and Canadian immigrant himself, Charles Coughlin, came out against communism and labor unions. Thus, the New Deal provided opportunities for Detroit's immigrants, but it also sparked a violent local backlash that furthered the tradition of espionage and nativism established in the previous decades. Ultimately, the clash between local anti-immigrant forces, the federal state, and the institutions it helped to create ensured that the cultural politics of nativism and intimidation that defined the 1920s would continue throughout the Depression era and become embedded in New Deal economic politics.

Anticommunism in Canada

As the Depression continued, the Canadian state advanced an anticommunist agenda that influenced the local anti-immigrant politics of Windsor and eventually Detroit. In 1932, the Canadian government tried and deported eight men who shared two things in common. They were members of the Communist Party and they were not Canadian citizens. Arvo Vaaro and Martin Parker were both Finns and editors of the widely circulated communist newspaper, *Vapaus.* Dan Holmes, whose real name was Dymitr Chomicki, left Ukraine to settle in Winnipeg, where he printed the *Ukrainian Daily Labor News.* John Farkas was born in Hungary and worked at Chrysler of Canada and became involved in labor activism. Scottish-born Ivan Sempley staged communist rallies and speeches across Edmonton, Ontario, and German-born Hans Kist and Conrad Cessinger headed western branches of the Communist Party in Vancouver and Winnipeg, respectively. In May, local police rounded up the communist activists and sent them to Halifax, Ontario, where an Immigration Board of Inquiry questioned the eight men and began processing their deportations to nations in Europe. In Canada, the deportations launched an era of anticommunism that would make immigrant removal a popular recourse for federal and local officials in their fight against radicalism.

By targeting the Halifax Eight, as they came to be called, Prime Minister Bennett reinforced his zero-tolerance policy on political radicalism. As examined in Chapter 4, Bennett had already begun to advocate deportations to relieve unemployment, but these practices could only target immigrants who had lived in Canada less than five years. In early 1932, however, the Canadian Supreme Court decision to outlaw the Communist Party gave Bennett and his administration the ability to prosecute, purge, and deport any known communists in Canada.[3] And across the border in Michigan, nativist organizations forming in opposition to American unions and welfare programs soon viewed Canada's hard-line deportation tactics as an appealing alternative to Franklin Roosevelt's New Deal.

The deportations and their widely publicized trials linked immigrants to political dissidence and criminality. On May 16, 1932, the Immigration Board of Inquiry tasked with determining the eight communists' guilt labeled Finnish Arvo Vaaro"a menace to Canada and to the existing economic and governmental structure." A few hours later, the same board decided that his compatriot John Farkas represented "a dangerous radical and prime mover of the Finnish Communist Party." In the case of Dymitr Chomicki, or Dan Holmes, the board struggled over what to do with the fact that he had emigrated from Ukraine with his family when he was just a child. Ultimately, they decided that the Ukrainian's leadership in Winnipeg's Working Women Group, Farmers Life Organization, and *Militant Youth Magazine* made him a "particularly dangerous type."[4] Like the deportation raids that had targeted anarchists in the United States just a decade before, news coverage of the Halifax Eight deportations associated new immigrants with dangerous politics and potential violence.[5]

As the Board of Inquiry negotiated the details of deporting the Halifax Eight, the Canada Club and hundreds of Canadians voiced their support.[6] N. R. Trickey wrote on behalf of the Salvation Army of Canada, warning Minister of Immigration Wesley Gordon that his organization often inadvertently offered jobs to communists but that instead of taking the work, they "criticized everyone in Canada from the Premier down." Trickey insisted that the eight symbolic deportations were necessary because "the eyes of our local communists are watching the present movements." Trickey reasoned that deporting the eight high-profile men would serve as a warning to communists across Canada.[7]

Canadian communist organizations staged mass protests against the deportations, but their outcry only encouraged government officials. By this period, Canada's Communist Party still numbered around 16,000 underground members, a figure that almost matched that in the United States, where communism remained a legal political option.[8] Toronto's main communist newspaper, the *Worker*, referred to Minister Gordon as the "Minister of Deportation" and accused Prime Minister Bennett of using an "iron heel" to violate the rights of workers in Canada.[9] In Ottawa, Toronto, Montreal, and Winnipeg, thousands of demonstrators picketed outside immigration offices, state buildings, and the Canadian Supreme Court. But instead of reversing the administration's stance, Minister Gordon viewed the protest as a sign that communists were "getting scared for once."[10] By December 1932, the Immigration Department scheduled the passage of the eight communists on ocean liners bound for Helsinki, Bremen, and Gdynia.[11]

The eight deportations terrified local communists in Windsor. Immigrant workers in the Border Cities of Windsor, Sandwich, Walkerville, and East Windsor paid particular attention to the trial of Hungarian John Farkas, a communist automobile worker from nearby Oshawa. In the early 1930s, the Border Cities had five to six thousand communist sympathizers, most of whom were of Finnish, Hungarian, or Polish origin. Windsor area communists had staged regular parades, distributed pamphlets, and organized walkouts at Ford of Canada.[12] When news spread that local police had raided John Farkas's house and held him for deportation after finding "literature of an extreme radical nature," Windsor communists became worried. Farkas, like thousands of Windsor's automobile workers, had emigrated from Hungary in 1926 as a farm laborer. But work in Saskatchewan was arduous and Farkas returned to Toronto for a few months before heading to Canada's Chrysler plant in Oshawa. The Depression put thousands of Chrysler workers out of jobs, Farkas included, and he soon became active in the Canadian Labour Defense League, the Unemployed Workers Association, and the Hungarian Workers Club. Farkas was certainly a communist, but he was not a key leader or newspaper editor, making his deportation even more concerning to local communists. East Windsor's Communist Party issued a warning to its members to "keep your heads down and your ears open. Farkas was first but you could be Bennett's next victim."[13] As the Bennett administration hoped, deporting the Halifax Eight sent a chilling warning to local communist groups.

Detroiters read about the deportations in local newspapers, which praised Canada's actions against communism. William Randolph Hearst's Detroit paper, the *Detroit Times*, reported that Canada had taken a "bold step" in finding and trying the Halifax Eight.[14] When Canada issued the deportation orders, the *Detroit News* lamented "America's inability to handle its communist problem," suggesting that the Department of Labor could learn from Canadian policies.[15] Just to the north in Port Huron, the *Times Herald* provocatively asked, "Canada has taken a stand against communism. Why is Washington waiting?"[16] Detroit and Port Huron's proximity to Canada meant their residents paid close attention to Canadian news and regularly compared the two North American nations' stances on foreigners and communism.

Communist deportations were only the beginning of Prime Minister Bennett's efforts to control communism and, by association, immigrants in Canada. Bennett knew he could not deport all noncitizens with ties to the Communist Party, so he established relief camps meant to contain the large populations of transient immigrant workers living in Canadian cities.[17] By 1932, the Depression meant 16,664 single men had lost their jobs in lumbering, mining, and agricultural regions and migrated to Toronto.[18] Of these, nearly 70 percent were born outside Canada, a fact that made the Bennett administration label the migrant problem an immigrant issue. Minister of Labor Gideon Robertson argued that transient workers endangered Canadian cities because "so large a proportion of them are of alien origin and Communistic sympathies." To keep transient workers from spreading communism, Minister Robertson suggested they be "put under supervision equivalent to semi-military control."[19] Major General A. G. L. McNaughton, head of the Department of National Defense, agreed and proposed a relief camp system that would contain transient workers in Canada's most remote regions and keep them under military supervision.[20]

Terrified the small army of unemployed migrants across Canada would cause political trouble, Prime Minister Bennett took his Minister of Labor's advice and established Canada's relief camp program. From 1932 to 1936, relief camps employed 170,248 "transient men," offering them twenty cents a day, a bunk, daily meals, clothing, and medical care in return for a forty-four-hour workweek in Canadian parks and wilderness areas. The Canadian government signed up "transient men" by the thousands, piling them into trains bound west for camps in British Columbia, Alberta, and Saskatchewan where they built roads and cleared avalanches and ice. Relief workers signed up voluntarily for camp work, but once in remote Canadian camps, many young men found themselves unprepared for demanding outdoor labor or harsh climates.[21]

In Windsor, the city government shipped several thousand immigrant and local men to camps across Ontario. The Rondeau Park Camp, a municipal park just under two hours east of the Border Cities, filled quickly with unemployed men living in Windsor. Here workers built picnic shelters, walking trails, and a pony barn, but they soon began to report poor conditions. Several men claimed they contracted colds because the bunkhouses had no heat or blankets. One man reported breaking a tooth on a piece of tough beef in the camp mess hall, where lead knives made black stains on workers' bread and caused many to become ill. The Bennett government sent regular inspectors to the camps to investigate working and board conditions, but relief workers reported, "There are really two camps up there. One for visitors, and one for the workers."[22] By 1934, it became clear that the Canadian government created the camp system less to feed and clothe the unemployed and more to mitigate political unrest and remove potential communists from cities.

Foreign-born camp workers fared worse than native-born Canadians at Rondeau Park. Because Canadian workers complained in the *Globe* that they had been "mixed in shacks with foreigners," camp officials separated the two groups. After the separation, immigrant workers routinely received sour potatoes and rotten meat, while the better provisions went to the Canadian workers.[23] Life at the camps no doubt emphasized to immigrants that though the Canadian state had solicited their labor, it valued their lives less than those of native-born Canadians.

Rondeau Park, however, looked like a leisurely summer camp when compared to the more distant camps to which the Windsor Welfare Board began sending unemployed men. In 1933, nearly a thousand men from the Canadian Border Cities boarded trains headed for northwestern points in Ontario on the Minnesota border, where the large Port Arthur and Kenora camps became known as "slave camps" among workers. At Camp Kenora, workers reported rotten meat, wage cuts, no fuel, and little shelter during the harsh winter months.[24] When Port Arthur camp workers complained to their supervisors that their meat was rotting, the camp head told them matter-of-factly, "It takes a long time to get here. What can you expect?" Beyond rotting meat, workers in remote northern regions endured winters with temperatures that rarely rose above freezing. When they returned to their huts after a day of clearing avalanches and icy roads, men crowded together for warmth under inadequate blankets while the wind cut through holes in the walls.[25]

If workers complained about harsh conditions, camp officials threated Canadians with unemployment and foreigners with deportation. In the winter of 1934, a Polish relief worker at Kenora decided that enough was enough and demanded a better blanket from the camp inspector. The inspector viewed the request as a sign of insolence and fired him on the spot. For severance, the inspector gave the Pole a paycheck that read, "Fired agitator, 3 months jail and deportation." In a fury, the Polish worker threw the worthless paycheck on the ground and left the camp. After the incident, the head officer posted the paycheck to the central board as a warning to other foreign-born relief workers who might complain about camp conditions.[26] At Port Arthur, camp officials regularly threatened immigrant relief workers with deportations, making many workers think twice about demanding better conditions.[27] When camp reports reached Prime Minister Bennett, he declared that removing foreign workers to relief camps had neutralized the threat of communism in Canada.[28]

To the prime minister's dismay, however, placing hundreds of young men in remote regions under rigid supervision turned relief camps into incubators for political radicalism. By 1934, strikes and protests erupted in Ontario and Manitoba camps, but the largest protest to camp conditions came from Canada's western provinces. In April 1935, just over fifteen hundred workers in British Columbia declared a general strike. Protesting the arduous working conditions, inedible food, and coercive immigration policies that characterized relief camps across Canada, the strikers planned a "March on Ottawa," a journey from Vancouver to Ottawa, where they hoped to bring their concerns before Prime Minister Bennett. As the men jumped trains and hitchhiked across the western provinces, they gained supporters from other camps along the way and captured the attention of North America. Newspapers from Toronto to New York reported eagerly on the mob of young men poised to descend on Prime Minister Bennett's residence.[29] Bennett blamed the strike on the "Communistic Societies of Canada" and used fear of radicalism to send the Royal Canadian Mounted Police to stop the strikers from making it past Regina, Saskatchewan.[30] Stranded in the prairie town, strikers staged a rally that devolved into a riot, resulting in three hundred arrests and the death of a city constable. The Regina Riot spelled the end of both Bennett's administration and the relief camp program. In October 1935, Liberal candidate William Lyon Mackenzie King won the general election and began to close the camps.[31]

In Windsor, however, many citizens resented camp closures because they brought thousands of immigrant men back to welfare lines. After Rondeau Park closed, Windsor's Canada Club staged a public rally demanding that "transient workers be sent away or deported," whichever would get them out of the Canadian municipality.[32] Windsor Welfare Commissioner Clyde Curry wrote to Windsor's Mayor David Croll, asking that the city furnish returning men with at least one week's wages to get them back on their feet and off the street.[33] When the mayor could not help, Commissioner Curry turned to the new prime minister, asking him to consider reopening the Rondeau Park camp, where, he argued, "men spoke of the wonderful conditions and steady employment." While Commissioner Curry's claims about Rondeau Park were clearly exaggerations, his letters reveal Windsor officials' reluctance to claim new migrants as local residents of the city.[34]

The migration of transient workers to small communities like Windsor most likely evoked gendered concerns about suspect sexuality. Margot Canaday has demonstrated that in the United States, the Federal Transient Program, a 1933 New Deal program meant to create camps and shelters for male migrants, earned a reputation as a "state-sponsored haven for sex perverts." Associating transient workers with having a particular "urge" that needed gratification or "wanderlust" and sexual perversion was widely held and promoted across the United States.[35] Given Windsor's proximity to the U.S. border and its long history of trade in not only people and goods but also ideas, it stands to reason that local residents would have feared transient workers for the economic and sexual threat they posed to the traditional family.

Local officials also feared returned workers would fuel the rise of Windsor's Communist Party. Commissioner Curry ended his letter by asking the prime minister, "What are we supposed to do now, as all the alien communists return to the city?"[36] Curry's suggestion that immigrants from relief camps were probably communists reinforced the connection between political radicalism and foreignness in the eyes of many Canadians. The tendency to connect immigrant Europeans and communism soon crossed the border. But in the United States, citizens and organizations concerned with foreignness became frustrated with a new administration that promised to dismantle xenophobic immigration policies.

A New Deal for Immigrants

In the United States, many immigrants hoped the election of President Franklin Roosevelt would mean a break from nativism and intolerance. Despite his reluctance to help Jewish refugees and the continuation of Mexican repatriation policies, Roosevelt's initial 1932 campaign united European immigrants, some African Americans, and native-born workers in a coalition of working-class Democratic voters.[37] Indeed, by 1935, thousands of alien workers in industrial centers like Chicago, New York, and Detroit had federal work, and those with industrial jobs could join unions made possible by New Deal labor laws. Ultimately, federal entitlements encouraged many foreign-born Europeans to place a measure of trust in the federal government and unions.

A reduction in deportations also signaled to many immigrants that the Roosevelt administration would break from its predecessor's immigration policy. In March 1933, President Roosevelt selected former settlement house worker and labor activist Frances Perkins to replace William Doak as secretary of labor. Secretary Perkins had long disapproved of Doak's coercive deportation policies, and in her first week as secretary of labor, she purged the department of prodeportation administrators and drastically decreased deportations. While in 1933, the United States had deported 19,865 immigrants, Secretary Perkins cut total deportations in half.[38]

Secretary Perkins also demonstrated a more tolerant stance on political radicalism by allowing anarchist Emma Goldman to return to the United States on a speaking tour. In 1919, the U.S. Department of Justice had deported Goldman alongside 248 fellow anarchists after a sensational public trial that stripped her of her citizenship on the grounds that she was married to noncitizen Alexander Berkman. Fourteen years later, however, Emma Goldman published a popular autobiography, *Living My Life*, and a group of American intellectuals launched a campaign to bring her back to the United States to speak. Indeed, in the same year the Canadian government deported the Halifax Eight, the U.S. Department of Labor organized a speaking tour featuring one of the world's most celebrated, infamous, and reviled political radicals, a woman known popularly as "Red Emma." Those who attended speeches on Goldman's ninety-day tour found her articulate yet largely uncontroversial, prompting criticism from many American radicals who thought she had become a pawn of the U.S. government.[39]

Communists in Detroit, however, viewed the Goldman tour as a positive step toward the acceptance of their political organization. In 1935,

Detroit's Communist Party had an official membership of 1,318, with another 2,600 belonging to affiliate organizations like the International Defense League or the International Workers Order.[40] Ever aware of their neighbors to the north, Detroit communists printed a flyer condemning Canada for deporting the "Halifax Eight." In the same sentence, the Detroit communists wrote in a hopeful tone, "Red Emma has returned as a special guest of Frances Perkins and the President. America will no longer use deportation to intimidate its masses." While Goldman's visa only lasted ninety days, to local communists, many of whom were foreign born, her tour represented a shift in American policies toward anarchists, communists, and socialists in America.[41]

Communism appealed to marginalized foreigners and African Americans because it was the first major organization to promote racial and ethnic acceptance. Historian Beth Bates notes that by the early 1930s, most black Detroiters continued to live isolated lives in Black Bottom and Paradise Valley and supported the Communist Party's unemployment councils in disproportionate numbers.[42] Like African Americans, foreign-born workers gravitated toward the Communist Party's inclusive doctrine. Instead of espousing Americanization or exclusion, in 1935, Detroit's Communist Party held meetings in Polish, Hungarian, Russian, Ukrainian, Finnish, Rumanian, Armenian, German, Lithuanian, and Bulgarian.[43] Ultimately, it was not a commitment to revolution or anticapitalist rhetoric but a unique vision of interracial unionism, antieviction activism, and a commitment to the unemployed that brought foreigners and black Americans to the Communist Party.[44]

The New Deal soon extended federal relief, at least on paper, to black workers and noncitizens. In his first hundred days in office, President Roosevelt provided direct aid to needy families with the Federal Emergency Relief Administration (FERA), and Secretary Perkins worked tirelessly with federal relief administrator Harry Hopkins to ensure that noncitizens would receive relief. Hopkins had years of experience working in immigrant neighborhoods of New York as a social worker and health care administrator and, like Secretary Perkins, felt that citizenship should not determine whether unemployed workers could feed their families.[45] For black workers, however, the Roosevelt administration's insistence on administering New Deal programs at the local level, as well as exclusion of domestic and farm workers from Social Security benefits, stymied black opportunities for economic advancement.[46]

New federal work programs did come with citizenship requirements, but even these programs helped noncitizens indirectly. In March 1933, President Roosevelt established the Civilian Conservation Corps (CCC), a work program that employed young men in military-like camps across rural America. In return for room, board, and a stipend of thirty dollars a month, men between 18 and 25 years of age donned uniforms, crowded into barracks, and worked clearing trails and roads in state and national parks across America. The CCC camps bore striking similarities to Canadian relief camps. But while Prime Minister Bennett established Canadian camps to isolate communist and foreign-born workers, the Roosevelt administration reserved the CCC for American citizens, giving CCC camps a patriotic rather than punitive reputation. Despite citizenship requirements, however, the CCC helped unnaturalized immigrants because many of their children worked in camps. In fact, 17 percent of CCC men had two foreign-born parents and 25 percent had one parent born outside the United States. Because CCC workers had to send 80 percent of their wages home to families, the camp program supported thousands of immigrants across the nation.[47]

When Canadian relief camps went on strike in 1935, American newspapers and policymakers used unrest in Canada to emphasize the desirability of CCC camps. The *New York Times* criticized Canada for grouping "communists, agitators and unassimilable drifters" together under harsh conditions in remote Canadian camps and then acting surprised when the workers "invaded Vancouver." In America, on the other hand, the newspaper noted that CCC camps offered good pay, fair wages, and night classes that "afforded the opportunity for improving the American workers' education."[48] When liberal William Lyon Mackenzie King replaced Bennett as Canada's prime minister, American newspapers reported with satisfaction that Canadian officials had begun to investigate the CCC camp system in the United States and suggested changing their relief camps to resemble the U.S. system.[49]

As the Depression continued, the Roosevelt administration began to loosen citizenship restrictions on federal work programs. The Public Works Administration and Civil Works Administration, which gave money to state and local governments to create jobs, came with preferences for citizens or immigrants who had taken out their first papers and declared their intention to naturalize. But by 1935, as more and more immigrants flocked to federal relief jobs, Secretary Perkins persuaded the administration to drop citizenship requirements for the Works Progress Administration (WPA), a popular program that created public jobs for unemployed workers.[50] In Detroit, WPA programs drew workers from the welfare rolls, many of whom had no citizenship and had not filed naturalization paperwork. Within a year, about 12,000 workers paved alleys, installed fire hydrants, and laid pipes across the city. The council also took advantage of federal funding to beautify Detroit. WPA workers planted trees, landscaped parks, and even renovated the Detroit Public Zoo, which WPA administrators noted was in a "sorry state." In 1936, about eight thousand noncitizens could be seen taking up shovels and pickaxes in the public parks, monuments, and streets of Detroit, a sign for all Detroiters that the Roosevelt administration had begun to employ those born outside America's borders and planned to include them in America's expanding welfare benefits.[51]

New Deal labor laws also allowed for the rise of ethnically and racially inclusive industrial unions. New federal protections under the National Industrial Recovery Act (NIRA) allowed for the rise of the Congress of Industrial Organizations (CIO), which organized workers in industrial unions in 1935 under the auspices of the American Federation of Labor (AFL). That same year in Detroit, labor leaders seized the moment to form the United Automobile Workers (UAW), a union devoted to industrial autoworkers and soon protected by the CIO. In 1936, future union president Walter Reuther organized workers into a series of strikes against small Detroit factories that provided auto parts to behemoths like Ford, Chrysler, and Packard.[52] With each successful strike, the UAW earned more support, but organizers struggled to unionize foreign-born workers. In most of these strikes, it was native-born and a handful of Anglo-Gaelic workers who put down their tools, but UAW leaders knew that to organize ethnically diverse Ford Motor Company or Polish-dominated Dodge, organizers needed the allegiance of immigrant workers regardless of their citizenship.[53]

Hoping to recruit immigrant workers, the UAW council hired second-generation Polish organizer Stanley Nowak as its envoy to Detroit's eastern European community. An avowed communist and supporter of the UAW, Nowak headed to Detroit's Polish, Slavic, and Russian neighborhoods armed with linguistic and cultural fluency and committed to persuading immigrants to join the UAW. Nowak wrote a weekly column in *Glos Lundony*, a leftist newspaper that called itself the "Only Polish Worker's Periodical in the U.S." and gave speeches on Polish radio broadcasts that urged Poles and the other Slavic groups, most of whom understood Polish, to join their fellow workers in protesting unfair wages and working conditions.[54]

But Nowak had trouble convincing first-generation immigrants to join the UAW. To Poles, Russians, and Hungarians, many of whom were middle aged and had lived through over a decade of deportation raids and Klan harassment, risking their livelihoods for the promises of a new union sounded foolhardy.[55] After returning from a particularly discouraging meeting at a Hungarian hall, Novak complained, "These men have no fire left. They would prefer to go home to their families than make change."[56] Indeed, Novak believed first-generation Hungarians might have been up to organizing in generations past, but by the 1930s, they had become tired of radical causes and tied to family life.

Other immigrant workers maintained allegiance to their employers. Historian Nelson Lichtenstein notes that a number of immigrant workers felt such gratitude toward Henry Ford that they kept a photograph of the auto magnate on their mantles next to photos of loved ones and depictions of the Virgin Mary.[57] Moreover, in an era marked by layoffs and deportations, a segment of foreign-born workers lived in constant fear of employer and government repercussions. Consequently, some immigrants who might have sympathized with the demands of strikers remained reluctant to put their jobs and families at risk.[58]

Black Detroiters tended to agree with foreign-born automobile workers and remained skeptical of labor, making the UAW overwhelmingly white and Anglo-Saxon. Like ethnic workers, many African Americans were reluctant to condemn Henry Ford, a man they credited with putting food on their tables and keeping them from eviction. And their feelings were not unfounded. During the early years of the Depression, while other factories slashed black workers first, Ford Motor Company added nearly 7,500 African Americans to its River Rouge workforce.[59] There is little evidence that African Americans participated in the Ford Hunger March mentioned in Chapter 5 or in early organizing efforts. Moreover, the Detroit Urban League and the local chapter of the National Association for the Advancement of Colored People (NAACP) urged black Detroiters to look upon the new union with caution. NAACP Secretary Walter White reminded black Detroiters of the debt they owed local factories for offering them "skills and better-paid jobs to a greater degree."[60]

Black and foreign-born Detroiters had reason to be skeptical of the UAW. Early on, the UAW's leadership committed blunders that most likely alienated them. Unions had traditionally excluded black workers or segregated them into Jim Crow locales, a trend that would be difficult to break in the 1930s.[61] Some early UAW leaders also believed southern and eastern

Europeans could not be committed activists. At a 1935 Labor Day picnic in Belle Isle Park, UAW organizing officer Richard Frankensteen condemned ethnic workers for associating respectable "American unions" with peasantry and communism. In his speech, which echoed Detroit Federation of Labor (DFL) President Frank Martel's brand of nativism, Frankensteen blamed employers for bringing southern European "illiterate, ignorant peasants to replace the good old Puritan stock." He asserted that Europeans had brought communism to the United States and with it a "flow of strikes, of sabotage, and of murders" that made even noncommunist unions appear suspicious.[62] News of Frankensteen's public nativism could not have helped the UAW's efforts to recruit foreign-born workers. This, coupled with African Americans' history of exclusion from unions in general, meant that the UAW would need to work hard to diversify its membership and organize the majority of automobile workers.

A reputation for strikebreaking also followed ethnic Europeans and African Americans into the 1930 union movement. Henry Ford relied on black strikebreakers to quell dissent in the early years of the Depression, and rumors circulated that factories also employed foreigners to keep native-born Americans from striking.[63] In early 1936, just after Frankensteen had taken his post in the UAW, he told radio listeners that "immigrants from Europe and coolies from the Far East" were "intolerable scabs." UAW council members who were more tolerant, or perhaps more politically savvy, encouraged Frankensteen to trade nativist rhetoric for a more inclusive language of working-class solidarity.[64] A few months later, Frankensteen stopped condemning ethnic groups, but Poles and Slavs remembered the leader's intolerance of their national groups.[65]

Religious and political ideologies gave other foreign-born ethnics further reason to avoid the new union. Because many of its leaders identified as communists, Detroit's Catholic Church denounced the UAW and encouraged its 300,000 constituents to follow suit.[66] Many Catholics did not question this decision from their religious leaders. When police made their rounds in Detroit's ethnic east side after a strike, they stopped Polish-born Josephine Kulesa for questioning. She told the officer that she was a housewife, her husband worked for Auto Tool and Die Company, and she had received her naturalization papers in 1932. When the interrogating officer asked whether she participated in UAW meetings or strikes, she answered in outrage, "I am a good Catholic and I do not support Bolshevik-led enterprises. They do not believe in God. There are not so many of those communists around here as you think."[67] Kulesa's response revealed the aversion many ethnic Europeans felt toward communism and that many Catholic immigrants actively resented being labeled politically radical.

As the UAW grew in power, however, it tapped into a base of ethnic, second-generation Polish workers. New to the shop floor, excited to work, and even more eager to strike, most of these workers were unmarried men and women who lived at home and gave their money to their families. In factories like the Detroit Parts Company, young Polish Americans formed tight-knit communities and encouraged foremen to hire their friends on the outside.[68]

Established networks of second-generation Poles provided the perfect opportunity for UAW organizers. In 1936, Stanley Nowak rallied young second-generation Polish women to wage a successful battle against the west side's largest factory, Ternstedt Auto Parts.[69] Meanwhile, in the Detroit Parts Company, Nowak's popularity among second-generation Polish men eclipsed that of the Catholic Church. While many first-generation Poles refused to set down their tools and strike, the company's new hires, an ethnic Polish group that composed 25 percent of its workers, eagerly followed Nowak to demand higher pay and fair conditions.[70]

In 1936, the UAW took over the administration of Detroit's WPA, giving the union the ability to offer loyal members concrete jobs. The partnership began when UAW officials learned that caseworkers in the Detroit Welfare Department had no time or resources to process the thousands of WPA applications pouring into their offices.[71] Sensing an opportunity, UAW Welfare Director George Edwards offered to help with the burden of administering WPA placements. Within a couple of months, Director Edwards and fellow UAW workers created uniform application forms and implemented a system of interviewing applicants to determine mutual fit in projects that demanded particular skills. They also developed a provision for recommending emergency relief in dire cases, particularly when a family's breadwinner was injured or sick. After UAW administrators proved their worth, the Detroit Welfare Department gladly turned all WPA administration over to the union. The alliance tied the New Deal to the new industrial union while giving the UAW the ability to offer its members secure federal work if they lost their jobs out on strike.[72] For instance, in 1937, when Tony Horval lost his Packard Motor Company job after attempting to incite a walkout, UAW administrators secured Horval a job painting federal buildings with the WPA.[73] The alliance between the New

Deal and the UAW helped legitimize the union, and it also proved to hesitant workers that the UAW had something concrete to offer them.

In December 1936, the UAW's efforts toward inclusion paid off when the union organized a sit-down strike against General Motors in Flint, Michigan. The strike lasted for over two months and would not have been possible without the participation of noncitizen workers employed at General Motors plants. For the duration of the strike, Stanley Nowak gave speeches across the eastern European neighborhoods of Detroit, reminding Polish, Russian, and other Slavic workers that Flint autoworkers were their "brothers in arms" and that their success would mean a triumph for Detroit workers. "The larger good of workers," he argued, "is more important than your jobs."[74] In February 1937, General Motors finally agreed to recognize the industrial union and Chrysler followed a month later, marking a major victory for the UAW.

While ethnic workers and foreign-born Detroiters began to turn toward the industrial union, black Detroiters remained notably absent from the strikes. UAW leaders appealed to black workers in 1937, but most sided with their factories and remained on the job, asking, "Will the union give us a square deal and a chance at some of the good jobs?" Consequently, when the UAW began its early attempts to organize Ford Motor Company, it appointed its first paid black organizer, a crane operator at the Michigan Steel Casting Company named Paul Kirk. The tactic worked, and as more black workers turned toward the union, the UAW appointed more and more black organizers, emphasizing the "nondiscrimination clause" within its bylaws as evidence that African Americans would receive full consideration and protection. Thus, in the wake of sit-down strikes, the UAW finally gained a membership that spoke more languages and came from more diverse racial backgrounds than it had in decades.[75]

Invigorated by its Detroit success, the UAW soon tried to extend its influence across the border, but in Canada, restrictive labor laws and immigration policies stymied organizing efforts. UAW Region 7 represented Canadian branch plants from Windsor to Oshawa, and in August 1938, the local organized a strike of foundry workers at Walker Metal Foundry in Windsor. The strike quickly spread to Dodge metalworkers in Oshawa, but because Canada had no laws against firing union members, employers dismissed the strikers and hired strikebreakers, many of whom were not Canadian citizens. Local UAW leader C. H. Millard wrote to the organization headquarters in Detroit that it was impossible to strike in Canada because the employers had all the power and no "New Deal exists here for them." Moreover, because employers insisted on hiring noncitizen workers, he argued that Canadian laws "sowed dissention and mutual suspicion" among workers.[76] Unlike in the United States, where New Deal labor laws allowed workers to band together regardless of citizenship, Canada's UAW fell apart when the ethnic divisions that had long plagued Detroit's union movement divided its workers. But the success of organized labor in Detroit incited a nativist backlash from groups that thought Canada, not the United States, provided a preferable model for dealing with immigrant aliens.

Opposing New Deal Inclusion

The New Deal gave Detroit's white ethnics access to federal work programs and an opportunity to unionize, but immigrant participation in these programs incited a nativist backlash. To combat the combined threat they thought communism, unions, aliens, and African Americans posed to the region, a group of angry white workers formed the Black Legion, an offshoot of the Ku Klux Klan that began to terrorize immigrants and African Americans and galvanized support among Americans who thought the New Deal coddled immigrants and had become too soft on communists.

The Black Legion developed as a more extreme and violent version of the Ku Klux Klan, and many of its earliest members were white southern migrants dismayed by race relations in the North.[77] Its founders, former Klan leaders Dr. William Jacob Shephard and Virgil "Bert" Effinger, formed the Black Legion in 1929 in Ohio because they thought the Klan had become too soft. Bert Effinger soon took full control of the Legion and expanded its influence to every industrial city in the Midwest, advocating the protection of "native-born, white, Protestant, Gentile American" citizenship.[78] By the mid-1930s, Effinger tapped into the economic concerns of white Americans, reinforcing the idea that immigrants and black migrants had taken their jobs and undermined white midwesterners' way of life. Effinger claimed that his organization had six million secret members with 122,000 in Michigan and ten thousand in the Detroit Metropolitan Area. And while this number may have been exaggerated, the Black Legion's influence on the city was very real.[79]

The Black Legion derived authority as a vigilante organization because many of its members were former or current police officers. Bert Effinger's right-hand man, Isaac "Peg Leg" White, had been a Detroit police officer and maintained a network within the Detroit Police Department and the Michigan State Police.[80] Local attorney and communist Maurice Sugar noted the "alarming extent of the Black Legion in public officialdom." He identified at least 100 Legionnaires in the Detroit Police Department itself, with dozens more working as deputy sheriffs, foremen, and Municipal Street Railway employees.[81] The large number of members with claims to law enforcement helped legitimize the Black Legion as an arm of the law not constrained by the rules and bureaucracy of local or federal government.

The Legion appealed to a segment of skilled, Protestant, native-born workers who feared the changes brought on by unions and new migrants and a president they saw as friendly to both these groups. In a call for members, the Black Legion reminded Detroiters, "The native-born white people of America are menaced on every hand from above and below." To combat the threat of "aliens, Negroes, Jews, and cults and creeds believing in racial equality," the organization advocated "fighting with whatever weapons come into our hands," a call that resonated with thousands.[82] By the mid-1930s, Maurice Sugar reported in alarm that up to six thousand men hooded in black often crowded into Cadillac Square outside the UAW offices. These eerie specters terrified ethnic and African American workers on their daily commutes and made others think twice before setting down their tools and joining the picket lines.[83]

The organization claimed to "follow in the footsteps of guerilla bands," but in practice, Legion members adhered to a strict set of rules.[84] Arranged under the same ranks as members of the U.S. Army, "officers" of the Legion took a "blood oath" swearing their Anglo-Saxon heritage, devotion, and secrecy. On the practical side of things, new members paid five dollars for a black hood and ten cents in monthly dues. They attended biweekly meetings in organizations with code names like the Wolverine Republican Club, the Bullet Club, and the Search Light Club. Moreover, every Monday night, Detroit's Legion held mandatory shooting practice at the Wayne County Rifle and Pistol Club.[85]

Legion members who stepped out of line faced draconian punishments. For instance, in late 1935, rumors surfaced that Legion member Charles A. Poole was born to a Catholic family. For having the gall to deceive the Anglo-Saxon integrity of the organization, Dayton Dean and seven fellow officers took Poole into the countryside and shot him in the back of the head assassination style. For a lesser offense, not attending regular meetings, Harley Smith faced a severe flogging that left him nearly dead.[86]

The Legion encouraged even more violence against its avowed "enemies." In 1935, Legionnaire Dayton Dean told police that he and his superior, "Col." Harvey Davis, were drinking on their porch one evening when they decided it would be fun to have a "bigger party and get ahold of a colored fellow." Stumbling from the porch, they threw beer bottles into the bushes, donned their black masks, and set out on the road toward an African American neighborhood. Within twenty minutes, they happened upon Silas Coleman, a black veteran of World War II headed home to his family. After kicking him to the ground, the Legionnaires took turns shooting him before rolling him into a pond and heading to a local party as if nothing out of the ordinary had transpired. The next morning, Coleman surfaced in a mill pond with five bullets in his head and chest.[87]

In Michigan, the Black Legion's primary target became the foreign born, communists, and members of the UAW, and Legionnaires worked under the presupposition that a member of one of these groups likely sympathized with another. Legion members soon began to attend strikes waving banners with "CIO IS COMMUNISM" written in red paint to simulate blood.[88] Many members believed that New Deal union policies would undermine American democracy and, worse still, its Anglo-Saxon hegemony. Thus, Legion leaders justified violence with the language of self-preservation. In the summer of 1936, the Legion forwarded a letter to the UAW's Civil Rights Committee, warning, "BE IT KNOWN that a State of Civil War exists in this city, country, and state, which will continue to exist till the alien and subversive elements are EXTERMINATED or until the last patriot is dead."[89] Rumors soon surfaced that during a Black Legion meeting, Michigan's Commander Arthur F. Lupp admitted he had two local scientists trying to figure out how to inject typhoid germs into milk and cottage cheese to be distributed throughout the Polish and Catholic neighborhoods of the city. And while this act of biological terrorism never transpired, the threat of arbitrary violence against white ethnics circulated in pamphlets, newspapers, and by word of mouth, creating panic within Detroit's immigrant neighborhoods.[90]

The Black Legion labeled Roosevelt a "communist tyrant" and urged its members to look to former Prime Minister Bennett's Canadian policies for evidence of "real, effective leadership." Black Legion flyers reminded

Detroiters that Bennett had not shied from deporting immigrants affiliated with communism or putting "foreign labor agitators in their place." In the United States, on the other hand, the Legion complained that the "communistic UAW" would soon rule the state of Michigan and spread across the nation. To prevent this from happening, the Black Legion argued that its duty was to act as "a police and deportation force in the face of an ineffective government."[91] Thus, the disparity between Canadian and U.S. immigration and labor policies in the early years of the Depression gave nativist Americans an example of how they thought an efficient state should be run.

The Black Legion backed its threats against the UAW with real violence. In December 1937, the hooded vigilante group became linked to a series of violent raids on UAW labor halls. Through the winter months, bricks shattered the windows of the Ford UAW office and powder bombs exploded in the halls of UAW Locals 157 and 235, forcing union members onto the cold streets. The Legion also targeted the homes of union leaders. After a long day of organizing city gas workers for the CIO, Walter Bolitho took the tram to his two-story brick home on Hazelwood Avenue in a region just south of Ford's Highland Park factory. But when he opened the door, a gas bomb exploded, forcing the union leader to the ground and destroying several rooms in the house. While no one was hurt in these attacks and union officials could not definitively tie the Black Legion to the violence, UAW leaders claimed, "The Black Legion was indisputably to blame."[92]

Labor leaders and civil rights groups could never concretely link employers or the police to the Black Legion, but rumors spread that major industrialists like Ford, Chrysler, and Briggs welcomed the hooded vigilante group into their factories. UAW officials complained that industrialists relied on the constant threat of violence to keep "Negroes, Jews, Catholics, and the foreign born divided" so that employers could exploit them.[93] But major industrialists balked when questioned about the Legion and local police feigned ignorance despite consistently arriving moments after a hooded mob had defaced a union member's car or launched stones at picketers.[94]

While perhaps the most extreme, the Black Legion represented one in a host of anti-CIO organizations that organized in the Roosevelt era and conflated the issues of foreignness, unions, and communism. The Prohibition Party of Michigan, which still had over ten thousand members, blamed aliens and idle strikers for the "prevalence of alcoholism in America." In 1936, the prohibitionists staged a play that became popular in Detroit and its suburbs called *The Green Tree* that featured a young boy named Bob who learns that the young "Wops from the city dumps" thought drinking whiskey prevented worms and drank it regularly with their parents.[95] Beyond highlighting the "abuses" of alcohol in Italian homes, the organization polled women on the effect of strikes on alcoholism. In the *Detroit Free Press*, the prohibitionists reported, "Sixty-six percent of the women said that strikes increased drunkenness and 80 percent said that strikes endangered the family life and health."[96] Thus, the prohibitionists concluded that alcohol consumption was not only linked to foreigners but also increased during times of labor upheaval and threatened immigrant families.

Father Charles Coughlin provided a voice for Catholic opposition to the UAW. Known popularly as the "radio priest" and infamously for his anti-Semitic tirades, Father Coughlin began his radio career in 1929 with a weekly Sunday evening broadcast from Royal Oak, Michigan, a suburb of Detroit.[97] Within several years, his sermons reached twenty-seven stations and several million Catholics across the nation. Coughlin claimed to speak for the ordinary Catholic worker. Like many of his listeners, he had faced Ku Klux Klan harassment and advocated a Catholic version of social justice that demanded fair treatment from bosses and anticommunism in the same breath. This appealed to the thousands of Catholics, many of whom were born in Europe yet remained skeptical of the UAW. In 1936, Coughlin began to devote constant airtime to discrediting the UAW, citing the organization's connections to the Communist Party and the "plutocratic salaries" the union paid its leaders as evidence of corruption.[98] Father Coughlin's broadcasts added to the voices of the Prohibition Party and the Black Legion to undermine the growing power of the UAW and link its members to communism, foreignness, and undesirability.

Detroiters targeted by vigilante violence and nativism did not accept it quietly. In the winter of 1938, the Detroit Civil Rights Federation packed Mayfair Auditorium for a scathing expose against Father Charles Coughlin. Many of the 1,200 audience members were communists, UAW members, or both, but others were ordinary workers unaffiliated with politics yet tired of the police constantly knocking on their doors. UAW Secretary George Addes, a second-generation Lebanese American himself, approached the podium to remind workers that "in Detroit, there are many groups and organizations, we must be aware of many of them as they are out to break the union and destroy our rights." Amid cheers, Addes chanted the names of workers who had been harassed or harmed by the Black Legion and police or killed during strikes.[99]

"Foreignness" soon became an accusation used by both police and unionists. On a crisp January morning in 1935, Mary Wolf, a DFL member and future wife of UAW President Walter Reuther, passed out the *Detroit Labor News* to Fisher Motor Company workers when Officer John Mulealy approached her and, in a thick Irish accent, demanded her newspapers. When she refused to turn them over, he dragged her to the local station, insisting that she was a communist foreigner who "should go back to Russia." Once at the station, Wolf sent for her birth certificate and was promptly released with a "disturbance of the peace" ticket.[100] To protest the ticket, Wolf condemned Officer Mulealy's own foreignness. After her altercation with the Irish officer, Wolf wrote a letter to the Detroit Police Department, demanding that the charges be dropped, adding, "Officer Mulealy speaks with a foreign accent, and I consider remarks of this kind from an alien a gross insult."[101] The confrontation between Wolf and Mulealy demonstrated the violence union supporters could expect to experience on a daily basis. But the fact that both police officer and union activists attempted to discredit the other with accusations of foreignness revealed the low status that foreign-born Detroiters occupied in Detroit's society.

As the UAW and larger CIO gained a foothold in industries across the nation, patriotic organizations renewed their concern over unauthorized immigrants. In 1936, American citizens flooded the White House mailroom with letters warning President Roosevelt of exaggerated numbers of illegal foreigners threatening American society from within. The American Legion of Connecticut told the president that if he did not deport the 7.5 million aliens living in the United States, they would break down the welfare system and incite labor unrest and strikes strong enough to collapse industry in America. Conflating all foreigners with illegal immigrants, the American Legion emphasized the growing sentiment that anyone not born within the boundaries of the United States was prone to criminal behavior and inherently suspect.[102] Similarly, Chicago's West Side Civic League urged Roosevelt to protect the "rights of American citizens" from the five million illegal aliens in the nation. Also exaggerating numbers of undocumented immigrants, the organization reinforced the growing fear among nativist groups that an entangled group of foreigners, illegal aliens, communists, and labor organizers threatened America from within its major cities.[103]

In Michigan, despite the fact that many European-born immigrants avoided unions, local police and nativists connected New Deal labor policies to foreignness, communism, and urban unrest. Otis Richmond of East Saugatuck, Michigan, warned Roosevelt that if he did not reverse his policies toward labor unions, the "3.5 million illegal immigrants across America" would overturn the democratic system. In order to restore industrial peace in Detroit, Richmond suggested that President Roosevelt sign an executive order to deport the aliens so they could "become a burden on their home countries."[104]

The Black Legion, Prohibition Party, and Father Coughlin represented members of a growing grassroots movement that pitted themselves against New Deal policies. Though they had separate followings and agendas, they shared the belief that by allowing unions to flourish, President Roosevelt had ceded to the demands of radical leftists. For the Black Legion, the most extreme of these groups, lax immigration and deportation policies compounded the union threat and allowed undesirable foreigners to challenge the region's Anglo-Saxon majority. Canada, the Black Legion reasoned, provided an excellent example of hard-line deportation and labor tactics that checked the power of foreigners. When Roosevelt refused to reverse pro-union, pro-foreign policies, however, local nativists pushed the Detroit Police Department to use its Red Squad to find and deport noncitizen communists. By the mid-1930s, the Red Squad legitimized the ideology and methods of vigilante nativists by using raids to legally terrorize local immigrant neighborhoods.

The Red Squad and State Violence

Profiling and coercion became part of the official Detroit Police Department when the city's Red Squad began monitoring, arresting, and deporting UAW members in the name of anticommunism. To combat the communist fears invoked by nativists, the Detroit Police Department poured resources into its "Special Investigation Squad," a unit devoted to uncovering "un-American" activities in the city. The unit, which became popularly known as the Red Squad, dated to the first Red Scare of the early 1920s and had long tracked leftists and anarchists in the city. As the Communist Party grew in membership and popularity, police departments in New York, Cleveland, Chicago, Los Angeles, and Detroit began funneling money and manpower into their Red Squads. Beginning in 1933, the Detroit Police

Department made its Red Squad an official department and designated three officers whose only job was to investigate instances of political radicalism across the city. In response to concerns about communism in the UAW, the police department designated two more full-time Red Squad investigators. By 1936, Detroit police officers frequented communist bookstores and meetings, taking note of speakers and license plate numbers of those in attendance.[105] The Red Squad modeled its espionage and information-gathering practices on the Border Patrol and deportation units of the police department, and because many communist suspects were foreign born, the police force worked to further alienate immigrants from state power in Detroit.

Despite the fact that Communist Party meetings took place across the city in fifty-seven subdistricts, the Red Squad focused its surveillance on immigrant neighborhoods and halls.[106] In the summer of 1936, the Red Squad placed permanent spies at the Ukrainian Workers' Hall and the Finnish Hall, both venues that held ethnic dances, immigrant organization meetings, and Communist Party meetings. Police attended all events at these halls and reported on who spoke and who was present, collected any pamphlets or printed materials, and sometimes followed speakers and attendees to local bars and parks to listen to conversations. Most of these meetings were mundane affairs. After a particularly boring Communist Party meeting at the Finnish Hall in October 1937, a Red Squad inspector reported nothing new "except the notable presence of foreign faces at the radical meetings." A few months later, an inspector noted the "Russian-looking" crowd at a Communist Party meeting at the Ukrainian Workers' Hall.[107] Ultimately, inspectors found and perceived large numbers of immigrants at Communist Party events because they spent more time at meetings in immigrant neighborhoods. These targeted searches reinforced their preconception that all foreigners had ties to political radicalism and all communists had something foreign in their pasts.

Unlike in Canada, membership in the American Communist Party was perfectly legal. Thus, Red Squad members kept close tabs on certain foreign-born members of the Communist Party in the hopes that they could deport them for committing a crime or missing key paperwork. For example, the Red Squad monitored Ferenz Unterwegner, a Hungarian who worked at Ford Motor Company as a machinist under the name Frank Wagner, keeping careful notes that contained his Ford badge number (S. 3166), vehicle (1941 Chrysler Royal), height (5′4″), and hair color (iron gray). The Red Squad called Unterwegner "one of the oldest Reds in the city of Dearborn" and wrote to Washington to check if he might have false or incomplete papers. The Department of Labor responded with a letter that assured the Red Squad that Unterwegner was indeed a naturalized citizen. Despite this information, Immigration Inspector L. K. Smith applauded the Detroit Police Department's tenacity and encouraged the Red Squad to continue "investigating suspicious characters in the name of Americanism."[108] The federal response to local espionage demonstrated how the U.S. government endorsed deportation as a way to control political unrest even as the New Deal extended benefits to immigrants. While the Canadian government could deport foreigners for membership in the Communist Party, the U.S. Department of State relied on local anticommunist forces to police and purge foreigners.

With the rise of the UAW, the Red Squad devoted much of its time to pinning down and exposing what it saw as the dual threats of communist and foreign influence within the automotive union.[109] In a report on the International Workers Order, a communist organization that backed UAW efforts, Detroit police noted, "They were all, with but few exceptions, Jews and foreigners who could hardly speak English plain enough to understand." The officer reported that the Jewish members dictated the terms of an upcoming strike while the foreigners nodded their heads and cheered whenever given the signal from their superiors.[110] Red Squad files reveal that officers had begun to conflate communism with foreignness and Jewishness, assuming any foreigner or Jew might be a member of the Communist Party and vice versa.

This assumption caused investigations to turn toward any foreigners who attended UAW meetings. For instance, when Polish Paul Stamtakis heard that Stanley Nowak had begun giving UAW speeches in his native tongue, he decided to see what the new industrial union was all about. After leaving his shift at Automotive Stamping Workers, where he had become dissatisfied with his hours and pay, Stamtakis headed to the Finnish Hall, where Stanley Nowak gave a rousing speech on workplace safety and employer accountability. However, Stamtakis did not know that an undercover Red Squad investigator had attended the same meeting and taken down his license plate number. Soon the Red Squad had a file on the Polish worker that noted he wore glasses and had "unruly coal black hair," blue eyes, and a "broad peasant face." Further investigation revealed that Stamtakis had no immigration papers, and though the Pole swore he entered the country legally from Canada, the Red Squad referred him to the INS for questioning. In the spring of 1938, the INS signed Stamtakis's deportation order, deeming him "likely to become a public charge" due to his radical tendencies.[111] Stamtakis was not officially a member of the Communist Party and had no prior affiliation with radical politics, but because the Red Squad had begun to conflate the UAW and communism, Stamtakis found himself caught up in the investigation.

Beyond espionage at local meetings, the Red Squad involved neighborhoods and communities in policing political radicalism by recruiting local informants. When Emily Baker's Polish neighbor, John Gielgud, asked her to join the Communist Party, she went directly to the Detroit Police Department to report him. She informed the police that Gielgud went to his job at the Auto Tool and Die Company each morning in a Dodge pickup truck and that he made suspicious deliveries for the shop next door. At the end of her report, Baker suggested that the police department take measures to "deport the Bokshevik who is ungrateful for his American life." The police sent Gielgud's name and information to the INS and learned that though he was a Polish citizen, he could not be deported because he had entered the United States legally through New York City on May 29, 1923. The police assured Baker that they would open a file on him and encouraged Baker to notify them if he began recruiting for the UAW or the Communist Party.[112] By asking local residents to spy on their neighbors, police reinforced local suspicions linking immigrants to communism and labor activism.

Growing suspicions and rumors fomented divisions within Detroit's immigrant communities, causing some immigrants to spy in an effort to prove their own claims to legitimacy and Americanness. Amelia Fronak, a Polish immigrant herself, sent the Detroit Police Department a series of reports on "suspicious communist Poles" who lived on her street near Hamtramck, Michigan. Fronak wrote the police that she had chosen to report potential communists in an effort to "clear the names of real American Poles who would never join a union or godless communism," revealing her concern that Polish immigrants had earned an unfair reputation as communists and labor activists.[113] And Poles were not the only national group that felt its members' reputations were at stake. In 1938, Hungarian John Bator wrote to the Detroit Police Department, asking them to stop "invading" his Hungarian neighborhood of Delray with police raids. "Most of my countrymen," he assured the police, "have no interest in communism or political extremes. We want only to be Americans."[114] Fronak and Bator's insistent claims to Americanness reveal that policing and red-baiting had alienated certain southern and eastern Europeans from American society.

Civil rights groups argued that the coercive policing undertaken by the Detroit Police Department threatened the civil rights of all Detroiters. In March 1938, the American Civil Liberties Union issued a report ranking Detroit behind Los Angeles as one of the "two worst big cities in the country for the protection of the Bill of Rights." Reverend J. H. Bollens, head of the local Civil Rights Federation, claimed the Detroit Police Department shouldered much of the blame for the report, condemning the department's "attitude on freedom of speech and assembly" and accusing the "so-called Red Squad" of being akin to an "Anti-Civil Liberties Squad."[115]

But the report did little to quash the Red Squad's zeal. In response to the civil rights report, Police Commissioner Pickert remarked, "I have important things to do, I am not interested. And the Civil Liberties Union doesn't amount to anything."[116] When the local Civil Rights Federation staged a meeting to address the issue, a coalition of nativists and Black Legionnaires picketed the event with signs reading "No Bill of Rights for any Communists," "Americanism Forever, Communism Never," and "Down with Nazi Communism."[117] Indeed, the intensity with which local citizens and police had begun to express their nativist views made foreignness a difficult marker to bear in Depression-era Detroit.

Despite the fact that at the federal level, New Deal administrators sought to help immigrants and their families, in Detroit, the foreign born continued to face stigmatization and police harassment. In America's Motor City, concerned nativists discussed Canadian deportation and relief camp policies as positive alternatives to what they viewed as Roosevelt's unacceptable insistence on including noncitizens in federal welfare policies. When new labor policies strengthened industrial unions, hundreds of Black Legionnaires insisted that communist foreigners were undermining American capitalism, and every evening, Father Charles Coughlin connected the CIO and communism in fiery radio broadcasts. Informal immigrant and communist harassment became official police policy when the Detroit Police Department sent its Red Squad into ethnic neighborhoods in search of communists. Ultimately, vigilante violence, nativist rhetoric, and official policing blurred the lines between who was an immigrant, communist, or member of the nascent UAW. Detroit labor activist and second-generation Syrian immigrant George Addes drove this point home when he told Detroit's mayor, "To the police I am a communist, to the Ku Klux Klan I am a foreigner. Really I am just an American worker who dares to ask for more from my country."[118] But the years that followed only brought Addes more anxiety as immigrant nationalities that had earned a local reputation for crime and illegality came under suspicion for cheating America's welfare system.

Chapter 7

Aliens and Welfare in North America

One October afternoon in 1938, Detroit's Mayor Richard Reading gave a radio address introducing the German-Jewish Wassermans, a family he claimed was "chiseling welfare from the city." According to the mayor, forty-eight-year-old Thomas Wasserman had not bothered to take out American citizenship, yet he had no problem supporting his family with taxpayers' dollars. Thomas worked part-time in a clothing store while his wife Minnie had a Works Progress Administration (WPA) job, and their youngest sons Simon and Nathan worked in Civilian Conservation Corps (CCC) positions outside the state. Together, the family made $150.25 each month, enough to pay the mortgage on their modest bungalow and offer occasional support to their eldest son Leo, who was a committed United Automobile Workers (UAW) organizer and bounced between jobs at automobile companies. Here the mayor paused to let listeners picture the Wassermans. They were Jewish immigrants, welfare recipients, and labor organizers, meaning they represented everything the mayor's Republican electorate feared about immigrants in Depression-era Detroit.

But a lack of citizenship papers and membership in the UAW, the mayor warned, were minor issues compared to the immigrant family's larger crime: the Wassermans were welfare cheaters. Taking a breath, the mayor began to explain how the family omitted their sons' CCC pay in reports to the Detroit Welfare Bureau yet still claimed all three sons as dependents. Next, he reported that the Wassermans housed a boarder in their back room, earning the family an extra $30 each month. Because the Wassermans did not report all their income, the family qualified for $44.05 in monthly welfare aid from the city. The Wassermans, Mayor Reading concluded, represented typical "welfare chiselers." They supported their immigrant family and "radical union son" with city funds that, the mayor claimed, could be better used to "support deserving American citizens."[1] Profiling the Wassermans helped Mayor Reading launch a campaign to discredit immigrant Americans, purge welfare rolls, and keep New Deal programs for U.S. citizens. The mayor's welfare purge drew on the discourse of the 1920s that had linked immigrants to illegality, crime, industrial unions, and communism to accuse the foreign born of a new crime: cheating the local and federal welfare system. Historians often frame the New Deal as a push to expand benefits and opportunities to the American people, but this narrative obscures the fact that it did so by leaving those without citizenship out of new programs. Examining the local administration of New Deal welfare programs reveals that excluding foreigners and those deemed foreign became embedded in America's emerging welfare state.

In the United States, the extension of federal benefits and labor rights to workers precipitated a conservative backlash that targeted noncitizens in ways that were not possible across the border in Canada, where welfare remained local and unions weak. When certain immigrants began joining industrial unions like the UAW, Detroit politicians cast them as ungrateful foreigners who had come to America to take advantage of the state's generosity. Stories of families like the Wassermans, who lied on welfare applications and sent money to a son in the UAW, made purging city welfare rolls popular in Detroit. Across the border in Canada, fiscally conservative politicians tried to initiate similar purges, but because Canada's federal government still allowed employer discrimination against unions, immigrant welfare recipients did not have a reputation as strikers. In fact, in Windsor, welfare purges modeled on Detroit backfired, and the politicians who proposed them appeared greedy and heartless for taking money from the most vulnerable Windsorites at the very moment they needed it most. The outbreak of World War II in 1939 accelerated Canada's move toward immigrant inclusion, while in the United States, local efforts to cast noncitizens as undesirable pushed the Roosevelt administration to exclude all immigrants from the WPA.[2] Ultimately, the practice of excluding or including noncitizens in welfare programs became entrenched in the policies of both North American nations.

America's anti-immigrant milieu of the 1920s and 1930s came to a head on the eve of World War II, when Congress passed the 1940 Alien

Registration Act, a measure that foreshadowed a series of federal civil liberties violations against those deemed "outsiders" in the name of national security. Historians tend to position the Registration Act as a wartime measure that gained traction amid fears of espionage from German and Italian aliens, and to a certain extent, this was true.[3] However, national alien registration would not have been possible without the prior two decades of continuous grassroots nativist activism. A long history of excluding and deporting foreigners made registering all noncitizens with the federal government a popular next step. When Congress declared war on Japan, Germany, and Italy in December 1941, excluding "foreigners" from American programs had become woven into the fabric of America's social structure, making barring refugees or incarcerating groups deemed "too foreign" an acceptable choice even for policymakers in support of a new liberal order.

Policing Local Welfare Fraud

Before congressmen debated WPA benefits and foreignness in Washington, D.C., Detroit's local politicians launched a campaign against welfare fraud that became central to efforts to curb the growing power of the UAW. By the fall of 1937, Detroit's United Automobile Workers played a key role in allocating WPA jobs and continued to celebrate its watershed victory at General Motors (GM) in Flint. Soon organizers began to imagine an international UAW that would span the U.S.-Canada border. On April 8, the union organized a strike at GM of Canada in Oshawa, Ontario, in which workers demanded an eight-hour day, better pay, and official recognition of their union. In Windsor, GM workers joined the strike eagerly, parading outside the factory each day under the leadership of P. M. Cappellini, an Italian American CIO organizer who had traveled to Canada after successfully organizing a union of West Virginia coal miners. Support also came from across the border when hundreds of Detroit UAW members traveled to Windsor to stand in solidarity with the Canadian workers.[4] After two weeks, GM capitulated, yielding to nearly all of the UAW's demands and signaling the union's first Canadian victory. Exhilarated by their international win, American leaders returned across the border and set their sights on Detroit's city government. But UAW organizers miscalculated the strength of nativism and open-shop politics across America's Motor City.

In 1937, Republican Richard Reading ran for mayor with a campaign that promised to curb the power of the UAW and end a new, yet he claimed, related problem to the city: welfare cheating. Reading was a city clerk who, in his seventeen years of political experience, had developed a vast network of local connections and a reputation for no-nonsense business dealings.[5] Reading appealed to city elites with the pledge "not to let the CIO take over City Hall," but he also gained traction with ordinary citizens when he promised to purge Detroit's welfare rolls in order to create space and resources for struggling Americans.[6] On the campaign trail, Reading faced Patrick H. O'Brien, a candidate who had served as Michigan's attorney general from 1933 to 1935, gained the endorsement of the UAW, and, therefore, thought he had the vote of ordinary working Detroiters in the bag.[7] What O'Brien failed to calculate, however, was the intensity with which American citizens of all classes had begun to blame noncitizens and migrants to the city for depleting welfare funds and taking jobs.

Reading tapped into this bitterness by reaching out to naturalized Europeans who did not want to be associated with crime, unions, or questionable legality. In the month before the city election, Reading appeared in front of the Italian American Political Federation, the Polish United Society, and the *Polish Daily News* staff, promising "fair wages and secure jobs" for those who "work hard and do not expect handouts." He even delivered speeches and sampled food at several Hungarian and Ukrainian picnics, always promising to retool city welfare to benefit those who deserved it, in this case, working ethnics with citizenship.[8] By emphasizing the thrift, hard work, and general desirability of ethnic Poles, Reading gave many established immigrants the acceptance they had long craved. In response, the *Polish Daily News*, a newspaper with a long-standing anti-UAW stance, offered him its highest endorsement, insisting that "hard working Poles" had everything to gain from a Reading administration.[9] Endorsing the conservative local candidate demonstrated certain Poles' desire to join the ranks of respectable society while also marking their repudiation of Franklin Roosevelt's New Deal labor and immigrant policies.

Patrick O'Brien, on the other hand, campaigned entirely on his UAW endorsement, assuming that because many ethnic Detroiters had joined the union, this would earn him the support of working and immigrant Americans. While rallying for votes, O'Brien attended dozens of UAW picnics and union locals, but he visited only one Hungarian orphanage and one Elks Lodge.[10] This undoubtedly reinforced his UAW base, but it did little to persuade first-generation ethnics or working-class whites who were not sure about industrial unionism. O'Brien's real downfall, however, began when the Detroit Federation of Labor (DFL) came out in favor of his opponent, Richard Reading. DFL President Frank Martel resented the UAW's quick rise to power and growing popularity, particularly as his own AFL-backed union lost membership. He claimed that "the city should remain unfettered from labor's grip" and promised Reading that the skilled laborers of the DFL would have his vote.[11]

The election gave Detroiters who were critical of federal New Deal policies a chance to voice their opposition. With DFL support, the Republican candidate could position himself as a moderate, prolabor, pro-ethnic candidate who would favor employers while clearing city welfare rolls for a to-be-determined set of "deserving Americans."[12] The tactic won Reading the election by over 90,000 votes.[13] The results crushed the UAW's hopes of controlling city politics and signaled to the Roosevelt administration that even in cities like Detroit, where record numbers of voters had supported the president, concern that undeserving immigrants might receive state handouts prompted thousands of native-born and immigrant voters to denounce the New Deal agenda.

After a bitter campaign, Mayor Reading asked the UAW to set aside past differences and cooperate with his administration to tackle Detroit's 41 percent unemployment rate. Over the next month, Mayor Reading worked with local administrators and UAW leaders to organize a demonstration that brought 100,000 men and women into Detroit's Cadillac Square to demand increased WPA jobs for Detroit. The demonstration lasted several days and joined members of the UAW, the DFL, and other unemployed workers to protest the proportionally low number of WPA jobs in Detroit and Michigan.[14] Hopeful UAW leaders saw the demonstration as a turning point in labor relations, particularly when President Roosevelt granted Detroit an unlimited number of WPA positions, a measure that translated to 40,000 immediate new WPA jobs for the unemployed in Detroit and its suburbs.[15] UAW leaders cheered and sent Mayor Reading their support, pleased that the new Republican administration had included the union in the fight.[16]

But before the ink had dried on Roosevelt's WPA increase in Detroit, Mayor Reading severed ties between the UAW and the WPA. After discussing the alliance with the Department of Public Welfare, Reading declared that the UAW operated WPA applications to "help men but also to show them that Welfare relief can more easily be obtained by belonging to the Union." In order to make good on his promise to keep the CIO-backed

UAW out of city politics, Reading announced that city welfare workers would no longer rely on "outside institutions" for city jobs.[17] Moreover, to ensure that WPA workers came from the ranks of the truly destitute, Reading instituted a "pauper's oath" that required clients to swear to their poverty before even receiving an application for relief.[18]

The establishment of a "pauper's oath" likened WPA work to charity, something that union leaders, politicians, and male workers had long associated with dependence and femininity.[19] The WPA, on the other hand, was supposed to support heads of households and instill men with a sense of masculine purpose. Historian Alice Kessler-Harris has demonstrated how New Deal programs and the emergence of a welfare state enshrined the conception that white men and, to a lesser extent, black men had the "right to work," while white women and children should rely on relief.[20] Mayor Reading's insistence that WPA recipients publicly declare their poverty not only appeared humiliating but also undermined the charade that WPA work was more than a way to keep idle men employed.

New regulations infuriated UAW leaders, who felt they had helped Reading secure more WPA jobs for Detroit only to be cut out of the entire system. Richard T. Leonard, the UAW's director of welfare, assured Reading that the union did not favor its own members but only wanted to "facilitate the work of taking care of the thousands of unemployed" across the city.[21] The union's assistant president, Richard Frankensteen, claimed the "pauper's oath" marked the "most backward step taken in relief administration since the Elizabethan poor laws." Poverty oaths, union leaders warned, represented one measure that was sure to become a larger effort to curb the power of the city's poorest inhabitants.[22]

It was not long before the Reading administration began to focus on the problem of individual welfare cheaters, people the mayor called "welfare chiselers." By early 1938, the city of Detroit gave direct aid to a total of 10,275 Detroiters. According to the mayor, thousands of these welfare recipients might be working other jobs or lying on their applications and, therefore, "chiseling" at the foundations of the welfare system. To remedy this purported drain on city resources, the mayor insisted, "We want to furnish welfare relief to all who deserve it, but we intend to eliminate the chiselers!"[23] The mayor's "antichiseler" campaign created hysteria across the city and a new charge to level on immigrant communities already associated with dependence and crime. It also conveniently shifted the blame for a worldwide economic crisis and mounting municipal debt to individuals who could be investigated and punished for their role in taking an unfair share of city resources.

Before fears surfaced over "welfare queens" in the 1970s, immigrant men and women earned an undeserved reputation for dishonesty and welfare fraud in the industrial North.[24] In reality, immigrants tended to avoid relief applications because they did not want to bring unnecessary government scrutiny upon themselves or family members.[25] In Detroit, just under 30 percent of welfare recipients were foreigners, but Mayor Reading exaggerated immigrants' participation in the welfare system and labeled them the group most likely to commit welfare fraud.[26] In March 1938, Mayor Reading tasked a squad on the police force to investigate and prosecute welfare recipients who committed fraud in any way. The Detroit Police Department's Lieutenant George McLelland began carrying out the mayor's request to "recheck every welfare case in order that we might be assured that not one dollar of relief was being expended unnecessarily."[27] But a list of ten thousand names presented an insurmountable task, and McLelland chose to investigate 1,363 welfare cases in the immigrant neighborhoods of northwest Detroit, regions already familiar to Detroit's Red Squad and deportation forces. In seven months, McLelland arrested 140 individuals and charged 115 with welfare fraud. Records do not denote the citizenship of those convicted, but about a third of them had eastern European names like Grabowski, Kaminski, and Nalepka.[28] Finding first- and second-generation immigrants connected to fraud became a self-fulfilling process. Because investigators looked for welfare fraud in immigrant neighborhoods, they naturally concluded that most welfare cheaters had immigrant backgrounds.

The welfare investigation squad worked in tandem with the established Red Squad to police communists, welfare cheaters, and potential deportees in the same rounds. In October 1938, in the hopes of finding welfare cheaters, policemen in the Special Investigation Squad attended a communist meeting at the Finnish Hall. The undercover policemen soon tired of tedious discussions of union dues and funding, but they noted the leaders and participants of the 120-person meeting and created a report for the Red Squad's files.[29] Thus, investigators of welfare fraud became part of Detroit's larger deportation apparatus, linking welfare fraud to both radical politics and the growth of the UAW and union power.

Welfare purges allowed police to punish ethnic Europeans not eligible for deportation. As the Red Squad patrolled ethnic neighborhoods for communist activity, they also investigated suspected welfare cheaters. Pursuing an anonymous tip, Red Squad patrolmen raided the Greek Minerva Restaurant and questioned business partner Gus Kapotas, interrogating him about his citizenship and political affiliations. When they determined the second-generation Greek was indeed an American citizen, investigators turned to his employment history. With the help of a neighbor's testimony, police determined that while Kapotas had worked as a welder at Murray and Briggs Body Companies, he was also on welfare. Evidently, the combination of sporadic wages and direct aid from the city had allowed Kapotas to save enough to covertly invest in a restaurant. The Red Squad charged Kapotas with "gaming the system" and regretted that they "could only fine him" rather than return him to Greece.[30] Kapotas's case demonstrates how investigators began to demonize anyone on city aid who was not struggling and impoverished, casting them as undeserving cheaters and criminals.

A segment of Depression-era Detroiters became angry when those on relief had what they perceived as luxuries. Many such reports came through hearsay and informants, fueling Detroiters' suspicions that foreign-born neighbors and friends might be welfare cheaters. After creating the investigation squad, Mayor Reading issued an appeal to "good taxpayers," asking, "If you know of any person who is receiving aid to which he is not entitled, please write me a letter about it and I shall see that the case is investigated at once."[31] In response, 110 Detroiters immediately wrote letters to report suspicious welfare activity.[32] In one case, Katherine Feeney reported that Anthony Kithas, the Greek-born cook living next door to her, might be abusing his welfare benefits. Through gossip or hearsay, Feeney seemed well aware that Kithas received twenty-five dollars a month from city welfare, but Feeney also noted that beginning in the winter of 1938, his household suddenly smelled of meat on a regular basis, a sure sign that he had money to spare. The charge drew the attention of Detroit's welfare investigation squad, which uncovered the fact that Kithas had found a part-time job sweeping the floors at Aviation Barber Shop. Because Kithas had neglected to inform the Welfare Department of his extra two dollars a week, he was convicted of welfare fraud and dropped from the city rolls.[33]

By 1938, noncitizens had endured over a decade of policy and policing linking their ethnic groups to crime, but welfare purges marked a first step in cutting them out of America's welfare state. Welfare had long been associated with dependence and stigmatized as something reserved for poor women or emasculated men.[34] Mayor Reading, however, invoked fears about immigrant crime to suggest that the same noncitizens who bootlegged liquor or smuggled across the border were also defrauding the city and robbing resources from American citizens. Rising concerns about fraud allowed the mayor to mobilize the police department, but while he could purge local immigrants from welfare with impunity, aliens could still get work in the Works Progress Administration. Within a few years, however, local welfare purges from places like Detroit popularized the idea that immigrants did not deserve aid from the state, and soon pressure to keep immigrants off welfare reached the Roosevelt administration and Congress. Ultimately, the nativist purges of the 1930s helped exclude certain individuals from a nascent welfare state. In contrast, the Canadian government took a relatively hands-off approach to relieving unemployment, and immigrants did not gain the reputation for dependence that plagued their counterparts to the south.

Canadian Progressivism

Across the border, Windsor relief workers shared concerns that the unemployed, many of whom were immigrants, had begun to take advantage of local welfare benefits. But in Windsor, politicians could not galvanize support for welfare purges because Canada's federal government maintained deportations and antiunion policies while insisting that relief was not the responsibility of the government in Ottawa.[35] In short, hardline national policies made native-born Canadians more likely to believe that immigrants posed little threat to their employment and welfare. When local leaders enacted Detroit-style welfare purges in Windsor, the local electorate rose in solidarity with the immigrant and working-class unemployed, who, they felt, had certainly endured enough. Comparing the Windsor case to Detroit, where federal efforts to include immigrants and legitimize unions incited local backlash, suggests that local drives for and against welfare played key roles in determining who would benefit from both nations' welfare states.

As in Detroit, unemployed immigrants represented a key issue for Canadian cities. After Prime Minister William Lyon Mackenzie King ended Canada's relief camp program, unemployed workers flooded into urban centers, and when they could not find work, thousands applied to local welfare agencies. By 1938 in Windsor, about 11,900 individuals qualified for relief in the form of cash or some combination of coal, milk, or groceries from the Provincial Department of Welfare. Because Canada had encouraged immigration to western farmlands into the 1930s, a large number of these unemployed workers were immigrants from Poland, Ukraine, and Hungary.[36] Windsor leaders looked just across the river, where the Reading administration had begun to investigate Detroit's welfare rolls and launched their own campaign to cut welfare and discourage labor unrest. In Windsor, however, leaders could not legitimize welfare cuts as a check on growing union power, and instead, they incited a working-class backlash that moved the city toward progressive reform.

After several years of progressive city politics, factory owners, middle-class businessmen, and patriotic women's organizations helped elect wealthy lawyer and World War I veteran Ernest Wigle to the office of mayor. Wigle won Windsor's mayoral race in December 1936 by promising to help the unemployed without bankrupting the city or succumbing to the demands of labor unions.[37] After his win, Mayor Wigle began to dismantle the welfare and housing programs instituted by his leftist predecessor, who had vacated the office for a position on Ontario Premier Mitchell Hepburn's cabinet. Former mayor David Croll's unemployment benefits, Mayor Wigle announced, represented the efforts of a Jewish immigrant who sought only to help other immigrants at the expense of hard-working and middle-class Canadians. The only way to help Canadian taxpayers, he reasoned, was to cut welfare and municipal spending.[38]

For inspiration, Mayor Wigle and his administration looked to Detroit's "antichiseler" campaign. Welfare Commissioner Clyde Curry, who spearheaded the welfare reform movement, called Mayor Reading "a visionary leader" and Detroit's "last hope to save herself from bankruptcy."[39] Commissioner Curry had already made a name for himself in the early 1930s when he went behind the back of Mayor Croll and deported several noncitizens on welfare, but this time, Curry worked under a mayor who fully supported his vision for reform.[40] He began the welfare cuts by working with the Windsor Police Department to investigate welfare recipients for fraud. Soon the Welfare Department announced it would slash benefits and reduce distribution dates from weekly to "semimonthly." The Windsor Cooperative Unemployed Association immediately staged a protest outside city hall, accusing the mayor and Welfare Department of "grave injustices" against Windsor's poor. In response, the mayor pointed out that Windsor paid "above average" when compared to welfare programs in Oshawa, London, Toronto, and even Detroit. Cutting welfare, he reasoned, would only bring the city's aid program to the level of cities in the surrounding region.[41]

Welfare reductions appealed to wealthy and middle-class Windsor residents who subscribed to the familiar idea that direct relief encouraged laziness and labor unrest among an immigrant working class. Gendered concerns that welfare would subvert family relations and turn hardworking men into effeminate dependents became a major concern of moneyed Windsorites. The Windsor Local Council of Women advised the mayor that welfare allowed the impoverished to fall into a cycle marked by "aimless days and an irregular life" that "make for mental, moral and physical softness." Immigrants and their children, the wealthy women's organization warned, were particularly susceptible to idleness and, if not engaged, would likely turn toward communism and labor organizing.[42] Thus, reformers began to position welfare cuts as a way to keep unemployed men from having the time to discuss political radicalism rather than developing a masculine work ethic.

A failed strike, however, emphasized the importance of local welfare programs to many Windsor workers. In August, one hundred thirty Walker Metal Foundry workers went on strike, confirming welfare reformers' fears that idle workers tended toward organizing. The strike began when a series of layoffs and wage cuts left over one hundred workers with few or no hours. Those who lost their jobs set up a picket outside and supported their families with municipal welfare rations.[43] The strikers claimed to be independent, but soon rumors spread that UAW leaders had traveled from Oshawa and Detroit to help organize the strikers.[44] Two weeks later, the UAW of Canada took credit for the two hundred foundry workers picketing the factory and encouraged Windsor's unemployed to join their ranks in solidarity.[45] When onlookers passed the foundry one afternoon, they witnessed hundreds of workers and unemployed singing "God Save the King" at the top of their lungs, screaming at police and urging them to make arrests.[46] The police restrained themselves, but as the strike lagged on, violent picketers targeted the strikebreakers they blamed for allowing the foundry to continue production. John Pitke, a thirty-three-year-old striker, became enraged when he saw his coworker John Uliene cross the picket lines, and that evening, Pitke threw a bomb through Uliene's window. The bomb did not explode, but it did land Pitke in prison and the *Windsor Evening Star* featured Pitke's efforts on its front page. The incident gave the strike a reputation for senseless violence, and it quickly lost popularity.[47]

After fourteen weeks of protest and several outbreaks of violence, the strikers reached an agreement with the foundry that could hardly be called a success. The UAW blamed both Windsor police's intimidation and immigrant strikebreakers for allowing the company to stay at full capacity. When the strike ended, Walker Metal Foundry promised to place strikers on a preferred list for rehire and not to discriminate against workers for union membership. Both sides declared a victory, but the company made no concessions on pay or hours, and hundreds of foundry workers returned home without jobs. And because in Canada, no laws existed to prevent employers from discriminating against union members, the company had no real incentive to hire troublesome workers back.[48]

City officials capitalized on the fact that a large number of Americans, immigrants, and unemployed welfare recipients participated in the Walker Metal Products strike to justify further cuts to relief. Just after the strike, an anonymous editorial to the *Windsor Evening Star* urged "cooperation between workers and leaders," condemning the strike as the product of "agitators from the United States and abroad" who "want nothing more than to stir up controversy."[49] Mayor Wigle tried to harness the anger a number of Canadians had begun to express toward unemployed and immigrant strikers with a new series of welfare cuts and citizenship requirements. He also suggested disenfranchisement of both relief recipients and tenants on the grounds that they "do not have Windsor's best interests at heart."[50] Such initiatives pleased middle- to upper-class property owners, but a proposal to disenfranchise anyone on welfare or renting a home proved too extreme for many workers. In a city where industrial unions had no power, the Walker Metal Products strike represented an isolated incident and a clear failure. Thus, Mayor Wigle's efforts to cast the strikers as dangerous agitators held less political sway than in Detroit, where UAW-backed strikes had begun to empower the city's working class and reshape employer-worker relations in major automobile companies.

Indeed, capitalizing on the failed strike backfired for Wigle. The growing sense that Mayor Wigle stood only for the moneyed elite generated a backlash movement that joined Canadian, immigrant, employed, and unemployed workers in an effort to oust the mayor and replace him with his predecessor, Mayor David Croll. Disturbed by the developments in his city, Croll agreed to challenge Wigle, and he announced his candidacy for mayor with promises to defend "the small man" and redress the wrongs committed by Mayor Wigle "in the name of wealth and privilege." Speaking to the concerns of workers across Windsor, Croll assured voters that he would keep the Canadian border region from becoming a site of raids and welfare purges, "like our sister city of Detroit."[51] Such statements earned him the support and following of ordinary workers, who felt Canadian politicians from Ottawa to Windsor had forgotten them. Moreover, because the UAW still had little power in Canada, no movement had developed to oppose it.

Croll's political record indicated that if elected, he would be a staunch advocate for poor and working Windsorites. He self-identified as a "liberal labor" candidate and had the credentials to back up this claim. In 1936, he lost his position as minister of municipal affairs when he sided with the UAW in its strike against GM of Canada, leaving him free to run for his old seat.[52] As mayor from 1930 to 1934, he had rolled out an ambitious set of social programs that provided allowances for widows, pensions for the blind, vocational schools for children, and green space for city workers with the construction of Jackson Park. In his second mayoral run, Croll spoke out against campaigns in both Windsor and Detroit that labeled the poor as "lazy."[53] In so doing, he united a broad coalition of union members, immigrants, and middle-class voters who hoped for U.S. New Deal–style reforms in Canada.

Croll won the election by over five thousand votes, capturing the attention of cities across Canada and the United States. The *Winnipeg Free Press* labeled the fight between Wigle and Croll "a duel that aroused countrywide interest," while the *Toronto Star* called it a victory for labor.[54] Mayor Croll's opponents feared he would allow the UAW and communism to spread further into Canada. As far north as Sault Sainte Marie, Ontario newspapers ran headlines warning, "CIO Sympathizer is Elected Windsor Mayor." The remote mining town's *Evening News* disparaged Croll as a "stormy petrel of Ontario politics," warning that their town could succumb to "communist pressure imminently."[55] Across the border, the *Detroit Free Press* worried about what a "labor sympathizer" would mean for border trade, and newspapers from New York to Boston followed the comeback of Windsor's Jewish immigrant labor mayor.[56] Unlike in Detroit, where a conservative mayor drew on decades of nativism to cast immigrants and labor activists out of America's welfare state, Windsor workers struggling to unionize joined together in opposition to what they came to view as U.S.-style welfare purges. Thus, the relatively weak state of industrial labor galvanized workers and the unemployed in a movement against city elites.

Local drives for progressive reform foreshadowed and shaped a wider Canadian move toward immigrant inclusion that was accelerated by Canada's entrance into World War II. For instance, as local municipalities like

Windsor refused to send immigrants to Ottawa for deportation, the practice declined. Moreover, news of Adolf Hitler's deportations in Europe prompted the Canadian government to stop deporting immigrants almost entirely.[57] As tensions mounted across the Atlantic, Canadian newspapers disparaged Hitler's plan to deport ten thousand Polish Jews from Germany, condemning the Gestapo's insistence that Germany would "no longer tolerate foreigners without passports" in their nation.[58] When the Canadian Legion launched a campaign that demanded the deportation of "foreign agents" from Canada, Prime Minister William Lyon Mackenzie King urged caution.[59] "Canada and her people," he warned a roomful of Canadian Legionnaires, "ought not stoop to the level of Germany."[60] Though the nation had made a practice of deporting immigrants for dependence on the state in the early 1930s, Canadian officials distanced its involvement in any activity that might draw parallels between Canada and Germany's Third Reich.

The Canadian government did, however, experiment with excluding "enemy aliens" from welfare. Canada followed Great Britain's lead and joined the war in September 1939, prompting Ontario's Canadian Legion to push even harder for the deportation of "enemy Germans who feel allegiance to Germany, not Canada."[61] Toronto's Acting Mayor Frederick Conboy addressed the Canadian Legion's concerns by working with the Ontario government to bar "enemy aliens" from Germany and Austria from relief and including an oath to the king of England mandatory in all relief applications.[62]

But determining who constituted an "enemy alien" became a difficult task for relief administrators. Changing national borders in post–World War I Europe meant that many immigrants who were born in regions considered Germany or Austria in 1939 identified as a different nationality. The *Ottawa Journal* reported that administrators had trouble determining whether an immigrant born in Bukowana, a province in Romania that had been part of Germany at the time of the man's birth, was a German or a Romanian. Other candidates for "enemy alien" status demonstrated no allegiance to and little knowledge of the Axis powers. When administrators asked one Austrian receiving relief about the war, he wrinkled his brow and replied, "No war. I not been there." The administrator concluded that the man knew nothing about the war in Europe and was more preoccupied with feeding his family.[63] Uncertainty over who constituted an "enemy alien" made the program fall apart, and the Ontario government began to focus much of its attention on wartime preparation. By 1939, all Canadian immigrants, regardless of citizenship, qualified for local and federal welfare benefits.

Thus, World War II brought efforts to close Canada's borders, but it also allowed noncitizens to relax and focus on their work and families. Municipalities stopped deporting immigrants for claiming public relief and even allowed aliens to apply for city funding. Zachary Levin, a Jewish assembly line worker in Windsor who had immigrated from Poland in 1929, remarked that the war "stopped the raids and questions" from local authorities. No longer afraid he would be deported or dropped from welfare, Levin claimed he could finally "breathe easy" and settle into his Canadian life.[64]

Aliens and Welfare in Washington, D.C.

Noncitizens in the United States, on the other hand, faced legal exclusions that made their place in American society precarious. As in Canada, deportations decreased with the outbreak war in Europe, but in the United States, nativist congressmen who had spent the 1920s and most of the 1930s lobbying for harsh immigration and deportation laws began to focus on the place of legal aliens in an emerging welfare state. Drawing on familiar refrains charging new immigrants with everything from communism to mob crime to fomenting labor unrest, these politicians pointed to the growing power of industrial labor and a perceived spike in welfare fraud to bar legal aliens from the Works Progress Administration. This move set a precedent for excluding those without citizenship from welfare programs in the decades that followed. Thus, excluding foreigners, legal or not, began to emerge at the heart of America's interwar liberal order.

As in Canada, the Roosevelt administration curbed deportations with the war, but fears of espionage gave nativists a new charge to level at foreigners. In 1938, Martin Dies, a Democrat from Texas who thought the New Deal undermined American institutions, established the House on Un-American Activities Committee. The committee became known as the Dies Committee and relentlessly attacked the president and his cabinet, particularly Secretary of Labor Frances Perkins, with accusations that they pandered to communist organizations.[65] One of the Dies Committee's first major cases concerned the deportation of Harry Bridges, an Australian communist CIO leader living in San Francisco. In 1934, Bridges had led fifteen thousand dockworkers across the United States in a successful strike, making him a key target for CIO opponents. When the committee learned he had never filed for American citizenship, Representative Dies insisted that the Department of Labor deport Bridges for advocating violence against the state, and the case soon turned into a highly publicized trial over the rights of noncitizens and labor organizers in the United States.[66] Secretary Perkins took the opportunity to emphasize that the Roosevelt administration respected the rights of citizens and noncitizens alike. "The fact that Communists are not popular," she reminded Representative Dies, "does not justify us in deporting them without scrupulous regard for due process of law." As in Canada, news of deportations and forced migration from Nazi Germany circulated in the American press, and Secretary Perkins insisted that "due process" set the United States apart from dictatorships in Europe.[67]

Local labor advocates rushed to defend Harry Bridges. In Detroit, the UAW circulated pamphlets and petitioned Congress for the California organizer's release.[68] Detroit's Labor's Non-Partisan League, a group devoted to ensuring the rights of laborers and the reelection of President Roosevelt, insisted that the Dies Committee was nothing more than a "witch hunting committee" with the purpose of helping businesses and defeating progressivism.[69] Detroit labor organizers cheered when Secretary Perkins appointed Harvard Law School Dean James Landis to investigate the Australian, and after a thorough examination, Landis found Bridges innocent of any and all offenses.[70] The verdict in the Bridges deportation case reflected the Department of Labor's shift from punitive deportations, but it did not signal an end to antiforeigner hysteria.

For instance, the Roosevelt administration kept America's gates firmly shut to refugees in Europe. When news of Nazi Germany's *Kristallnacht* pogrom reached the United States in November 1938, President Roosevelt heeded the advice of Frances Perkins and indefinitely extended all German Jews' visitor visas in the United States. President Roosevelt then attempted to negotiate the resettlement of 500,000 Jews in the United States, Palestine, and other allied nations over a five-year period, but he faced an uncooperative Congress and an international response that ranged from apathetic to downright anti-Semitic. Cabinet advisors also warned him to avoid further alienating the Ku Klux Klan or angering his key base, the American labor movement, by changing immigration quotas. In 1938, Secretary Perkins and human rights organizations worked tirelessly to fill twenty thousand

German and Austrian quotas with Jews, but President Roosevelt dropped his vision of resettling hundreds of thousands of Jews across the world and maintained an isolationist stance.[71]

A conservative backlash to the 1937 economic recession meant immigration debates in Congress shifted from a focus on issues of deportation and refugees to the rights of noncitizens living within the boundaries of a growing welfare state.[72] Immigrants' participation in strikes and industrial unions made many politicians cast them as ungrateful and politically dangerous. Noncitizens with jobs were still welcome to pay into Social Security and even receive unemployment and Aid to Families with Dependent Children benefits, all entitlements linked to work and personal contribution.[73] However, many politicians objected to noncitizens' participation in the Works Progress Administration (WPA), the entitlement most connected to relief. Moreover, because the WPA required participants to work in public, local politicians became particularly concerned with visibly employing foreigners over citizens. These debates over alien WPA workers invariably centered on two themes: funding and union activism.

Senators from across the United States objected to the burden noncitizens placed on the American economy. As early as February 1938, the Senate began discussing amendments to WPA funding bills that barred aliens from federal work programs. Democratic Senator James Byrnes of South Carolina argued that because each WPA job cost sixty-five dollars a month, while direct aid cost around thirty dollars a month, "the privilege of work should not be extended to aliens." Senator Byrnes, a close friend and confidante of President Roosevelt, assured the president and Congress that he supported noncitizens "receiving direct aid" but that the WPA should be reserved for male breadwinners who were citizens. Senator Henry Ashurst from Arizona took a harsher stance and blamed the Department of Labor for becoming "remiss in the performance of its duty in connection with the deportation of criminal aliens." If the Department of Labor refused to deport aliens, Senator Ashurst argued that cutting off their benefits represented the next best solution.[74] Though they differed on precisely what should be done with noncitizens, Senators Ashurst and Byrnes agreed that regardless of legal status, they did not deserve the same benefits as American citizens, placing them in the category of dependent alongside women and children.

Purging noncitizens from the WPA held particular appeal in the rural Midwest, where white citizens who had little contact with immigrants resented the perceived money sent to foreigners in cities such as Chicago, Cleveland, and Detroit. In fact, congressmen from rural Michigan led the charge against aliens in the House, resting their arguments on the perceived foreignness of the labor movement in industrial centers across America. Clare Hoffman of Michigan's Fourth District, a rural region just north of Lansing, asserted, "The alien in this country is organizing to demand his rights, but he has no right to wreck our industries." He claimed that giving noncitizens federal benefits allowed them to "live in idleness and be supported by our taxpayers."[75] Representative George O'Brien from Kalamazoo, Michigan, agreed, arguing that "propaganda spread by outside radicals" had precipitated strikes in Lansing, Flint, and Detroit. Neither Senator O'Brien nor Hoffman represented voters from these cities, but their constituents resented tax hikes in their state as stories of urban sit-down strikes and hunger marches became front-page news.[76] Thus, the alien ban found support in rural regions with a history of Klan organizing, where residents blamed communism and foreigners for the rise of the UAW and, in some cases, America's economic decline.[77]

The alien ban's only vocal opponent in the House, Representative Vito Marcantonio (D-NY), likened the measure to Nazism. Marcantonio represented a New York district of Italians where many of his constituents did not have the money or language skills to apply for naturalization. Reminding his fellow congressmen of Hitler's cruelty, Marcantonio emphasized the hypocrisy of making naturalization difficult and costly, then punishing those who had not filed for citizenship. Linking welfare purges and deportations to Nazism had worked in Canada as the nation prepared for war, but the United States had yet to enter the war and congressmen worried more about Jewish refugees' threat to American jobs than abstract concerns about Hitlerism and democracy.[78]

Consequently, the alien ban sailed through the House and met minor opposition in the Senate. A number of senators worried that requiring a birth certificate or naturalization papers from WPA registrants would create chaos in an organization employing three million workers, so the two branches reached a compromise that required WPA workers to make "an affidavit of American citizenship" to continue their jobs.[79] On March 4, 1939, WPA Administrator Francis Harrington ordered all state administrators to drop noncitizens from the WPA regardless of their legal status. To ensure compliance, Harrington asked states to provide the names and numbers of barred aliens within the month.[80] As a result, over forty-five

Figure 10. Detroit Works Progress Administration workers repaving Grand River Avenue near Lothrop Street. Before 1939, thousands of these workers were not American citizens, and the very visible nature of the work caused local politicians and citizens to demand that the government purge foreigners from the federal work program. Courtesy of the Walter P. Reuther Library, Archives of Labor and Urban Affairs, Wayne State University.

thousand legal immigrants lost their WPA jobs, 60 percent of whom lived in the immigrant-heavy states of Ohio, Illinois, California, New York, and Michigan.[81]

The WPA Purge in Detroit

The WPA ruling affected hundreds of thousands of immigrants across the nation, but in Detroit, where Mayor Reading had already tasked a police squad with finding "welfare chiselers," the WPA purge proved particularly effective. Within four months, Detroit's city government, police, and immigration authorities cooperated to end the employment of over five thousand WPA workers.[82] Beyond those who lost jobs directly, the purge affected immigrants who hoped for a WPA position. By 1939, Detroit had about seventy thousand legal immigrants with no naturalization papers and another thirty thousand who had filed for their papers within the past two years, all of whom found themselves barred from the benefits of the state-sponsored relief program.[83] Moreover, a single WPA worker often supported an entire family, meaning that the purge cost hundreds of thousands of dependents their only means of support. In short, the measure crippled Detroit's ethnic communities, reinforcing nativist rhetoric that noncitizens brought nothing but poverty and dependence to the streets of American cities.

Local immigrants and their children implored the city and federal government to reconsider the ban. A twenty-year-old girl wrote a letter to the editor of the *Detroit News* under the name "a foreigner's daughter" that objected to her father's expulsion from his WPA position. She claimed that though he was not a citizen, her father was an upstanding worker who had resided in Detroit for thirty-five years. He spoke good English, complied with American laws, and therefore, she argued, deserved the same opportunity to support his wife and seven children afforded to those with full citizenship papers. She closed her letter by writing, "Most of us have foreigners for parents," reminding readers of the ubiquitous presence of immigrants in Detroit.[84] The letter emphasized the difficulties new restrictions placed on entire immigrant families, including those born in America.

Many native-born Detroiters welcomed the WPA purge. A self-pronounced "full-blooded American" named R.C.K. responded to the "foreigner's daughter" a couple days later with his own *Detroit News* letter that began, "It is surely wonderful how the patriotism of some people increases when it looks as if Uncle Sam has something to give them without too much effort on their part."[85] The *Detroit Free Press* also featured editorials from readers who insisted, "Our own should come first for jobs." Automobile worker Carl Wright scoffed at the suggestion that "these furniers [sic]" undertook the "dirty work of the past," insisting that "they received nice hard round American dollars for it."[86] The letters revealed the resentment many Detroiters still harbored toward the foreign born, a group that had become a convenient scapegoat for the unemployment caused by a complex financial crisis. Such sentiments were not confined to Detroit. In 1939, when Gallup asked the American public to cite the main causes of unemployment, "too many aliens working" made the top of national lists.[87]

Detroiters also claimed the alien ban would curb alien smuggling and the employment of illegal immigrants. Congress had officially barred undocumented immigrants from WPA work since 1936, and official reports suggested that the Great Depression had greatly reduced immigrant smuggling to Detroit.[88] Nevertheless, in a letter to the *Detroit Free Press*, a man who signed his name H.N. insisted, "Thousands of aliens are smuggled into this city every year" in search of "real American jobs." The alien ruling, he argued, would keep these "free loaders" from taking the federal jobs meant to get American citizens back on track.[89] H.N.'s letter revealed the extent to which fear of illegal immigrants persisted into the New Deal era and also the tendency to conflate unnaturalized legal immigrants with their undocumented counterparts.

The alien ban meant that legal immigrants without citizenship faced federal restrictions that had once only applied to the undocumented, pushing even legal immigrants toward poverty. Detroit resident Mrs. William Hammond expressed her exasperation with the federal government in a letter that recounted how her husband had been "crippled from a factory accident" at fifty-five and, as an Irish citizen, had lost his WPA job painting Detroit street signs. Because automobile factories rarely hired men over forty, she wrote that it would be impossible for him to find a good job. In closing, she reminded WPA authorities, "I am getting terribly ill, he is crippled, and Xmas will come soon."[90] Mrs. Hammond's letter emphasized the desperation and resentment many immigrants had begun to feel at suddenly being categorized alongside undocumented immigrants and denied benefits. In this case, a woman who, as a female worker, could not earn the wages to support her family found herself pleading with the federal government on behalf of her disabled husband.

The WPA ruling encouraged police and welfare administrators to scour Detroit's immigrant neighborhoods in ways that echoed the deportation raids of the 1920s. While by 1939, Detroit's foreign-born population had decreased to 25 percent of the city's total population, in many regions, the percentage remained much higher. In one ethnic, west side neighborhood 64 percent of residents over the age of twenty-five were born outside the United States. Of these, 51 percent were aliens, meaning they had not taken final steps toward naturalization.[91] In such regions, Detroit police officers knocked on doors and visited worksites to question potential WPA violators. Most of these individuals could prove legal residency and, therefore, could not be deported. However, legal aliens did face public humiliation when they were discharged from federal work programs. Frick Widdas, a Scotsman who had lived in Detroit since 1908, supported himself as a WPA book binder until welfare administrators checked his workplace and his supervisor fired him on the spot. Widdas promised he was a "patriotic American citizen," but his declaration made no difference, and the Scot turned over his badge in what he called a "humiliating process of removal."[92]

Not content to let thousands lose their jobs, the UAW stepped forward in defense of alien Detroiters. One early evening in June 1939, George Addes, secretary-treasurer of the UAW, voiced the position of the union on WJR radio station. Speaking to a wide audience, Addes lamented the "Detroit workers, most of them with wives and families," who were "cut off from their only means of support" by federal and local antialien drives. A child of Lebanese immigrants himself, Addes felt the WPA purge at a personal level and charged the government with "selecting the people whom they thought were best qualified to starve" and determining that "the right to live depended on the location of one's birth."[93]

But because Congress had sold the purge partly as a way to check the power of labor unions, local police and politicians paid little mind to UAW protest. In fact, the Detroit police took every opportunity to denounce protesters as communist radicals. When the UAW held a meeting in conjunction with the communist Civil Rights Commission to discuss the unfairness of new WPA regulations, police informants seized the moment to label the protest as one of "the typical one of Jews, aliens, foreigners, and communists." Police assured their superiors and Mayor Reading that UAW protest meant the WPA purge was working and that foreign-born strikers would soon lose their access to government jobs.[94]

In a city that was still rife with nativism and crippled by economic depression, the UAW faced an uphill battle. Nevertheless, the union continued to fight for the economic rights of aliens. One UAW pamphlet entitled "The Aliens Are Persecuted!" reminded Detroiters that "many thousands of men and women in this country are good tax paying citizens, have been in the country for some 20 years or more, have worked and done constructive jobs, and have raised children as good American citizens." Emphasizing that many citizenship issues arose from simple misunderstandings, the UAW claimed, "Often [immigrants] are too busy acting as good citizens to be aware of the fact that they should legalize their status."[95] The great lengths UAW activists went to emphasize the desirability, hard work, and patriotism of noncitizens, however, revealed the intensity and persistence of antialien sentiments in America's Motor City.

City newspapers reinforced connections between aliens, laziness, and cheating the new government system. The *Detroit News* profiled Scottish-born Alva Baxter in an article entitled "WPA Laborer Is Too Lazy to Lean on Spade." Baxter was a shoveler on a WPA project, and according to his ex-wife, when he worked on the WPA earning $13.95 a week, "he'd report for work then come to my house till it was time to check out." Baxter defended his actions by claiming, "I didn't do any worse than the others. They all loafed around gas stations." Such reports made it seem that WPA workers, particularly foreigners, performed little work on useless jobs. After listening to Baxter's case, Judge Vincent Brennan agreed by saying, "This seems to bear out reports we have heard concerning WPA workers."[96]

Stories of fraud also helped solidify the association between aliens and welfare cheating. In 1939, the *Detroit Free Press* profiled a sensational case involving Michael Fedytnik, head of the Michigan Steamship Agency, who had for years conspired with Welfare Department employees John Kock-wicz and Joseph Mowatt to arrange the voluntary removal of Detroit aliens. But instead of returning these impoverished individuals to Europe, the men pocketed the government's money and gave participating immigrants a cut.[97] During the trial, fourteen aliens "found on the relief rolls and WPA after the government had paid for their transportation back to their native lands" testified against Fedytnik, Kockwicz, and Mowatt. Judge John Maher found the defendants, two of whom had conspicuously eastern European names, guilty, charging them with defrauding the state and costing the department nearly two thousand dollars.[98]

With the WPA closed to aliens, Detroiters without citizenship found themselves left with few options. They could seek direct aid from the city, and indeed, in the months after the ban, noncitizens flooded the Detroit Welfare Bureau with applications. By May, just under five thousand aliens had their relief petitions approved by the Welfare Bureau, meaning one-fifth of all welfare recipients in the city had no citizenship.[99] The sharp rise made welfare officials fear that the city would go bankrupt, and they began to slow the distribution process to conserve resources.[100] Thus, immigrants found themselves waiting months for small city allowances of milk and coal that were hardly enough to sustain a family.

Regardless of relief amounts, many immigrants hesitated before apply-ing for direct aid. John Gorsky, a Polish alien, reported that working for the WPA had given him a sense of pride, while "going on the dole" made him feel like a failure and, given welfare's association with dependent women, perhaps emasculated. Moreover, Gorsky was afraid that registering for city welfare might make him a candidate for deportation if laws changed.[101] Gorsky had reason to be concerned. Gorsky may have remembered how deportation drives in Windsor, Canada, sent thousands of workers back to Europe in the early 1930s. And by 1939, Michigan's State Relief Commission had begun lobbying the Lansing legislature to have all noncitizens on Michigan relief rolls deported immediately. State Relief Commissioner Louis Mariani insisted that the idea was illegal, but rumors and news coverage still made many noncitizens wary of signing their names to direct aid requests.[102]

Aliens' next option was to apply for full citizenship. When Detroit's Department of Welfare recorded a rise in requests for direct aid, personnel began to encourage those dropped from WPA jobs to apply for citizenship so they could regain their positions.[103] In 1939, Detroit's Legal Aid Bureau stepped in to guide aliens through the naturalization process. The Bureau instructed aliens to take out their first papers at the city courthouse and helped them verify acceptable documents to prove they had lived in the United States for the five years required for final naturalization.[104]

Helping immigrants through complicated paperwork allowed organizations like the Young Women's Christian Association (YWCA) and the International Institute to draw on an established tradition of Americanization, which in the 1910s and 1920s had focused on social uplift and assimilating immigrants.[105] Their new efforts, however, approached naturalization as a way to shift immigrants eligible from city welfare rolls to federal work programs.[106] The Detroit Welfare Department even attempted to pay for the naturalization fees of aliens as part of its relief program, arguing that a one-time payment of $10 cost the city less than the monthly welfare checks many immigrants received during the Depression. When the city asked the state of Michigan to help with fees, the State Welfare Commission refused to fund the practice. Louis Mariani, the member of the commission in charge of Detroit, asked rhetorically, "Do people starve for lack of paper; are they in better health for lack of being naturalized?" Mariani encouraged the state to reject Detroit's petition, reinforcing the idea that welfare existed not to provide social uplift or better people's lives but to keep them from starving in the streets.[107] Moreover, Mariani emphasized a growing trend that insisted no extra state benefits should go to those without citizenship.

Proving legal entry and time of residence in the United States was difficult for many immigrants. The Legal Aid Bureau's Glen Munro claimed a large number of aliens, most of them Poles, had no record of their crossing into the United States and, therefore, could not prove they had entered legally. Munro cited the case of a particular Polish man who traveled to the United States in 1905 but could not remember the name of the boat on which he came.[108] Similarly, Karl Kaufman, a German-born Detroiter who immigrated to the United States in 1913 with his parents and two sisters, claimed he did not apply for citizenship because he thought he was covered under his father's naturalization. Evidently in New York, misinformed immigration workers told his father that the entire family would receive citizenship under one application. But because Karl and his sister Fanny were over twenty-one when their father filed for naturalization, his citizenship did not transfer. This detail had not mattered to Karl, who lived and worked in Detroit's factories thinking he was a citizen, but when the Welfare Department demanded his papers, the oversight meant he lost his WPA job.[109] Similar petitions for lost, misfiled, or misinformed citizenship situations poured into the federal welfare office. Swamped administrators responded with a form letter, lamenting the "many precisely similar inquiries and limited personnel" designated to carry out citizenship paper requests.[110] In an era of inconsistent recordkeeping on land borders and missing ship records, such immigrants had little beyond their own word to prove the legality of their presence in America.

Excluded from federal relief programs, many noncitizens turned to illegal work, particularly in the liquor industry.[111] Despite the end of Prohibition, a market for inexpensive, untaxed liquor continued the production of unauthorized alcohol in homemade stills. In fact, the Detroit press noted a spike in illegal liquor production in 1939, charging "foreign neighborhoods" with distilling gallons of unregulated whiskey and moonshine for distribution across the city.[112] For instance, Casmir Fronceck, an unnaturalized Pole ineligible for the WPA, began to distill and distribute illegal alcohol. In 1939, Michigan police raided Fronceck's boarding house and found a fifteen-gallon still, thirty gallons of whiskey, and one-half pint of illegal moonshine behind the bed he shared with four other Polish immigrants. When Judge Arthur Tuttle questioned Fronceck's decisions, the bootlegger shrugged and said he had come to Michigan to work in sugar beets and chicory. When farm work dried up with the Depression, he supported himself digging ditches for the WPA. The 1939 alien ruling meant Froncek lost his only means of support, and instead of returning to Poland, he turned to illegal distilling, a move he said was his "only chance to make a life."[113] While he had a clean record during his early years in America, campaigns labeling foreigners welfare chiselers or criminals prompted the federal government to exclude Fronceck from work programs, a move that, ironically, turned the Polish immigrant toward crime.

Local judges reinforced the link between foreigners and crime, thereby justifying and solidifying their exclusion from the American welfare state. Arthur Tuttle, the judge who presided over Casmir Fronceck's case, drew on his own background as a naturalization judge to mete out strict sentences that emphasized the immorality of prohibition violations. The judge worked as a key founder and member of the Americanization Committee of Detroit throughout the 1910s and presided over Detroit's naturalization court in the 1920s, where he emphasized the importance of not only becoming American on paper but also adopting key moral traits such as Christian piety, cleanliness, and sobriety. As an adjudicator of naturalization cases, Tuttle considered an immigrant's legal marital status, history of sexual (mis)conduct, and adherence to mainstream political norms to determine his or her loyalty to the United States.[114] Tuttle practiced little sympathy after the WPA purge, when cases involving unemployed aliens and bootlegging appeared in his courtroom by the dozens. For instance, when Beitler Gottfried, a seventy-five-year-old Russian alien and widower, was caught with a ten-gallon copper still and several bottles of moonshine, he faced Judge Tuttle for sentencing. Gottfried was ineligible for government-sponsored work, but he told the judge he had to find some way to repay his cousin, who generously fed him and let him sleep in a back room of his home. The whiskey, which he claimed to share only with his family and neighbors, allowed him to make a little money. Though it was clear the Russian produced a limited amount of alcohol, Judge Tuttle rebuked Gottfried and sentenced him to two years' probation, a punishment that would make it nearly impossible for the elderly man to secure a job. The judge reasoned that a "hearty punishment" would serve as a "warning to other men considering immoral acts."[115]

Judge Tuttle's sentences tended to ignore circumstances all together and drew on Detroit's history of policing and deportation in the 1920s to presuppose the innate criminality of foreigners. When police caught John Kryczka, a Polish immigrant who ran a small bootlegging business in the city's Polish West Side, Tuttle ignored the fact that Kryczka had worked steadily for Briggs Body Company and only began distilling after losing his position to citizenship regulations. Instead of considering circumstances, Tuttle stressed the Pole's criminality, stating, "This is not only a big, bad bootlegger, but he is an all-around bad man." After having established Kryczka's innate criminal tendencies, Tuttle sentenced him to two years of imprisonment.[116] Many of these "basement bootleggers," as they came to be called, only began bootlegging when new citizenship requirements barred them from more legitimate work. Nevertheless, Judge Tuttle portrayed them as inveterate criminals, suggesting that foreigners tended naturally toward bootlegging and other crimes.[117]

But during the late 1930s, many immigrants turned toward petty crime only to support their families. Seventeen-year-old Edward Kaminski, a child of Polish Detroiters, landed in the Detroit Police Department after being apprehended stealing coal, lumber, and lathes in a lumberyard. Investigation revealed that Kaminski had stolen the supplies to repair the single-frame Hamtramck home where he lived with his parents that welfare service workers admitted was in a "poor state of repair." When his father had lost his job due to citizenship requirements, Kaminski said he turned to theft, a choice that earned him a twenty-five-dollar fine and sixty days in prison.[118] Similar cases dot Detroit's police and judicial records of the late 1930s, suggesting that as full citizens took federally funded work, those without papers and even their children turned to theft in an effort to feed and house their families.[119]

While the New Deal offered opportunities and benefits to thousands of Americans, it also made citizenship a requirement for participation in a growing welfare state. New exclusions meant noncitizen workers joined their undocumented family members, neighbors, and friends in underpaid, part-time employment. And while these workers were not deportable, they were certainly exploitable. Mike Chaykoswki, a Ukrainian who entered the United States before 1924 immigration restrictions yet never completed his final citizenship papers, lost his job at Ford in 1933. For the next several years, he bounced between Hudson, Briggs, Fisher, and Dodge plants, always taking jobs on a contract basis for what he considered "low pay." For two months, he held a position in the foundry at Peninsula Stove Company, a division known for its hot fumes, molten iron, and lack of regulations. Excluded from federal benefits, the only choice for Chaykoswki and countless others became this part-time contract work in the most dangerous jobs across the city.[120]

Chaykoswki, Kaminski, and Kryczka's turn from gainful employment to federal work to Detroit's criminal underground revealed the constrained world in which noncitizens could operate. As the New Deal reversed harsh deportations and encouraged union growth in Washington, D.C., the left-ward turn incited a nativist backlash that was perhaps unsurprising when considering the enduring presence of the Ku Klux Klan and Black Legion in Michigan. Despite many immigrant Detroiters' desperate financial straits and reluctance to join industrial unions, local politicians used the growing power of the UAW and concern over welfare cheating to cast recent immigrants as either ungrateful strikers or dishonest manipulators of federal generosity and tolerance. In contrast, Canada's relatively hardline stance on immigrants and unions made local citizens more likely to view impoverished foreigners with sympathy. Thus, the federal policies that helped curb deportations and allowed industrial unions to organize ethnic workers also generated nationwide momentum for curtailing benefits to immigrants without citizenship. Establishing citizenship as the bar for inclusion in an expanding welfare state cast those without it as second-class residents in American society.

Wartime Registration Internment

When America entered World War II, a history of conflating "foreignness" and criminality at the local level helped legitimize federal efforts against noncitizens. During the war, federal policymakers easily transitioned from denying noncitizens welfare to registering and imprisoning groups perceived as "foreigners" and, therefore, disloyal to American interests.

Decades of nativist immigration policy culminated in the Alien Registration Act of 1940. Labor Secretary Frances Perkins had stalled the implementation of national immigrant registration for several years, but rising concerns over wartime espionage pressured the president to sign the act by the end of June. The Registration Act contained two basic parts. The first enacted strict punishment for subversive political activity, and the second required all noncitizens to register and be fingerprinted with the federal government. Aliens would be required to carry a registration card at all times and had to notify the INS in writing of any change of address.[121] In a speech broadcast over the radio, President Roosevelt insisted, "The registration and identification of approximately three and one-half million aliens who are now within our borders do not carry with them any stigma or implication of hostility towards those who, while they may not be citizens, are loyal to this country and its institutions."[122] But by insisting that registration would not stigmatize the foreign born, the president only reminded noncitizens of their outsider status. Between late August and December 26, 1940, over 3.6 million foreign born people over the age of fourteen waited in long lines outside local post offices, where they registered their names and answered a set of questions about their criminal and political activities in the United States.[123] And despite the fact that President Roosevelt signed the law at the federal level, immigrants learned about registration in local newspapers and filed into long post office lines in cities like Detroit, New York, and Los Angeles.

Impending war presented the perfect moment for the passage of the 1940 Alien Registration Act, and the momentum generated by over fifty years of antialien legislation made it nearly impossible for a Democratic Congress and president to oppose the bill.[124] By the late 1930s, noncitizens had become a major concern to many Americans. In 1939, fear of foreign spies caused Congress to consider over one hundred antialien bills, including one to curtail immigration by over 90 percent, another to halt it all together, and thirty-eight demanding alien registration.[125] Perhaps the most drastic, a bill introduced by Senator Kenneth McKellar, a Democrat from Tennessee, required that aliens register every six months and face deportation if they did not become citizens within six years.[126] Amid mounting pressure to take a hard line on immigration, President Roosevelt vetoed several bills aimed at making deportation easier but finally relented by transferring the Immigration and Naturalization Service (INS) from the Department of Labor to the Department of Justice. This presidential directive aligned the policies and practices of police and Border Patrol in cities like Detroit to federal immigration policy, officially changing immigration from a labor issue to one concerning public safety and crime.[127]

Registration advocates drew on the previous two decades of associating European immigrants with illegal entry, political radicalism, and welfare fraud to gain support. Representative Samuel Dickstein, a Democrat from New York, chaired the House Immigration Committee, testified that he had sources claiming "well-organized groups were smuggling 'millions' of aliens into the United States annually," and insisted that registration represented the only way to end the practice.[128] In Senate hearings over the bill's passage, Senator Robert Reynolds, a Democrat from North Carolina, presented the Senate a petition from the Veterans of Foreign Wars (VFW) reminding his colleagues that aliens had been involved in sabotage during World War I and had a robust tradition of political radicalism.[129] Registration, the VFW reasoned, represented a way to curb the actions of "dangerous revolutionary groups of alien extraction." Senator Theodore Bilbo, a Democrat from Mississippi, agreed that alien registration could deter communist aliens who "attempt to destroy us." Beyond fearmongering, Senator Bilbo echoed the refrain that had sounded in Depression-era cities for years. He presented the Senate an American Legion report suggesting that registration might help "aliens be taken off the relief rolls."[130] Those in favor of registration positioned the law as a way to stop the threat they perceived illegal, communist, and dependent immigrants brought to the United States. So when President Roosevelt assured aliens that registration would only "preserve and build up the loyalty and confidence of those aliens within our borders who desire to be faithful to its principles," many foreigners would have found it difficult to overlook the nativist underpinnings of the new law or trust a Democratic Party that, in this era, comprised southern statesman clinging to laws promoting segregation and Anglo-Saxon supremacy.[131]

Leftist activists decried the new measure. The ACLU and the National Council for the Protection of Foreign Born Workers viewed the act as a major blow to the civil liberties of America's most vulnerable inhabitants.[132] Jack Harrison Pollack, a prominent freelance writer and press liaison officer on alien registration in the Department of Justice, called the law the manifestation of a nativist "germ [that] refused to die" and the "most far reaching legislation affecting aliens in the history of the United States."[133] In an article in the *American Scholar* entitled "America Registers Her Immigrants," he commended Roosevelt's efforts to reassure immigrants, but he maintained that "the registration process needlessly terrified countless aliens, young and old, many of whom feared dismissal by unsympathetic employers—or worse, deportation and separation from their families."[134] And indeed, tens of thousands of noncitizens were terrified registration might represent a first step in a series of wartime antialien measures. The *New York Herald Tribune* confirmed that on the first day of registration, a "stampede of frightened aliens" crowded into post offices in Manhattan, Pelham, and the Bronx.[135]

Prominent progressive white women, the first lady among them, also came out in opposition to registration. The General Federation of Women's Clubs issued a statement that called registration the "regimentation of American democracy." Signers included First Lady Eleanor Roosevelt; Dr.

Mary Woolley, president of Mount Holyoke College; Dr. Mildred McAffe, president of Wellesley College; Dr. Marion Parks, president of Bryn Mawr College; University of Chicago's Dr. Grace Abbot; and novelist Fannie Hurst. Drawing on a tradition of women's civic engagement, these women lobbied the president and Congress, but their efforts represented a small minority and ultimately failed.[136]

The language of patriotism made 95 percent of Americans support alien registration, and ultimately, even labor and ethnic organizations backed the measure.[137] Despite the fact that registration would affect many of their members, the UAW and other CIO-affiliated unions stayed silent on the measure. In the first weeks of registration, prominent ethnic organizations across the country stepped in to help. The American Jewish Committee, American Jewish Congress, B'nai Brith, and Jewish Welfare Board ran informational sessions and published literature on registration for distribution to members in Boston, Chicago, and Philadelphia.[138] In Detroit, radio station WJR's "Polish Hour" offered a special foreign-language program on how to register at the post office.[139] In these publications and broadcasts, Jewish, Russian, and Polish Americans insisted that registration would help their ethnicities become accepted as legal, law-abiding Americans.

Ethnic Americans began peddling registration as a patriotic way for noncitizens to show their loyalty to the United States. Charles Boyer, a Frenchman and romantic lead in a number of 1930s films, publicized his own experience registering at the Hollywood post office. Boyer released photographs of a post office official taking his fingerprints as he stood next to his wife, British actress Pat Paterson, assuring Americans that registration protected the "preciousness of their democratic heritage." In a press release for the News Enterprise Association (NEA) Service, Boyer urged "bewildered aliens and naturalized citizens" to embrace the "American way of life" and prove their loyalty. And indeed, news that the romantic lead from popular films like *The Garden of Allah* (1936), *Algiers* (1938), and *Love Affair* (1939) was also subject to new regulations may have calmed certain noncitizens.[140]

In Detroit, the city with America's third largest alien population, registration proceeded smoothly.[141] By December 27, 1940, the city's postmaster, Roscoe B. Hurston, announced that 174,408 aliens had registered in the city, three thousand of whom had scrambled to post offices on the registration deadline of December 26. Hurston warned noncitizens that failure to register came with a one thousand dollar fine or six months in jail, but certainly thousands of undocumented Detroiters had certainly stayed as far from the post office as possible.[142] To those without papers, the *Port Huron Times Herald* published a statement issued by Attorney General Robert Jackson urging them to come forward to face what he promised would be a "square deal." But without details or evidence, few illegal immigrants volunteered their information.[143] Most were terrified local police and inspectors would sign their immediate deportation warrants, but wholesale deportations of Europeans never came to pass, and the Alien Registration Act marked the beginning and the end of white ethnic groups' concerns with policing.[144]

In December 1941, Congress declared war on Germany, Italy, and Japan, causing renewed suspicion toward foreigners from enemy nations. But two years before a formal declaration of war, President Roosevelt had designated the FBI the group that would investigate espionage and sabotage in the United States. A large part of their investigation centered on ethnic Europeans, particularly German and Italian nationals who were suspected to have affiliations with fascist Europe.[145] As in so many moments of panic over noncitizens, the FBI looked to Canada, where, in 1940, the Royal Canadian Mounted Police (RCMP) had registered sixteen thousand "enemy aliens" and designated a special branch to surveil them.[146] In the spring of 1941, the RCMP coordinated the internment of 847 Germans, 800 Italians, and several hundred communist and Nazi Canadians, a small number compared to these groups' relative population within Canada.[147] Nevertheless, FBI Director J. Edgar Hoover thought interning European spies was an excellent idea, and in the first years of the war, the FBI set up relocation and internment camps across the United States, with the largest camps established in North Dakota and New Mexico. Agents interrogated and held 11,000 Germans and 4,000 Italians throughout the course of the war.[148] FBI investigations drew on the policies and tactics developed by INS and U.S. Border Patrol officers on America's northern border, where enforcers had spent two decades investigating undocumented and communist aliens.

European internment camps also relied on INS officers' local expertise to manage the practical, day-to-day aspects of internment. After all, no one knew better where particular immigrants lived, worked, and worshiped than the officials who had spent the previous two decades policing them. In Detroit, the FBI put INS Director John Zurbrick, the same man who ran deportation drives in the 1920s and 1930s, in charge of the "temporary detention phase" of interning enemy Europeans. On October 10, 1941, two months before the United States officially entered the war, Special Assistant to the Attorney General Lemuel Schofield wrote to Director Zurbrick, placing him in charge of a temporary Detroit facility that he estimated would accommodate sixty new German and Italian "enemies" each month.[149] By December 17, Director Zurbrick had investigated and incarcerated fifty-seven Germans, twenty-two Italians, and two Argentines.[150] Most internees were Nazi or Mussolini sympathizers, and reports suggest that they were treated well and usually were only kept in the camps for several months at a time. After their internment, "enemy Europeans" were released on parole and watched closely by INS inspectors and local police, who reported their activities directly to J. Edgar Hoover. By July 1944, the Detroit INS was monitoring just over one hundred fifty former internees, most of whom were German or Italian.[151] Director Hoover's use of local INS agencies drew on the experience and methods of officials in local districts like Detroit to monitor aliens thought to be subversive.

But instead of inciting resentment and fear of German and Italian Americans, European incarceration was isolated and rare, representing the INS's last major involvement in policing European immigrants. European internment is often overlooked, and perhaps rightly so, because it paled when compared to the incarceration of the 120,000 Japanese and Japanese Americans living on America's West Coast. And while all people of Japanese ancestry living in the United States were considered potential enemies, American policymakers and the press were careful to differentiate between "enemies" and their ethnic American counterparts, a nuance never afforded to Japanese Americans. Thus, when President Roosevelt signed Executive Order 9066 and relocated ethnically Japanese men, women, and children to internment camps in the interior of the United States, local INS inspectors never granted them the parole or freedoms that had been given to the small number of European internees.[152] By the end of World War II, Japanese and soon Mexicans and other nonwhite immigrants became associated with foreignness, crime, and political subversion.

Between World War I and World War II, however, new laws assigned the category of "the foreigner" or "the alien," constructing this person as someone fundamentally distinct from "the citizen" and with a disadvantaged relationship to the welfare state and the world of labor. While this process is often obscured by studies that focus on immigration policy in Washington, D.C., examining the dynamic borderland straddling Detroit,

Michigan, and Windsor, Canada, reveals how local politicians, police, employers, and activists defined the process of marginalizing and excluding "the foreigner" through daily acts. Local and, considering Detroit's relationship to Canada, transnational decisions dictated where Border Patrol sent police, who foremen employed, when immigrants could cross the border, and what sort of welfare they could expect when they reached either side. In interwar Detroit, the category of "foreigner" largely stigmatized southern and eastern Europeans, but after World War II, as these immigrants gained access to housing and benefits, new immigrants on America's southern border faced reputations as smugglers, welfare cheaters, and threats to local economies. Ultimately, by expanding benefits and opportunities to citizens and denying them to noncitizens, America's New Deal set a precedent that would write the exclusion of foreigners and those perceived as foreign into an emerging liberal order.

The Legacy of Restrictive Immigration

Unauthorized immigration continues to be a flashpoint in U.S. politics in the twenty-first century. In 2016, Donald Trump won the U.S. presidential election with promises to build a "great, great wall on our southern border."[1] In a campaign replete with nativism, Trump claimed a border wall would keep out the drugs, crime, and rapists crossing the border from Mexico.[2] Beyond closing the physical border, Trump also promised that the moment he took office, he would deport three to four million immigrants.[3] Despite criticism from politicians on both sides of the aisle, Donald Trump's hard-line immigration policies appealed to many white voters, including those in Michigan, who feared an influx of foreigners threatened the "American way of life."[4] On November 8, 2016, millions of Americans signed off on Trump's nativist policies by electing him the forty-fifth president of the United States.

Once in office, President Trump continued to attack immigrants and foreigners. In his very first month, Trump signed Executive Order 13769, banning immigrants from seven predominantly Muslim nations in the name of "protecting the nation from foreign terrorist entry."[5] Just a few days later, in his first State of the Union Address, the president connected undocumented immigrants to criminality by pointing to parents whose son had been "viciously murdered by an illegal immigrant gang member."[6] Trump's contention of a connection between Muslims and terrorism and Latin Americans and gangs resonated with a segment of Americans, exposing the nativist undercurrents that persist in American society. Indeed, in June 2017, as many as 45 percent of polled Americans reported they thought immigration made the "crime situation" worse in the United States.[7]

Bootlegged Aliens has demonstrated that Trump's worldview is neither new nor particularly surprising. Instead, it fits into a long narrative of U.S. nativism that dates to early immigration restrictions and became—and has remained—embedded in discussions about crime, the economy, and welfare. Nearly one hundred years before Donald Trump proposed selective immigration laws that would privilege "merit-based immigration," Senator David Reed introduced immigration quotas that he claimed would preserve "the Nordic integrity of America."[8] In both cases, federal leaders promoted regulations that privileged immigrants from a particular nation, deeming all others "foreign" and, therefore, undesirable. Like the framers of the 1924 Immigration Act, who cast southern and eastern Europeans as immigrants from poor nations predisposed to crime, in 2018, President Trump disparaged America's diversity lottery program for privileging immigrants from the "shithole countries" of Haiti and those in Africa.[9] Indeed, for over a century, policymakers have waged racially charged campaigns against certain Europeans, Latin Americans, and Africans on the grounds that their nations of origins were deemed too underdeveloped to provide immigrants deserving of American citizenship.

While federal discourse matters, local border politics has always shaped the lives of individual immigrants and wider immigration policy. Just as local immigration directors like John Zurbrick launched a "deportation war" on the Detroit-Windsor border in the late 1920s, local law enforcement, politicians, and judges on the U.S. border with Mexico have helped craft hard-line immigration policies in the twenty-first century. For instance, just outside Phoenix, Arizona, Maricopa County sheriff Joe Arpaio detained undocumented immigrants in what he called a "concentration camp" from 1993 to 2017. When the Justice Department accused him of "racially profiling Latinos on his patrols and denying prisoners basic human rights in jails," he laughed and reminded leaders, "I still keep getting re-elected."[10] Also at the local level, when city mayors across the Southwest promised not to investigate the immigration status of its residents, judges in Texas and Arizona issued rulings that banned these "sanctuary cities" and allowed police to check the immigration status of the individuals they detained.[11] Thus, in the twenty-first century, the practices and policies of local leaders continue to shape the meaning of immigration laws. While in the 1920s, ethnic Europeans faced profiling and harassment on America's northern border, by the twentieth-century, Sheriff Joe Arpaio, a second-generation Italian himself, policed immigrants with brown skin on the U.S. border with Mexico.[12]

In the World War II years, ethnic Europeans like Sherriff Joe Arpaio's Italian-born parents shed the popular perception of their ties to illegal immigration, crime, and foreignness. These Americans benefited from the state's efforts to recognize particular types of European diversity. Throughout the war, government publications celebrated America as a place where Protestant, Catholic, and Jewish immigrants came together, a move meant to set Americans apart from the homogeneity espoused by European fascism.[13] Moreover, state officials aimed patriotic wartime propaganda disproportionately at ethnic and African American workers, a move that, historian Gary Gerstle notes, made them feel accepted and tied to the wartime project. By the end of the war, 12 percent of America's population had served in the military, meaning that hundreds of thousands of immigrants had brothers, aunts, and cousins serving abroad. Thus, participating in a collective wartime project brought thousands of ethnic European Americans closer to acceptance, distancing the concerns and stigmas about foreignness that had dominated local politics in the prior decades.[14]

For white ethnics, postwar America was marked by steps toward consensus and unity. Historian Wendy Wall has argued that this development was not a natural result of the war but a political project undertaken by businesses, interfaith activists, government officials, and cultural elites.[15] In the postwar era, ethnic groups and cultural elites promoted "cultural pluralism and a unifying American way" as a uniquely American construct. And throughout the era, the specter of communism and fascism provided a foil for America's "nation of immigrants."[16] During the war, even the Congress of Industrial Organizations (CIO) had begun touting "an American Way," a political project that allowed predominantly white Jews, Catholics, and Protestants to come together in a "tri-faith" American identity.[17] By the Cold War era, this tri-faith construction united white ethnic and Protestant Americans, while racial divisions between black, white, and brown Americans became the dominant fault lines in American society.[18]

Throughout this era of supposed consensus, however, immigrant Americans continued to resent the quotas that barred their relatives from immigrating to the United States. In the 1940s, immigration advocacy groups successfully lobbied for the repeal of certain exclusions against Chinese, Indians, and Filipinos, efforts that resulted in the War Brides Act of 1945, the Alien Fiancées and Fiancés Act of 1946, and the Displaced Persons Act of 1948.[19] But what Jewish and Italian organizations really wanted was a repeal of quotas against southern and eastern Europeans. When restrictionists in Congress proposed the McCarran-Walter bill in 1950, a measure that allowed a small number of Asians and refugees entrance in exchange for retaining the quota system and tightening exclusion, ethnic organizations prepared their protest. The American Jewish Congress claimed the bill proved that American policymakers had no intention of living up to their postwar promises of ethnic acceptance and unity. Italian groups also lobbied for the repeal of their quotas, while the National Catholic Welfare Conference remained neutral yet refused to testify in favor of the bill, a clear sign that the Catholic organization felt slighted by quotas against nationalities associated with Catholicism. The CIO, a labor organization with a large percentage of southern and eastern European members, criticized the bill as divisive and unfair toward groups who were supposed to be accepted as American workers.[20] Despite ethnic protest and President Harry Truman's veto, a House and Senate override passed the Immigration and Nationality Act in 1952. The new law confirmed to many Jewish and Catholic Americans that they would continue to be labeled "foreigners" or not-quite "citizens" into the postwar era of supposed tri-faith unity and diversity. In the wake of the 1952 law, President Truman established the Commission on Immigration and Naturalization that comprised white ethnic religious (particularly Jewish) organizations, organized labor, and a handful of native-born Protestant liberals who took on the task of recommending new immigration policy.[21]

Consequently, many ethnic Americans clung to European identities and remained politically active even as they moved to suburbs and participated in postwar consumer culture. Italian Americans, in particular, felt that continued restrictions against their groups served as evidence that they were valued less than Anglo-Saxon Americans in postwar America.[22] Thus, during the 1950s and 1960s, Italians used the politics, culture, and ideology of the Cold War to push for incremental immigration reform, a movement that finally resulted in the 1965 repeal of quotas. The American Committee on Italian Migration (ACIM) and the National Catholic Welfare Conference (NCWC) both argued that family reunification, accepting refugees, and admitting more immigrants from European nations would improve America's image in the world and stem the rising tide of communism.[23] In 1965, President Lyndon Johnson signed the Immigration and Naturalization Act, repealing the quota system that had shaped American politics and ethnic life for over forty years.

During World War II, new labor and migration patterns also shifted policymakers' attention to border crossing on America's border with Mexico. In July 1942, an executive agreement between the United States and

Mexico filled a wartime demand for agricultural labor with the bracero program, admitting 215,000 agricultural and 75,000 railroad workers for temporary work in the United States.[24] After the war, despite the return of American laborers, the federal government extended the program, bringing about 200,000 braceros to California, Texas, and other southwestern states each year.[25] The Truman administration hoped braceros would represent a solution to rising concerns about illegal immigration, but as historian Mae Ngai has shown, the program generated an influx of undocumented labor. First of all, because of segregation laws, Mexico did not allow braceros to work in Texas, Arkansas, or Missouri, and growers in those stated began to recruit unauthorized labor. Moreover, there were not enough bracero spots for the workers who hoped to fill them, generating more and more migration across the southern border. Soon, much like previous southern and eastern Europeans on the U.S.-Canada border, Mexicans gained a reputation as dangerous criminals who undercut wages and threatened the American welfare state.[26]

Along with illegal immigration, the bracero program led to the rise of another pattern of migration that mirrored and drew legal legitimacy from commuting practices established on America's northern border. As U.S. border cities began to seek access to braceros and demand for their labor exceeded the supply offered by the legitimate program, local border crossers used the precedent set on the Detroit-Windsor border and General Order 86 (as outlined in Chapter 3 of this book) to begin commuting daily for work. This first began in Tijuana, where local residents secured the right to cross daily into San Diego for jobs in factories and businesses. San Diego employers argued that they had no money or space to provide barracks and food for braceros but that they were in dire need of labor. Mexican President Ávila Camacho expressed concern that commuters might drain Baja California of its labor force, but when workers produced General Order 86 as evidence for the legality of the practice, the U.S. government pressured Mexico to allow the new system of legal work.[27]

Just as automobile industries had employed Canadians to undercut unions in the 1920s, businesses on the U.S.-Mexico boundary began to maintain low wages with workers who legitimized their daily commute with a border regulation established in the North. In the 1950s and 1960s, Ciudad Juárez–El Paso, Matamoros-Brownsville, and Nuevo Laredo–Laredo joined Tijuana–San Diego to employ thousands of commuters in agriculture and local businesses. These regions established an interdependence that made border crossing integral to the economies of both sides. In the 1960s, labor unions brought a series of court cases against commuters, but the INS upheld local border crossers' right to work in the United States. Thus, while only several thousand commuters continued to cross the U.S.-Canada border, the practice became permanently embedded in the local economies of the U.S.-Mexico border.[28]

By the 1970s, border cities in Mexico grew exponentially, and unlike braceros, commuters gained a permanent place as "semilegal" foreigners on the southern border.[29] In 1964, Department of Justice officials concluded that braceros were no longer profitable and encouraged a surge of "illegal immigrants" or, as they were derisively termed at the time, "wetbacks" and terminated the program.[30] The commuters who had begun to cross the border alongside braceros, however, managed to carve out a space for themselves on the border. And despite the fact that the 1965 Immigration Act imposed a ceiling on Western Hemisphere immigration, the law permitted commuters to continue to cross as exempt workers.[31] In the decades that followed, between 100,000 and 160,000 Mexican workers commuted to jobs on the U.S. side of the border each day.[32] For local employers, these border crossers represented an ideal alternative to braceros or illegal workers. Local businesses neither had to house and feed braceros nor worry about fines for employing those without papers. Kitty Calavita suggests that commuters represented "a labor supply stripped of its most human needs," a group of workers stuck between the categories of "citizen" and "illegal alien."[33] Thus, by the 1970s, Mexico, not Canada, became the border nation on which U.S. policymakers focused their concerns about immigrants.

On the U.S.-Mexico border, local concerns about braceros, "illegal wetbacks," and commuters incited a wave of policing on the southern border that continues to stigmatize Latino/a migrants in the Unites States as potential noncitizens. In the postwar era, the U.S. Border Patrol and the Mexican government cooperated to deport over one hundred thousand Mexicans to inland farms, operating under the supposition that transporting them into Mexico's interior would make returning difficult.[34] By the 1970s, officers traded tactics that used brute force and periodic deportation for a process marked by fencing, bussing, train lifts, airlifts, and broad systematic control.[35]

At the federal level, presidential efforts to punish and incarcerate led to unprecedented levels of policing on the U.S.-Mexico border. Kelly Lytle Hernández argues that Richard Nixon's War on Crime "primed the pump" for an age of mass incarceration, while Ronald Reagan's War on Drugs "turned the spigot . . . that deluged U.S. communities with extraordinary levels of arrests, surveillance, and violence."[36] Thus, the U.S.-Mexico border became a major focus of policymakers and Border Patrol, launching debates about profiling and policing that cast Mexican and other Latino/a crossers as drug runners, gang members, and threats to the safety of white American citizens.[37] And as in Detroit, hard-line federal policies were carried out by Border Patrol officers, judges, and lawmakers who waged local wars on drugs and crime in California, Texas, and Arizona border regions.

Unauthorized immigrants also lost their access to state welfare benefits, completing a trend that began with the 1930s WPA purge (see Chapter 7). Thirty years after Roosevelt banned noncitizens from the federal work program, the Nixon administration barred unauthorized immigrants from nearly all welfare programs, including Medicare.[38] And by the 1990s, states led the charge to deny benefits to immigrants without papers. In California, Proposition 187 denied most nonemergency services to unauthorized immigrants, a move that scholars claimed led to the 1996 Personal Responsibility and Work Opportunity Reconciliation Act, or welfare reform. This act denied federal funding to states when they provided Medicaid and welfare to recent legal immigrants. And as in the 1930s, immigrants barred from social services turned toward underpaid, unauthorized work.[39]

Deportations also increased exponentially after the 1990s. President Bill Clinton's election promised a reprieve from the hard-line policies of his predecessors, but when public opinion shifted against immigrants, Clinton signed the Violent Crime Control and Law Enforcement Act of 1994, which established a criminal alien center to investigate crimes tied to noncitizens and make it easier to deport them.[40] By Barack Obama's presidency, terrorist attacks on the World Trade Center and wars in the Middle East heightened concerns about Muslim foreigners, meaning that for many Americans, anyone with a dark beard or headscarf became a potential terrorist.[41] And despite President Obama's promises to Latino/a voters, his homeland security oversaw the arrest and expulsion of 2.7 million people, more than any president in U.S. history.[42] Indeed, by the 2010s, restrictive immigration policies had become the rule rather than the exception for U.S. leaders.

A national history of hard-line immigration policy and xenophobia, however, does not make the rise of extreme nativism inevitable in our modern era. Canada, for instance, had a history of hard-line immigration policy, but after World War II, the Canadian public's zeal for relief camps and deportation drives ceded to a more multicultural vision of the nation.[43] A postwar economic boom also prompted Canada to accept over two million immigrants and a quarter of a million refugees between 1946 and 1962.[44] In 1967, the Canadian Parliament rolled out its "points system," in what the *Toronto Star* claimed marked an effort at eliminating "outright racial discrimination."[45] In 1976, Canada passed a progressive new immigration law that exempted refugees, families, and assisted relatives from the points system and offered all those subject to removal to a full and impartial inquiry.[46] New laws opened the door to a diverse group of immigrants, and while critics rightly point to lingering discrimination and racism embedded in national policies, outright nativism has lost much of its political purchase in Canadian discourse.[47] For instance, when in 2018, right-wing populist Doug Ford ran a successful campaign for premier of Ontario, sending Canadian and U.S. newspapers into a tailspin over the prospect of Trumpism in Canada, Ford's campaign avoided the xenophobic tropes that worked so well for Donald Trump.[48] Despite the United States and Canada's shared history of racialized immigration and deportation laws, Canada emerged as a nation committed, not just on paper, to a certain measure of multiculturalism and inclusion.

President Donald Trump's rhetoric, on the other hand, has continued a legacy of nativism in U.S. immigration policy. And while Trump has focused on Latino/a and Muslim migrants, *Bootlegged Aliens* demonstrates that in the years before World War II, southern and eastern Europeans faced condemnation as criminals, terrorists, and burdens on an emerging welfare state. Barring these Europeans from the nation and attempting to deport thousands more led to their exclusion from labor unions and welfare programs in the decade that followed. And though ethnic Europeans managed to shed their ties to foreignness in the 1950s, the mechanisms of exclusion set in place in the 1920s soon targeted nonwhite immigrants on the U.S. border with Mexico. By the 1980s, Latino/a migrants who had also endured decades of exclusion became the group most associated with foreignness in American society. And though overt racism fell out of fashion, Americans began to express their anxieties about these migrants by condemning them for taking jobs or committing crimes. Thus, President Trump, who has called for a wall on the U.S.-Mexico border and a ban on immigrants from Muslim nations, presents another chapter in an American narrative of restricting, excluding, and punishing those without citizenship.

Notes

Introduction

1. "U.S. Adding Prosecutors Judges, to Process Immigrants at the U.S.-Mexico Border," *Reuters*, May 2, 2018.

2. *Bootlegged Aliens* draws on both contemporary and historical terminology when discussing immigrants and their various statuses. Politicians of the 1930s rarely used the term "illegal immigrant" and never referred to immigrants as "undocumented" or "illegal aliens," or "illegal Europeans." Instead, newspapers and policymakers preferred to call immigrants who crossed the border without papers "bootlegged aliens" or simply "aliens." To streamline language and stress contemporary relevance, the book refers to immigrants who violated 1920s immigration laws as "illegal" or "undocumented," terms that stress the fact that those in power treated these immigrants as criminals. "Legal immigrant" or "noncitizen" indicates immigrants who had legally entered the United States yet had not completed the naturalization process, and "foreigner," "alien," "foreign born," or "European" refers to any immigrant without citizenship, regardless of legal status. Because police, politicians, and organizers often elided the differences between these categories, the book sometimes slips between terms, demonstrating that an immigrant's perceived legal status often became more important than the evidence provided in documents or papers.

3. Original reference to Andrew Boyko (pseudonym used at the request of Benson Ford Research Library) found in Andrew Boyko File, August 2, 1932, Box 22, Accession 55, Sociological Department Records, BFRC. Information on Boyko's entrance and marriage found in Ancestry.com, *Michigan, Marriage Records, 1867–1952* [database online] (Provo, Utah: Ancestry.com, Operations, Inc., 2015) and National Archives at Washington, D.C., *Card Manifests (Alphabetical) of Individuals Entering Through the Port of Detroit, Michigan, 1906–1954; Records of the Immigration and Naturalization Service, 1787–2004*, Record Group Number 85 (Provo, Utah: Ancestry.com, Operations, Inc., 2015).

4. Deportation Record of Filip Kucharski, Deportation Record of Artur Kucharski, December 12, 1929, File 55044/127, NARAI.

5. In 1924, Detroit had 638,068 foreign-born Europeans, meaning that more than 46 percent of the city's inhabitants were born abroad. Albert Mayer, "A Study of the Foreign-Born Population of Detroit, 1970–1950" (PhD diss., Wayne State University, 1951). Historians have explored how politicians, police, and local organizations in major urban regions negotiated large immigrant populations, often casting immigrants as second-class citizens in the 1910s and 1920s. For a sampling of studies focusing on immigrant issues in Chicago, see

James Barret, *Work and Community in the Jungle: Chicago's Packinghouse Workers, 1894–1922* (Urbana: University of Illinois Press, 2002); Lizabeth Cohen, *Making a New Deal: Industrial Workers in Chicago, 1919–1939* (New York: Cambridge University Press, 1990), chaps. 1–2; Thomas Guglielmo, *White on Arrival: Italians, Race, Color, and Power in Chicago, 1890–1945* (New York: Oxford University Press, 2003); Dominic Pacyga, *Polish Immigrants and Industrial Chicago: Workers on the South Side, 1880–1922* (Chicago: University of Chicago Press, 2003). For recent studies of immigrants, crime, and nativism in New York, see Jennifer Fronc, *New York Undercover: Private Surveillance in the Progressive Era* (Chicago: University of Chicago Press, 2009); Hidetaka Hirota, *Expelling the Poor: Atlantic Seaboard States and the 19th-Century Origins of American Immigration Policy* (New York: Oxford University Press, 2003).

6. Cohen, *Making a New Deal*; Cybelle Fox, *Three Worlds of Relief: Race, Immigration, and the American Welfare State* (Princeton, N.J.: Princeton University Press, 2012); Gary Gerstle, *American Crucible: Race and Nation in the Twentieth Century* (Princeton, N.J.: Princeton University Press, 2017).

7. The following scholars offer excellent treatments of immigration policy and laws as they developed at the federal level: Katherine Benton-Cohen, *Inventing the Immigration Problem: The Dillingham Commission and Its Legacy* (Cambridge, Mass.: Harvard University Press, 2018); Roger Daniels, *Guarding the Golden Door: American Immigration Policy and Immigrants Since 1882* (New York: Hill and Wang, 2004); Bill Ong Hing, *Defining America Through Immigration Policy* (Philadelphia: Temple University Press, 2004); Erika Lee, *At America's Gates: Chinese Immigration During the Exclusion Era, 1882–1943* (Chapel Hill: University of North Carolina Press, 2003); Lucy E. Salyer, *Laws Harsh as Tigers: Chinese Immigrants and the Shaping of Modern Immigration Law*, 2nd ed. (Chapel Hill: University of North Carolina Press, 1995). Libby Garland analyzes the emergence of Jewish illegal immigrants, but her work focuses on Jewish organizers and the ways their groups ultimately escaped the stigma of illegality through legal efforts. Libby Garland, *After They Closed the Gates: Jewish Illegal Immigration to the United States, 1921–1965* (Chicago: University of Chicago Press, 2014). *Bootlegged Aliens* shows how in Detroit, police and Border Patrol used their discretion to label ethnic Europeans "likely to become a public charge," excluding them from the nation. Legal scholars such as Kunal Parker and Barbara Welke have emphasized how federal laws combined with local practice to privilege moneyed, white men at the expense of foreigners, the poor, women, and minority groups. Kunal Parker, *Making Foreigners: Immigration and Citizenship Law in America* (Cambridge: Cambridge University Press, 2015); Barbara Welke, *Law and the Borders of Belonging in the Long-Nineteenth-Century United States* (Cambridge: Cambridge University Press, 2010). Margot Canaday examines the "likely to become a public charge" of the 1882 Immigration Act in particular to demonstrate how policing homosexuality at America's borders labeled anyone deemed "sexually deviant" as second-class citizens. Examining southern and eastern European ethnic communities in New Deal Detroit reveals that their nationalities faced similar bouts of policing, profiling, and criminalization. Margot Canaday, *The Straight State: Sexuality and Citizenship in Twentieth-Century America* (Princeton, N.J.: Princeton University Press, 2009).

8. Mae Ngai, *Impossible Subjects: Illegal Aliens and the Making of Modern America* (Princeton, N.J.: Princeton University Press, 2004).

9. Ngai, *Impossible Subjects*, chap. 2.

10. Mae Ngai notes that in 1933 and 1934, liberals began a new legislative strategy that sought to facilitate naturalization for "relatively harmless and deserving people," all of whom were of European descent. Ngai, *Impossible Subjects*, 81.

11. Jeremy Adleman and Stephen Aron, "From Borderlands to Borders: Empires, Nation-States, and the Peoples in Between in North American History," *American Historical Review* 4, no. 103 (June 1999): 814–841; Katherine Benton-Cohen, *Borderline Americans: Racial Division and Labor War in the Arizona Borderlands* (Cambridge, Mass.: Harvard University Press, 2011); Geraldo L. Cadava, *Standing on Common Ground: The Making of a Sunbelt Borderland* (Cambridge, Mass.: Harvard University Press, 2013); Kelly Lytle Hernández, *Migra! A History of the U.S. Border Patrol* (Berkeley: University of California Press, 2010); Miguel Antonio Levario, *Militarizing the Border: When Mexicans Became the Enemy* (College Station: Texas A&M Press, 2012); S. Deborah Kang, *The INS on the Line: Making Immigration Law on the US-Mexico Border, 1917–1954* (New York: Oxford University Press, 2017); Rachel St. John, *Line in the Sand: A History of the Western U.S.-Mexico Border* (Princeton, N.J.: Princeton University Press, 2012); Samuel Truett, *Fugitive Landscapes: The Forgotten History of the U.S.-Mexico Borderlands* (New Haven, Conn.: Yale University Press, 2008).

12. For a representative example of the recent historical scholarship on the carceral state, see Michelle Alexander, *The New Jim Crow: Mass Incarceration in the Age of Colorblindness* (New York: New Press, 2010); Ruth Wilson Gilmore, *Golden Gulag: Prisons, Surplus, Crisis, and Opposition in Globalizing California* (Berkeley: University of California Press, 2007); Marie Gottschalk, *The Prison and the Gallows: The Politics of Mass Incarceration in America* (Cambridge: Cambridge University Press, 2006); Elizabeth Hinton, *From the War on Poverty to the War on Crime: The Making of Mass Incarceration in America* (Cambridge, Mass.: Harvard University Press, 2016); Julilly Kohler-Hausmann, *Getting Tough: Welfare and Imprisonment in 1970s America* (Princeton, N.J.: Princeton University Press, 2017); Khalil Gibran Muhammad, *The Condemnation of Blackness: Race, Crime, and the Making of Modern America* (Cambridge, Mass.: Harvard University Press, 2011); Heather Ann Thompson, "Why Mass Incarceration Matters: Rethinking Crisis, Decline, and Transformation in Postwar American History," *Journal of American History*, 97, No. 3 (December 2010): 703–734; Heather Ann Thompson, *Blood in the Water: The Attica Prison Uprising of 1971 and Its Legacy* (New York: Pantheon, 2016).

13. Kelly Lytle Hernández, *City of Inmates: Conquest, Rebellion, and the Rise of Human Caging in Los Angeles, 1771–1965* (Chapel Hill: University of North Carolina Press, 2017).

14. Recently, Lisa McGirr's *War on Alcohol: Prohibition and the Rise of the American State* (New York: Norton, 2016) and Nora Krinitsky's "The Politics of Crime Control: Race, Policing, and Reform in Twentieth-Century Chicago" (PhD diss., University of Michigan, 2017) have taken up the issue of policing Europeans. McGirr's work, however, focuses on federal efforts to castigate European violators of liquor laws and Krinitsky's study examines day-to-day policing in Chicago.

15. Matthew Frye Jacobson, *Whiteness of a Different Color: European Immigrants and the Alchemy of Race* (Cambridge, Mass.: Harvard University Press, 1999); David R. Roediger, *The Wages of Whiteness: Race and the Making of the American Working Class* (New York: Verso, 2007).

16. The book draws on the "whiteness" argument set forth by Thomas Guglielmo's *White on Arrival: Italians, Race, Color, and Power in Chicago, 1890–1945* (New York: Oxford University Press, 2004), which claims Italian immigrants may have faced prejudices but that the American state never cast them as nonwhite.

17. "Immigration Officials State Detroit Receives More Illegal Aliens Than Any City in the U.S.," July 10, 1928, *Detroit News*, File 55166/379, NARAI.

18. On numbers of foreign born in Detroit between 1925 and 1930, see "Nationalities in Detroit," *Detroiter*, May 21, 1931.

19. McGirr's *The War on Alcohol* examines how ethnic immigrants in northern industrial centers got caught up in the liquor business, and Marni Davis investigates how American Jews disavowed alcohol to integrate into the mainstream. Marni Davis, *Jews and Booze: Becoming American in the Age of Prohibition* (New York: NYU Press, 2012). Holly Karibo's *Sin City North: Sex, Drugs and Citizenship on the Detroit-Windsor Borderland* (Chapel Hill: University of North Carolina Press, 2015) explores the underground world in the postwar Detroit-Windsor borderland.

20. For exceptions to this dearth of literature on smuggling along the U.S.-Canada border, see Kornel Chang, *Pacific Connections: The Making of the U.S.-Canadian Borderlands* (Berkeley: University of California Press, 2012); Garland, *After They Closed the Gates*; Lee, *At America's Gates*.

21. For an excellent treatment of naturalization laws, see Dorothee Schneider, "Naturalization and United States Citizenship in Two Periods of Mass Migration: 1894–1930, 1965–2000," *Journal of American Ethnic History* 21, no. 1 (2001): 50–82.

22. James Davis, "The Men Without a Country," *Dearborn Independent*, August 13, 1927.

Chapter 1

1. Statement of Earl F. Coe, inspector in charge at Detroit, January 20, 1923. Coe's report notes the practice of a Belgian smuggling ring that took immigrants across the ice "shrouded in white," File 55234/510, NARAI.

2. "Aliens' Tricks Trip Up US Trap," *Detroit News*, February 9, 1930.

3. Just as modern *coyotes* lead Mexican and Central American migrants across the Rio Grande today, the 1920s "ghost-walking gangs" guided Europeans across the Detroit River. Nancy Foner, *From Ellis Island to JFK: New York's Two Great Waves of Immigration* (New Haven, Conn.: Yale University Press, 2002); Jeffrey Kaye, *Moving Millions: How Coyote Capitalism Fuels Global Immigration* (New York: John Wiley & Sons, 2010).

4. "Aliens Find Devious Ways into States," *Border Cities Star*, December 12, 1928.

5. Roger Daniels, *Guarding the Golden Door: American Immigration Policy and Immigrants Since 1882* (New York: Hill and Wang, 2005), 49–52.

6. Statement of Earl F. Coe, inspector in charge at Detroit, January 20, 1923, File 55234/510, NARAI.

7. While this chapter seeks to understand how actors on the ground shaped quota policies, literature discussing 1920s immigration quotas tends to focus on the ways nativist congressmen, lawyers, and cabinet members conceived of and implemented new quota laws in ways that ended Asian immigration and slashed European entries. For excellent policy analyses focusing on the congressional debate over quotas, see Daniels, *Guarding the Golden Door*, chap. 3; Ngai, *Impossible Subjects*, chap. 1; and Aristide R. Zolberg, *A Nation by Design Immigration Policy in the Fashioning of America* (Cambridge, Mass.: Harvard University Press, 2006), chap. 8. Kelly Lytle Hernández's work takes up questions of immigration laws and their grassroots enforcement, but her study remains focused on America's border with Mexico. Hernández, *Migra!*

8. "The Gateways to Detroit," *Detroiter*, November 16, 1925, BDPL.

9. Population numbers for all immigrant groups found in Mayer, "A Study of the Foreign-Born Population of Detroit, 1970–1950," 18. On Italians, see "Italians Folder," 1940,

Committee on the Study of Foreign Language Groups, Box 1, BDPL, and Carole Eberly, *Our Michigan: Ethnic Tales & Recipes* (East Lansing, Mich.: Shoestring Press, 1979), 171–172. After 1920, ten thousand Belgians migrated from the sugar beet fields of the Upper Peninsula to settle the far east side, sharing streets and beer houses with the Germans who fled factory regions now inhabited by other ethnic groups. Eberly, *Our Michigan*, 178–179. Five thousand Greeks settled right downtown, where some worked in factories but most opened their own restaurants, florists, and grocery stores, selling "huge tubs of olives preserved in oil and great slabs of goat and sheep's milk cheese." "Greeks Folder," 1930, Committee on the Study of Foreign Language Groups, BDPL. And by 1910, five thousand Croatians migrated from Dalmatia and the islands near the Croatian coast, settling along Russell Street and Harper Avenue on the east side. Many Croatians were devoutly Catholic, but a significant number held radical political views and attended communist meetings at the Workers' Hall on East Ferry Street, a development that could not have pleased employers. "Croatians Folder," 1930, Committee on the Study of Foreign Language Groups, BDPL.

10. Jeremy Williams, *Detroit: The Black Bottom Community* (Mount Pleasant, S.C.: Arcadia Publishing, 2009), 11.

11. Hungarians had their own doctors, lawyers, notaries, pastors, grocers, butchers, tailors, shoemakers, and undertakers and could choose between St. Janus, Holy Cross, and St. John Cantius churches, all within several blocks of each other. Malvina Hauk and James Abonyi, *Hungarians of Detroit* (Detroit, Mich.: Wayne State University Press), 24–26, 42.

12. Olivier Zunz, *The Changing Face of Inequality: Urbanization, Industrial Development, and Immigrants in Detroit, 1880–1920* (Chicago: University of Chicago Press, 1982), 349.

13. Eberly, *Our Michigan*, 114.

14. Zunz, *The Changing Face of Inequality*, 288.

15. Dennis Badaczewski, *Poles in Michigan* (East Lansing: Michigan State University Press, 2002), 13; Zunz, *The Changing Face of Inequality*, 13; Committee on the Study of Foreign Language Groups, Box 1, BDPL.

16. "Poles Folder," 1940, Committee on the Study of Foreign Language Groups, Box 1, BDPL; on the Polish Republican League, see "Polish Republican League to Frank Murphy," March 20, 1923, Correspondence Folder, Box 1, Frank Murphy Papers, BHL.

17. "Russian and Ukrainian Folder," 1940, Committee on the Study of Foreign Language Groups, Box 1, BDPL.

18. Eberly, *Our Michigan*, 147–148.

19. Sidney Bolkosky, *Harmony and Dissonance: Voices of Jewish Identity in Detroit, 1914–1967* (Detroit, Mich.: Wayne State University Press, 1991), 19.

20. Zunz, *The Changing Face of Inequality*, 350.

21. Henry Ford, *The International Jew, the World's Foremost Problem, a Reprint of a Series of Articles Appearing in the* Dearborn Independent *from May 22 to October 2, 1920* (Dearborn, Mich.: Dearborn Independent, 1920), chaps. 14, 17, and 19.

22. Beth Bates, *The Making of Black Detroit in the Age of Henry Ford* (Chapel Hill: University of North Carolina Press, 2012), 16.

23. For information on white southerners' migration to Detroit, see James Gregory, *The Southern Diaspora: How the Great Migrations of Black and White Southerners Transformed America* (Chapel Hill: University of North Carolina Press), 31–32.

24. Williams, *Detroit: The Black Bottom*, 14.

25. "The Negro Population in Detroit," 1930, Box 74, Detroit Urban League Papers, BHL.

26. Bates, *The Making of Black Detroit*, 16.

27. August Meier and Elliot Rudwick, *Black Detroit and the Rise of the UAW* (Oxford: Oxford University Press, 1979), 6–7.

28. Meier and Rudwick, *Black Detroit*, 7.

29. On early Syrian migrants to Detroit, see Sally Howell, *Old Islam in Detroit: Rediscovering the Muslim American Past* (New York: Oxford University Press, 2014), 33. For more on Syrian immigrants and whiteness, see Sarah Gualtieri, *Between Arab and White: Race and Ethnicity in the Early Syrian American Diaspora* (Berkeley: University of California Press, 2009).

30. Howell, *Old Islam*, 34–36.

31. Emiko Ohniki, "The Detroit Chinese: A Study of Socio-Cultural Changes in the Detroit Chinese Community from 1872 Through 1963" (MA thesis, University of Wisconsin, 1964), 15.

32. "Detroit's First Chinese Restaurant," *Detroit News*, July 9, 1934.

33. Ohniki, "The Detroit Chinese," 19.

34. Howell, *Old Islam*, 35.

35. Year: 1920; Census Place: Detroit, Wayne, Michigan; Roll: T625_804; Page: 4A; Enumeration District: 90, accessed on Ancestry.com, *1920 United States Federal Census* [database online] (Provo, Utah: Ancestry.com Operations, Inc., 2010).

36. Vivek Bald, *Bengali Harlem and the Lost Histories of South Asian America* (Cambridge, Mass.: Harvard University Press, 2013), 6, 120.

37. Zaragosa Vargas, *Proletarians of the North: A History of Mexican Industrial Workers in Detroit and the Midwest, 1917–1933* (Berkeley: University of California Press, 1993), 45.

38. Vargas, *Proletarians of the North*, 48.

39. Vargas, *Proletarians of the North*, 61.

40. Vargas, *Proletarians of the North*, 64–67.

41. Vargas, *Proletarians of the North*, 135.

42. Roger Daniels, *Coming to America: A History of Immigration and Ethnicity in American Life* 2nd ed. (New York: Perennial, 2002), chaps. 7–8.

43. Bates, *The Making of Black Detroit*, 19–21.

44. Vargas, *Proletarians of the North*, 13–19.

45. "Detroit Mecca of Immigrants," *Detroit Free Press*, September 29, 1920.

46. Zunz, *The Changing Face of Inequality*, 1.

47. Richard Walter Thomas, *Life for Us Is What We Make It: Building Black Community in Detroit, 1915–1945* (Bloomington: Indiana University Press, 1992), 25; Library and Archives Canada, *Sixth Census of Canada, 1921* (Ottawa, Ontario, Canada: Library and Archives Canada, 2013), 367.

48. Eberly, *Our Michigan*, 45–46.

49. U.S. Department of Labor, *Annual Report of the Commissioner General of Immigration to the Secretary of Labor* (Washington, D.C.: Government Printing Office, 1919 and 1923); "Border Cities Advancement Association to Mayor Martin in Detroit, on Detroit-Windsor Ferries," July 29, 1924, File 55280/11, NARAI.

50. Janet Langlios claims that smuggling goods between Windsor and Detroit was not only an economic endeavor but also a folk art. She notes that smuggling connected border

dwellers in a joint Windsor-Detroiter identity, allowing them to share "concomitant cultural and national identities." Janet Langlios, "Smuggling Across the Windsor-Detroit Border: Folk Art, Sexual Difference, and Cultural Identity," *Canadian Folklore* 13, no. 1 (1991): 23.

51. Register of Marriages, St. Alphonsus Church Records, 1911–1917, DLA.

52. For analyses of Chinese smuggling on both borders immediately after the Chinese Exclusion Act, see Peter Andreas, *Smuggler Nation: How Illicit Trade Made America* (New York: Oxford University Press, 2013), chap. 12; Lee, *At America's Gates*, chap. 5; and Chang, *Pacific Connections*, chap. 5.

53. Lee, *At America's Gates*, 14.

54. Beth Lew-Williams, *The Chinese Must Go: Violence, Exclusion, and the Making of the Alien in America* (Cambridge, Mass.: Harvard University Press, 2018); William H. Siener, "Through the Back Door: Evading the Chinese Exclusion Act Along the Niagara Frontier, 1900 to 1924," *Journal of American Ethnic History* 27, no. 4 (July 1, 2008): 34–70.

55. "Guarding Uncle Sam's Back Door," *Detroit Free Press*, January 21, 1912.

56. In 1918, wartime laws required immigrants to obtain visas from American consulates abroad before journeying to the United States. Those who could not do so found other ways in. For instance, along the Detroit-Windsor border, inspectors frequently complained of Russian Jewish, Spanish, and Polish immigrants who did not possess proper visas, yet slipped past overburdened immigration inspectors on the ferries that crossed the Detroit River. Patrick Ettinger, *Imaginary Lines: Border Enforcement and the Origins of Undocumented Immigration, 1882–1930* (Austin: University of Texas Press, 2009), 147; Craig Robertson, *The Passport in America: The History of a Document* (New York: Oxford University Press, 2012), 27. For discussion of Poles, Russians, and Spaniards coming in via Canada without a quota visa, see "U.S. Commissioner of Immigration at Montreal to W. W. Husband," File 55166/379, NARAI.

57. "Chinese Smuggler's Gang Broken Up and Overscore Arrested," *Detroit Free Press*, November 24, 1911.

58. "Alien Traffic Grows Rapidly," *Detroit News*, July 2, 1928.

59. Philip P. Mason, *Rum Running and the Roaring Twenties: Prohibition on the Michigan-Ontario Waterway* (Detroit, Mich.: Wayne State University Press, 1995), 35. For more on liquor smuggling in Michigan, see Larry Engelmann, *Intemperance, the Lost War Against Liquor* (New York: Free Press, 1979).

60. Thomas Reppetto, *American Mafia: A History of Its Rise to Power* (New York: Holt Paperbacks, 2004), 102; Camille Chidsey, "The Purple Gang," July 30, 2012, Walter P. Reuther Library, https://www.reuther.wayne.edu/node/8731.

61. Ford, *The International Jew*, chap. 12.

62. For classic literature on Americanization, see John Higham, *Strangers in the Land: Patterns of American Nativism, 1860–1925* (New Brunswick, N.J.: Rutgers University Press, 1955, reprinted 1988), and Edward George Hartmann, *The Movement to Americanize the Immigrant* (New York: Columbia University Press, 1948).

63. Nicole Greer Golda has demonstrated the gendered nature of the Americanization project, which attempted to turn immigrants into "proper" American men and women. "To Shape the Future of the Nation: Gender and Family Order in the Age of Americanization" (PhD diss., University of Michigan, 2016).

64. "Melting Pot Ceremony at Ford English School," July 4, 1917, Accession 106481, BFRC.

65. Beverly Gage, *The Day Wall Street Exploded: A Story of America in Its First Age of Terror* (New York: Oxford University Press, 2009), 233–234.

66. Major employers in the city had consolidated control of hiring practices and the city government in the 1910s. In 1912, Cadillac Motors the Employer's Association of Detroit (EAD) created a labor bureau that vetted potential employees before sending them to specific industries. For more on this, see Thomas Klug, "Employers' Strategies in the Detroit Labor Market, 1900–1929," in *On the Line: Essays in the History of Auto Work*, ed. Nelson Lichtenstein and Stephen Meyer (Urbana: University of Illinois Press, 1989), 43–44. Chrysler President Henry Leland also worked with industrialists to restructure Detroit's municipal government in favor of industry. Afraid Detroit's ward system and increasingly segmented ethnic population might foster the growth of a political machine or, worse, a powerful union movement, Leland proposed a revision of the city's charter, cleverly arguing that the revisions had to be carried out by a nonpartisan committee of elite businessmen, men he claimed were more attuned to the growing needs of Detroit than seasoned politicians. The committee abolished the ward system in favor of a special city council to be chosen directly by the mayor, a system that ensured elite men would retain power over the city and local ethnics would have little power to elect their own leaders. Raymond R. Fragnoli, *The Transformation of Reform: Progressivism in Detroit—and After, 1912–1933* (New York: Garland, 1982), 132–136.

67. Howard Abramowitz, "Historians and the Red Scare of 1919–1920 in Detroit," in *Anti-Communism: The Politics of Manipulation*, ed. Judith Joël and Gerald M. Erickson (Minneapolis, Minn.: MEP Publications, 1987), 99.

68. Fred Yonce, "The Big Red Scare in Detroit, 1919–1920" (University of Michigan, History 770 Seminar Paper, May 24, 1963), 34, BHL.

69. JoEllen Vineyard, *Right in Michigan's Grassroots: From the KKK to the Michigan Militia* (Ann Arbor: University of Michigan Press), 29.

70. Kevin Boyle, *Arc of Justice: A Saga of Race, Civil Rights, and Murder in the Jazz Age* (New York, 2004), 140.

71. Craig Fox, *Everyday Klansfolk: White Protestant Life and the KKK in 1920s Michigan* (East Lansing: Michigan State University Press, 2011), xxviii.

72. Fox, *Everyday Klansfolk*, 26.

73. Kenneth T. Jackson, *The Ku Klux Klan in the City, 1915–1930* (New York: Oxford University Press, 1970), chap. 3.

74. For more on urban housing riots, see the Ossian Sweet case as described in Boyle, *Arc of Justice*.

75. "Study of Census Reports Show Dangers of Lax Immigration Law," *Imperial Nighthawk*, September 17, 1924; "Vice Rights Operated by Foreigners," *Imperial Nighthawk*, March 26, 1924.

76. A good example of this is a description of an initiation ceremony in Bakersfield, California, in which "approximately one hundred aliens were naturalized into the realm of the Invisible Empire." "Klan Stages First Outdoor Naturalization Ceremony," *Imperial Nighthawk*, March 5, 1924.

77. "Ku Klux Klan valtaa sijaa Kanadassakin" (Ku Klux Klan Takes Over Canada Too), *Vapaus*, June 26, 1923, translation courtesy of Raija, Hanninen, Helsinki, Finland.

78. "Horrors! Fiery Cross Blazes Merrily on the Star's Lawn," *Border Cities Star*, August 21, 1925.

79. Bolkosky, *Harmony and Dissonance*, 59.

80. "Higher Alien Bars Urged," *Detroit Free Press*, January 1, 1921.

81. "Sons of the American Revolution, Detroit Chapter," February 11, 1921, and "Daughters of the American Revolution to Washington," March 12, 1923, File 55639/576, NARAI.

82. Gary Gerstle, *American Crucible: Race and Nation in the Twentieth Century*, 2nd ed. (Princeton, N.J.: Princeton University Press, 2017), 95.

83. Daniels, *Guarding the Golden Door*, 28.

84. Daniels, *Guarding the Golden Door*, 46.

85. Katherine Benton-Cohen, *Inventing the Immigration Problem: The Dillingham Commission and Its Legacy* (Cambridge, Mass.: Harvard University Press, 2018).

86. Daniels, *Guarding the Golden Door*, 48–49.

87. Salvatore LaGumina, *Wop! A Documentary History of Anti-Italian Discrimination* (New York: Straight Arrow Books, 1973), 227.

88. Gage, *The Day Wall Street Exploded*, 233–234.

89. "Chapter XXXXVIII, Immigration Reform," Origins Folder, Box 1, John Bond Trevor Papers, BHL.

90. "Origins of Immigration Reform by John Bond Trevor," Origins Folder, Box 1, John Bond Trevor Papers, BHL.

91. "Johnson to John Bond Trevor," January 2, 1922, Origins Folder, Box 1, John Bond Trevor Papers, BHL.

92. Albert Johnson, "For Immigration Reform," *New York Times*, February 17, 1922; also see Albert Johnson, "On Immigration," *Daily World*, January 14, 1922, Origins Folder, Box 1, John Bond Trevor Papers, BHL.

93. H. H. Laughlin, *Analysis of America's Melting Pot* (Washington, D.C.: Government Printing Office, 1923); U.S. House of Representatives Committee on Immigration, 67th Congress, "An Analysis of the Racist Origins of the National Origins Quota System of the Immigration Act of 1924," Folder 4, Box 25, U.S. Conference of Catholic Bishops, ACHR.

94. Daniels, *Guarding the Golden Door*, 51.

95. Daniels, *Guarding the Golden Door*, 52–53.

96. "Immigration Investigated by Board," *Detroiter*, October 2, 1920, BDPL.

97. David Roberts, *In the Shadow of Detroit: Gordon M. McGregor, Ford of Canada, and Motoropolis* (Detroit, Mich.: Wayne State University Press, 2006), 14–30, 45.

98. Roberts, *In the Shadow of Detroit*, 100.

99. "U.K. Government Report on Windsor for 1926–1927," Public Record Office, DO 53/4, NAUK.

100. Significant layoffs in Windsor's Bayer Aspirin Factory and the General Motors Corporation of Walkerville forced many Canadians to seek work in Detroit. "U.K. Government Report on Windsor for 1925–1926," DO 53/4, NAUK. On numbers of commuters in the early 1920s, see Donald Avery, "Canadian Workers and American Immigration Restriction: A Case Study of the Windsor Commuters, 1924–1931," *Mid America: An Historical Review* 80, no. 3 (Fall 1998): 235–263.

101. Ninette Kelley and Michael Trebilcock, *The Making of the Mosaic: A History of Canadian Immigration Policy* (Toronto: University of Toronto Press, 2010), 186–188.

102. "Relief Matters, Anton Winowski File, August 1927," MS 19 I-8/5, WPLA.

103. "A Forgotten Heritage Rediscovered," *Windsor Star*, August 17, 1974.

104. Correspondence, November 21, 1925, Father Krupa File, Box 15, Bishop Fallon Papers, DLA. Consequently, instead of joining the Windsor Catholic or Canada's growing immigrant community, Ukrainian and Russian churchgoers crossed into Detroit for ethnic festivals or to attend Sunday services. Father Sembratovick, a Ukrainian priest in Detroit, often boarded the ferry to visit families in Windsor, administering sacraments and holding mass for those unable to make the boat ride themselves. Correspondence, November 21, 1925, Father Krupa File, Box 15, Bishop Fallon Papers, DLA.

105. General File, St. Anthony of Padua, Windsor publication, 1928, DLA.

106. "Ford Report on Plant Life," September 1927, MS 27 I 2/3, Windsor Municipal Archives, WPLA.

107. Dennis Gruending, "They Didn't Want Handouts" and "Croatians Mark Club Anniversary," *Windsor Star*, November 14, 1977, Croatian Clippings File, WPLA.

108. "Cecil Jackson to the Canada Club of Windsor," May 9, 1929, MS 28 ¼, Windsor Municipal Archives, WPLA.

109. General File, St. Anthony of Padua, Windsor publication, 1928, DLA.

110. "Massena, NY Smuggling Reports, 1924," File 55773/134, NARAI.

111. "John Thibault File, February 22, 1924," File 55773/726, NARAI.

112. U.S. Department of Labor, *Annual Report* (1923), 25.

113. "Alien Traffic Grows Rapidly," *Detroit News*, July 2, 1928.

114. "$100 and a Password, Another Alien Slips In," *Detroit News*, July 1, 1928.

115. "Deportation File of Innocenzo Blanco," December 28, 1925, File 55477/776, NARAI.

116. "Deportation Record of Napolis Usoris," July 15, 1928, File 55714/485, NARAI.

117. The *Detroit Labor News* noted that the average wage in eastern Europe for farm laborers and carpenters ranged from $1 to $1.50 a week. "Protect American Standards," *Detroit Labor News*, August 21, 1928, File 55598/453, NARAI.

118. "Deportation Hearing of Jacob Smoor," January 24, 1926, File 55477/763, NARAI.

119. Meier and Rudwick, *Black Detroit*, 6–7.

120. "1932 District 11 Report," File 55778/911, NARAI.

121. USCIS History Office, *Overview of INS History* (Washington, D.C.: USCIS History Office and Library, 2012), 4.

122. Lytle Hernández, *Migra!*, 33–34.

123. "Deportation Hearing of Jacob Smoor," January 24, 1926, File 55477/763, NARAI.

124. Though policymakers and smugglers had yet to use the term "illegal alien," I employ the modern terminology in order to situate Europeans within the longer history of illegal "alienness" in American history. For more on use of this term in the 1920s context, see Garland, *After They Closed the Gates*; Ngai, *Impossible Subject*.

125. For examples of the many press reports referring to Europeans as "alien bootleggers" and "undesirable aliens" or "alien gangsters," see "Anti-Alien Cry Raised in House," *Baltimore Sun*, February 17, 1929; "Teeth for Alien Law," *Los Angeles Times*, December 2, 1927; and "Anti-Alien Cry Raised in House," *Baltimore Sun*, February 17, 1929. On the other hand, the *Coalitionist*, a prominent nativist paper, referred to aliens only as Europeans, while it called Mexican entrants "Mexican immigrants" or simply "Mexicans." Found in "The Mexican Immigration Question," *Coalitionist*, August, 1929, Box 2, John Bond Trevor Papers,

BHL. In regards to the Chinese, Secretary of Labor Davis himself noted that 23,000 undesirable aliens (meaning Europeans) resided in the United States and placed the nation's 40,000 "illegal Chinamen" in a separate category. "Davis Wants Aliens Registered," *New York Times*, February 21, 1922.

126. Howell, *Old Islam*, 63.

127. "Answers to American Foreign Service Report Issued December 8, 1924," report from Damascus, Syria, May 18, 1925, State Department Records 150.01/1159, NARAII.

128. INS stood for Immigration and Naturalization Services, a division under the Department of Labor. "Detroit Inspector in Charge Report," December 7, 1924, File 53990/160, NARAI.

129. G. W. Titus, Citizen of Mishawaka, Indiana to Washington's Immigration Department, April 21, 1923, File 53990/160, NARAI.

130. Nineteen-year-old Albert Robinet, who was captured as a smuggling accomplice, testified that there were approximately seventy-five individual smuggling operations running through the Border Cities between 1924 and 1928. "Vast Alien Smuggling Ring Bared as U.S. Nabs 5," *Detroit Free Press*, August 26, 1928, File 55601/676, NARAI.

131. George T. Montague, Inspector in Charge to P. L. Prentis, District Director, January 5, 1926, NARAI.

132. "Deportation Record of Joseph Alias Sebastian Alias Sam Zeleski," April 6, 1928, File 55489/468, NARAI.

133. "Alien Traffic Grows Rapidly," *Detroit News*, July 2, 1928.

134. "Detroit District Is Easiest to Enter; Smuggling Extensive Trade," *Border Cities Star*, December 17, 1928; "Run Runners Smuggle Aliens and Narcotics," *Toronto Daily*, November 7, 1928.

135. "Alien Traffic Grows Rapidly," *Detroit News*, July 2, 1928.

136. Libby Garland notes that organized crime, including smuggling, "was perceived to be a profoundly ethnic world," giving ethnic and foreign-born Americans a reputation for crime in the American imagination. *After They Closed the Gates*, 95.

137. For literature on the connection between Latinos on the U.S.-Mexican border and the drug trade, see Peter Andreas, *Drug War Politics: The Price of Denial* (Berkeley: University of California Press, 1996), and Timothy Dunn, *The Militarization of the U.S.-Mexico Border, 1978–1992: Low-Intensity Conflict Doctrine Comes Home* (Austin: University of Texas Press, 1995).

138. "Smuggling Prices Vary by Destination," *Detroit News*, July 4, 1928.

139. Though a wealth of scholarship examines the development of federal enforcement on the U.S.-Mexico border, little attention has been given to the U.S. Border Patrol's role on the northern border. For scholars who address the establishment of the U.S. Border Patrol along the U.S.-Mexico border, see Peter Andreas, *Border Games: Policing the U.S.-Mexico Divide* (Ithaca, N.Y.: Cornell University Press, 2000); Dunn, *The Militarization of the U.S.-Mexico Border*; Lytle Hernández, *Migra!*. Andrew Graybill analyzes policing the U.S.-Canada border but focuses on the Royal Canadian Mounted Police in 1919. Andrew Graybill, *Policing the Great Plains: Rangers, Mounties, and the North American Frontier, 1875–1910* (Lincoln: University of Nebraska Press), 2007.

140. For statistics, see U.S. Department of Labor, *Annual Report of the Commissioner General of Immigration to the Secretary of Labor* (Washington, D.C.: Government Printing Office, 1925).

141. "Chief of Border Patrol Tells of Uncle Sam's Work," September 7, 1929, File 55598/453, NARAI.

142. "Report on District 11," May 7, 1924, File 55391/237, Subject Correspondence, Records of the Immigration and Naturalization Service, RG 85, National Archives, Washington, D.C.; "Crashing America's Back Gate," *New York Herald Tribune*, July 31, 1927.

143. Nora Krinitsky, "The Politics of Crime Control: Race, Policing, and Reform in Twentieth-Century Chicago" (PhD diss., University of Michigan, 2017), 11–12.

144. Denis Halpin, *A Brotherhood of Liberty: Black Reconstruction and Its Legacies in Baltimore, 1865–1920* (Philadelphia: University of Pennsylvania Press, 2019); Khalil Muhammad, *The Condemnation of Blackness: Race, Crime and the Making of Modern Urban America* (Cambridge, Mass.: Harvard University Press, 2011).

145. "How Employees and Officers at Bridge Will Be Dressed," *Detroit News*, November 19, 1929.

146. "They Guard Uncle Sam's Boundary," *Port Huron Times Herald*, July 8, 1927.

147. Graybill, *Policing the Great Plains*, 12–15.

148. Steve Hewitt, "Policing the Promised Land: The RCMP and Negative Nation Building in Alberta and Saskatchewan in the Interwar Period," in *The Prairie West as Promised Land*, ed. Douglas Frances and Chris Kitzan (Calgary: University of Calgary Press, 2007), 317.

149. On the RCMP's Ford City headquarters, see "Provincial Officer Seeks Views of Border Chiefs," *Border Cities Star*, December 18, 1923.

150. "How Uncle Sam Is Outwitting the Smuggler," *Detroit Free Press*, July 26, 1926.

151. "'Bootleggers in Humanity' Prey on Helpless Aliens," *Detroit Free Press*, October 19, 1924.

152. "Michigan State Police Pursue Outlaws on Land and Sea," *Detroit Free Press*, August 16, 1925.

153. For literature that investigates the role of police in furthering the goals of local politicians and political machines during this era, see Frank J. Donner, *Protectors of Privilege: Red Squads and Police Repression in Urban America* (Berkeley: University of California Press, 1990); Robert M. Fogelson, *Big-City Police* (Cambridge, Mass.: Harvard University Press, 1977).

154. "Immigration Officers Arrest 'Bible Student' Lass from Germany on Clue," *Detroit Free Press*, December 28, 1927.

155. On aliens hidden in the compartment of a truck, see "Rum, Alien Runners Are Bitter Foes," *Border Cities Star*, December 18, 1928; on aliens in Pullman cars, see "Aliens Find Devious Ways into States."

156. "Aliens Find Devious Ways into States."

157. Numbers of unsanctioned entries prove difficult to quantify, but local press and government reports suggest that illegal operations catered to several thousand illegal entrants per year. In 1928, the *Detroit Free Press* reported that smugglers successfully managed to bring around two hundred European aliens into the United States per month. A year later, when the Detroit police apprehended a major smuggling ring, newspaper reports claimed that the gang had trafficked over one thousand immigrants into the United States in less than two years. "Vast Alien Smuggling Ring Bared as U.S. Nabs 5"; also see "Alien Runners Sent to Prison."

158. "Aliens Find Devious Ways into the States."

159. For a thoughtful treatment of European smuggling in Havana, El Paso, and Cuba, see Garland, *After They Closed the Gates*; Lee, *At America's Gates*.

160. "Border Patrolmen Take Four Aliens," *Port Huron Times Herald*, April 12, 1924, File 55601/676, NARAI.

161. Immigrants from Russia tended to speak these four major languages. Albert Mayer, "A Study of the Foreign-Born Population of Detroit, 1870–1950" (PhD diss., Wayne State University, 1951), 30.

162. Craig Robertson examines the American state's increasing demand for universal documentation, which he notes increased after the passage of the 1921 and 1924 Immigration Acts. Craig Robertson, *The Passport in America: The History of a Document*, reprint ed. (New York: Oxford University Press, 2012), 13.

163. "Answers to the American Service Report, American Consulate in Warsaw, December 8, 1924"; "Answers to the American Service Report, American Consulate in Prague, February 24, 1925"; "Answers to the American Service Report, American Consulate in Rome, May 8, 1925"; and "Answers to the American Service Report, American Consulate in Damascus, May 18, 1925," State Department Records, File 150.01/1159, NARAII.

164. "Answers to the American Service Report," State Department Records, File 150.01/1159, NARAII.

165. "Rum Runner Terror of Alien Smuggler," *Border Cities Star*, December 21, 1928, File 55598/452, NARAI; "$100 and a Password, Another Alien Slips In."

166. For discussions of criminality and foreignness in Chicago and Philadelphia, see "Alien Murderers in Chicago," *Chicago Daily Tribune*, September 10, 1928; "Alien Gangsters," *Washington Post*, September 13, 1928.

167. For examples of this, see "Alien Murderers in Chicago," *Chicago Daily Tribune*, September 10, 1928; "Alien Gangsters," *Washington Post*, September 13, 1928; "Alien Criminals," *Washington Post*, October 6, 1928; "Too Many Criminal Aliens," *Washington Post*, August 22, 1927.

168. "William Burns to W. W. Husband," February 14, 1924, File 53990/160A, NARAI.

169. For an example, see "Communists 90% Aliens," *Coalitionist*, November 1930, Correspondence Folder, Box 1, John Bond Trevor Papers, BHL.

170. "Report on Detroit: Smuggling of Aliens Hit by Border Patrol," *Wyandotte Ontario*, April 7, 1927, File 55598/453A, NARAI.

171. Enforcers regularly referred to Detroit as the "back door" to the United States. For an example, see the memoir of Howard Blakemore, *Special Detail* (Philadelphia: Dorrance and Company, 1944), 296.

172. Harry E. Hull claimed, "The only basis that we have so far as we know, for the computation is that in the application for re-entry permits about 25 percent have been rejected for lack of verification. Now you apply that to the number of aliens that we know are in the country, and you can make a rough guess that it will run over 1,300,000." From "Say 1,300,000 Aliens May Be Deportable," *New York Times*, February 16, 1926.

173. "O. Adams, Inspector in Charge to J. S. Fraser, Esq., Division Commissioner," May 28, 1931, Windsor, Ontario, Department of Immigration and Colonization of Canada, Reel C-4723, Library and Archives of Canada.

174. "Catholic Vigilance Committee to Henry Ford," June 20, 1924, Box 30, Nevins and Hill Collection, Accession 572, BFRC.

175. "Deportation Hearing of Constantine Polos," January 4, 1926, File 55477/777, NARAI.

176. "George Smith File (pseudonym)," October 1931, Box 16, Accession 55, Sociological Department Records, BFRC.

177. The Border Patrol uses the term "legion of friends" to describe its informants, who seem to have been varied. U.S. Department of Labor, *Annual Report of the Commissioner General of Immigration to the Secretary of Labor* (Washington, D.C.: Government Printing Office, 1930), 36.

178. Howell, *Old Islam*, 68–69.

179. Daniels, *Guarding the Golden Door*, 52.

180. Vargas, *Proletarians of the North*, 110–111.

181. Vargas, *Proletarians of the North*, 130–132.

182. "Letter to Right Reverend Bishop Gallagher," July 1927, Box 1, Our Lady of Guadalupe Parish Records, ADA.

183. *Daughters of the American Revolution of Michigan Yearbook* (Albion, Mich.: D.A.R. Printing, 1929), 37.

184. *DAR Yearbook*, 67.

185. "Care in Immigration Is Urged by Nesbit," *Globe*, July 2, 1927.

186. "Lovat Says Lack of Immigration May Cloud Immigration Question," *Globe*, August 23, 1928.

187. "Annual Report of the National Catholic Welfare Conference, 1930–1931," Folder 9, Box 25, Bruce Mohler Papers, CUA.

188. U.S. Department of Labor, *Annual Report of the Commissioner General of Immigration to the Secretary of Labor* (Washington, D.C.: Government Printing Office, 1925), 9.

189. For an examination of how informal border policing developed on the U.S.-Mexico border, see Lytle Hernández, *Migra!*

190. Charging the streamliner for deportations became common practice in state-level immigration policies from 1819 to 1822, especially in port states from Maine to Florida, where alien seamen and stowaways often escaped at city ports. Aristide R. Zolberg, *A Nation by Design Immigration Policy in the Fashioning of America* (Cambridge, Mass.: Harvard University Press, 2006), 117.

191. Casabella's case is found in "Deportation Hearing of Luca Casabella," December 17, 1928, File 55477/943, NARAI. For similar deportation cases, see "Testimony of Pete Kogian," September 27, 1922, File 55210/54, NARAI; "Deportation Hearing of Sylvester Piwnicki," December 30, 1940, File 56029/196, NARAI; and "Deportation of Tanasi Liutyk," January 25, 1926, File 55477/920, NARAI. Deportation scene is described in "Aliens Find Devious Ways into States."

192. Lucy Salyer examines early Chinese exclusion and deportation cases to shed light on the enormous discretion of INS inspectors and the lack of judicial review afforded Chinese aliens during the 1890s. Salyer, *Laws Harsh as Tigers*, chap. 8.

193. For an excellent treatment of modern deportation policy, see Daniel Kanstroom, *Deportation Nation: Outsiders in American History* (Cambridge, Mass.: Harvard University Press, 2010).

194. St. Louisa's chapter of the DAR offers information on both police station and Woodward Avenue detention centers, where ladies conducted social work among foreign-born women. *DAR Yearbook*, 37.

195. "Complaints Re: Deportation Camps in U.S.," June 15, 1928, RG 25 vol. 1474, LAC.

196. Canaday, *The Straight State*, 21–22.

197. Anna R. Igra, "Likely to Become a Public Charge: Deserted Women and the Family Law of the Poor in New York City, 1910–1936," *Journal of Women's History* 11, no. 4 (2000): 59–81.

198. Leopold Drapal File, June 15, 1927, 55713/513, NARAI; Peter Kojanian File, August 24, 1925, File 55210/54, NARAI.

199. Robert Van De Voore File, January 25, 1926, File 55477/930, NARAI.

200. For examples, see Peter Limina File, January 29, 1926, File 55477/944, NARAI; Tanasi Liutyk File, January 25, 1926, File 55477/920, NARAI; Yakob Dwarok File, November 26, 1930, File 55715/925, NARAI; Peter Grabowiecki File, March 25, 1926 File 55489/472, NARAI.

201. "Alien Smugglers Find Devious Ways In," *Border Cities Star*, April 14, 1928; "On the Border," *Detroit News*, April 12, 1927; "Rum Runners Smuggle Aliens and Narcotics," *Toronto Daily Star*, November 24, 1928.

Chapter 2

1. Leopold Drapal File, June 15, 1927, File 55713/513, NARAI. For other examples of northern Europeans deported because of arrest for border crossing or other crimes, see Peter Limina File, January 29, 1926, File 55477/944, NARAI; Thomas O'Conner File, May 25, 1926, File 55558/259, NARAI; Godfrey Scott File, October 10, 1925, File 55457/863, NARAI; Horace Hopper File, April 30, 1925, File 55489/792, NARAI.

2. Clementi Palazzola File, March 3, 1927, File 5547/477, NARAI.

3. Revealing the ways southern and eastern European immigrants faced continued and systematic policing at the local level revises Mae Ngai's argument that "a critique of deportation policy emerged among social welfare advocates and legal reformers" that helped distance all Europeans from being stigmatized as illegal immigrants. In Detroit, northern European groups' efforts to emphasize their own desirability functioned to cast southern and eastern Europeans alongside Asians as the groups most likely to be illegal in Detroit. Mae Ngai, "The Strange Career of the Illegal Alien: Immigration Restriction and Deportation Policy in the United States, 1921–1965," *Law and History Review* 21, no. 1 (Spring 2003): 90.

4. Matthew Frye Jacobson argues that racial ideologies depicting Anglo-Saxons as racially superior to Celts, Teutons, and Slavs shifted toward a pattern that emphasized "Caucasian unity" in the mid-1920s. Jacobson, *Whiteness of a Different Color*, 92. For more on European ethnicity and assimilation during this period, see Gerstle, *American Crucible*; Daniel Roediger, *Working Toward Whiteness: How America's Immigrants Became White. The Strange Journey from Ellis Island to the Suburbs* (New York: Basic Books, 2005).

5. As outlined in the Introduction, this study relies on Thomas Guglielmo's intervention into the debate on whiteness and ethnicity, which argues that despite being considered inferior, ethnic Europeans were "widely accepted as white by the widest variety of people and institutions." Guglielmo, *White on Arrival*, 6.

6. Translation from the Yugoslav newspaper *Svijet*, "Release from the Foreign Language Information Service," February 29, 1924, 150.01/870, U.S. State Department Records, National Archives, College Park, Maryland.

7. "Report on the State of New U.S. Laws," June 11, 1925, The National Archives: Public Record Office, FO 115/2991, NAUK.

8. "Report from the Dominion of Canada," July 5, 1925, The National Archives: Public Record Office, FO 115/2991, NAUK.

9. "Romanian Report to the Undersecretary of State, Sir Joseph Pope on the 1924 Immigration Act," February 11, 1924, Reel C-4721, LAC.

10. "Report to L. C. Moyerm Esq., Private Secretary to W. L. Mackenzie King," November 22, 1926, Reel C-4722, LAC.

11. Tara Zahra, *The Great Departure: Mass Migration from Europe and the Making of the Free World* (New York: Norton, 2017).

12. "American Consular Report, Rome, May 8, 1925," File 150.01/1159, U.S. State Department Records, State Department Records, NARAII.

13. "Report from Prague, February 24, 1925; Warsaw to the U.S. Department of State, March 7, 1925," File 150.01/1159, NARAII.

14. "Detroit Board of Commerce Minutes," December 11, 1924, Box 1, Detroit Board of Commerce Papers, BHL.

15. "Readers of the Detroiter," *Detroiter*, March 19, 1928.

16. "Immigration Investigated by Board," *Detroiter*, October 2, 1920, BDPL.

17. "Help Prevent a Labor Shortage," Bulletin No. 750, December 5, 1922, Box 1 of 1922 minutes, Michigan Manufacturers Association Papers, BHL.

18. "Minutes of the Twenty-first Annual Banquet, Michigan Manufacturers Association, Hotel Statler, Detroit," April 25, 1923, Box 1, Michigan Manufacturers Association Papers, BHL.

19. Charles T. Gwyne, "Cheap Labor Un-American," *Coalitionist*, October 1929, File 150.01, State Department Records, NARAII.

20. "Detroit League of Urban Conditions Among Negroes," 1918, Box 28, Nevins and Hill Collection, Accession 572, BFRC.

21. Bates, *Black Detroit*, 64–65.

22. Bates, *Black Detroit*, 99–100.

23. Howell, *Old Islam*, 70.

24. For more on the *Chicago Defender*'s circulation across the urban North and even the South, see James Grossman, *Land of Hope: Chicago, Black Southerners, and the Great Migration* (Chicago: University of Chicago Press, 1991), 78–79.

25. "Out Foreign Friends," *Chicago Defender*, April 23, 1927.

26. "Know Your Neighbor and His Language," *Chicago Defender*, July 31, 1926.

27. "Urban League Report on Negro Workers, 1923," Box 74, Detroit Urban League Papers, BHL.

28. Daughters of the American Revolution Pamphlet, March 7, 1924, Origins Folder, Box 1, John Bond Trevor Papers, BHL; National Immigration Legislative Committee Pamphlet, November 1923, Origins Folder, Box 1, John Bond Trevor Papers, BHL.

29. "NCWC Protest to Congress Against the 1924 Immigration Bill," January 1924, U.S. Catholic Bishops and Immigration Documents, National Catholic Welfare Conference Papers, ACHR.

30. For more on Syrian American lobbies against quotas, see Gualtieri, *Between Arab and White*; Ariela Gross, *Guess What Blood Won't Tell: A History of Race on Trial in America* (Cambridge, Mass.: Harvard University Press, 2008); Lisa Suhier Majaj, "Arab American Ethnicity: Locations, Coalitions and Cultural Negotiations," in *Arabs in America: Building a New Future*, ed. Michael Sulieman (Philadelphia: Temple University Press, 1999).

31. Howell, *Old Islam*, 68–69.

32. Quotation from the *Novoye Russkoye Slovo*, a national Jewish paper with a circulation of over 700,000. Its Detroit circulation was cited at 20,000 in 1927, Report on Naturalization Folder, Box 2, Carl M. Weidman Papers, BHL.

33. Translations of foreign papers cited from report in the Foreign Language Information Service, February 29, 1924, File 150.01/870, State Department Records, NARAII.

34. On Czechs, see *Svet*; on Lithuanians, see *Draugas*; and on Poles, see *Nowy Swiat*. Translations from report in the Foreign Language Information Service, February 29, 1924, File 150.01/870, State Department Records, NARAII.

35. On racial discrimination, see *Amerikai Magyar Hepszaba*, a Polish newspaper based in Chicago. From report in the Foreign Language Information Service, February 29, 1924, File 150.01/870, State Department Records, NARAII.

36. Daniels, *Guarding the Golden Door*, 54–55.

37. Daniels, *Guarding the Golden Door*, 54.

38. "An Analysis of the Racist Origins of the National Origins Quota System of the Immigration Act of 1924," Folder 4, Box 25, U.S. Conference of Catholic Bishops, ACHR.

39. Daniels, *Guarding the Golden Door*, 55.

40. "An Analysis of the Racist Origins."

41. Ngai, *Impossible Subjects*, 25.

42. Ngai, *Impossible Subjects*, 26–27.

43. "Deportation File on Heinrich Petersen," File 55549/627, NARAI.

44. Daniels, *Guarding the Golden Door*, 57.

45. "Origins, 1930," Box 1, John Bond Trevor Papers, BHL.

46. Hing, *Defining Immigration Policy*, 43.

47. "An Analysis of the Racist Origins."

48. "Minutes from the Annual Meeting of the Michigan Manufacturers Association," September 1927, Box 1, Michigan Manufacturers Association Papers, BHL.

49. "Objectives," *Detroiter*, October 1927.

50. "La quota immigratoria aumenta da 3,845 a 5,802," *Tribuna Italiana d'America*, June 28, 1929.

51. "Nuove Disposizione di Immigraxione e Citadinanza," *La Voce del Popolo*, July 5, 1929, translated by Charles Keenan. Boston College biographical information on Reverend Joseph Ciarrochi is found in "Dared the Blackhand: Italian Priest Started Educational Newspaper," March 1923, Folder 22, Box 1, Santa Maria Detroit Parish Collection, ADA.

52. For quotes by Saperti and Bommarito, see "Sons of Italy Correspondence, Lodge 215, July 1927," National Origins Folder, File 55639/576B, NARAI. For wider information on the Sons of Italy in Detroit, see "The Americanization Committee of Detroit Annual Report, 1925," pp. 4–5, BHL.

53. "City of Chelsea, Mass. Board of Aldermen Joint Resolution," February 25, 1929, File 55639/576, NARAI. For more on petitioners from New York, Boston, and Connecticut, see File 55639/576 and File 55639/576A, NARAI.

54. "Anti-National Origins Clause League to Frank X. Martel," January 3, 1928, Anti-National Origins Clause League Folder, Box 1, CIO-AFL Papers, RL.

55. Solveig Zempel, *In Their Own Words: Letters from Norwegian Immigrants* (Minneapolis: University of Minnesota Press, 1991), 173.

56. "Anti National Origins Clause League to Hoover," March 20, 1929, File 55639/577, NARAI.

57. "Anti National Origins Clause League to Hoover."

58. "Anti National Origins Clause League to Hoover."

59. "Anti National Origins Clause League Letter," June 6, 1929, File 55639/576C, NARAI.

60. Information on Otto Shultz's life and living situation is found in the following: 1940; Census Place: Detroit, Wayne, Michigan; Roll: T627_1875; Page: 9A; Enumeration District: 84–1197, accessed on Ancestry.com, *1940 United States Federal Census* [database online] (Provo, Utah: Ancestry.com Operations, Inc., 2012). For Shultz's Klan "naturalization," see "L. J. Black to Mr. Otto Shultz," February 4, 1927, KKK Correspondence Folder, 1927–1940, Box 16, Civil Rights Congress of Michigan Records, RL.

61. "J. A. Moorehead, Executive Director of the American Relief Organization to Herbert Hoover," 1928, File 55639/576B, NARAI.

62. "Alien-Minded Groups in the 1928 Campaign," published by the Immigration Restriction Association, File 55639/577, NARAI, and an article from the *New York Times*, October 22, 1928.

63. "North American Civic League correspondence," February 21, 1929, and "Sons of the American Revolution, Detroit Chapter," February 11, 1929, File 55639/577, NARAI.

64. "Mr. Hoover and National Origins," *New York Times*, March 1, 1929.

65. "Anti-National Origins Clause League," June 6, 1929, File 55639/576C, NARAI.

66. "Anti-National Origins Clause League President Joseph Carey to Robe Earl White, Assistant Secretary of Labor," June 28, 1929, File 5639/576C, NARAI.

67. "Anti-National Origins Clause League President Joseph Carey to Robe Earl White, Assistant Secretary of Labor," June 28, 1929, File 5639/576C, NARAI.

68. "Protest Against Alien Law Clause," *New York Times*, February 16, 1929.

69. "Gladys A. Rohl to President Herbert Hoover," June 8, 1929, File 55639/576, NARAI.

70. Marshall Roderick, "The Box Bill, Public Policy, Ethnicity, and Economic Exploitation in Congress" (MA thesis, Texas State University, San Marcos, 2011), 2.

71. Patrick D. Lukens, *A Quiet Victory for Latino Rights: FDR and the Controversy over "Whiteness"* (Tucson: University of Arizona Press, 2012), 56–59.

72. "No Bars Are Raised Against Emigration from Great Britain," *Globe*, November 28, 1927.

73. "From Serbia to the 'Ford City . . .,'" *Windsor Star*, July 6, 1974; "They Didn't Want Handouts," *Windsor Star*, August 4, 1974.

74. "They Came, They Saw, They Built a Community," *Windsor Star*, September 4, 1987.

75. "Windsor Spark Plug Plant Is Operating on Important Scale," *Border Cities Star*, May 4, 1929.

76. "Allied Patriotic Societies," March 6, 1929, File 55639/576C, NARAI.

77. "Allied Patriotic Societies Bulletin on the National Origins Act," March 6, 1929, File 55639/576, NARAI.

78. "Albert Johnson to John Bond Trevor," March 26, 1929, Correspondence Folder, Box 1, John Bond Trevor Papers, BHL.

79. "Joseph Carey to Robe Earl White," July 28, 1929, File 5639/576C, NARAI.

80. INS inspectors did not patrol immigrant Scandinavian or Irish neighborhoods and British immigrants tended to live alongside established, native-born workers. For examples of

Finn, Swede, and Irish immigrants who faced deportation for being arrested for another crime, see the files of Godfrey Scott (File 55457/863), Harlon Fairchild (File 55477/447), Nick O'Conner (File 5558/259), and Per Peterson (File 55475/958), NARAI.

81. Unlike northern Europeans, who faced deportation when inspectors took the time to look into their legal statuses, Polish, Italian, and Russian immigrants were often picked up in the streets of their immigrant neighborhoods and in immigrant halls. For examples, see Conor Palazzola (File 55477/447), Ray Solucci (File 55558/260), Vasile Carmanos (File 55558/68), Mihail Szakacs (File 55475/717), and Peter Graboweicki (File 55489/472), NARAI.

82. "Klan and Rival Candidate Neck in Neck in Detroit," *Baltimore Sun*, November 6, 1929.

83. The Bowles election uncovers the importance of the Klan and vigilante nativists into the late 1920s. Historians argue that the formal power of the midwestern Ku Klux Klan peaked in 1924 when Bowles received one-third of Detroit's vote in his first attempt to run for mayor. Nancy MacLean notes that by 1926, the official Klan had "smaller numbers and a dwindling influence," eventually crumbling under the burden of tax evasion and bankruptcy. But even if Klan headquarters began to lose power in the mid-1920s, Bowles's successful election, an event rarely discussed in literature on the Klan or Detroit, ensured that Klan power continued in local industrial regions, especially in the urban Midwest. Kenneth T. Jackson, *The Ku Klux Klan in the City, 1915–1930* (New York: Rowman and Littlefield, 1967), 127–144; Nancy MacLean also uses the Bowles case to demonstrate the ideological hold the Klan had on Detroit, "America's fourth largest city," in 1924. Nancy MacLean, *Behind the Mask of Chivalry: The Making of the Second Ku Klux Klan* (New York: Oxford University Press, 1994), 184. A notable exception is Sidney Fine, whose pivotal work on the life of Frank Murphy details the Bowles case. Sidney Fine, *Frank Murphy: The Detroit Years* (Ann Arbor: University of Michigan Press, 1975), 210–223.

84. "KKK Gift, $100,000," *Detroit Owl*, September 28, 1929, Box 1, Carl Weidman Papers, BHL.

85. "Newspaper Clipping on Charles Bowles," September 1929, Clippings Folder, Box 1, Carl Weidman Papers, BHL.

86. Robert A. Hill, ed., *The Marcus Garvey and Universal Negro Improvement Association Papers*, vol. 9 (Berkeley: University of California Press, 1983).

87. "Newspaper Clipping on Charles Bowles."

88. An African American paper, the *Detroit People's News*, "refused to accept campaign advertising from Bowles on the grounds that Bowles was a member of the Ku Klux Klan and that the paper would be a traitor to the race." Reported in "Detroit Paper 'Tricked' to Aid Klan Candidate," *Pittsburgh Courier*, November 16, 1929, and "Radio Slaying Is Linked with Bowles Recall," *Baltimore Sun*, July 24, 1930.

89. "Bowles in Office," *Baltimore Sun*, September 24, 1929.

90. "Irish for Bowles," *Detroit Owl*, October 14, 1929, Box 1, Carl Weidman Papers, BHL.

91. "Klan and Rival Candidate Neck in Neck in Detroit," *Baltimore Sun*, November 6, 1929.

92. "Bowles Cites Smith Record," *Detroit News*, October 22, 1929.

93. "Meet John Smith, the Man—the Mayor," newspaper clipping from 1929, Clippings Folder, Box 1, Carl Weidman Papers, BHL.

94. "Elezioni," *La Tribuna Italiana D'America*, November 1, 1929.

95. On Bowles's victory, see "Detroit Elects Bowles Mayor in Close Race," *Chicago Daily Tribune*, November 6, 1929. On the "criminal element" in urban centers, see the statement of Secretary of Labor James Davis, which was distributed throughout the nation: "Alien Criminal Hard to Catch, Davis Explains," *Chicago Tribune*, July 1, 1929.

96. For examples of Michigan newspapers suggesting deportation would help mitigate urban crime, see "Chicago Nabs Sicilian Gang: 21 Marked for Deportation as Italian Gunmen," *Detroit Free Press*, February 24, 1926; "Moscow Radical Faces Deportation," *Detroit Free Press*, September 24, 1924; "Deportation of Alien Criminals Noted as Good," *Lansing State Journal*, December 20, 1930; "A Rusty Italian Weapon," *Battle Creek Enquirer*, August 9, 1929.

97. Hirota, *Expelling the Poor*, 5.

98. Nora Krinitsky, "The Politics of Crime Control: Race, Policing, and Reform in Twentieth-Century Chicago" (PhD diss., University of Michigan, 2017), 239–240.

99. "Drop in Detroit's Alien Crime Credited to Deportation Policy," *New York Herald Tribune*, March 15, 1931.

100. "US Steps in to Aid Police," *Detroit News*, January 7, 1930.

101. The article also noted that Detroit had twice as many deportable aliens in its prison than Chicago. "Deport the Undesirables," *Detroit Saturday Night Magazine*, September 14, 1929.

102. "Deporting Undesirables," *Detroit News*, January 9, 1930.

103. Numbers are difficult to quantify, but the Department of Labor reported 3,401 deportations across the U.S.-Canada border between June 30, 1929, and 1930. U.S. Department of Labor, *Annual Report* (1930), 51.

104. "Drop in Detroit's Alien Crime Credited to Deportation Policy," *New York Herald Tribune*, March 15, 1931.

105. Peter Wiconciwski File, November 5, 1929, Box 48, Arthur Tuttle Papers, BHL.

106. "Deport Alien Rummers," *Detroit Times*, August 4, 1930.

107. "Many Hang on Rim of U.S. Melting Pot," *Detroit Free Press*, September 29, 1929.

108. "Many Hang on Rim of U.S. Melting Pot."

109. "Many Hang on Rim of U.S. Melting Pot."

110. Peggy Pascoe, *What Comes Naturally: Miscegenation Law and the Making of Race in America* (New York: Oxford University Press, 2009), 181.

111. "Many Hang on Rim of U.S. Melting Pot."

112. Howell, *Old Islam*, 76–79.

113. "U.S. Relents, Alien to Stay," *Detroit Free Press*, March 11, 1930.

114. On the consideration of Syrian Christians as acceptable immigrants because of their religion, see Gualtieri, *Between Arab and White*, 3–4.

Chapter 3

1. Registering as a "nonquota" immigrant meant Yates was exempt from the quotas set forth by the 1924 Immigration Act. "Allotment by Quota Increased by 1,200 at Windsor Border," *Globe*, June 11, 1927.

2. "7 Ask Injunctions," *Border Cities Star*, October 16, 1928.

3. "250 Aliens After Visas," *Border Cities Star*, October 30, 1928.

4. "Action Urged Against Delegates Against Quota Law," *Border Cities Star*, May 7, 1927; "Detroit Board of Commerce Supports Commuters," May 5, 1927, State Department, File 150.01, NARAII.

5. "Frank Martel to Frank Morrison," November 1926, "Report by Frank Martel," December 1, 1926, Immigration Folder, Box 2, AFL-CIO Records, RL.

6. Fine, *Frank Murphy*, 100.

7. LaGumina, *Wop!*, 227.

8. Lee, *At America's Gates*, 32–33.

9. Daniels, *Guarding the Golden Door*, 35–36.

10. Thomas Klug, "Residents by Day, Visitors by Night: The Origins of the Alien Commuter on the U.S.-Canadian Border During the 1920s," *Michigan Historical Review* 34, no. 2 (Fall 2008): 86.

11. "Frank Martel Address," January 15, 1927, File 150.01, State Department Records, NARAII.

12. "Memorandum—General Review of Detroit Border Crossing Situation as Affecting Business and Immigration by the Border Cities Chamber of Commerce, Windsor," 1927, File 150.01, State Department Records, NARAII.

13. "List of Non-Quota Aliens Coming into Detroit," December 9, 1927, File 150.01, State Department Records, NARAII.

14. "Case of Fedor Bachila," Commuting Cases 1931, Commuting File 150.01, State Department Records, NARAII.

15. "Threatened Suspension of Commuting Privilege Following Protests of Union Labor," from Consul H. F. Hawley, January 6, 1927, File 150.01, State Department Records, NARAII.

16. Klug, "Residents by Day," 83–84.

17. "Detroit Gives Aid to Border," *Border Cities Star*, January 8, 1927.

18. "Report on Commuting," December 13, 1939, R. B. Bennett Papers, Reel M-1072, LAC.

19. *U.S. City Directories, 1822–1995 and Michigan, Death Records, 1867–1950* [database online] (Provo, Utah: Ancestry.com Operations, Inc., 2011).

20. United States Census Year: 1910; Census Place: Detroit Ward 17, Wayne, Michigan; Roll: T624_680; Page: 1B; Enumeration District: 0250, accessed on Ancestry.com, *1910 United States Federal Census* (Provo, Utah: Ancestry.com Operations, Inc., 2006).

21. "Unions Protest Entry of Canadian Workers," *Detroit Labor News*, November 12, 1926.

22. "Is Immigration Department to Permit Continued Violation of U.S. Law?" *Detroit Labor News*, January 14, 1927.

23. The DFL had wanted to organize the automobile workers and had petitioned the AFL multiple times for support in organizing the skilled workers of the industry. Joyce Shaw Peterson, *American Automobile Workers, 1900–1932* (Albany: SUNY Press, 1997), 122.

24. "Frank Martel to Frank Morrison," November 1926, Immigration Folder, Box 5, Metropolitan Detroit AFL-CIO Collection, RL.

25. "Frank Morrison to Frank Martel," November 20, 1926, and "Frank Morrison to Frank Martel," November 23, 1926, Immigration Folder, Box 5, Metropolitan Detroit AFL-CIO Collection, RL.

26. "News Encouraged Violation of U.S. Immigration Laws," *Detroit Labor News*, December 31, 1926.

27. "Detroit Federation of Labor to E. H. Dunnigan, Special Representative Department of Labor," December 1, 1926, Immigration Folder, Box 5, Metropolitan Detroit AFL-CIO

Collection, RL; "Threatened Suspension of Commuting Privilege Following Protests of Union Labor," from Consul H. F. Hawley, January 6, 1927, File 150.01, State Department Records, NARAII.

28. For letters from Martel to officials in Washington, New York, and Detroit, see "DFL's Frank Martel to Frank Morrison, Secretary of the AFL," November 1926, and "DFL to E. H. Dunnigan, Special Representative Department of Labor," December 1, 1926, Immigration Folder, Box 5, Metropolitan Detroit AFL-CIO Collection, RL.

29. "DFL to E. H. Dunnigan, Special Representative to the Department of Labor."

30. "Plan to Limit Labor Coming from Canada," *Detroit Labor News*, April 22, 1927.

31. "General Order No. 86, Bureau of Immigration," April 1, 1927, Immigration Folder, Box 5, Metropolitan Detroit AFL-CIO Collection, RL.

32. Klug, "Residents by Day," 89.

33. "Memo to Office of Foreign Control from H. T. Nugent," April 11, 1927, File 150.01, NARAII.

34. "Correspondence Between Mr. L. J. Flint, Detroit Board of Commerce to the Department of Labor," early 1927, File 150.01, NARAII.

35. "Resolutions Pass Councils; Special Meeting Is Called," April 1927, File 150.01, NARAII.

36. McGregor, *In the Shadow of Detroit*, 226–230.

37. "Border Cities Chamber of Commerce Report on 1927 Situation," December 16, 1930, R. B. Bennett Papers, Microfilm Reel M-1072, LAC.

38. "Actions Urged by Delegates Against Quota Laws," *Globe*, May 7, 1927.

39. RG 2A—Clerk Council Records, 1927, Windsor Municipal Archives, WPLA.

40. "Border Cities Chamber of Commerce Report," January 6, 1927, File 150.01, NARAII.

41. "Detroit Gives Aid to Border," *Border Cities Star*, January 8, 1927.

42. "Treaty Halts Passage Bar," *Border Cities Star*, January 4, 1927.

43. "Treaty Rights Unearthed," *Detroit Times*, January 9, 1927.

44. Detroit Chamber of Commerce to the State Department, January 1927, File 150.01, NARAII.

45. "Courageous Actions Urged by Delegates Against Quota Law," *Border Cities Star*, May 7, 1927.

46. Detroit Chamber of Commerce to the State Department, January 1927, File 150.01, NARAII.

47. "John L. Zurbrick, District Director of Immigration to Frank Martel," November 30, 1930, Box 5, AFL-CIO Files, RL.

48. "Report on the Commuter Situation, May 1927," File 150.01, NARAII.

49. "Notes on Meeting with the Windsor Delegation," May 6, 1927, File 150.01, NARAII.

50. Correspondence May 1922, R. B. Bennet Papers, Reel M-1072, LAC.

51. "Day Laborers from Canada," FO 115/3354, January 22, 1927, NAUK.

52. Donald Avery, "Canadian Workers and American Immigration Restriction: A Case of the Windsor Commuter, 1924–1931," *Mid-America: An Historical Review* 80 (Fall 1998): 239–240.

53. "Elizabeth Smith to President Hoover," May 4, 1927, File 55639/576C, NARAII.

54. "Higher Alien Bars Urged," *Detroit Free Press*, January 1, 1927.

55. "William Green to Frank Martel," March 22, 1927, Police Department Folder, Box 53, AFL-CIO Papers, RL.

56. "DFL to Secretary of State Frank Kellogg," April 29, 1927, File 150.01, U.S. State Department Records, NARAII.

57. "Affronting Canada," *New York Journal of Commerce*, June 10, 1927, RG 76, Vol. 593, File 840629, LAC.

58. "Canada and 'Grave Results,'" *Boston Transcript*, June 10, 1927, RG 76, Vol. 593, File 840629, LAC.

59. "Allotment by Quota Increased by 1,200 at Windsor Border," *Globe*, June 11, 1927.

60. "Bar Right to Enter States," *Border Cities Star*, November 8, 1927.

61. "Immigration Order of Department Officials Nullifies U.S. Law," *Detroit Labor News*, June 17, 1927.

62. "Immigration Order of Department Officials Nullifies U.S. Law," *Detroit Labor News*, June 17, 1927.

63. "Prepare for the Invasion," *Detroit Labor News*, July 1, 1927.

64. "Commuters Go to Court," *Globe*, November 8, 1927.

65. "Bar Right to Enter States."

66. "Frank Martel to Secretary of State Frank Kellogg," December 8, 1927, File 150.01, U.S. State Department Records, NARAII.

67. "The American Mussolini," *Detroit Labor News*, December 2, 1927.

68. "St. Clair Daughters of American Revolution to Secretary of State Frank Kellogg," December 15, 1927, File 150.01, U.S. State Department Records, NARAII.

69. "Allied Patriotic Societies to Secretary of State Frank Kellogg," December 15, 2017, File 150.01, U.S. State Department Records, NARAII.

70. "Bar Right to Enter States."

71. "250 Aliens After Visas," *Border Cities Star*, October 20, 1928; "Windsor Commuters Win Fight in Detroit," *Globe*, November 20, 1928.

72. "Commuting Injunctions Report," November 1928, R. B. Bennet Papers, Reel M-1072, LAC.

73. "250 Aliens After Visas."

74. "Report on the Commuting Situation," June 1928, File 150.01, NARAII.

75. "Memorandum—Review of Detroit Border Crossing Situation by the Border Cities Chamber of Commerce, Windsor," 1929, File 150.01, State Department Records, NARAII.

76. "Martel to Mr. E. D. Williams," November 14, 1929, November 22, 1929, and November 25, 1929, Box 2, AFL-CIO Records, RL.

77. "Martel to Mr. E. D. Williams," December 10, 1929, December 17, 1929, January 3, 1930, and February 12, 1930.

78. "Cases of Commuters," 1930, File 150.01, U.S. State Department Records, NARAII.

Chapter 4

1. Holly Karibo, *Sin City North: Sex, Drugs, and Citizenship in the Detroit-Windsor Borderland* (Chapel Hill: University of North Carolina Press, 2015), 15.

2. Peterson, *American Automobile Workers*, 132.

3. President of Park and Davis Pharmaceuticals, Owen Smith, claimed the new bridge "will bring us closer to our neighbor than ever before." Smith hoped the bridge would link

the company with its Canadian suppliers and perhaps provide a new pool of skilled pharmacists and chemists to foster innovation in Detroit's pharmaceutical industry. "On Ambassador Bridge, 1929," MS 19 I-8/1 Citizenship File, Windsor Municipal Archives, WPL. Automobile companies agreed. Chrysler's Vice President K. T. Keller predicted that an easier route across the border would "heretofore economically benefit both the United States and Canada" by facilitating the transportation of workers and goods between factories and branch plants. "Ambassador Bridge," *Detroit Free Press*, November 11, 1929; "Detroit International Bridge: The Ambassador Bridge, 1929," Ambassador Bridge Records, UMSC. In Canada, realtors and property developers responded to the bridge with full-page advertisements in the *Detroit Free Press* promoting Windsor subdivisions as "Detroit adjacent" or as "right next to River Rouge." The advertisements reminded Detroiters, "The bridge is here. Now is the time to buy, before prices go up!" In Windsor, the same relators and businesses lobbied for the bridge's potential to bring much-needed American money to Canadian border towns. "Nations Hail Opening of Bridge," *Detroit Free Press*, November 10, 1929.

4. For work on Canadian deportation drives, see Barbara Roberts, *Whence They Came: Deportation from Canada, 1900–1935* (Ottawa: University of Ottawa Press, 1988); Kelley and Trebilcock, *Making of the Mosaic*. For scholarship on Mexican repatriation, see Abraham Hoffman, *Unwanted Mexican Americans in the Great Depression: Repatriation Pressures, 1929–1939* (Tucson: University of Arizona Press, 1974); Dennis Nodín Valdés, *Al Norte: Agricultural Workers in the Great Lakes Region, 1917–1970* (Austin: University of Texas Press, 1991); Zaragosa Vargas, *Proletarians of the North: A History of Mexican Industrial Workers in Detroit and the Midwest, 1917–1933* (Berkeley: University of California Press, 1993).

5. Cohen, *Making a New Deal*; Gerstle, *American Crucible*; Jacobson, *Whiteness of a Different Color*.

6. Peterson, *American Automobile Workers*, 131.

7. "Report on Unemployment in Detroit, January 4, 1930," Welfare Folder, 1930, Mayor's Papers, BDPL.

8. In 1930, census records show that 403,721 foreign-born residents lived in Detroit, and the total city population was 1,568,662. Albert Mayer, "A Study of the Foreign-Born Population of Detroit, 1870–1950" (PhD diss., Wayne State University, 1951), 20.

9. "Discouraging Underworld Support," *Detroit Times*, August 18, 1930; "Bowles Comes Out for Death Penalty," *Detroit Times*, August 19, 1930; Beth Tompkins Bates, *The Making of Black Detroit in the Age of Henry Ford* (Chapel Hill: University of North Carolina Press, 2012), 127.

10. "Murphy Runs for Mayor," *Detroit Times*, August 20, 1930.

11. For more on the complex development of laws categorizing European, Asian, and African American groups by race, see Peggy Pascoe, "Miscegenation Law, Court Cases, and Ideology of 'Race' in Twentieth Century America," *Journal of American History* 83, no. 1 (June 1996): 44–69.

12. For more on the Ossian Sweet case, which encouraged civil rights *activists* to focus on the problem of de facto segregation and working-class racial violence in housing in the urban North, see Kevin Boyle, *Arc of Justice: A Saga of Race, Civil Rights, and Murder in the Jazz Age* (New York: Holt, 2004).

13. "Walter White of the NAACP to Frank Murphy," September 2, 1930, Box 2, Frank Murphy Papers, BHL.

14. Bates, *Black Detroit*, 128.

15. In Spanish: "Vote por el juez, Frank Murphy para Mayor. Un hombre que comprende y representara a todo el pueblo. Siempre ha demostrado especial interés en los derechos de las minorías," "G. G. Lopez, Notary Public, 2620 Baker Street to Frank Murphy," September 8, 1930, Box 2, Frank Murphy Papers, BHL.

16. Fine, *Frank Murphy*, 227.

17. For Bund organization information, see "Deutschen Unterstützungs-Bundes Bezirk Detroit to Frank Murphy," September 4, 1930, Box 2, Frank Murphy Papers, Bentley Historical Library, Ann Arbor, Michigan; Albert Mayer, "A Study of the Foreign-Born Population," 20.

18. The Catholic Church, which represented nearly 60 percent of Detroit's population, threw its energy into rousing Catholic voters, but Murphy's religious base did not stop with his own church. Secular ethnic organizations also rallied behind Murphy like no previous mayoral candidate. In particular, the Sons of Italy and the Ukrainian American Citizens League agreed with Murphy's stance on the familiar issues of relaxing immigration, overturning Prohibition, and solving unemployment. On Catholics, see Fine, *Frank Murphy*, 221. On Italians for Murphy, see "Nicholas Rovengo of the Detroit Fire and Marine Insurance Company to Frank Murphy," undated; on Poles for Murphy, see "Leopold Koscincki, Attorney to Frank Murphy," September 10, 1930; on Hungarians for Murphy, see "A. J. Hirlap, Hungarian News to Frank Murphy," September 12, 1930; and on Ukrainians, see "Ukrainian American Citizens Club to Murphy," September 11, 1930. All found in Box 2, Frank Murphy Papers, BHL. On Jewish support for Murphy, see "Max Silverman to Frank Murphy," August 29, 1930, Box 2, Frank Murphy Papers, BHL.

19. Bates, *Black Detroit*, 132.

20. Martin Edward Sullivan, "'On the Dole': The Relief Issue in Detroit, 1929–1939" (PhD diss., University of Notre Dame, 1974), 91.

21. For more on the Welfare Department and the Ford Sociological Department, see Box 16, Sociological Department Records, Accession 55, BFRC.

22. Sullivan, "On the Dole," 91.

23. Sullivan, "On the Dole," 72.

24. Nowak, *Two Who Were There*, 15.

25. Wladyslav Sciecki File, October 23, 1933, File 55840/306, NARAI.

26. Vargas, *Proletarians of the North*, 170.

27. Bates, *Black Detroit*, 124.

28. Wolcott, *Remaking Respectability*, 169–170.

29. Formed in 1930, the mayor's unemployment committee united a disparate group of leaders across Detroit in order to address the problem of unemployment in the city. Members included Mayor Frank Murphy; Rabbi Leon Fram of Temple Beth El; the DFL's Frank Martel; M. A. Cudlip, vice president of Packard Motor; Walter Briggs of Briggs Body Company; and Charles E. Sorenson of Ford Motor Company. Mayor's Unemployment Committee Meeting Notes, 1930, Box 9, Detroit Urban League Papers, BHL.

30. Peterson, *American Automobile Workers*, 136–137.

31. Bates, *Black Detroit*, 138.

32. Peterson, *American Automobile Workers*, 136–137.

33. Elizabeth Esch, *The Color Line and the Assembly Line: Managing Race in the Ford Empire* (Oakland: University of California Press, 2018), 103; Bates, *Black Detroit*, 145.

34. Esch, *The Color Line*, 104.

35. Bates, *Black Detroit*, 145.

36. Esch, *The Color Line*, 105.

37. Esch, *The Color Line*, 109.

38. Bates, *Black Detroit*, 156.

39. "Welfare Program Strongly Indicted," *Detroit Free Press*, June 29, 1931.

40. "Two Papers Criticize Welfare Policy Here," *Detroit Free Press*, June 26, 1931.

41. Jonathan Plaut, *The Jews of Windsor, 1790–1990: An Historical Chronicle* (Toronto: Dundurn, 2007), 94.

42. Jonathan Plaut, "Reforming and Conforming: A History of the Jews of Windsor, 1790–1940" (PhD. diss., Hebrew Union College, Jewish Institute of Religion, 1977), 451.

43. *Census of Canada*, 1931, 294.

44. On President Hoover and the Smoot Hawley tariff, see Komiko Koyama, "The Smoot Hawley Tariff Act: Why Did the President Sign the Bill?" *Journal of Policy History* 21, no. 2 (2009): 163–186; Richard N. Kottman, "Herbert Hoover and the Smoot-Hawley Tariff: Canada, a Case Study," *Journal of American History* 62, no. 3 (December 1975): 609–635. On the consequences of American tariffs on Canada's economy, see David Jacks, "Defying Gravity: The Imperial Economic Conference and the Reorientation of Canadian Trade," *Explorations in Economic History* 53 (July 2014): 22.

45. Plaut, *Jews of Windsor*, 100.

46. "Mayoral Candidates Speak," *Detroit News*, November 7, 1930.

47. "Mayor Moves for Change," *Border Cities Star*, January 14, 1931.

48. "Mayor's Municipal Fund," *Border Cities Star*, February 2, 1931.

49. "To Make Check of Alien Labor," *Border Cities Star*, February 16, 1931.

50. "Report of Sub-Committee on Welfare Statistics, July 25, 1932," Box 114, Accession 6, Edsel Ford Office Papers, BFRC.

51. "Annual Report of the National Catholic Welfare Conference," 1930–1931, Folder 9, Box 25, Bruce Mohler Papers, ACHR.

52. "Detroit Police Chief, Backed by Drys Ousted," *Baltimore Sun*, January 11, 1931.

53. "District 11 Report for the Fiscal Year," June 30, 1932, File 55778/911, NARAI.

54. Krinitsky, "The Politics of Crime Control," 239–240.

55. For more on John Zurbrick's "deportation war," see Chapter 2 of this book.

56. "3,000 Expected to Flee Alien Welfare Check," *Detroit Free Press*, June 14, 1931.

57. Greer Golda, "To Shape the Future of the Nation," 213; Dennis Nodín Valdés, *Al Norte: Agricultural Workers in the Great Lakes Region, 1917–1970* (Austin: University of Texas Press, 1991), 3.

58. Vargas, *Proletarians of the North*, 178.

59. Greer Golda, "To Shape the Future of the Nation," 210–211.

60. Canaday, *The Straight State*, 21–22.

61. Valdés, *Al Norte*, 13.

62. Department of Labor, *Annual Report of the Secretary of Labor, Fiscal Year Ended June 1933*, 44.

63. Greer Golda, "To Shape the Future of the Nation," 213.

64. Vargas, *Proletarians of the North*, 186.

65. Ohnuki, "The Detroit Chinese," 77.

66. "Hunt Alien Ring Here," *Detroit Free Press*, October 27, 1931.

67. Department of Labor, *Annual Report of the Secretary of Labor* (Washington, D.C.: Government Printing Office, 1932), 73.

68. "Removal Hearing of Panto Corovich," October 1933, File 55840/284, NARAI.

69. "Removal Hearing of Giuseppe Morano," October 21, 1933, File 55840/313, NARAI.

70. Department of Labor, *Annual Report of the Secretary of Labor*, 73.

71. "Removal Hearing of Istvan Meszano," May 24, 1934, File 55840/258, NARAI.

72. "Removal Hearing of Ivan Petrumajanez," February 15, 1930, File 55740/395, NARAI.

73. "Remarks by John Zurbrick," July 26, 1933," File 55778/911, NARAI.

74. Howell, *Old Islam*, 106–107.

75. Cohen, *Making a New Deal*, chap. 4.

76. Windsor Welfare Reports, 1930–1935, MS 27 I 12, Windsor Municipal Archives, WPL.

77. Barbara Roberts, *Whence They Came: Deportation from Canada, 1900–1935* (Ottawa: University of Ottawa Press, 1988), 18; Pierre Berton, *The Great Depression, 1929–1939* (Toronto: Anchor Canada, 1990), 145.

78. Kelley and Trebilcock, *Making of the Mosaic*, 229.

79. Kelley and Trebilcock, *Making of the Mosaic*, 14.

80. "Welfare Department Deports Foreigners," *Border Cities Star*, June 3, 1930; "Foreigners Out," *Border Cities Star*, February 10, 1931; "A New System," *Border Cities Star*, March 12, 1931. For information on deportations from East Windsor, see RG 8 DII-1/3, East Windsor Prisoner's Register, 1930–1931, Windsor Municipal Archives, WPL.

81. For information on deportations from East Windsor, see RG 8 DII-1/3, East Windsor Prisoner's Register, 1930–1931, Windsor Municipal Archives, WPL.

82. "Oshawa to Deport Jobless Aliens," *Border Cities Star*, June 4, 1932.

83. "Mayor Bucks Deportations," *Border Cities Star*, June 6, 1932.

84. "On Welfare, So Deported," *Border Cities Star*, July 16, 1932.

85. "Mayor Bucks Deportations."

86. "Mayor and Curry Talk Deportation," *Border Cities Star*, June 11, 1932.

87. In Windsor, the Italian Falcons and Polish American League wrote to Mayor Croll voicing their support. The Detroit Magyar Association, a Hungarian group, wrote from across the river, lamenting the fact that "Detroit cannot have a mayor so sympathetic to immigrants." Found in "Immigrants to the Mayor," June 1, 1932, MS 12 I-8/8 Mayor's File, Windsor Municipal Archives, WPL.

88. "On Welfare, So Deported."

89. Immigrant Canadians expressed their concern that the threat of deportation left their communities in constant fear. "Immigrants to the Mayor," June 1, 1932, MS 12 I-8/8 Mayor's File, Windsor Municipal Archives, WPL.

90. "On Welfare, So Deported."

91. "On Ambassador Bridge, 1929," MS 19 I-8/1 Citizenship File, Windsor Municipal Archives, WPL; "Ambassador Bridge," *Detroit Free Press*, November 11, 1929; "Detroit International Bridge: The Ambassador Bridge, 1929," Ambassador Bridge Records, Special Collections Library, Transportation History Collection, UMSC.

92. "Nations Hail Opening of Bridge," *Detroit Free Press*, November 10, 1929.

Chapter 5

1. "House Enrolled Act No. 176, Signed by Wilber M. Brucker, Gov. of Michigan (for release to press)," May 31, 1931, Union League of Michigan Folder, Box 20, AFL-CIO Collection, RL.

2. Thomas A. Klug, "Labor Market Politics in Detroit: The Curious Case of the Spolansky Act of 1931," *Michigan Historical Review* 14, no. 1 (Spring 1988): 4.

3. "Joseph Kowalski to the Detroit Welfare Department," March 12, 1931, Alien Folder, Box 7, Mayor's Records 1931, Burton Historical Collection, DPL.

4. "Labor Opposes Bridge Project," *Detroit Labor News*, June 17, 1927; "Immigration from Canada Shows Gain; Mexico a Decrease," *Detroit Labor News*, November 22, 1929.

5. For historians who suggest the Briggs strike launched an era of automobile organizing, see Peterson, *American Automobile Workers*, 128, Robert H. Zieger, *American Workers, American Unions, 1920–1985* (Baltimore: Johns Hopkins University Press, 1986), 24. Steve Babson takes a more nuanced approach, arguing that the Briggs strike and the Depression gave "native-born and immigrant workers of Detroit a new sensibility, one which rapidly narrowed the gap between Anglo-Gaelic activists and their increasingly militant co-workers."*Building the Union: Skilled Workers and Anglo-Gaelic Immigrants in the Rise of the UAW* (New Brunswick, N.J.: Rutgers University Press, 1991), 117.

6. For labor's role in anti-immigrant activism, including its efforts in favor of Chinese exclusion and European immigration quotas, see Chapter 3 of this book.

7. "Martel to ACLU," March 10, 1930, ACLU Folder, Box 1, AFL-CIO Papers, RL.

8. "Roger N. Baldwin to Frank Martel," March 6, 1930, ACLU Folder, Box 1, AFL-CIO Papers, RL.

9. Klug, "Labor Market Politics," 7.

10. "Mass Letter from Frank Martel to Detroit Employers," November 20, 1929; "Frank Martel to Mayor John C. Lodge," November 22, 1929; and "Frank Martel to Wilber Brucker," November 30, 1929, Detroit Mayor's Papers, 1929, BDPL.

11. Gage, *The Day Wall Street Exploded*, 254.

12. For a discussion of the Detroit Communist Party's involvement in protesting the Sacco and Vanzetti case, see "Workers Rally Behind the Gastonia Prisoners," *Industrial Intelligence Bulletin*, July 1, 1929.

13. "Detroit Leads the Country in Getting New Members for the Reds," *Industrial Intelligence Bulletin*, March 3, 1930, BHL.

14. "Communists Making Progress in Michigan. Meetings Are Well Attended," *Industrial Intelligence Bulletin*, April 21, 1930, Bentley Historical Library, Ann Arbor, Michigan. The Communist Party passed out special editions of the *Fisher Body Worker*, the *Chevrolet Worker*, the *Hudson Worker*, and the *Ford Worker* in corresponding automobile plants. "Thousands of Shop Workers Distributed to Workers Here Last Week," *Industrial Intelligence Bulletin*, February 17, 1930, BHL.

15. Klug, "Labor Market Politics," 21.

16. Thomas Klug, "The Eyes of the Country Are Again on Detroit! The Michigan Alien Registration Law of 1931 and the Arrowsmith Case," unpublished paper (used with permission of author), Marygrove College (September 22, 2013), 15.

17. Klug, "The Eyes of the Country," 15–16.

18. For a sampling of literature on African Americans and the Communist Party, see Robin Kelley, *Hammer and Hoe: Alabama Communists During the Great Depression* (Chapel

Hill: University of North Carolina Press, 1990); Meier and Rudwick, *Black Detroit*; Mark Niason, *Communists in Harlem During the Depression* (Urbana: University of Illinois Press, 1983); Cedric Robinson, *Black Marxism: The Making of the Black Radical Tradition* (Chapel Hill: University of North Carolina Press, 1983); Mark Solomon, *The Cry Was Unity: Communists and African Americans, 1917–36* (Oxford: University of Mississippi Press, 1998).

19. "American Legion to the Detroit Federation of Labor," October 29, 1932, American Legion Folder, Box 1, RL.

20. "Roger N. Baldwin to Frank Martel," March 6, 1930, ACLU Folder, Box 1, AFL-CIO Papers, RL.

21. "Communists Plan to Hold Jobless Mass Meeting in Detroit," *Industrial Intelligence Bulletin*, December 23, 1930, BHL.

22. On advisory council, see "Detroit Council for the Protection of Foreign-Born Workers," *Industrial Intelligence Bulletin*, April 2, 1928, No. 26, Box 2, Frank Murphy Papers, BHL.

23. "Prepare for Legal Battle Against Alien Registration Bill; Governor Is Certain to Approve of the Measure," *Jewish Daily News*, May 22, 1931.

24. "Memo from the Detroit Council for the Protection of Foreign Born Workers," April 2, 1928, and DCPFBW Conference Call, Sunday 10 a.m., April 22, 1928, International Institute of Detroit, 1921–1928 Folder, Box 6, AFL-CIO Papers, RL.

25. "Protest to Registration," 1931–1932, File 56044/99, NARAI.

26. "House Enrolled Act No. 176."

27. Klug, "Labor Market Politics," 4.

28. "Department of Immigration and Colonization Canada," Windsor, Ontario, May 28, 1931, Reel C-4723, LAC; Klug, "The Eyes of the Country," 17.

29. "Detroit Council for the Protection of Foreign Born Workers"; International Institute of Metropolitan Detroit Papers, "Lithuanian Workers of Detroit," February 14, 1932, File 56044/99, NARAI.

30. "House Enrolled Act No. 176."

31. "House Enrolled Act No. 176"; "Union League of Michigan Copy of Registration Bill, State of Michigan, Session of 1931," Reel C-4723, LAC.

32. Klug, "Labor Market Politics," 18.

33. Klug, "Labor Market Politics," 13.

34. "Minutes of the Meeting of the Detroit Employment Manager's Club," March 13, 1930, Box 1, Human Resource Association of Detroit Papers, BHL.

35. Klug, "The Eyes of the Country," 27.

36. Frank E. Carter, *Michigan Manufacturers and Financial Record*, vol. 29 (Lansing, Mich.: Manufacturing Industries, 1922), 14.

37. "Alien Listing Law Assailed," *Detroit News*, May 31, 1931.

38. Klug, "Labor Market Politics," 28.

39. "Open Fight on Enforcement of Alien Registry," *Detroit Times*, May 30, 1931.

40. Peterson, *American Automobile Workers*, 132.

41. "Demonstration at Grand Circus Park, June 19, 1931," Communist 1930s Folder, AFL-CIO Papers, Box 1, RL.

42. Libby Garland points out that high-powered Jewish lobbies saw overturning registration as pivotal to their path to whiteness and acceptance in mainstream American life. Garland, *After They Closed the Gates*.

43. Klug, "Labor Market Politics," 2; Garland, *After They Closed the Gates*, chap. 5.

44. On the American Legion and DAR's tendency to elide the differences between communists, Jews, Catholics, and foreigners, see "American Legion Invades Detroit," *Second Baptist Church Herald*, September 28, 1931; "DAR on Immigrants," July 10, 1930, Race Relations Folder, Box 28, Accession 572, Nevins and Hill Research, BFRC.

45. "The Rabbi Rants," *Detroit Labor News*, July 2, 1931; "Judges Denison, O'Brien, and Simons Hear Constitutionality Arguments of Michigan Alien Registration Bill," *Detroit Jewish Chronicle*, July 3, 1931.

46. "Organize to Fight Registration Bill at July 1 Hearing," *Detroit Jewish Chronicle*, June 12, 1931.

47. Klug, "The Eyes of the Country," 33–34.

48. Klug, "The Eyes of the Country," 38.

49. "Fred M. Butzel's Attack on the Alien Registration Bill," *Detroit Jewish Chronicle*, June 5, 1931.

50. "On Hearings Before the District Court on Registration. Report by the British Consulate in Detroit," July 22, 1931, Reel C-4723, LAC.

51. Klug, "The Eyes of the Country," 36.

52. "Judges Denison."

53. "Lessons of the Registration Bill Fight," *Detroit Jewish Chronicle*, July 10, 1931.

54. "Lessons of the Registration Bill Fight."

55. "Michigan Manufacturer's Association to Frank Januszweiski," July 1931, Box 31, Nevins and Hill Research Collection, Accession 572, BFRC.

56. Sanford Jacoby, *Modern Manners: Welfare Capitalism Since the New Deal* (Princeton, N.J.: Princeton University Press, 1997), 4.

57. In 1930, census records show that 403,721 foreign-born residents lived in Detroit and the total city population was 1,568,662. Mayer, "A Study of the Foreign Born," 20.

58. "Ford Official Documents, 1933," Sociological Department Records, Procedural Manuals Subseries, Accession 280, BFRC.

59. "March 30, 1930 Minutes," Detroit Personnel Management Association Folder, Box 1, Human Resource Association of Greater Detroit Papers, BHL.

60. Peterson, *American Automobile Workers*, 135.

61. "Questionnaire for Case Study, 1932 Cases," Box 114, Sociological Department Records, Accession 55, BFRC.

62. "George Duffy (pseudonym) to Ford Motor Company," July 20, 1936, Investigation Subseries Folder, Box 19, Employee Account Series, Sociological Department Records, Accession 55, BFRC.

63. Fine, *Frank Murphy*, 246.

64. Fine, *Frank Murphy*, 403–404.

65. Fine, *Frank Murphy*, 404–406.

66. "The Ford Plant Riot," *Los Angeles Times*, March 9, 1932.

67. "Mailed Fist for Communists," *Record Eagle*, August 30, 1932.

68. "U.S. Gets a Plea to Apprehend Riot Leaders," *Detroit Free Press*, March 9, 1932.

69. "Ford Tells of Red Stand," *Detroit News*, July 27, 1930.

70. "Detroit Drive on Aliens," *Evening Independent*, July 21, 1932.

71. Thomas Kostopoulos is a pseudonym for a Greek worker found in the restricted files of the Ford Sociological Department Records, case file taken on November 14, 1932, Box 17, Sociological Department Records, Accession 55, BFRC.

72. Mike Kovacevich is a pseudonym for a Yugoslavian worker found in the restricted files of the Ford Sociological Department Records, case file taken on October 27, 1932, Box 16, Sociological Department Records, Accession 55, BFRC.

73. "Deportation Record of Maria Belenko," April 12, 1931, File 56898/455, NARAI.

74. "Deportation Record of Maria Belenko," April 12, 1931, File 56898/455, NARAI.

75. In 1930, census records show that 403,721 foreign-born residents lived in Detroit. Mayer, "A Study of the Foreign Born," 20.

76. "Correspondence from Frank X. Martel to Carl Weidman," June 9, 1933, Correspondence 1933 Folder, Box 1, Carl Weidman Papers, BHL.

77. "Correspondence from Frank X. Martel to Carl Weidman," June 9, 1933, and "Correspondence Between Frank Martel and Carl Weidman," March 29, 1933, Correspondence 1933 Folder, Box 1, Carl Weidman Papers, BHL.

78. "Correspondence Between Frank Martel and Patrick Hurley, Secretary of War," November to December 1930, Box 13, Selfridge Field Folder, AFL-CIO Papers, RL.

79. Babson, *Building the Union*, 107.

80. Peterson, *American Automobile Workers*, 141.

81. Zieger, *American Workers*, 25.

82. "The Briggs Disaster," *Ford Worker*, June 1, 1927.

83. "What Caused the Briggs Fire?" *Auto Workers News*, May 1927.

84. Approximately 10 percent or 1,300 workers at Briggs were African American, making the body plant the fourth largest employer of African American workers in Detroit. Meier, *Black Detroit*, 6.

85. "What Caused the Brigg's Fire?"; Zieger, *American Workers*, 24.

86. Babson, *Working Detroit*, 61.

87. Fine, *Frank Murphy*, 412.

88. Peterson, *American Automobile Workers*, 144.

89. Fine, *Frank Murphy*, 412.

90. Zieger, *American Workers*, 24.

91. For examples of cities across the nation covering the Briggs strike, see "Briggs Strike End Seen," *Philadelphia Enquirer*, January 28, 1933; "Strikers Asked to Return to Jobs," *Chicago Tribune*, February 9, 1933; "Briggs Plant Resumes Work on Ford Bodies," *Brooklyn Daily Eagle*, January 31, 1933; "Ford Marking Time as Strike Fails to End," *Tampa Tribune*, January 31, 1933; "Red Plot Stirs Detroit Strife," *Los Angeles Times*, March 22, 1933.

92. "Federation of Labor Demands Withdrawal of State Troops at Briggs," *Detroit Labor News*, February 3, 1933.

93. "Briggs Strike Contributions," *Detroit Labor News*, February 24, 1933.

94. Fine, *Frank Murphy*, 416; Peterson, *American Automobile Workers*, 122–123.

95. "Report of Proceedings Before the Mayor's Committee for Investigation into Causes of Strike at Briggs Manufacturing Company Held at the City Hall, Detroit, Michigan, on Thursday, January 31, 1933, at one o'clock p.m.," p. 79, BHL.

96. Babson, *Building the Union*, 107.

97. Meier, *Black Detroit*, 7–8.

98. Meier, *Black Detroit*, 19.

99. Meier, *Black Detroit*, 30.

100. Fine, *Frank Murphy*, 412.

101. Babson, *Working Detroit*, 62.

102. "Briggs Picket Song," February 13, 1933," Box 34, Joe Brown Collection, RL.

103. "Tizenotezer automunkas strajkol Detroitban," *Canadai Magyar Munkas*, February 22, 1933.

104. "Report of Proceedings Before the Mayor's Committee," pp. 88–94, BHL.

105. Babson, *Building the Union*, 107.

106. Babson, *Working Detroit*, 62.

107. "Auto Workers Union Organizes for Strike," January 22, 1933, Box 1, Henry Kraus Papers, RL.

108. "Auto Workers Union Organizes for Strike."

109. Mayer, "The Foreign Born in Detroit," 30.

110. "Publicznose Detroicka Spieszy z Pomoca Strajukajacym Robotnikom Briggsa," *Polish Daily News*, January 31, 1933. For more in the *Polish Daily News* on the Briggs strike, see articles on February 1, 1933, February 2, 1933, February 4, 1933, February 6, 1933, and February 10, 1933.

111. For details on violence during the strike, see "Rozruchy Strajkowe Przy Fabryce Briggsa Na Mack Ulicy," *Polish Daily News*, February 6, 1933.

112. "Bosses Agents Betray Mack Briggs Strike," *East Side Auto Worker*, April–May 1933; see also Jack Stachel, "The Strikes of the Auto Industry," *Labor Unity*, March 1933, Communism Folder, Box 6, Joe Brown Collection, RL.

113. "Maurice Sugar to Frank Martel," March 27, 1933, Maurice Sugar Folder, Box 18, AFL-CIO Papers, RL.

114. Phil Raymond, "The Brigg's Auto Strike Victory," *Labor Unity*, March 1933, Briggs Strike Folder, Box 1, Henry Kraus Papers, RL.

115. "Frequent Layoffs Lashed; 'Foreign Labor' Attacked," *Detroit Times*, December 15, 1934, National Recovery Administration Folder, Box 17, Joe Brown Collection, RL.

116. "Welfare Record of Mike Ozols (pseudonym), August 1, 1940," Box 117, Accession 55, Employee Account Series, Sociological Department Records, BFRC.

117. "Federal Men Nab 105 Aliens," *Detroit Free Press*, July 22, 1932.

Chapter 6

1. "Report to the Detroit Police Department," December 8, 1935, Box 7, Detroit Red Squad File, UMSC. On June 10, 1933, President Franklin Roosevelt issued Executive Order 6166, which merged the separate Bureau of Immigration and Bureau of Naturalization into a single bureau, which was to be headed by the commissioner of immigration and naturalization. USCIS History Office, *Overview of INS History* (Washington, D.C.: USCIS History Office and Library, 2012), 7.

2. Examining the marginal space noncitizens occupied in Depression era society challenges Lizabeth Cohen's argument in particular. Her seminal examination of Chicago posits that while in the 1910s, managers used a "divide-and-conquer" method to keep ethnic European, Mexican, and native-born Americans under control, by the Depression era, the same workers lost faith in ethnic businesses and mutual aid societies and banded together to begin "championing an expanded role for the state and the organization of national-level industrial unions." This chapter demonstrates that while certain ethnic Europeans certainly joined the labor movement, concerns about employer retaliation and nativism within the movement on

the whole kept many ethnic Europeans on the edges of American society. Cohen, *Making a New Deal*, 43, 253, 333.

3. "Deportation of Members of the Communist Party," 1932, RG76, Vol. 738, File 513057, LAC.

4. R. Munroe, Assistant Commissioner, Department of Immigration and Colonization Halifax, NS, May 11, 1932, Minutes of a Board of Inquiry, RG76, Vol. 738, File 513057, Deportation of Members of Communist Party, LAC.

5. On how Italian anarchist bombings in the 1910s led to America's first Red Scare and a wave of deportations that associated immigrants with crime, see Gage, *The Day Wall Street Exploded*. For examples of newspaper reports associating the Halifax Eight with violence, see "Inquiry Board to Hear Cases Men Arrested," *Ottawa Journal*, May 7, 1932; "Supreme Court Dismisses Communists' Appeal," *Ottawa Journal*, November 29, 1932; "Stay Asked in Deportation of Eight Communists," *Winnipeg Tribune*, November 30, 1932.

6. Deportation File, 1932, RG76, Vol. 738, File 513057, Deportation of Members of Communist Party, LAC.

7. "N. R. Trickey, Major to Wesley Gordon, Minister of Immigration," June 17, 1932, RG76, Vol. 738, File 513057, Deportation of Members of Communist Party, LAC.

8. Ivan Avakumovik, *The Communist Party in Canada: A History* (Toronto: McClelland and Stewart Limited, 1975), 115. In 1932, U.S. membership in the Communist Party hovered just under twenty thousand. "Communist Party USA History and Geography," Mapping American Social Movements Through the Twentieth Century, University of Washington, http://depts.washington.edu/moves/CP_intro.shtml (accessed March 11, 2019).

9. "Deportation Faces Eight," *Worker*, December 17, 1932.

10. "Inspector at Montreal to Commissioner of Immigration at Ottawa," November 9, 1932, RG76, Vol. 738, File 513057, Deportation of Members of Communist Party, LAC.

11. Deportations Scheduled, December 7, 1932, RG76, Vol. 738, File 513057, Deportation of Members of Communist Party, LAC.

12. Ford and Packard of Canada kept records of all political parades and literature found at Ford of Canada. Moreover, Ford of Canada had extensive lists detailing the suspected political affiliations and nationalities of their workers. Resume of Report on Communism Prepared by the Canadian Chamber of Commerce, September 10, 1930, RG13, Vol. 344, File 1930–1534, RCMP, LAC.

13. Communist Pamphlets, 1932, RG 2A, Clerk Council Records, Windsor Municipal Archives, WPLA.

14. "Canadian Communists Face Trial," April 12, 1932, *Detroit Times*.

15. "Communists to Be Deported from Canada," *Detroit News*, November 12, 1932.

16. "Canada Slates Deportation of Eight Communists," *Times Herald*, November 10, 1932.

17. Blair Neatby, *The Politics of Chaos: Canada in the Thirties* (Toronto: Macmillan of Canada, 1972), 34.

18. Lorne A. Brown, "The Bennett Government, Political Stability, and the Politics of the Unemployment Relief Camps, 1930–1935" (PhD diss., Queens University, 1979), 20.

19. David Carter, "The State Responds to Communism: Single, Homeless Unemployed and Federal Relief Camps, 1930–36" (PhD diss., University of Waterloo, 1982), 7.

20. Thomas William Tanner, "Microcosms of Misfortune: Canada's Unemployment Relief Camps Administered by the Department of Defense, 1932–1936" (M.A. thesis, University of Western Ontario, 1965), 3.

21. Tanner, "Microcosms of Misfortune," 53.

22. "Relief Workers Deny Pork Chops Served at Camps," *Globe*, February 23, 1934.

23. "Complaint Is Made of Relief Camp," *Globe*, April 3, 1934; "Charges About Camp Found to Be Wrong," *Globe*, April 18, 1934.

24. "Intimidation Is Common in Kenora Slave Labor Camp," *Toronto Worker*, February 12, 1934.

25. "Slave Camp Union Holds Wage Meet," *Toronto Worker*, October 13, 1934.

26. "Intimidation Is Common in Kenora Slave Labor Camp."

27. "Slave Camp Union Holds Wage Meet."

28. Carter, "The State Responds to Communism," 92.

29. "Relief Strike Out of Control," *Globe*, May 29, 1935; "Bennett Says Reds Lead Relief March," *New York Times*, June 25, 1935; "Mounties Quell Relief Strike Riots," *Des Moines Tribune*, July 2, 1935.

30. "Bennett Says Reds Lead Relief March," *New York Times*, June 25, 1935.

31. On the Regina riot and march, see Tanner, "Microcosms of Misfortune," chap. 4.

32. Canada Club Rally Notes, November 1, 1935, RG 2A, Clerk Council Records, WPLA.

33. "Commissioner Clyde Curry to Mayor David Croll," November 5, 1935, RG 2A, Clerk Council Records, WPLA.

34. "Commissioner Clyde Curry to Prime Minister William Lyon MacKenzie King," December 10, 1935, RG 2A, Clerk Council Records, WPLA.

35. Canaday, *The Straight State*, 92–93, 98–99.

36. "Commissioner Clyde Curry to Prime Minister William Lyon MacKenzie King."

37. For histories that explore the intricacies of the Roosevelt administration's refusal to admit refugees during the Nazi era, see Richard Breitman and Alan Lichtman, *FDR and the Jews* (New York: Belknap, 2013); Leonard Dinnerstein, *Antisemitism in America* (New York: Oxford University Press, 1995); David Wyman, *The Abandonment of the Jews: America and the Holocaust, 1941–1945* (New York: Pantheon, 1984). On how Mexican repatriations continued into Roosevelt's administration and were used by agricultural employers to break strikes, see Abraham Hoffman, *Unwanted Mexican Americans in the Great Depression: Repatriation Pressures, 1929–1939* (Tucson: University of Arizona Press, 1974), chaps. 6–7. Francisco Balderrama and Raymond Rodriguez, however, note that after Franklin Roosevelt's New Deal, deportations "assumed a more humane aspect." Francisco Balderrama and Ramon Rodriguez, *Decade of Betrayal: Mexican Repatriation in the 1930s* (Albuquerque: University of New Mexico Press, 2006), 82. On how Roosevelt's campaign united ethnic and black workers, see Cohen, *Making a New Deal*, chap. 6.

38. Cybelle Fox, *Three Worlds of Relief: Race, Immigration, and the American Welfare State from the Progressive Era to the New Deal* (Princeton, N.J.: Princeton University Press, 2012), 202; Daniels, *Guarding the Golden Door*, 65.

39. Oz Frankel, "Whatever Happened to 'Red Emma?' Emma Goldman, from Alien Revel to American Author," *Journal of American History* 83, no. 3 (December 1996): 903–942.

40. "A Survey of Communist Activities in the City of Detroit and Vicinity," July 1, 1936, Communist Party, 1926–1930 Folder, Box 1, AFL-CIO Metropolitan Detroit Records, RL.

41. "Communist Report, 1935," Communism Folder, Box 16, Accession 44, William J. Cameron Papers, BFRC.

42. Bates, *Black Detroit*, 151.

43. "Communist Report, 1935," Communism Folder, Box 16, Accession 44, William J. Cameron Papers, BFRC.

44. Bates, *Black Detroit*, 123–124.

45. Fox, *Three Worlds of Relief*, 202.

46. For scholarship chronicling how black Americans were excluded from New Deal federal programs, see Ira Katznelson, *When Affirmative Action Was White: An Untold History of Racial Inequality in Twentieth-Century America* (New York: Norton, 2006).

47. Fox, *Three Worlds of Relief*, 206–207.

48. "Unrest Stirs Canadian CCC," *New York Times*, June 16, 1935.

49. "Canadians Turn to New Program," *New York Times*, February 3, 1936.

50. Fox, *Three Worlds of Relief*, 214–215.

51. On the number employed by the WPA, see "WPA Helps Many," *Detroit News*, July 18, 1937; on particular projects, see "Do the WPA Projects Which the Cities Have Sponsored Represent Useful and Desirable Work of Public Benefits?" 1939, WPA Folder, Box 8, Mayor's Papers, BDPL.

52. Nelson Lichtenstein, *The Most Dangerous Man in Detroit: Walter Reuther and the Fate of American Labor* (New York: Basic Books, 1995), 63.

53. Babson, *Building the Union*.

54. Lichtenstein, *The Most Dangerous Man in Detroit*, 62.

55. Nelson Lichtenstein notes that Polish autoworkers played "a relatively muted role in the organizing era." *The Most Dangerous Man in Detroit*, 63.

56. "Stanley Novak to Richard Frankensteen, November 14, 1936," Welfare Folder, Box 9, Mayor's Papers, 1936, BDPL.

57. Lichtenstein, *The Most Dangerous Man in Detroit*, 82.

58. Peter Friedlander, *The Emergence of a UAW Local, 1936–1939: A Study in Class and Culture* (Pittsburgh: University of Pittsburgh Press, 1975), 43; Lichtenstein, *The Most Dangerous Man in Detroit*, 82.

59. Bates, *Black Detroit*, 167.

60. Meier and Rudwick, *Black Detroit*, 5.

61. Bates, *Black Detroit*, 190–191.

62. Bruce Nelson, "Autoworkers, Electoral Politics, and the Convergence of Class and Race, Detroit, 1937–1945," in *Organized Labor and American Politics, 1894–1994: The Labor-Liberal Alliance*, ed. Kevin Boyle (Albany: SUNY Press, 1998), 131.

63. Meier and Rudwick, *Black Detroit*, 88–91.

64. Bruce Nelson, "Autoworkers," 131.

65. Frank Januszweiski, the editor of the *Polish Daily News*, used Frankensteen's actions as evidence that, like the DFL, the UAW was "no friend to Poles or other Slavs in Detroit." Found in "Memo from the Detroit Protection of Foreign Born Workers to the AFL," June 12, 1935, Box 9, Detroit Red Squad Papers, UMSC.

66. In its early days, the majority of UAW leaders identified or sympathized with communism. Its larger umbrella organization, the CIO, comprised about 25 percent communists. Judith Stepan-Norris and Maurice Zeitlin, *Left Out: Reds and America's Industrial Unions* (Cambridge: Cambridge University Press, 2003), 19; Friedlander, *Emergence of a Union Local*, 4.

67. John Wanat File, September 30, 1935, Box 7, Detroit Red Squad Files, UMSC.

68. Friedlander, *Emergence of a Union Local*, 27.

69. Lichtenstein, *Walter Reuther*, 93.

70. Friedlander, *Emergence of a Union Local*, 15–19.

71. "UAW-WPA Welfare Department Report, 1938," Box 11, Series II, George Edward Senior Collection, RL.

72. "Information Sheet," UAW Welfare Activities Folder, Box 33, Joe Brown Collection; "UAW-WPA Welfare Department Report, 1938," Box 11, Series II, George Edward Senior Collection, RL.

73. "George Edwards Report on WPA," March 12, 1937, Welfare Folder, Box 7, Mayor's Papers, 1937, BDPL.

74. "Stanley Novak on the Flint Strike," January 1937, Box 12, Mayor's Papers, 1937, BDPL.

75. Meier and Rudwick, *Black Detroit*, 34–41.

76. Report from C. H. Millard, September 1938, Folder 1, Box 70, UAW Region 7 Canadian Regional Office Records, RL.

77. James Gregory notes that though Detroit's southern migrants bore the brunt of the blame for the Black Legion's violence and many of its founding members migrated from southern states, the organization was not dominated or controlled by southern migrants alone. Gregory, *The Southern Diaspora*, 295.

78. Kenneth R. Dvorak, "Terror in Detroit: The Rise and Fall of Michigan's Black Legion" (PhD diss., Bowling Green State University, 2000), 103; "Black Legion Oath and Initiative," 1936, Black Legion Folder, Box 7, Henry Kraus Papers, RL.

79. "Memo on the Black Legion by Maurice Sugar," 1937, Black Legion Folder, Box 7, Henry Kraus Papers, RL.

80. Dvorak, "Terror in Detroit," 102.

81. "Memo on the Black Legion by Maurice Sugar," 1937, Black Legion Folder, Box 7, Henry Kraus Papers, RL.

82. "Black Legion Oath and Initiative."

83. "Memo on the Black Legion by Maurice Sugar."

84. "Black Legion Oath and Initiative."

85. "Memo on the Black Legion by Maurice Sugar."

86. "Memo on the Black Legion by Maurice Sugar."

87. "Memo on the Black Legion by Maurice Sugar."

88. "A Ku Klux Klan History," *Detroit News*, August 26, 1940, Box 16, Don Binkowski Papers, RL.

89. "Army and Navy Club of Detroit to the Conference for the Protection of Civil Rights," June 12, 1936, Box 7, Henry Kraus Papers, RL.

90. "Memo on the Black Legion by Maurice Sugar."

91. "UAW Report on the Black Legion," 1936, Box 16, Don Binkowski Papers, RL.

92. "Civil Rights Federation to Police Department, December 21, 1937," Box 1, Detroit Red Squad Files, UMSC.

93. "UAW Report on the Black Legion," 1936, Box 16, Don Binkowski Papers, RL.

94. Dvorak, "Terror in Detroit," 128, 154.

95. "The Green Tree: A Play in Three Acts Dealing with the Problem of Liquor by Stanley B. Niles," Michigan, 1936, Prohibition Party Folder, Box 7, Prohibition National Committee Papers, BHL.

96. "Eyes of the Nation on Detroit Vote," *Detroit Free Press*, November 2, 1937.

97. Donald Warren, *Radio Priest: Charles Coughlin, the Father of Hate Radio* (New York: Free Press, 1996).

98. JoEllen McNergney Vinyard, *Right in Michigan's Grassroots: From the KKK to the Michigan Militia* (Ann Arbor: University of Michigan Press, 2011), 99, 165.

99. "Meeting of International UAW-CIO meeting. Advertised by the Civil Rights Federation, expose of Rev. Coughlin," December 19, 1938, Box 9, Red Squad Files, UMSC.

100. "Mary Wolf and DFL to the Detroit Police Department," January 27, 1935, Police Department 1920–1944 Folder, Box 14, AFL-CIO Papers, RL.

101. "Mary Wolf and DFL to the Detroit Police Department."

102. "American Legion of Connecticut to President Franklin Roosevelt," August 10, 1936, File 55883/700A, NARAI.

103. "West Side Civic League of Chicago to President Franklin Roosevelt," November 12, 1937, File 55883/700A, NARAI.

104. "Otis Richmond to Franklin Roosevelt," December 13, 1937, File 55883/700A, NARAI.

105. For files that detail Red Squad surveillance of communist bookstores, particularly the Modern Book Store, the Family Drug Company, and the Polish Book Store, see "Communist Party Book Stores File, October 1935," Box 1, Detroit Red Squad Files, Michigan Special Collections, Labadie Collection. For information on meeting houses, see "Communist Meetings Exposed, May 1935," Box 1, Detroit Red Squad Files, UMSC. For surveillance of particular individuals, see "Potential Communists in Detroit, 1935–1936," Box 2, Detroit Red Squad Files, UMSC.

106. "A Survey of Communist Activities in the City of Detroit and Vicinity," July 1, 1936, Communist Party Folder, Box 2, AFL-CIO Papers, RL.

107. "DPD Special Investigation Squad Report," October 14, 1937, Box 6, Red Squad Papers, UMSC.

108. "Detroit Police Department Investigation of Ferenz Unterwegner," October 9, 1941, Box 7, Red Squad Papers, UMSC.

109. "Report on Communist Activities, September 26, 1935," Box 6, Detroit Red Squad Files, UMSC.

110. "Report on the International Workers Order," February 13, 1936, Box 8, Detroit Red Squad Files, UMSC.

111. "Deportation of Paul Stamtakis, April 12, 1938," File 55963/336, NARAI.

112. "John Gielgud Investigation," October 30, 1938, Box 7, Red Squad Files, UMSC.

113. "Amelia Fronak to Detroit Police Department," February 16, 1938, Box 8, Detroit Red Squad Files, UMSC.

114. "John Bator to Detroit Police Department," January 5, 1938, Box 8, Detroit Red Squad Files, UMSC.

115. "Detroit Rated Low in Rights," *Detroit News*, March 6, 1938.

116. "Detroit Rated Low in Rights."

117. "Meeting of International UAW-CIO meeting. Advertised by the Civil Rights Federation, expose of Rev. Coughlin," December 19, 1938, Box 9, Detroit Red Squad Files, UMSC.

118. "George Addes to Mayor's Office," December 19, 1936, Welfare Folder, Box 9, Mayor's Papers, 1936, BDPL.

Chapter 7

1. "Welfare Speech," October 1938, Welfare Folder, Box 7, Mayor's Papers 1938, BDPL.

2. Histories of Canadian immigration policy tend to position World War II as the catalyst for a national move toward immigrant inclusion. For instance, see Kelley and Trebilcock, *The Making of the Mosaic*; Valerie Knowles, *Strangers at Our Gates: Canadian Immigration and Immigration Policy, 1540–1997* (Toronto: Dundurn Press, 1997). At the local level, however, this book shows how Depression-era poverty prompted many municipal governments to promote inclusive immigration policies as a humanitarian measure. In Detroit, on the other hand, local actors worked to dismantle what they viewed as the New Deal's lax immigration and labor policies, meaning federal policy and local pressures yielded separate outcomes on either side of the Detroit-Windsor border.

3. Carl Bon Tempo, *Americans at the Gate: The United States and Refugees During the Cold War* (Princeton, N.J.: Princeton University Press, 2008), 19; Daniels, *Guarding the Golden Door*, 83.

4. "Wait on Oshawa," *Ottawa Journal*, April 12, 1937.

5. "Office Seekers Wait a Record Vote," *Detroit Free Press*, October 5, 1937.

6. Steve Babson, *Working Detroit: The Making of a Union Town* (New York: Adama Books, 1984), 93–96.

7. "Nominees Gird for Busy Drive to Seek Votes," *Detroit Free Press*, October 7, 1937.

8. "Mayoral Foes Busy on Talks," *Detroit Free Press*, September 1, 1937; "Mayoral Race at Busy Stage," *Detroit Free Press*, September 5, 1937.

9. "Memo from the Detroit Protection of Foreign Born Workers on the Political Endorsements of the *Polish Daily News*," October 4, 1937, Box 9, Detroit Red Squad Papers, UMSC.

10. "Mayoral Foes Busy on Talks"; "Mayoral Race at Busy Stage."

11. "Reading Hails Labor Backing," *Detroit Free Press*, October 23, 1937.

12. Just before the election, Reading called himself the representative of the "great class of working men and women in Detroit who have the interests and the welfare of the city at heart." "Reading Hails Labor Backing."

13. "Reading Winds in Landslide; All CIO Candidates Lose," *Detroit Free Press*, November 3, 1937.

14. "Massive WPA Protest in Detroit," *Detroit News*, February 15, 1938; Babson, *Working Detroit*, 93.

15. The UAW called it the "the greatest demonstration that was ever staged by one union, particularly in Detroit, once the haven of the open shop." "UAW-WPA Welfare Department Report, 1938," Box 11, Series II, George Edward Sr. Collection, RL.

16. "40,000 WPA Jobs Promised to State," *Detroit Free Press*, February 17, 1938.

17. "Department of Public Welfare Report to Richard Reading," February 26, 1938, Welfare Folder, Box 9, Mayor's Papers, 1938, BDPL.

18. "40,000 WPA Jobs Promised to State."

19. Alice Kessler-Harris, *In Pursuit of Equity: Women, Men, and the Quest for Economic Citizenship in 20th Century America* (New York: Oxford University Press, 2001); Gwendolyn Mink, *The Wages of Motherhood: Inequality in the Welfare State, 1917–1941* (Ithaca, N.Y.: Cornell University Press, 1995); Linda Gordon, *Pitied but Not Entitled: Single Mothers and the History of Welfare, 1890–1935* (New York: Free Press, 1994); Joanne Goodwin, *Gender and the*

Politics of Welfare Reform: Mothers' Pensions in Chicago, 1911–1929 (Chicago: University of Chicago Press, 1997).

20. Kessler-Harris, *In Pursuit of Equity*, 143. Most black women were encouraged to work, but the terms of the 1935 Social Security Act trapped them in domestic training programs. Mary-Elizabeth Murphy, *Jim Crow Capital: Women and Black Freedom Struggles in Washington D.C., 1920–1945* (Chapel Hill: University of North Carolina Press, 2018), 123.

21. "Richard Leonard to Richard Reading," February 8, 1938, Welfare Folder, Box 9, Mayor's Papers, 1938, BDPL.

22. "40,000 WPA Jobs Promised to State," *Detroit Free Press*, February 17, 1938.

23. "Mayor Scores Dole Chiselers," *Detroit Free Press*, February 16, 1938.

24. For an excellent treatment of 1970s welfare politics and the origins of the African American woman portrayed as "welfare queen," see Julilly Kohler-Hausmann, "Welfare Crises, Penal Solutions, and the Origins of the 'Welfare Queen,'" *Journal of Urban History* 41, no. 5 (September 2015): 756–771; Annelise Orleck, *Storming Caesar's Palace: How Black Mothers Fought Their Own War on Poverty* (Boston: Beacon, 2006), 85.

25. Martha Gardner, *The Qualities of a Citizen: Women, Immigration, and Citizenship, 1870–1965* (Princeton, N.J.: Princeton University Press, 2005), 195.

26. "Department of Public Welfare Report, City of Detroit, May 1938," Welfare Folder, Box 7, Mayor's Papers 1938, BDPL.

27. "Richard Reading Address," March 2, 1938, Welfare Folder, Box 7, Mayor's Papers 1938, Detroit Public Library.

28. "Detroit Special Investigation Squad Report," October 1, 1938, Welfare Folder, Box 7, Mayor's Papers 1938, BDPL.

29. "Detroit Police Department Special Investigation Squad," October 14, 1938, Box 1, Red Squad Files, UMSC.

30. "Information Received on Welfare Cheaters, November 10, 1938," Box 1, Detroit Red Squad Files, UMSC.

31. "Mayor Seeks to Find Chiselers," *Detroit News*, February 17, 1938. On European-sounding names, see "Special Investigation Squad, October 1938, Detective File," Welfare Folder, Box 7, Mayor's Papers 1938, BDPL.

32. "Welfare Chiselers Found in Detroit," *Detroit News*, February 27, 1938.

33. "City of Detroit Department of Public Welfare Report to Richard Reading, March 24, 1938," Welfare Folder, Box 7, Mayor's Papers 1938, BDP.

34. Mimi Ambramovitz, *Regulating the Lives of Women: Social Welfare and Policy from the Colonial Times to the Present*, 3rd ed. (London: Routledge, 2017); Linda Gordon, *Pitied but Not Entitled: Single Mothers and the History of Welfare, 1890–1935* (New York: Free Press, 1994).

35. For an overview of the laissez-faire approach taken by Depression-era federal policy-makers in Canada, see Pierre Berton, *The Great Depression, 1929–1939* (Toronto: Anchor Canada, 1990); Blair Neatby, *The Politics of Chaos: Canada in the Thirties* (Toronto: Macmillan of Canada, 1972).

36. "Annual Report Windsor Local Council of Women," January 31, 1938, Relief Matters Folder, MS 19 I-8/5, WPLA.

37. "New Mayor in Windsor," *Windsor Evening Star*, December 7, 1936.

38. "Welfare Investigated," *Windsor Evening Star*, March 13, 1938, Welfare Matters, 1938, MS 19 I-8/5, WPLA.

39. "Welfare Investigated."

40. For more on Mayor Croll's first mayoral election, see Chapter 4.

41. "Relief Crowd Dispersed by Police," *Windsor Evening Star*, August 29, 1938.

42. "Annual Report Windsor Local Council of Women."

43. "On the Walker Metal Strike," August 12, 1938, Relief Matters Folder, MS 19 I-8/5, WPLA.

44. "Windsor Plant Picketed as Agreement Runs Out," *Windsor Evening Star*, August 4, 1938.

45. "Report by C. H. Millard," September 1938, Folder 1, Box 70, UAW Region 7, Canadian Regional Office, RL.

46. "A Vocal Test Case," *Windsor Evening Star*, August 12, 1938.

47. "Strike Picket Held as Bomb Suspect," *Windsor Evening Star*, September 1, 1938.

48. "Metal Products Strike Settled," *Windsor Evening Star*, November 1, 1938.

49. "Work Is Better," *Windsor Evening Star*, November 2, 1938.

50. "More Protest to Welfare Cuts," *Windsor Evening Star*, November 5, 1938.

51. "Won't Attack His Rival," *Windsor Evening Star*, November 2, 1938.

52. "Croll Spurns 'Red' Tenets," *Windsor Evening Star*, November 3, 1938.

53. "Croll Spurns 'Red' Tenets."

54. "Ontario Cities Hold Elections," *Winnipeg Free Press*, December 5, 1938; "Croll and Labor Win," *Toronto Star*, December 6, 1938.

55. "CIO Sympathizer is Elected Windsor Mayor," *Evening News*, December 6, 1938.

56. "Wigle Is Ousted by Croll," *New York Herald Tribune*, December 7, 1938; "Croll Begins Comeback," *Boston Jewish Advocate*, December 23, 1938.

57. On the sharp decrease of Canadian deportations during World War II, see Roberts, *Whence They Came*, Conclusion.

58. "New Nazi Move to Rid Reich of Foreign Jews," *Ottawa Journal*, June 8, 1939; "British Say Hitler Speech at Danzig a 'Travesty,'" *Ottawa Journal*, September 20, 1939.

59. "To Ask Deportation of Foreign Agitators," *Winnipeg Tribune*, July 25, 1939.

60. "William Lyon Mackenzie King to Ministry of Labor," August 12, 1939, William Lyon Mackenzie King Correspondence, Microfilm Reel C-3748, LAC.

61. "Royal Canadian Legion to Mayor Conboy," September 26, 1939, VIMY Branch, Box B562, File 10, Western Archives, University of Western Ontario.

62. "Province Cuts off Enemy Aliens from Relief Rolls," *Ottawa Journal*, November 2, 1939.

63. "Aliens on Relief Must Seek Naturalization Here," *Ottawa Journal*, October 24, 1939.

64. "Remembering the War," *Polish Society Bulletin*, May 1970, Polish Clippings, Windsor Public Library Clippings Files, WPLA.

65. Richard Polenberg, "Franklin Roosevelt and Civil Liberties: The Case of the Dies Committee," *Historian* 30, no. 2 (February 1968): 165–166.

66. Daniel Piliero, "The Attempts to Deport Harry Bridges," *Georgetown Immigration Law Journal* 5, no. 237 (1991): 238–239.

67. "Miss Perkins Refuses to Seek Bridges Deportation," *New York Times Herald*, August 31, 1938.

68. For discussion of protest concerning the imprisonment and trial of Harry Bridges, see Correspondence, 1939, Box 1, Richard Frankensteen Collection, RL.

69. "Miss Perkins Refuses to Seek Bridges Deportation."

70. "Hands in Finding on CIO Leader," *Detroit Free Press*, December 30, 1939.

71. Breitman and Lichtman, *FDR and the Jews*, 110–116.

72. In the 1938 midterm elections, the Democratic Party lost an overwhelming seventy-two seats in the House of Representatives and seven in the Senate, meaning the Roosevelt administration had to negotiate with the Republican Party. David Kennedy, *Freedom from Fear: The American People in Depression and War, 1929–1945* (New York: Oxford University Press, 2001), 352.

73. For more on the benefits the New Deal conferred on immigrants and ethnics as opposed to Mexicans and African Americans, see Cybelle Fox, *Three Worlds of Relief: Race, Immigration, and the American Welfare State from the Progressive Era to the New Deal* (Princeton, N.J.: Princeton University Press, 2012).

74. "Senate Congressional Record," Seventy-fifth Congress, Session Three, February 2, 1938.

75. "House Congressional Record," Seventy-fifth Congress, Session Three, June 16, 1938.

76. George O'Brien of Michigan's Thirteenth District (Detroit), Carl Mapes of Michigan's Fifth District (Flint), and Fred Crawford from Michigan's Eighth District (Lansing) refrained from discussing immigration in the debates over how to restructure the WPA.

77. "House Congressional Record," Seventy-sixth Congress, Session Five, February 3, 1939. Beyond condemning foreigners, Clare Hoffman condemns President Roosevelt for acting like a "tyrant in Washington." "House Congressional Record," Seventy-fifth Congress, Session Three, June 16, 1938.

78. Fox, *Three Worlds*, 238–239.

79. Fox, *Three Worlds*, 239.

80. "Thousands Dropped from Relief Lists," *Lansing State Journal*, March 5, 1939.

81. Fox, *Three Worlds*, 240.

82. Official numbers of WPA workers dropped are difficult to calculate. Allen Soris, the Detroit WPA personnel director, claimed to have dropped 3,500 workers in the first month of the ban, but welfare department workers calculated the number closer to 5,000. UAW leader and labor organizer George Addes claimed the number was closer to twenty thousand, but the official federal report that 45,000 aliens lost their jobs nationally suggests that the number leaned closer to 5,000. "City Presented Problem by WPA Ban on Aliens," *Detroit Free Press*, March 5, 1939; "Radio Speech by George F. Addes, Wed., June 14th, 1939, WJR at 5:30pm," WPA File, Box 33, Joe Brown Collection, RL.

83. "1940 Census Information" found in "The Jewish Community Prior to the War," Jewish Welfare Federation Papers, Microfilm 925, Reel 1, BDPL.

84. "Daughter Irked by Rule That Cost Father a Job," *Detroit News*, March 2, 1939.

85. "35 Years Long Enough to Decide on Citizenship," *Detroit News*, March 4, 1939.

86. "Alien Relief Controversy Draws Fire of Readers," *Detroit Free Press*, March 26, 1939.

87. George Gallup, "The Gallup Poll: View of Reliefers," *Sun*, June 25, 1939.

88. Fox, *Three Worlds of Relief*, 225–228.

89. "Word 'Free' Misused," *Detroit Free Press*, March 26, 1939. H.N. was not alone in his assumptions that aliens still smuggled regularly into Detroit. A 1939 *Detroit Free Press* letter to the editor argued, "Alien smuggling appears to have reached new proportions under the present Administration in Washington." While the author provided no evidence for this

claim, it reflected a sustained concern many Detroiters felt about undocumented immigration. "This Is No Dumping Ground," *Detroit Free Press*, April 3, 1939.

90. "William Hammond File," February 17, 1939, File 23/30675, NARAI.

91. Sixteenth Census of the United States, 1940, *Population and Housing: Statistics for Census Tracks*, 82.

92. "Frick Widdas File," July 3, 1941, Box 7, Detroit Red Squad Papers, UMSC.

93. "Radio Speech by George F. Addes."

94. "Notes on Civil Rights Federation Meeting, UAW Hall, 51 Sproat Street," Monday, March 6, 1939, Box 9, Detroit Red Squad Papers, UMSC.

95. "The Aliens are Persecuted!" Box 11, Series II, George Edward Sr. Collection, RL.

96. "WPA Laborer Is Too Lazy to Lean on Spade," *Detroit Free Press*, February 17, 1939.

97. "Aliens Testify in Fraud Trial," *Detroit Free Press*, March 24, 1939.

98. "Aliens to Testify in Fraud Hearing," *Detroit Free Press*, March 23, 1939.

99. "Citizenship Status of Head of Family, April 1939," Welfare Folder, Box 8, 1939, BDPL.

100. "City Presented Problem by WPA Ban on Aliens," *Detroit Free Press*, March 5, 1939.

101. "John Gorsky to the Detroit Welfare Department," April 9, 1939, Welfare Folder, Box 8, 1939 Mayor's Papers, BDPL.

102. "Drive Opened on Alien Relief," *Detroit Free Press*, April 14, 1939.

103. "City Presented Problem by WPA Ban on Aliens."

104. "WPA Firings Hard on Aliens," *Detroit Free Press*, March 8, 1939.

105. For more on Americanization, see Chapter 1 of this book.

106. For studies on how businesses and social welfare organizations attempted to Americanize Europeans through formal institutions, see John Higham, *Strangers in the Land: Patterns of American Nativism, 1860–1925* (New Brunswick, N.J.: Rutgers University Press, 1955, reprinted 1988); Edward George Hartmann, *The Movement to Americanize the Immigrant* (New York: Columbia University Press, 1948); Jeffrey Mirel, *Patriotic Pluralism: Americanization, Education, and European Immigrants* (Cambridge, Mass.: Harvard University Press, 2009). Nicole Greer Golda offers a fresh perspective on these programs in Detroit by bringing gender into our understanding of the process. Greer Golda, "To Shape the Future of the Nation."

107. "State Will Check City's Welfare Plan," *Detroit Free Press*, May 10, 1940.

108. "WPA Firings Hard on Aliens."

109. Karl Kaufman File, File 23/30625, NARAI.

110. The Welfare Department warned individuals like naturalized Italian Carlo Di Cicco that replacing his papers could take six months to a year. This meant that Di Cicco and thousands of others would be ineligible for federal works programs while the department took the steps to find his paper. Carlo Di Cicco File, July 13, 1939, File 23/30625, NARAI.

111. Lisa McGirr's work examines how immigrants became caught up in discourses about illegal liquor and vice during the 1920s, but it focuses the majority of its attention on explaining how African Americans gained a reputation for bootlegging during this era. McGirr, *The War on Alcohol*. Examining Detroit in the late 1930s reveals that both immigrants who had entered the United States illegally and immigrants without citizenship turned to liquor smuggling after the Prohibition era as a means of support.

112. "Liquor Industry Grows," *Detroit Owl*, July 19, 1939, Clippings Folder, Mayor's Papers, 1939, BDPL.

113. Casmir Froncek File, June 15, 1939, Box 48, Arthur Tuttle Papers, BHL.

114. Greer Golda, "To Shape the Future of the Nation," 173–174.

115. Beitler Gottfried File, May 28, 1940, Box 48, Arthur Tuttle Papers, BHL.

116. John Kryczka File, May 28, 1939, Box 48, Arthur Tuttle Papers, BHL.

117. For similar reports on aliens illegally distilling alcohol after prohibition, see Box 48, Arthur Tuttle Papers, BHL.

118. Edward Kaminski, July 17, 1939, Box 48, Arthur Tuttle Papers, BHL.

119. Similarly, Serbian Stanley Brayovich and Duane Grekonitz teamed up with another friend to break into a railroad car of Goodyear tires meant for Chevrolet's Jefferson Street Plant. The men broke the railroad car's seal, stole ninety-six tires, and sold them on the street for cash. In interrogations, both men admitted to turning this money over to their families to pay rent, buy groceries, and clothe their children. Case investigators focused on the perpetrators' "poor to average intelligence," emphasizing the fact that they "could not pass a simple English test" and did not deserve the mercy of the courts. Stanley Brayovich File, January 13, 1939; Duane Grekonitz File, January 13, 1939, Box 48, Arthur Tuttle Papers, BHL.

120. Mike Chaykoswki File, March 11, 1939, Box 48, Arthur Tuttle Papers, BHL. For more examples of noncitizens convicted of bootlegging and stealing, see Michalina Baberacki File (November 4, 1939), William Barraco File (December 28, 1939), Beitler Gottfried File (May 28, 1940), Fernando Belmarcz File (June 14, 1939), Stanley Brayovich File (January 13, 1939), and Edward Kaminski File (July 17, 1939), all found in Box 48, Arthur Tuttle Papers, BHL.

121. Daniels, *Guarding the Golden Door*, 83.

122. Franklin D. Roosevelt, "Statement on Signing the Alien Registration Act," June 29, 1940,

The American Presidency Project, https://www.presidency.ucsb.edu/node/209766.

123. Scott Martelle, *The Fear Within: Spies Commies, and American Democracy in Trial* (New Brunswick, N.J.: Rutgers University Press, 2011), 2.

124. Carl Bon Tempo, *Americans at the Gate: The United States and Refugees During the Cold War* (Princeton, N.J.: Princeton University Press, 2008), 19; Daniels, *Guarding the Golden Door*, 83.

125. Martelle, *Fear Within*, 5.

126. J. H. Pollack, "America Registers Her Aliens," *American Scholar* 10, no. 2 (Spring 1941): 198.

127. Smith, *Guarding the Golden Gate*, 83.

128. "Claims 'Millions' Smuggled into the U.S. Annually," *Herald Palladium*, March 7, 1939.

129. Senator Reynolds, introducing a document from the Veterans of Foreign Wars of North Carolina, 76th Cong., 3rd Sess., *Congressional Record*, June 21, 1940, 8762.

130. Senator Bilbo, introducing a document from Indianola Post No. 2 of the American Legion, 76th Cong., 3rd Sess., *Congressional Record*, June 21, 1940, 8762.

131. Roosevelt, "Statement on Signing the Alien Registration Act."

132. Daniel Tichenor, *Dividing Lines: The Politics of Immigration Control in America* (Princeton, N.J.: Princeton University Press, 2009), 165.

133. Pollack, "America Registers Her Aliens," 198–200.

134. Pollack, "America Registers Her Aliens," 203.

135. "Registry Starts Here Today for 650,000 Aliens," *New York Herald Tribune*, August 27, 1940.

136. "Registration of Aliens Opposed by First Lady," *Battle Creek Enquirer*, November 26, 1939.

137. George Gallup, "Public in Favor of Registration of Aliens 'Just to Play It Safe,'" *Atlanta Constitution*, June 10, 1940.

138. "Organizations Aid Aliens in Registration," *Jewish Advocate*, September 20, 1940; "American Jewish Congress Aids in Alien Registration," *Chicago Tribune*, October 20, 1940; "President Signs Bill for Registration," *Jewish Exponent*, July 5, 1940.

139. "What the Radio Offers Today," *Detroit Free Press*, August 12, 1940.

140. Charles Boyer, "Many of Them Are Confused," *Lansing State Journal*, November 15, 1940.

141. Throughout the 1930s, Detroit had the highest alien population behind New York and Chicago, respectively. Clifford A. Prevost, "Report from the Free Press Washington Bureau," *Detroit Free Press*, July 30, 1940. Letters to the *Detroit Free Press* expressed overwhelming support for the Registration Act. For an example, see "Voice of the People," *Detroit Free Press*, June 2, 1940.

142. "Aliens Sign Up in a Late Rush," *Detroit Free Press*, December 27, 1940.

143. "Urges Illegal Entrants to Confess," *Port Huron Times Herald*, December 12, 1940.

144. Attorney General Jackson reminded illegal immigrants who had entered before 1922 that they were eligible to naturalize and that he would consider leniency to all others. "More Aliens Than Estimated," *Herald Palladium*, January 2, 1941.

145. John Joel Culley, "Enemy Alien Control in the United States During World War II: A Survey," in *Alien Justice: Wartime Internment in Australia and North America*, ed. Kay Saunders and Roger Daniels (Queensland: University of Queensland Press, 2000), 139.

146. Reg Whitaker and Gergory Kealy, "A War on Ethnicity: the RCMP and Internment," in *Enemies Within: Italian and Other Internees in Canada and Abroad*, ed. Franca Iacovetta, Robert Perin, and Angelo Principe (Toronto: University of Toronto Press, 2000), 129.

147. Whitaker and Kealy, "A War on Ethnicity," 137.

148. Stephen Fox, *America's Invisible Gulag: A Biography of German American Internment and Exclusion in World War II* (New York: Peter Lang, 2000), xvi; Jorg Nagler, "Internment of German Enemy Aliens in the United States During the First and Second World Wars" and George Pozzeta, "Alien Enemies or Loyal Americans? The Internment of Italian-Americans" in *Alien Justice: Wartime Internment in Australia and North America*, ed. Kay Saunders and Roger Daniels (Queensland: University of Queensland Press, 2000), 78–83.

149. "Attorney General Lemuel Schofield to Director Zurbrick," October 10, 1941, File 56116/764, NARAI.

150. "Director Zurbrick to FBI," December 17, 1941, File 56116/764, NARAI.

151. "Report on Paroled Enemy Aliens, Detroit District," July 17, 1944, File 56125/8, NARAI.

152. John Dower, *War Without Mercy: Race and Power in the Pacific War* (New York: Pantheon, 1986), 78–79.

Conclusion

1. "Donald J. Trump: Presidential Candidate on the Issues," *New York Times*, December 15, 2015.

2. "What Donald Trump Has Said About Mexico and Vice Versa," *Time*, August 31, 2016.

3. "What Donald Trump's Vow to Deport up to 3 Million Immigrants Would Mean," *New York Times*, November 4, 2016.

4. Daniel Cox, Rachel Leinesch, and Robert P. Jones, "Beyond Economics: Fears of Cultural Displacement Pushed the White Working Class to Trump," *PRRI, the Atlantic Report*, May 9, 2017.

5. Richard Wolff, "Travel Ban Timeline," *USA Today*, June 26, 2019.

6. "Trump's Address to Joint Session of Congress, Annotated," *NPR News*, February 28, 2017.

7. "In Depth Topics, A to Z: Immigration," *Gallup*, https://news.gallup.com/poll/1660/immigration.aspx (accessed March 4, 2019).

8. For Trump's policy, see "Trump Uses Vulgar Language to Refer to African Countries, Sources Say," *NPR News*, January 11, 2018. For Senator Reed's discussion of immigration, see "Origins of Immigration Reform by John Bond Trevor," Origins Folder, Box 1, John Bond Trevor Papers, BHL.

9. "Trump Referred to Haiti and African Nations as Shithole Countries," *NBC News*, January 11, 2018.

10. Valeria Fernandez, "Arizona's 'Concentration Camp': Why Was Tent City Kept Open for 24 Years?" *Guardian*, August 21, 2017.

11. Tom Dart, "Texas Immigration Law 'More Dangerous' Than Infamous Arizona Bill, Critics Say," *Guardian*, May 9, 2017.

12. Matt Pearce, "Timeline: The Rise and Fall of Arizona Sherriff Joe Arpaio," *Los Angeles Times*, August 1, 2017.

13. Gerstle, *American Crucible*, 195.

14. Gerstle, *American Crucible*, 196–197.

15. Wendy Wall, *Inventing the "American Way": The Politics of Consensus from the New Deal to the Civil Rights Movement* (New York: Oxford University Press, 2008), 5.

16. Wall, *Inventing the "American Way,"* 7.

17. Wall, *Inventing the "American Way,"* 7, 103.

18. Kevin Schultz, *Tri-Faith America: How Catholics and Jews Held Postwar America to Its Protestant Promise* (New York: Oxford University Press, 2011), 7.

19. Maddalena Marinari, "Divided and Conquered: Immigration Reform Advocates and the Passage of the 1952 Immigration and Nationality Act," *Journal of American Ethnic History* 35, no. 3 (Spring 2016): 11.

20. Marinari, "Divided and Conquered," 15–16.

21. Ngai, *Impossible Subjects*, 239–240.

22. Danielle Battisti, "American Committee on Italian Migration, Anti-Communism, and Immigration Reform," *Journal of American Ethnic History* 31, no. 2 (Winter 2012): 12; Ngai, *Impossible Subjects*, 227–254.

23. Battisti, "American Committee on Italian Migration," 31.

24. For more on bracero agricultural workers, see Kitty Calavita, *Inside the State: The Bracero Program, Immigration, and the I.N.S.* (New York: Routledge, 1992); Ngai, *Impossible Subjects*, chap. 4. For a study of bracero railroad workers, see Erasmo Gamboa, *Bracero Railroaders: The Forgotten World War II Story of Mexican Workers in the U.S. West* (Seattle: University of Washington Press, 2016).

25. Ngai, *Impossible Subjects*, 138–139.

26. Ngai, *Impossible Subjects*, 147–149.

27. María Balandrán Castillo, "Commuters, Green-Carders, and Semi-Legal Wetbacks: The History of a Border Immigration Practice, 1927–1968" (unpublished working paper, Latin American History Workshop, University of Chicago, 2010), 13–15. Used with the author's permission.

28. Lawrence Hertzog, "Border Commuter Workers and Transfrontier Metropolitan Structure Along the United States-Mexico Broder," *Journal of Borderlands Studies* 5, no. 2 (November 2001): 3–4.

29. For an excellent study chronicling the personal side of commuting, see Sergio Chávez, *Border Lives: Fronterizos, Transnational Migrants, and Commuters in Tijuana* (New York: Oxford University Press, 2016).

30. Calavita, *Inside the State*, 81, 152.

31. Hertzog, "Border Commuter Workers," 6.

32. Balandrán Castillo, "Commuters, Green Carders," 22; Hertzog, "Border Commuter Workers," 6.

33. Calavita, *Inside the State*, 152.

34. Numbers of returned Mexicans in the postwar era are staggering. In 1946, the United States returned 91,456 migrants, and from 1947 to 1948, the number rose to nearly 200,000. The number continued to rise steadily until 1954. Lytle Hernández, *Migra!*, 122.

35. Lytle Hernández, *Migra!*, 147–148.

36. Kelly Lytle Hernández, *City of Inmates: Conquest, Rebellion, and the Rise of Human Caging in Los Angeles, 1771–1965* (Chapel Hill: University of North Carolina Press, 2017), 195.

37. In 1986, President Reagan signed the Immigration Reform and Control Act (IRCA), which legalized three million illegal immigrants living in the United States but included "get tough" provisions that led to warrantless raids and arrests in Mexican communities. Daniels, *Guarding the Golden Door*, 224–225. For examples of articles in newspapers from across the country profiling drug running and crime on the border, see H. G. Reza, "Mexican Man Guilty of Shootout at Border," *Los Angeles Times*, October 25, 1985; Mary Thorton Washington, "Murder at the Border of No Man's Land," *Washington Post*, April 16, 1986; Poppa Terrence, "A Drug Smuggler's World," *Boston Globe*, March 29, 1987; Arthur Rotstein, "Smugglers' Tunnel Discovered on Mexican Border," *Baltimore Sun*, May 19, 1990.

38. Cybelle Fox, "Unauthorized Welfare: The Origins of Immigrant Status Restrictions in American Social Policy," *Journal of American History* 102, no. 4 (2016): 1052.

39. The Supreme Court ruled Proposition 187 unconstitutional, but it launched decades of political controversy over excluding unauthorized immigrants from state services. Kitty Calavita, "The New Politics of Immigration: 'Balanced-Budget Conservatism' and the Symbolism of Proposition 187," *Social Problems* 43 (August 1996): 284–305; Robin Dale Jacobson, *The New Nativism: Proposition 187 and the Debate over Immigration* (Minneapolis: University of Minnesota Press, 2008).

40. Daniels, *Guarding the Golden Door*, 241–242.

41. For examples of Islamophobia in the Obama era, see Shibley Telhami, "Cartoon Villains: A Look at American Media Since 9/11 Makes the Case That Muslims Have Been Unjustly Demonized," *New York Times*, January 6, 2008; David Sanger, "Islamophobia: Juan

Coal Says American Approaches to the Middle East Have Been Shaped by Fear," *New York Times*, May 10, 2009.

42. Sarah Gonzalez, "No One Expected Obama Would Deport More People Than Any U.S. President," *WNYC News*, January 19, 2017.

43. In 1950s Canada, prominent academics, members of the media, liberal religious and ethnic organizations, trade unions, and civil liberties groups demanded less racist immigration policies, and their points gained real traction against the backdrop of an American civil rights movement and the decolonization of Asia and Africa. In 1947, Canada also repealed the Chinese Exclusion Acts. Triadafilos Triadafilopoulos, *Becoming Multicultural: Immigration and the Politics of Membership in Canada and Germany* (Vancouver: University of British Columbia Press, 2013), 86.

44. Kelley and Trebilcock, *Making of the Mosaic*, 318.

45. Under this new law, immigration officers assigned points in nine categories, including education, employment opportunities in Canada, age, personal characteristics, and his or her degree of fluency in English or French. While this new law paved the way for an influx of skilled Asian, African, and Middle Eastern migrants, critics pointed to the problems of privileging so-called high-quality immigrants. Triadafilopoulos, *Becoming Multicultural*, 102.

46. Two years later, a complementary act revised the points system to emphasize practical training and experience alongside formal education. Knowles, *Strangers at Our Gates*, 195, 208–210.

47. In the face of Donald Trump's overt xenophobia, Canadian reporters and scholars have sought to thwart the idealization of Canada's policies, which perhaps look good in practice but produce lengthy delays for refugees and continue to rely on discretionary decisions. Tony Keller, "Canada Has Its Own Ways of Keeping Out Unwanted Immigrants," *Atlantic*, July 12, 2018. Moreover, studies demonstrate that on the ground in Canada, nativism is as virulent as in the United States. This is not to say Canadians do not express nativist views but that nativism is less visible and influential in political discourse. On nativist Canadians in Montreal, see "Canadian Employers Need Workers but Balk at Hiring Immigrants," *Montreal Gazette*, September 5, 2018. A 2017 University of Toronto study also found that one in five Canadians wanted to end all immigration and a higher number favored discriminating against Muslims. Celine Cooper, "Canadian Exceptionalism: Are We Good or Are We Lucky?" (paper presented at the Annual Conference of the McGill Insitute for the Study of Canada, February 9–10, 2017, Montreal).

48. On Doug Ford as the Canadian Donald Trump or "Donald Trump Lite," see Catherine Porter, "Will a Canadian Donald Trump Become Ontario's Leader?" *New York Times*, June 2, 2018; Scott Reed, "Doug Ford, Donald Trump, and the Humility Crisis in Politics," *Globe and Mail*, September 11, 2018; Ashifa Kassam, "Canada's Trump Movement? Doug Ford Rises in Conservative Party," *Guardian*, April 30, 2018. Despite the parallels between Ford and Trump, political scientist Myer Siemiatycki claims, "One of the differences is their orientation towards immigration and populations of diversity." John Lorinc, "Doug Ford Could Bring Trumpism to Ontario," *Washington Post*, April 22, 2018.

Index

Acknowledgments

I am indebted to the institutions and individuals who have helped me research, write, and revise this book over the past ten years. Libraries and archives, although undervalued and underfunded, allow historians to uncover the past. I have encountered excellent archivists across the United States and Canada and could not have completed the book's research without the help of Bill Creech at the National Archives, who screened hundreds of deportation files in the Immigration and Naturalization Service Records. The Walter Reuther Library offered me a Sam Fishman Travel Grant and the staff, including Mike Smith, provided invaluable insight into the history of labor. Likewise, the Benson Ford Research Center welcomed me to the Henry Ford Museum with a Clark Travel-to-Collections Grant. Archivists at the Bentley Historical Library also helped locate and digitize collections for this book, and a Mark C. Stevens Fellowship made frequent visits to Ann Arbor financially possible. I also appreciate the help from my institutions' research librarians, Harriet Lightman at Northwestern and Julia Nims at Eastern Michigan University, as well as countless interlibrary loan staff who worked behind the scenes to locate books, articles, and documents that proved invaluable to the project.

At Northwestern University, I had the good fortune to work with some of the greatest scholars and teachers in the discipline. I am grateful to Michael Allen, who saw potential in this project from its earliest days and provided feedback on countless drafts that guided me toward broader arguments about America's welfare state. I also thank Gerry Cadava, Kevin Boyle, and Susan Pearson, whose thoughtful comments and careful critique strengthened the project. I benefited greatly from seminars with Dylan Penningroth, Nancy MacLean, Henry Binford, Tim Breen, Alex Owen, and Deborah Cohen, all of whom taught me to think and express myself in more refined ways. I also owe a debt to Northwestern's Americanist Workshop, where, under the careful guidance of Mike Sherry, I learned to critique others and defend my own ideas. Beyond intellectual rigor and mentorship, Northwestern also provided substantial financial support. I am particularly grateful to the Chabraja Center for Historical Research and its director, Sarah Maza, and assistant director, Elzbieta Foeller-Pituch, for offering me a fellowship that allowed me to revise my manuscript and pursue a career in academia.

Camaraderie helped me succeed at Northwestern. Alex Lindgren-Gibson, Andy Baer, Matt Kahn, Wen-Qing Ngoei, Charlie Keenan, Ian Saxine, and Don Johnson provided companionship, critique, and laughter at every stage. Later on, Beth Healy, Rachel Thomas, Emma Goldsmith, Katie Gustafson, Keith Rathbone, and Marlous Van Waijenburg became dear friends. In a year living and researching in Michigan, I was lucky to meet Austin McCoy, Nora Krinistky, and Nicole Greer Golda, whose friendship has continued to this day. I am also grateful to Helen Plass, Liz Bacon, Katie Bahr, Lauren Finucane, and Monica Salas, who offered a reminder that life existed outside the academy.

I am also fortunate to have received continued support from Mount Holyoke College. In 2014, the history department granted me a Joseph Skinner Award that allowed me to write and research for an entire summer. My thanks also go to Dan Czitrom, who has served as a constant champion from my earliest days in the academy and continues to read and comment on my work.

A year as a visiting assistant professor at Binghamton University taught me the art of teaching and time management. Life as a contingent faculty member can be alienating at best, but I am grateful to the members of the Binghamton History Department for welcoming me and treating me as a valued colleague. I am particularly indebted to Steve Ortiz, who mentored me as I taught my first enormous lecture classes and took the time to read parts of this manuscript. That year would have been lonely indeed without the friendship of Meg Leja, with whom I shared the frustrations and joys of teaching for the first time.

I could not have found a better permanent home department than Eastern Michigan University (EMU), and I am grateful to the new colleagues, who have welcomed me to the History and Philosophy Department. Jim Egge, John McCurdy, Jesse Kauffman, Richard Nation, Mark Higbee, Mary Strasma, and Steven Ramold have all taken time out of their busy schedules to answer questions and offer thoughtful advice. I also appreciate the collegial friendships of Laura McMahon and especially Mary-Elizabeth Murphy, who have eased my transition to Michigan and permanent faculty life. Teaching at EMU has become a true delight, and I am indebted to my students, whose critical discussions have influenced my own thinking and writing.

This book has also benefited from critique from colleagues in the history discipline. Mae Ngai's illuminating thoughts on an earlier article version of this project for the *Journal of Urban History* helped me refine my argument. The Newberry Library is a haven for scholars in Chicago, and chapters of this book benefited from feedback at the Newberry Urban History Dissertation Group and the Seminar in Labor History. Co-creating the Midwestern Borderlands Reading Group with friend and colleague Nicole Greer Golda gave me the opportunity to get to know a bright group of young midwestern scholars, and my book's arguments benefited from the thoughts and critique of Sergio González, Katie Rosenblatt, Jesse Gant, and Jesse Nasta. As experts on Detroit, Tom Klug and Steve Babson strengthened the details of the narrative, and Keli Boyd worked as a careful copy editor. When it came time to revise final chapters, Alison Efford and Brendan Shanahan provided invaluable critique on chapters, and JoEllen Vineyard and Libby Garland both volunteered to read and comment on the whole draft. The final book is much better for their suggestions.

Working with the University of Pennsylvania Press has been a gratifying experience. Bob Lockhart has been a stellar editor, reader, and critic, and his advice improved the manuscript. The editorial board of the Politics and Culture in Modern America series provided thoughtful insights into the book's arguments and implications. The book also benefited from two thorough and very constructive reader's reports, one anonymous and one from Tracy Neumann. These reports helped me reframe the book's arguments, and they have been integral to the revision process.

Finally, those closest to me have been with this book for the longest, and I owe them the largest debt of gratitude. My dearest friends Joy Bhaskar, Leslie Crain, Sasha Sherman, and Kelly Chernin provided over a decade of encouragement. My in-laws, Chris and Rich Bavery; Brad, Julia, and Cory Bavery; and Jacinda Cuniff welcomed me into their loving family. My aunt and uncle, Kirk Campbell and Dominique Grandclaudon, always served as models of intellectual thought and curiosity. My grandmother, Nanette Campbell, a skilled story teller in her own right, taught me the importance of history and the written word at an early age. I could not have finished this project without the enduring love and support of my parents. Dean Johnson taught me to value hard work and commitment, while Melanie Johnson introduced me to a world of reading, museums, and travel that made me want to ask questions and learn. My sister Kristin Johnson has been a constant friend and champion, and I have enjoyed watching her become a scholar in her own right. Finally, I thank Ryan Bavery for his love, companionship, and dedication as a partner and now as a father. This book is for Christopher Kirk Bavery, who came into the world during the last stages of this project and helped put everything in perspective.